INJUSTICE

GODS AMONG US: YEAR FOUR

VOLUME 1

INJU

GODS AMON

Brian Buccellato
Writer

Bruno Redondo Mike S. Miller
Xermanico Juan Albarran Tom Derenick
Artists

J. Nanjan (NS Studios) Rex Lokus
Colorists

Wes Abbott
Letterer

Howard Porter and Rex Lokus
Cover Artists

STICE

G U S: YEAR FOUR

VOLUME 1

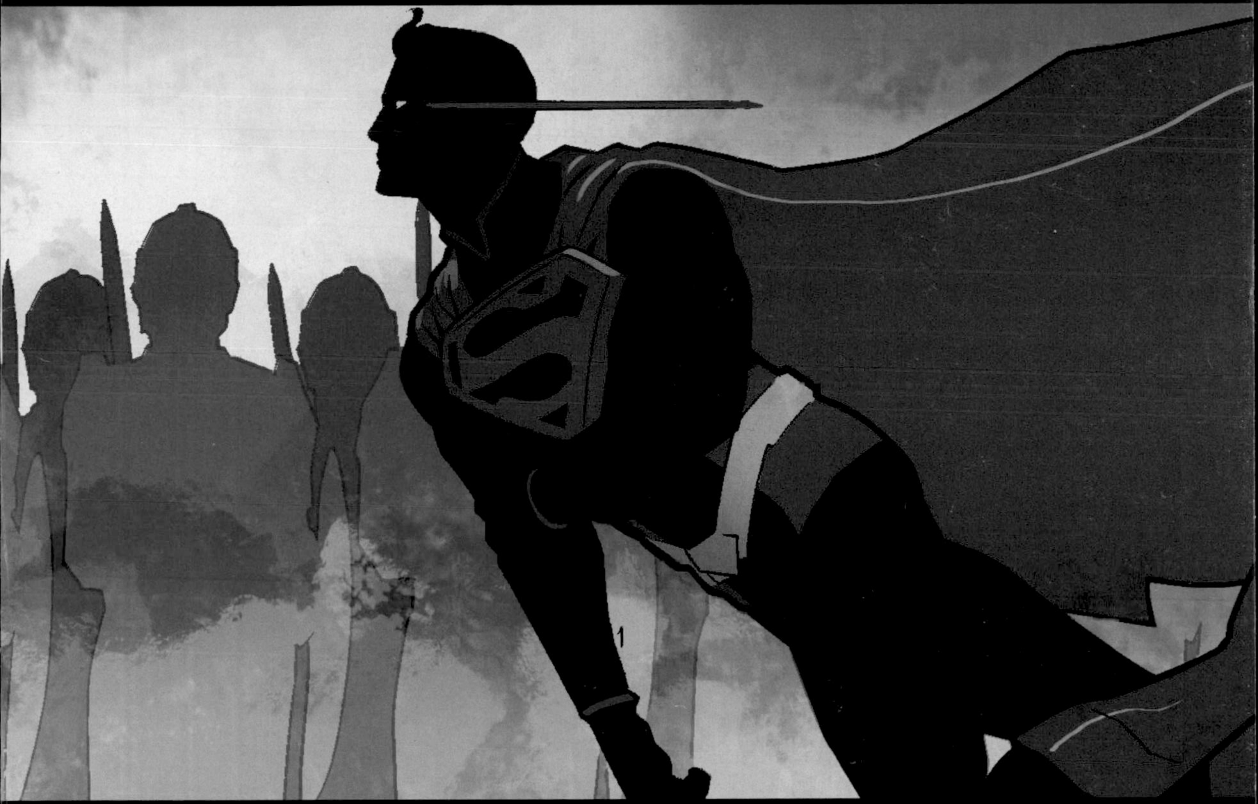

Jim Chadwick Editor – Original Series
David Piña Assistant Editor – Original Series
Jeb Woodard Group Editor – Collected Editions
Paul Santos Editor – Collected Edition
Steve Cook Design Director – Books
Louis Prandi Publication Design

Bob Harras Senior VP – Editor-in-Chief, DC Comics

Diane Nelson President
Dan DiDio and Jim Lee Co-Publishers
Geoff Johns Chief Creative Officer
Amit Desai Senior VP – Marketing & Global Franchise Management
Nairi Gardiner Senior VP – Finance
Sam Ades VP – Digital Marketing
Bobbie Chase VP – Talent Development
Mark Chiarello Senior VP – Art, Design & Collected Editions
John Cunningham VP – Content Strategy
Anne DePies VP – Strategy Planning & Reporting
Don Falletti VP – Manufacturing Operations
Lawrence Ganem VP – Editorial Administration & Talent Relations
Alison Gill Senior VP – Manufacturing & Operations
Hank Kanalz Senior VP – Editorial Strategy & Administration
Jay Kogan VP – Legal Affairs
Derek Maddalena Senior VP – Sales & Business Development
Jack Mahan VP – Business Affairs
Dan Miron VP – Sales Planning & Trade Development
Nick Napolitano VP – Manufacturing Administration
Carol Roeder VP – Marketing
Eddie Scannell VP – Mass Account & Digital Sales
Courtney Simmons Senior VP – Publicity & Communications
Jim (Ski) Sokolowski VP – Comic Book Specialty & Newsstand Sales
Sandy Yi Senior VP – Global Franchise Management

Published by DC Comics. Cover and compilation Copyright © 2016 DC Comics. All Rights Reserved.

Originally published in single magazine form in INJUSTICE: GODS AMONG US: YEAR FOUR 1-7. Copyright © 2015 DC Comics. All Rights Reserved. All characters, their distinctive likenesses and related elements featured in this publication are trademarks of DC Comics. The stories, characters and incidents featured in this publication are entirely fictional. DC Comics does not read or accept unsolicited ideas, stories or artwork.

DC Comics, 2900 West Alameda Ave., Burbank, CA 91505
Printed by RR Donnelley, Salem, VA, USA. 6/17/16. First Printing.
ISBN: 978-1-4012-6267-9

Library of Congress Cataloging-in-Publication Data is Available.

THE STORY SO FAR

This is not the world as you know it. This is a world where the Joker destroyed Metropolis in an atomic attack that claimed the lives of Lois Lane and her unborn child with Superman. This is a world where the Man of Steel, mad with grief, murdered the Joker in cold blood as Batman looked on in horror.

From that moment on, everything changed. Superman started going further and further to bring justice to the entire world, even involving himself in civil wars. As Batman became concerned about Superman's increasing global power, the Justice League found themselves split between members loyal to Superman and those who shared Batman's concerns.

Soon, Superman's team came into conflict with the U.S. government, and the battle between the two former friends started to see casualties mount on each side. Batman's resistance team stole a Kryptonite-powered pill that grants the user superpowers, to even the fight between Superman's super-powered troops and Batman's allies in the Gotham City Police Department.

Meanwhile, Superman found himself with an unexpected new ally: Sinestro, the former rogue Green Lantern who formed his own fear-powered Sinestro Corps. Sinestro recruited both Superman and Hal Jordan into the Sinestro Corps, and a huge war with the Green Lantern Corps and Batman's resistance followed, with casualties on both sides. Batman's team captured Raven, Flash and Robin from Superman's side and put Wonder Woman into a magical coma, but, despite these setbacks, Superman now seemed unstoppable.

To combat a Superman empowered with a yellow power ring, Batman turned to the one force he knew can damage Superman—magic. Teaming up with John Constantine, who wanted revenge on Superman for causing the events that lead to the death of his daughter's mother, Batman gathered an impressive array of magic-user to his side and took to the Tower of Fate to plan his attack on Superman.

But Superman found himself with an unlikely magical ally—The Spectre, the Spirit of Vengeance. With the Spectre on his side, Batman's team couldn't dare attempt an assault on Superman. But as the Spectre began acting erratically, killing powerful beings like Deadman and the demon Etrigan's human host Jason Blood, Batman and Constantine hatched a plan to counter him. While Batman became the new human host for Etrigan, Constantine tricked the demon Trigon into thinking Superman, not Batman, had kidnapped Trigon's daughter Raven.

But all was not as it seemed. The Spectre had been controlled by Mr. Mxyptlk, the fifth-dimensional being who was obsessed with Superman. As the war between Mxyptlk and Trigon threatened to unravel reality, a desperate final plan—executed with the help of Dick Grayson, now the new Deadman—banished both Mxyptlk and Trigon to another dimension, but left Batman without his new magical allies.

Now, Batman is hidden deep underground, his team reduced to just a handful of stalwarts. And Superman's team is reunited—Flash, Raven and Robin were rescued, and Wonder Woman was awoken from her coma when her mother Hippolyta made a deal with the goddess Hera. With Diana back by his side, Superman rejected Sinestro's ring.

Times have never been brighter for Superman's team, or looked darker for Batman. But in this world, things have a habit of changing quickly...

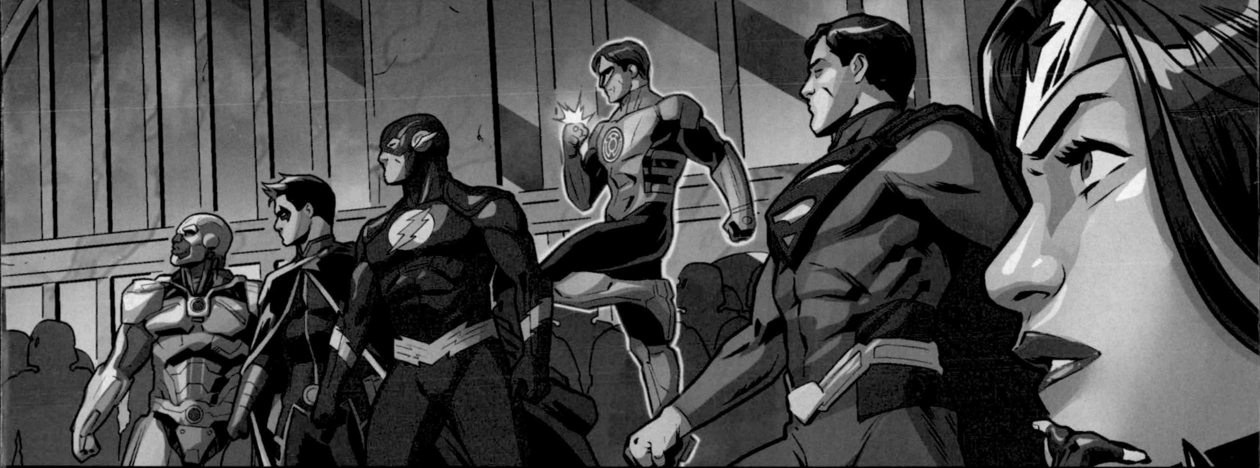

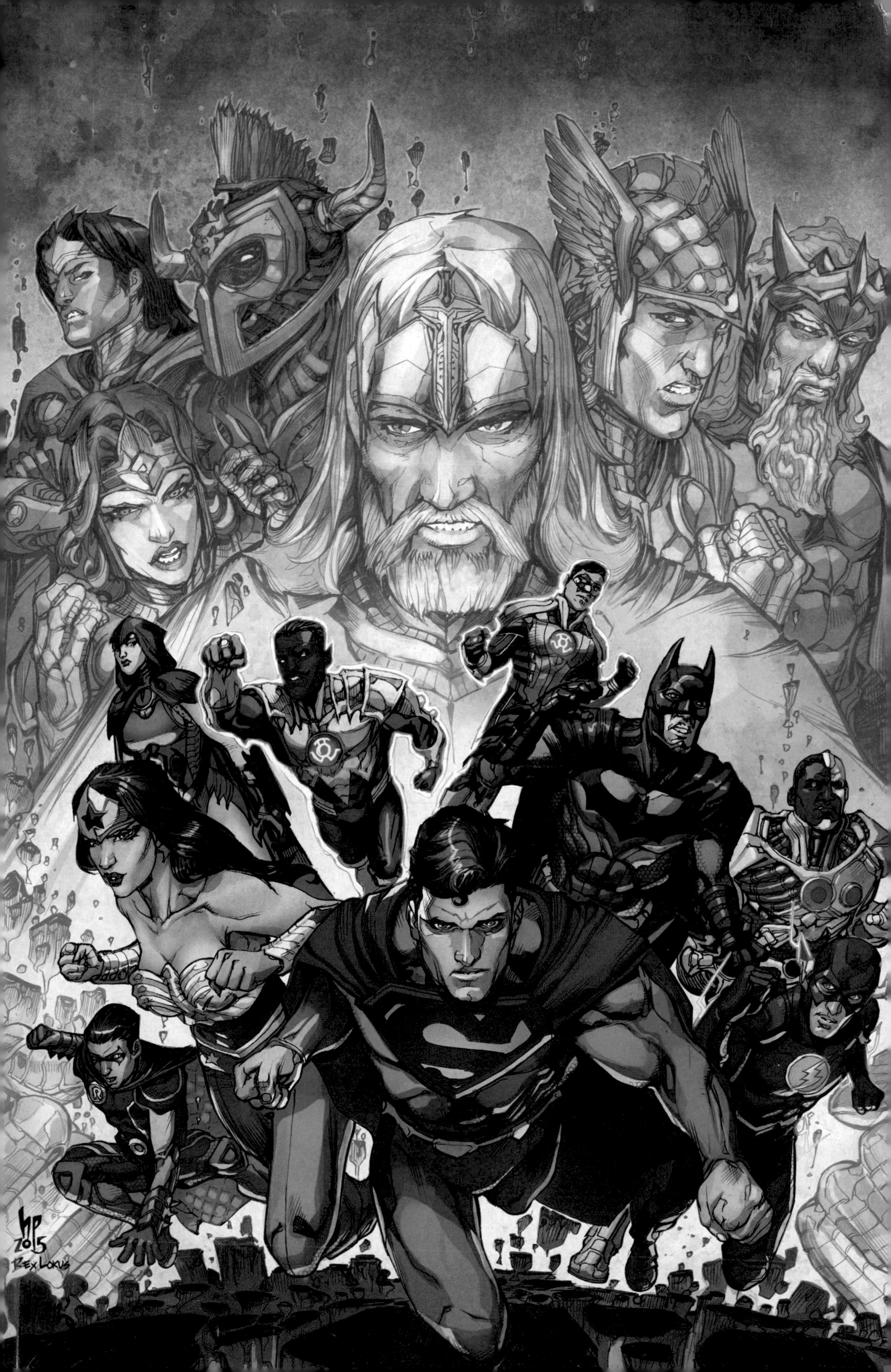
hp
2015
Rex Lokus

"The Gods Themselves" **Bruno Redondo** Penciller **Juan Albarran** Inker **Rex Lokus** Colorist
Cover Art by **Howard Porter & Rex Lokus**

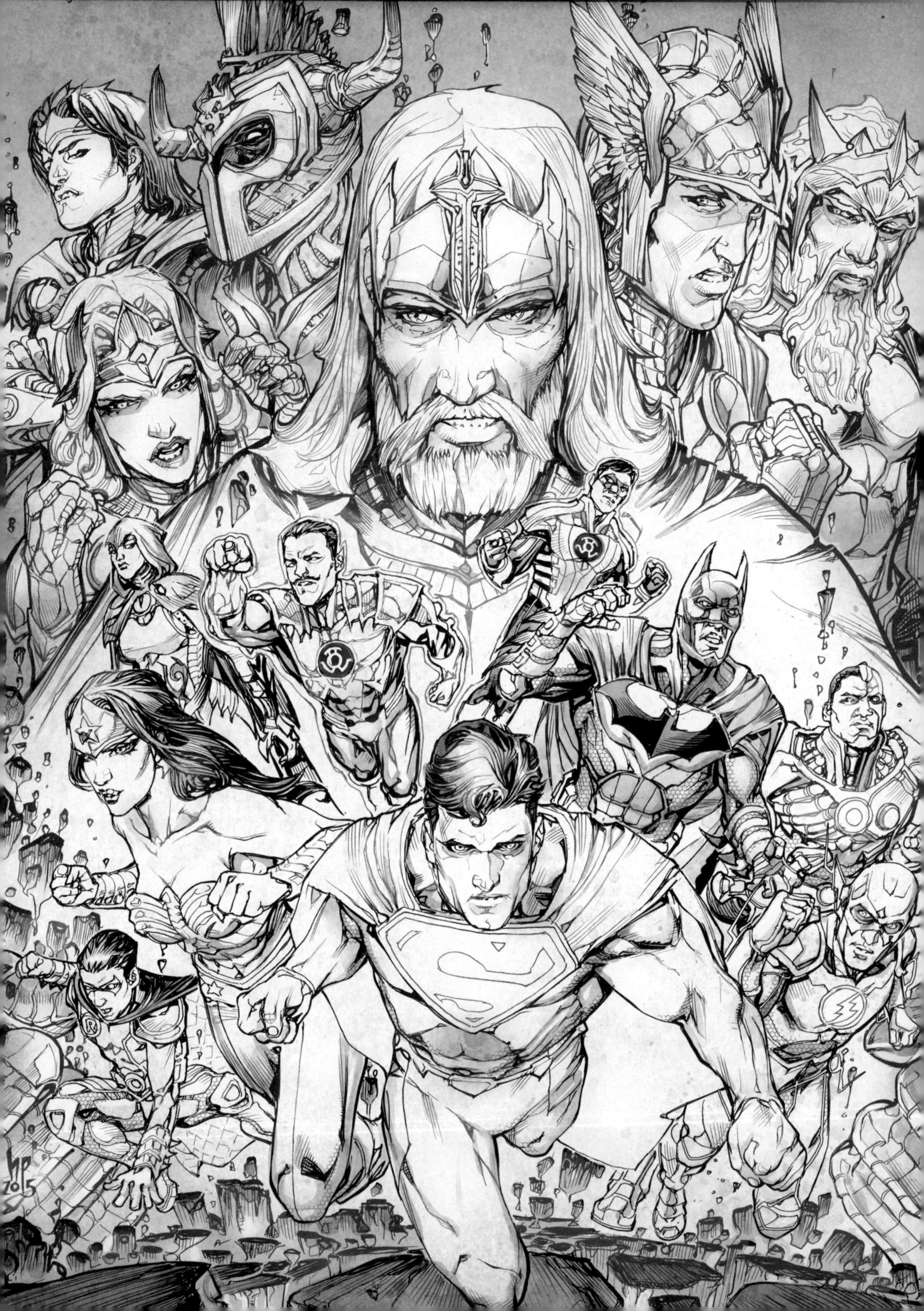

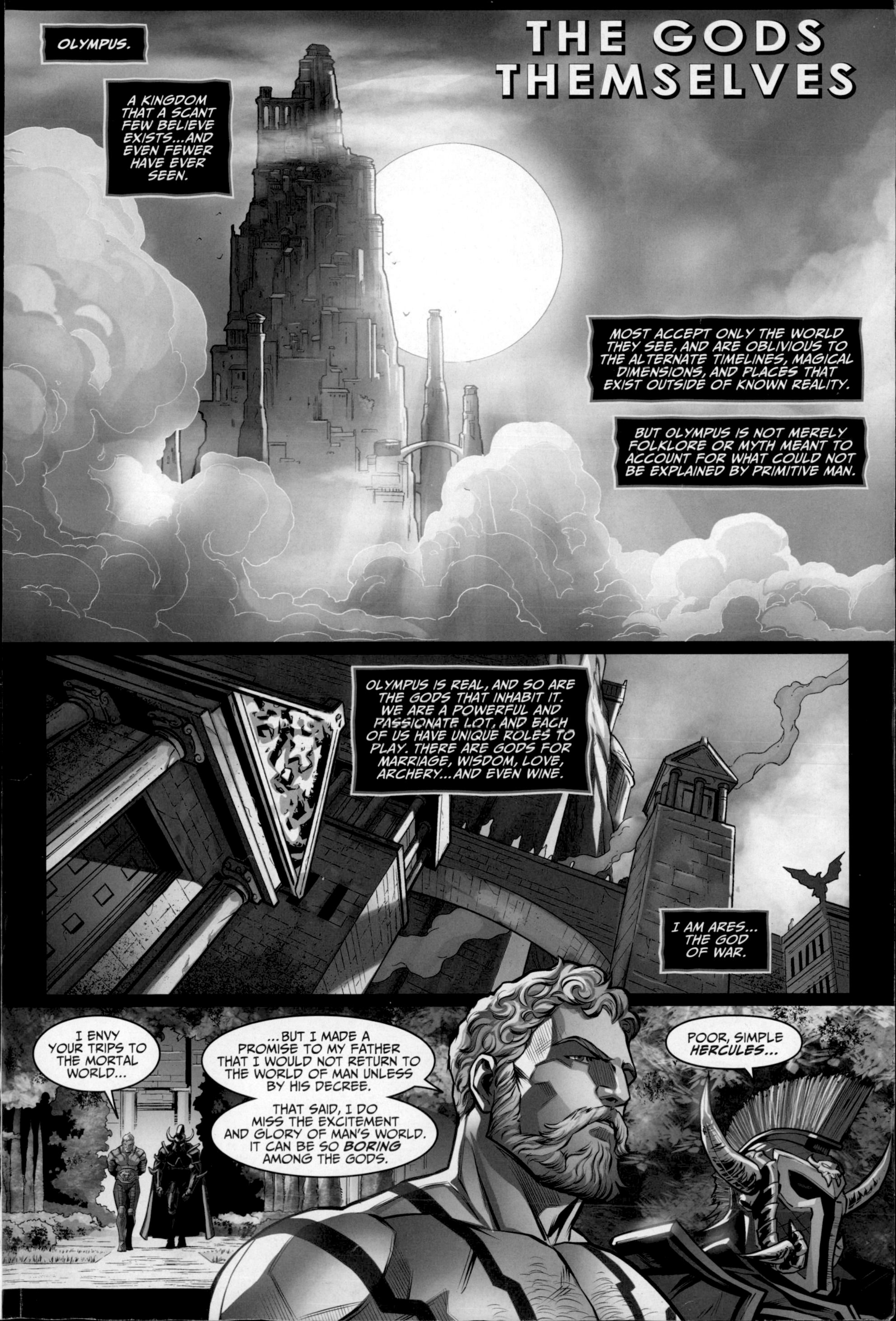
THE GODS THEMSELVES
OLYMPUS.
A KINGDOM THAT A SCANT FEW BELIEVE EXISTS...AND EVEN FEWER HAVE EVER SEEN.
MOST ACCEPT ONLY THE WORLD THEY SEE, AND ARE OBLIVIOUS TO THE ALTERNATE TIMELINES, MAGICAL DIMENSIONS, AND PLACES THAT EXIST OUTSIDE OF KNOWN REALITY.
BUT OLYMPUS IS NOT MERELY FOLKLORE OR MYTH MEANT TO ACCOUNT FOR WHAT COULD NOT BE EXPLAINED BY PRIMITIVE MAN.
OLYMPUS IS REAL, AND SO ARE THE GODS THAT INHABIT IT. WE ARE A POWERFUL AND PASSIONATE LOT, AND EACH OF US HAVE UNIQUE ROLES TO PLAY. THERE ARE GODS FOR MARRIAGE, WISDOM, LOVE, ARCHERY...AND EVEN WINE.
I AM ARES... THE GOD OF WAR.
I ENVY YOUR TRIPS TO THE MORTAL WORLD...
...BUT I MADE A PROMISE TO MY FATHER THAT I WOULD NOT RETURN TO THE WORLD OF MAN UNLESS BY HIS DECREE.
THAT SAID, I DO MISS THE EXCITEMENT AND GLORY OF MAN'S WORLD. IT CAN BE SO BORING AMONG THE GODS.
POOR, SIMPLE HERCULES...

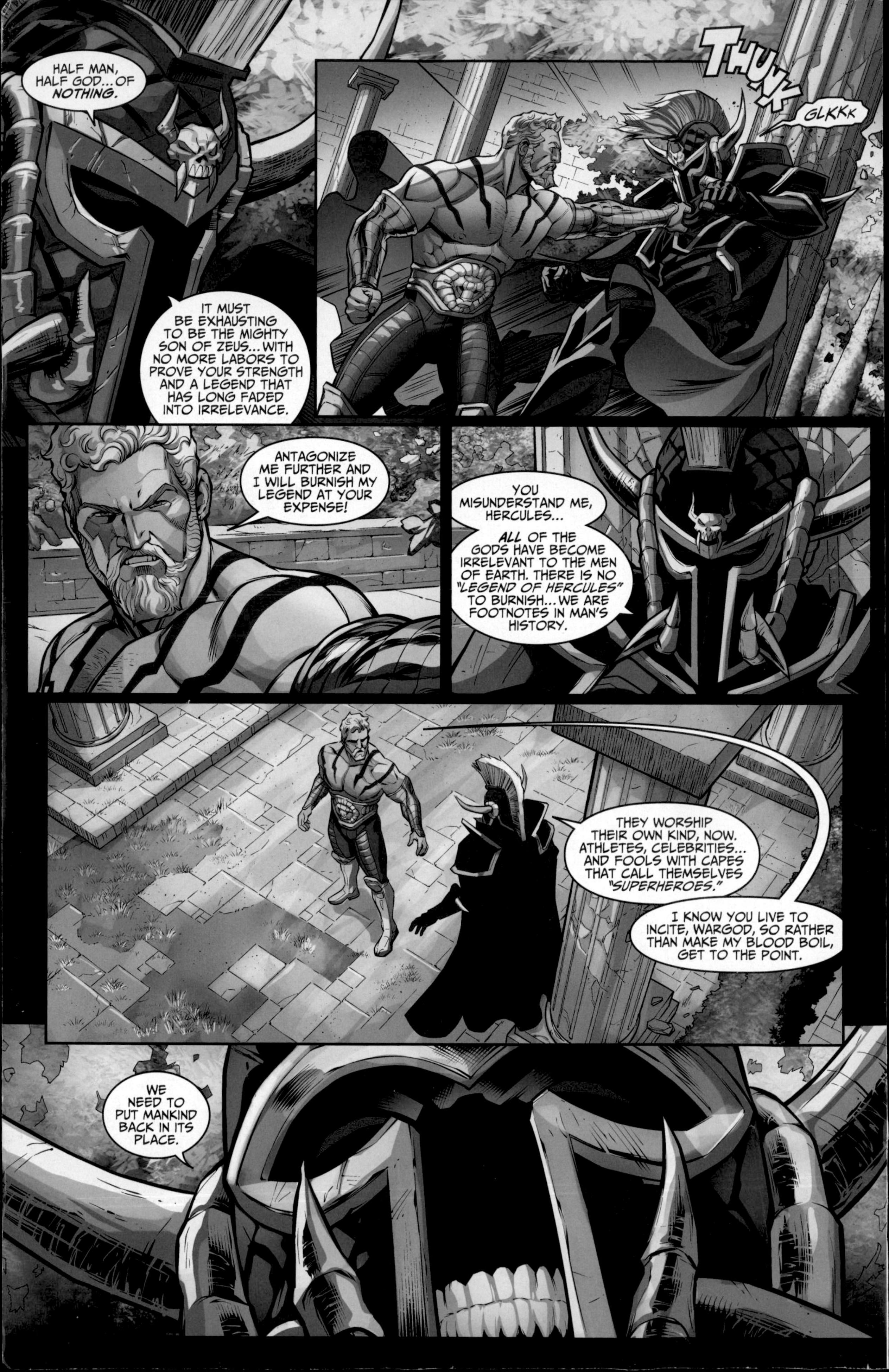
HALF MAN, HALF GOD...OF NOTHING.
THUNK
GLKKK
IT MUST BE EXHAUSTING TO BE THE MIGHTY SON OF ZEUS...WITH NO MORE LABORS TO PROVE YOUR STRENGTH AND A LEGEND THAT HAS LONG FADED INTO IRRELEVANCE.
ANTAGONIZE ME FURTHER AND I WILL BURNISH MY LEGEND AT YOUR EXPENSE!
YOU MISUNDERSTAND ME, HERCULES...
ALL OF THE GODS HAVE BECOME IRRELEVANT TO THE MEN OF EARTH. THERE IS NO "LEGEND OF HERCULES" TO BURNISH...WE ARE FOOTNOTES IN MAN'S HISTORY.
THEY WORSHIP THEIR OWN KIND, NOW. ATHLETES, CELEBRITIES... AND FOOLS WITH CAPES THAT CALL THEMSELVES "SUPERHEROES."
I KNOW YOU LIVE TO INCITE, WARGOD, SO RATHER THAN MAKE MY BLOOD BOIL, GET TO THE POINT.
WE NEED TO PUT MANKIND BACK IN ITS PLACE.

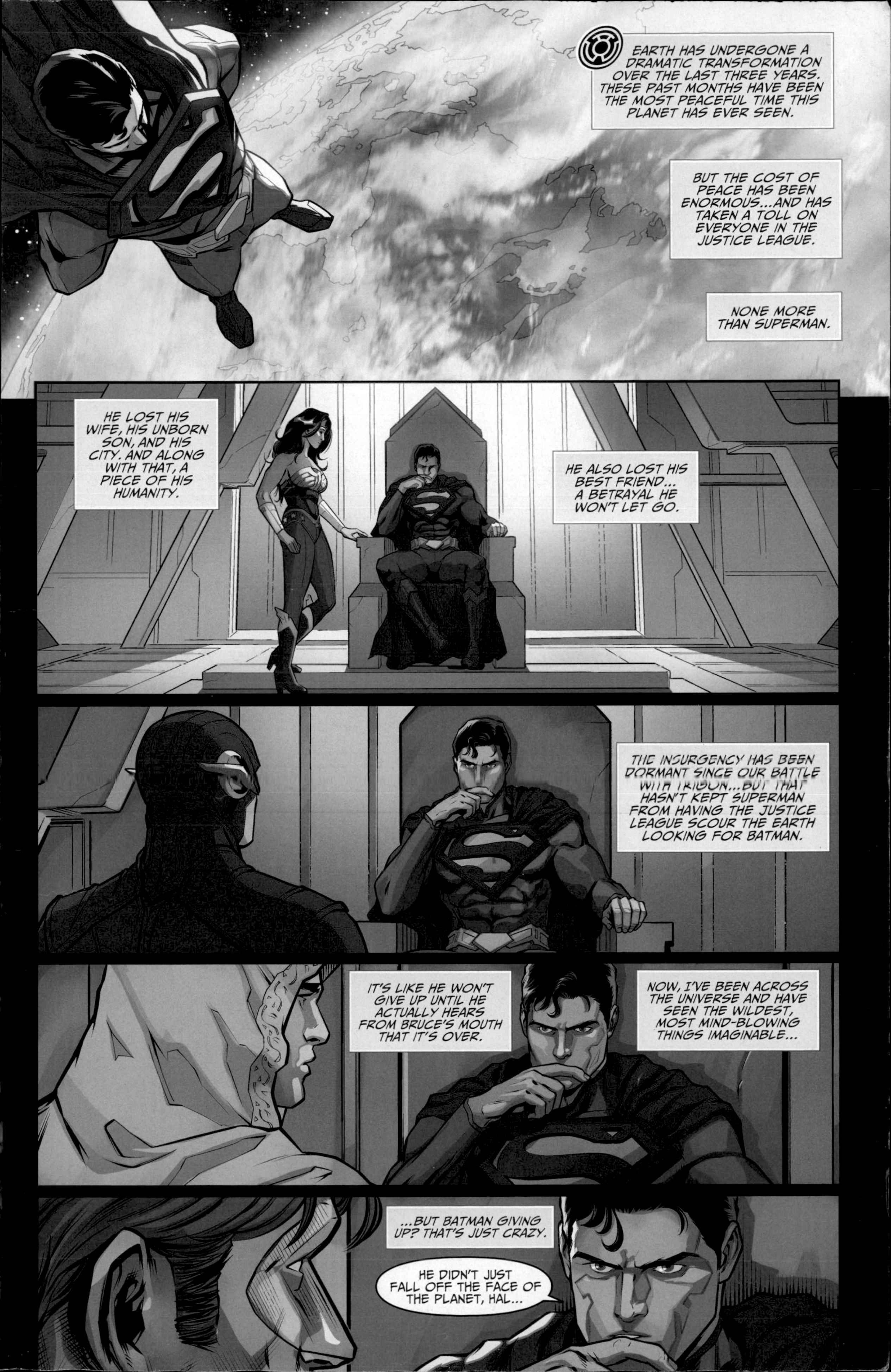
EARTH HAS UNDERGONE A DRAMATIC TRANSFORMATION OVER THE LAST THREE YEARS. THESE PAST MONTHS HAVE BEEN THE MOST PEACEFUL TIME THIS PLANET HAS EVER SEEN.
BUT THE COST OF PEACE HAS BEEN ENORMOUS...AND HAS TAKEN A TOLL ON EVERYONE IN THE JUSTICE LEAGUE.
NONE MORE THAN SUPERMAN.
HE LOST HIS WIFE, HIS UNBORN SON, AND HIS CITY. AND ALONG WITH THAT, A PIECE OF HIS HUMANITY.
HE ALSO LOST HIS BEST FRIEND... A BETRAYAL HE WON'T LET GO.
THE INSURGENCY HAS BEEN DORMANT SINCE OUR BATTLE WITH TRIGON...BUT THAT HASN'T KEPT SUPERMAN FROM HAVING THE JUSTICE LEAGUE SCOUR THE EARTH LOOKING FOR BATMAN.
IT'S LIKE HE WON'T GIVE UP UNTIL HE ACTUALLY HEARS FROM BRUCE'S MOUTH THAT IT'S OVER.
NOW, I'VE BEEN ACROSS THE UNIVERSE AND HAVE SEEN THE WILDEST, MOST MIND-BLOWING THINGS IMAGINABLE...
...BUT BATMAN GIVING UP? THAT'S JUST CRAZY.
HE DIDN'T JUST FALL OFF THE FACE OF THE PLANET, HAL...

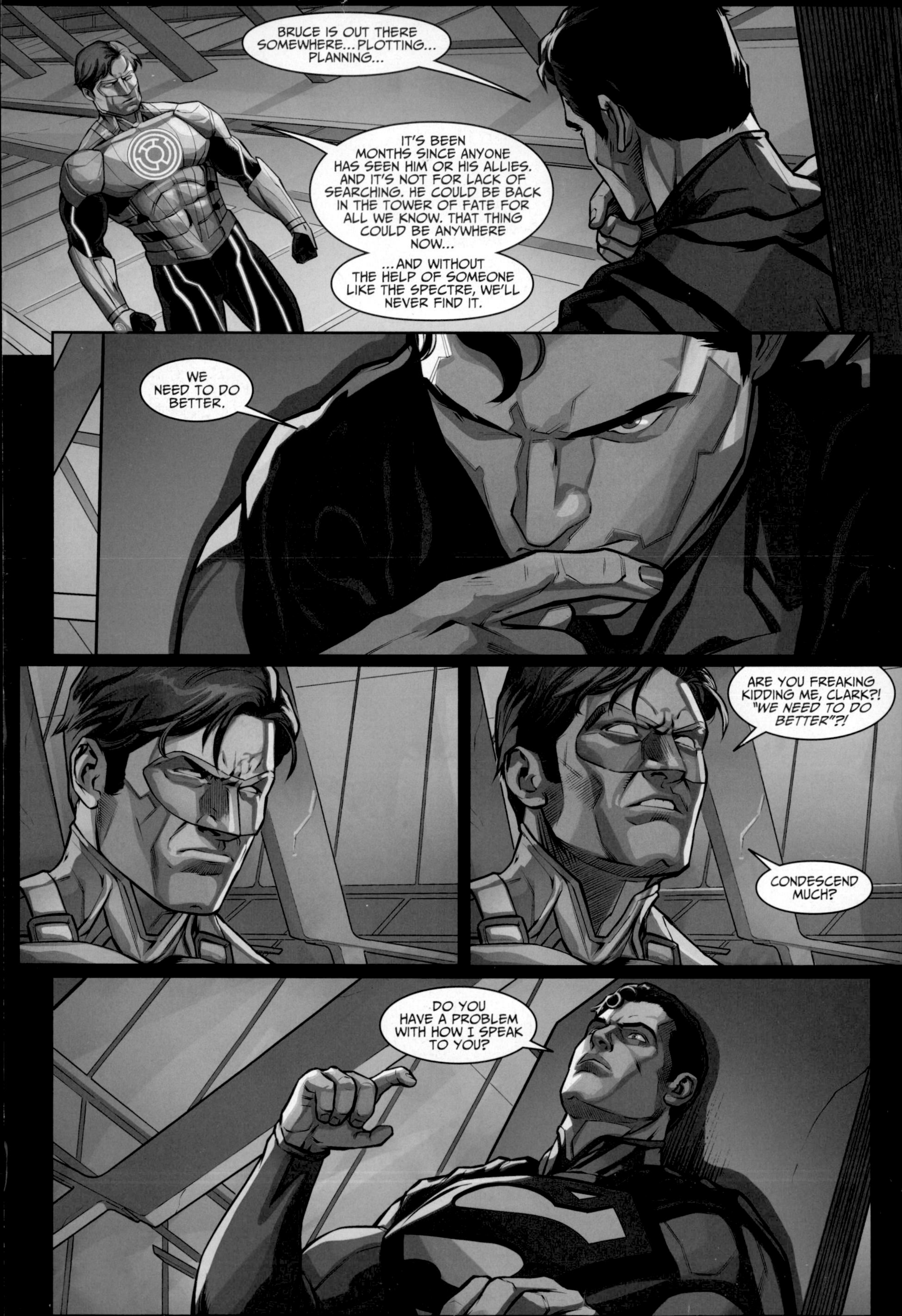
BRUCE IS OUT THERE SOMEWHERE...PLOTTING... PLANNING...
IT'S BEEN MONTHS SINCE ANYONE HAS SEEN HIM OR HIS ALLIES. AND IT'S NOT FOR LACK OF SEARCHING. HE COULD BE BACK IN THE TOWER OF FATE FOR ALL WE KNOW. THAT THING COULD BE ANYWHERE NOW...
...AND WITHOUT THE HELP OF SOMEONE LIKE THE SPECTRE, WE'LL NEVER FIND IT.
WE NEED TO DO BETTER.
ARE YOU FREAKING KIDDING ME, CLARK?! "WE NEED TO DO BETTER"?!
CONDESCEND MUCH?
DO YOU HAVE A PROBLEM WITH HOW I SPEAK TO YOU?

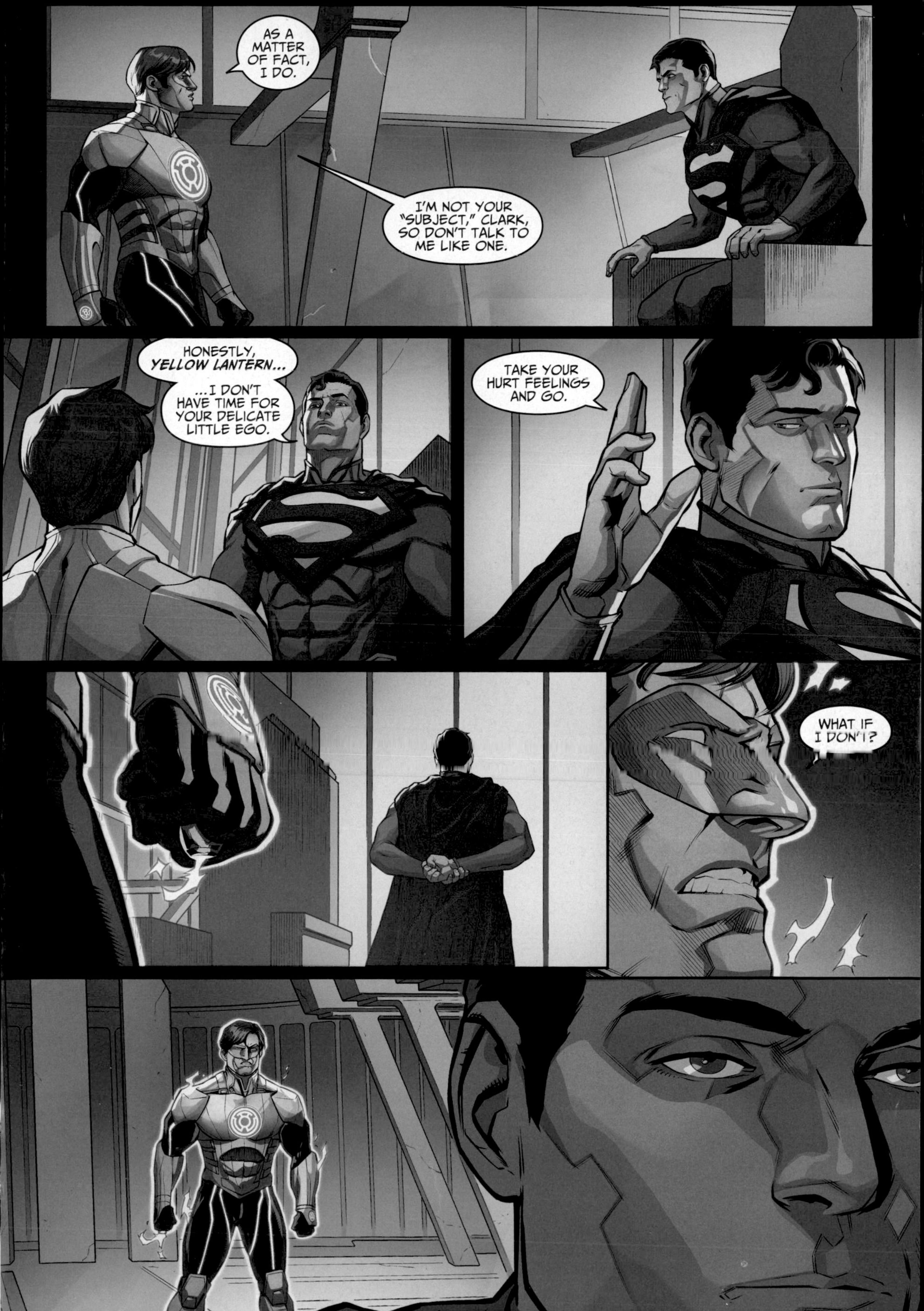
AS A MATTER OF FACT, I DO.
I'M NOT YOUR "SUBJECT," CLARK, SO DON'T TALK TO ME LIKE ONE.
HONESTLY, YELLOW LANTERN...
...I DON'T HAVE TIME FOR YOUR DELICATE LITTLE EGO.
TAKE YOUR HURT FEELINGS AND GO.
WHAT IF I DON'T?

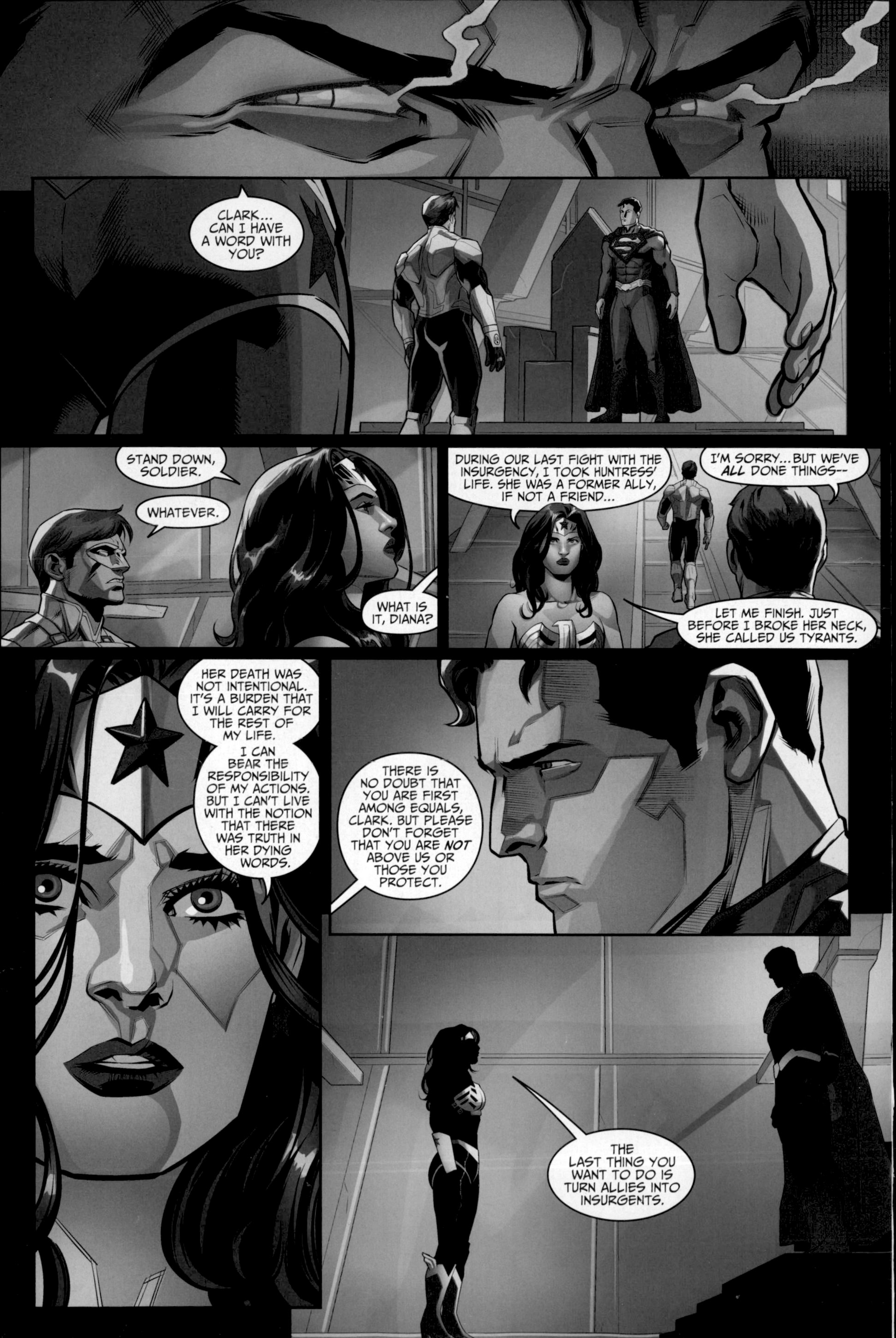
CLARK... CAN I HAVE A WORD WITH YOU?
STAND DOWN, SOLDIER.
WHATEVER.
WHAT IS IT, DIANA?
DURING OUR LAST FIGHT WITH THE INSURGENCY, I TOOK HUNTRESS' LIFE. SHE WAS A FORMER ALLY, IF NOT A FRIEND...
I'M SORRY... BUT WE'VE ALL DONE THINGS--
LET ME FINISH. JUST BEFORE I BROKE HER NECK, SHE CALLED US TYRANTS.
HER DEATH WAS NOT INTENTIONAL. IT'S A BURDEN THAT I WILL CARRY FOR THE REST OF MY LIFE.
I CAN BEAR THE RESPONSIBILITY OF MY ACTIONS. BUT I CAN'T LIVE WITH THE NOTION THAT THERE WAS TRUTH IN HER DYING WORDS.
THERE IS NO DOUBT THAT YOU ARE FIRST AMONG EQUALS, CLARK. BUT PLEASE DON'T FORGET THAT YOU ARE NOT ABOVE US OR THOSE YOU PROTECT.
THE LAST THING YOU WANT TO DO IS TURN ALLIES INTO INSURGENTS.

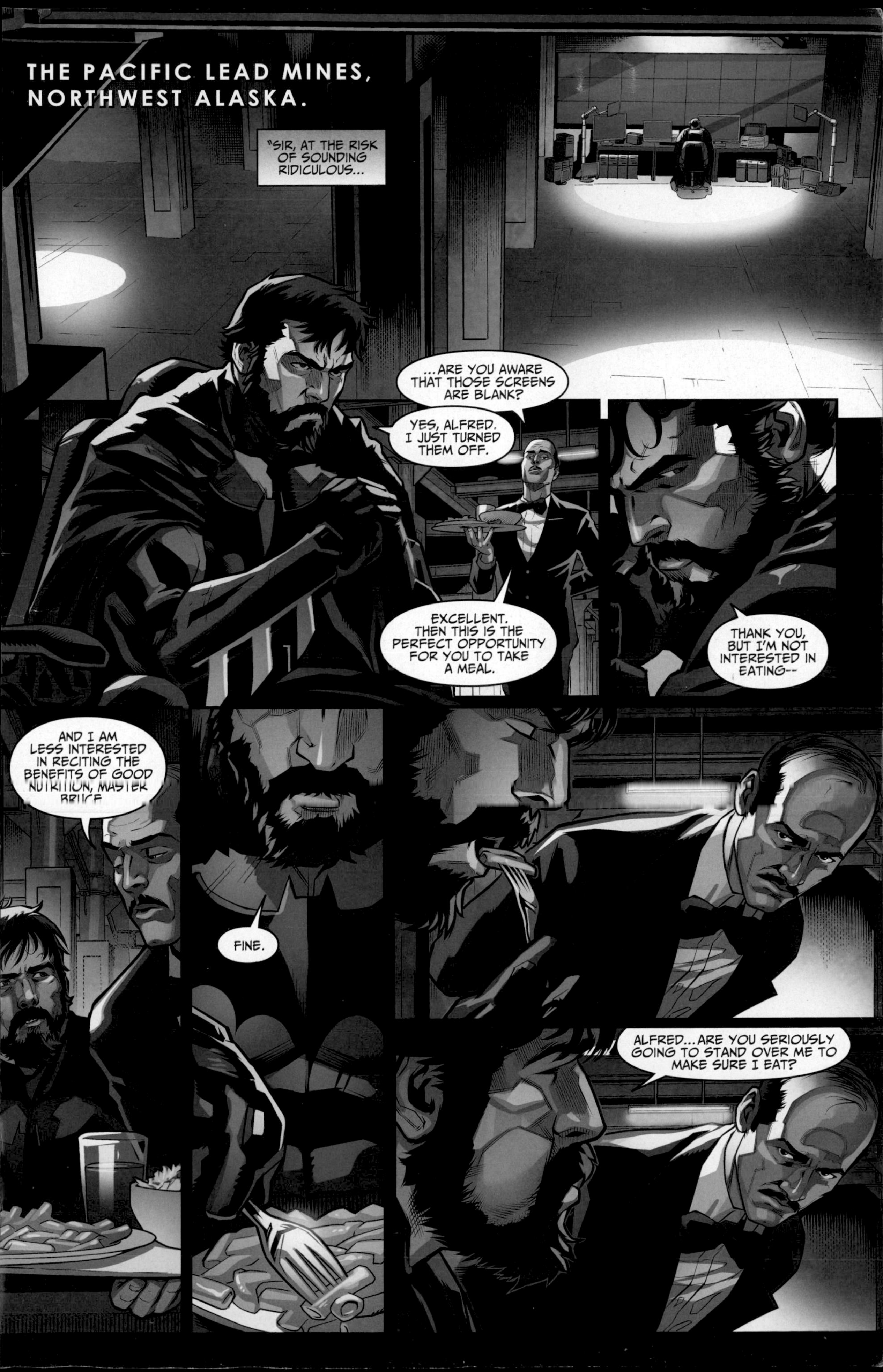
THE PACIFIC LEAD MINES, NORTHWEST ALASKA.
"SIR, AT THE RISK OF SOUNDING RIDICULOUS...
...ARE YOU AWARE THAT THOSE SCREENS ARE BLANK?
YES, ALFRED. I JUST TURNED THEM OFF.
EXCELLENT. THEN THIS IS THE PERFECT OPPORTUNITY FOR YOU TO TAKE A MEAL.
THANK YOU, BUT I'M NOT INTERESTED IN EATING--
AND I AM LESS INTERESTED IN RECITING THE BENEFITS OF GOOD NUTRITION, MASTER BRUCE.
FINE.
ALFRED...ARE YOU SERIOUSLY GOING TO STAND OVER ME TO MAKE SURE I EAT?

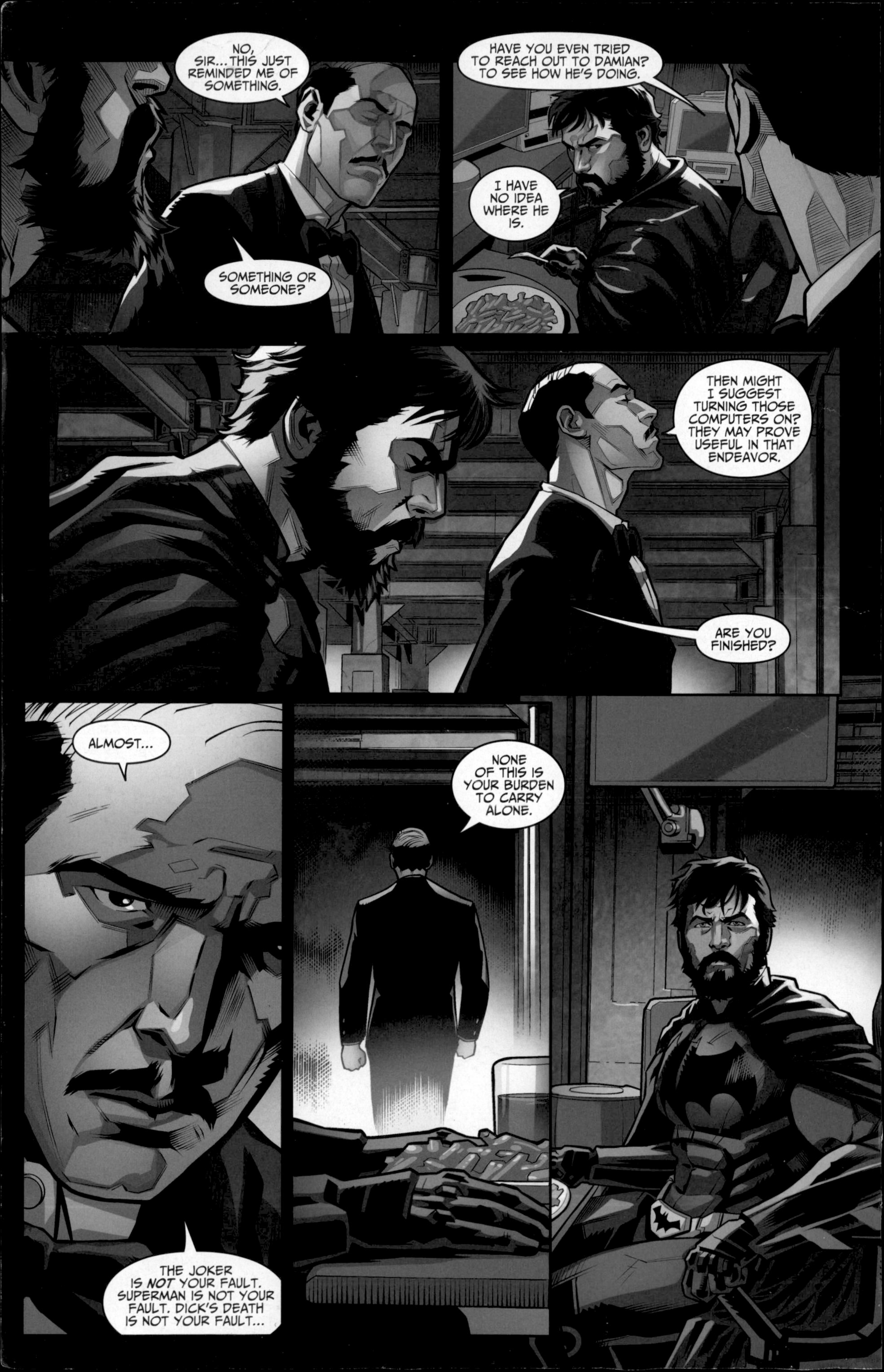
NO, SIR... THIS JUST REMINDED ME OF SOMETHING.
SOMETHING OR SOMEONE?
HAVE YOU EVEN TRIED TO REACH OUT TO DAMIAN? TO SEE HOW HE'S DOING.
I HAVE NO IDEA WHERE HE IS.
THEN MIGHT I SUGGEST TURNING THOSE COMPUTERS ON? THEY MAY PROVE USEFUL IN THAT ENDEAVOR.
ARE YOU FINISHED?
ALMOST...
THE JOKER IS *NOT* YOUR FAULT. SUPERMAN IS NOT YOUR FAULT. DICK'S DEATH IS NOT YOUR FAULT...
NONE OF THIS IS YOUR BURDEN TO CARRY ALONE.

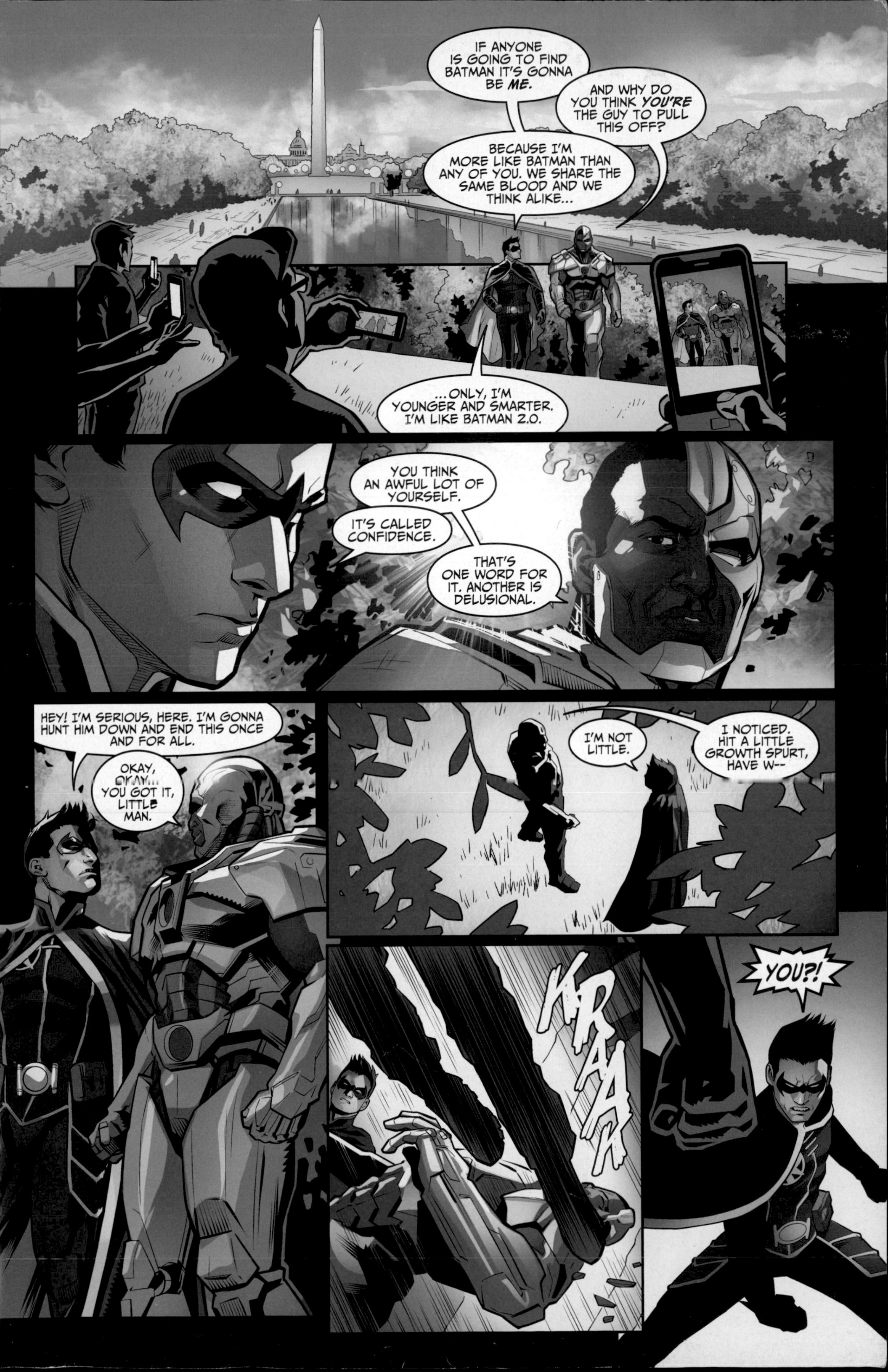
IF ANYONE IS GOING TO FIND BATMAN IT'S GONNA BE ME.
AND WHY DO YOU THINK YOU'RE THE GUY TO PULL THIS OFF?
BECAUSE I'M MORE LIKE BATMAN THAN ANY OF YOU. WE SHARE THE SAME BLOOD AND WE THINK ALIKE...
...ONLY, I'M YOUNGER AND SMARTER. I'M LIKE BATMAN 2.0.
YOU THINK AN AWFUL LOT OF YOURSELF.
IT'S CALLED CONFIDENCE.
THAT'S ONE WORD FOR IT. ANOTHER IS DELUSIONAL.
HEY! I'M SERIOUS, HERE. I'M GONNA HUNT HIM DOWN AND END THIS ONCE AND FOR ALL.
OKAY, OKAY... YOU GOT IT, LITTLE MAN.
I'M NOT LITTLE.
I NOTICED. HIT A LITTLE GROWTH SPURT, HAVE W--
KRAAK
YOU?!

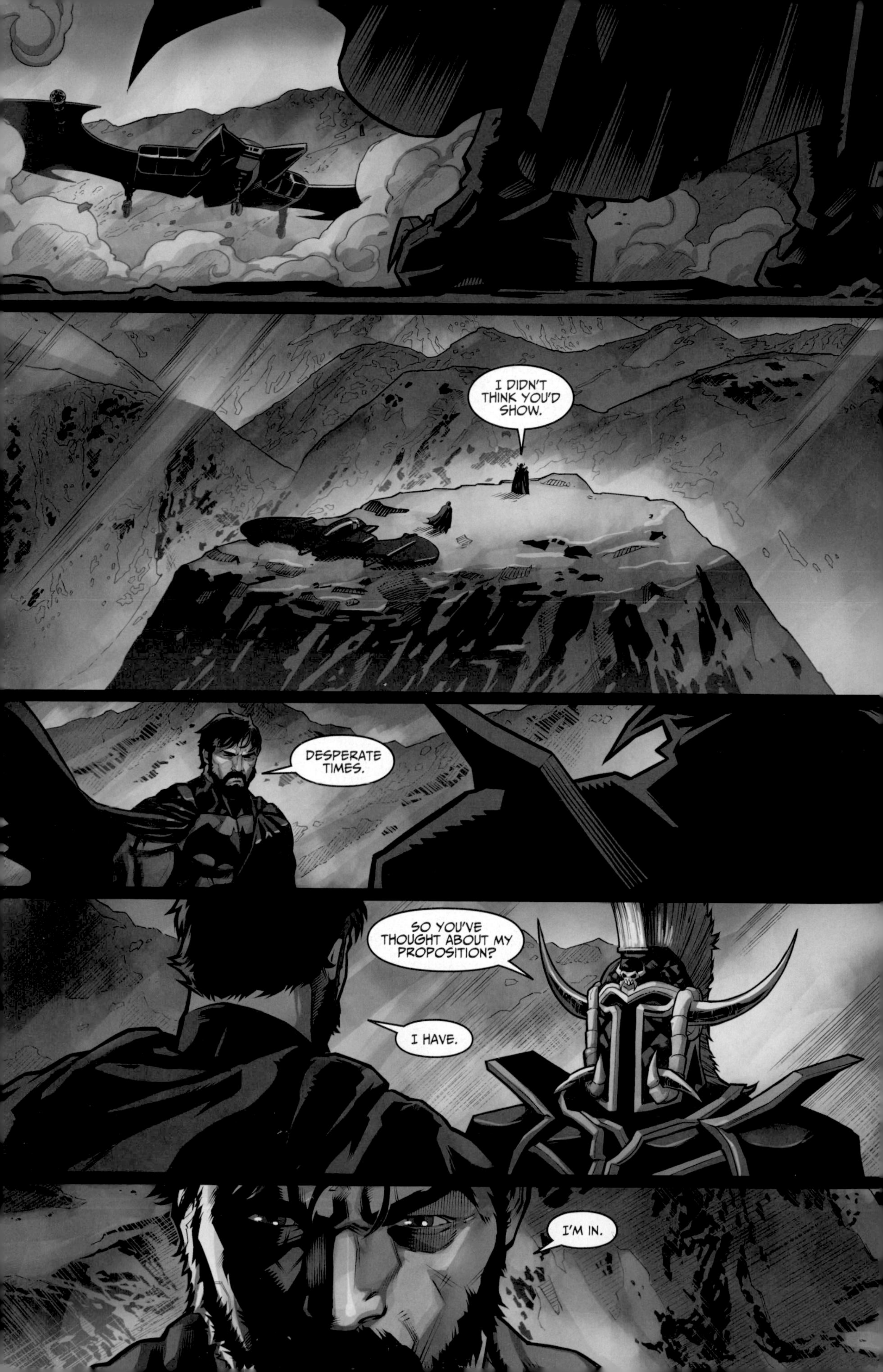
I DIDN'T THINK YOU'D SHOW.
DESPERATE TIMES.
SO YOU'VE THOUGHT ABOUT MY PROPOSITION?
I HAVE.
I'M IN.

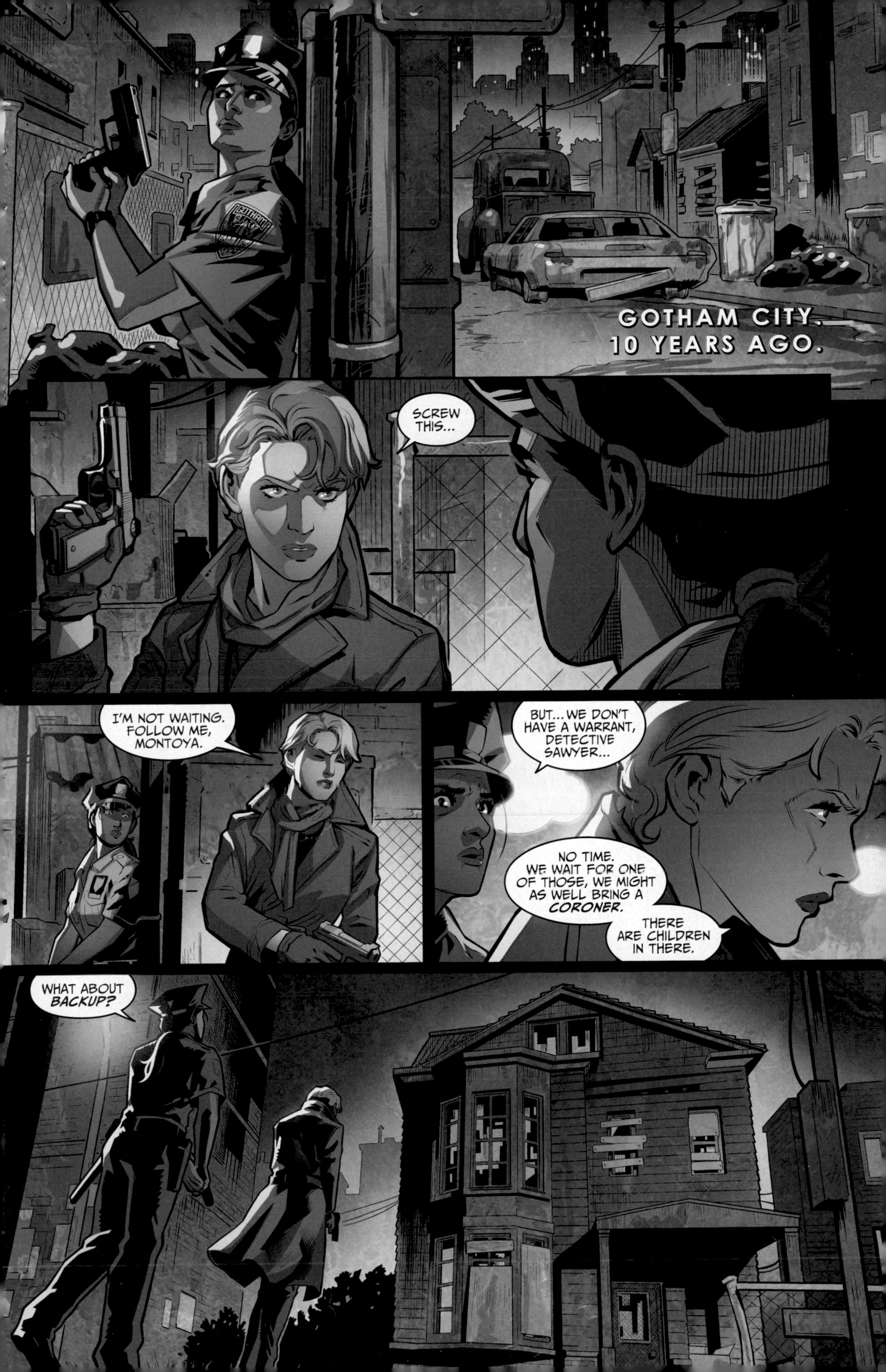
GOTHAM CITY.
10 YEARS AGO.
SCREW THIS...
I'M NOT WAITING. FOLLOW ME, MONTOYA.
BUT...WE DON'T HAVE A WARRANT, DETECTIVE SAWYER...
NO TIME. WE WAIT FOR ONE OF THOSE, WE MIGHT AS WELL BRING A *CORONER.*
THERE ARE CHILDREN IN THERE.
WHAT ABOUT *BACKUP?*

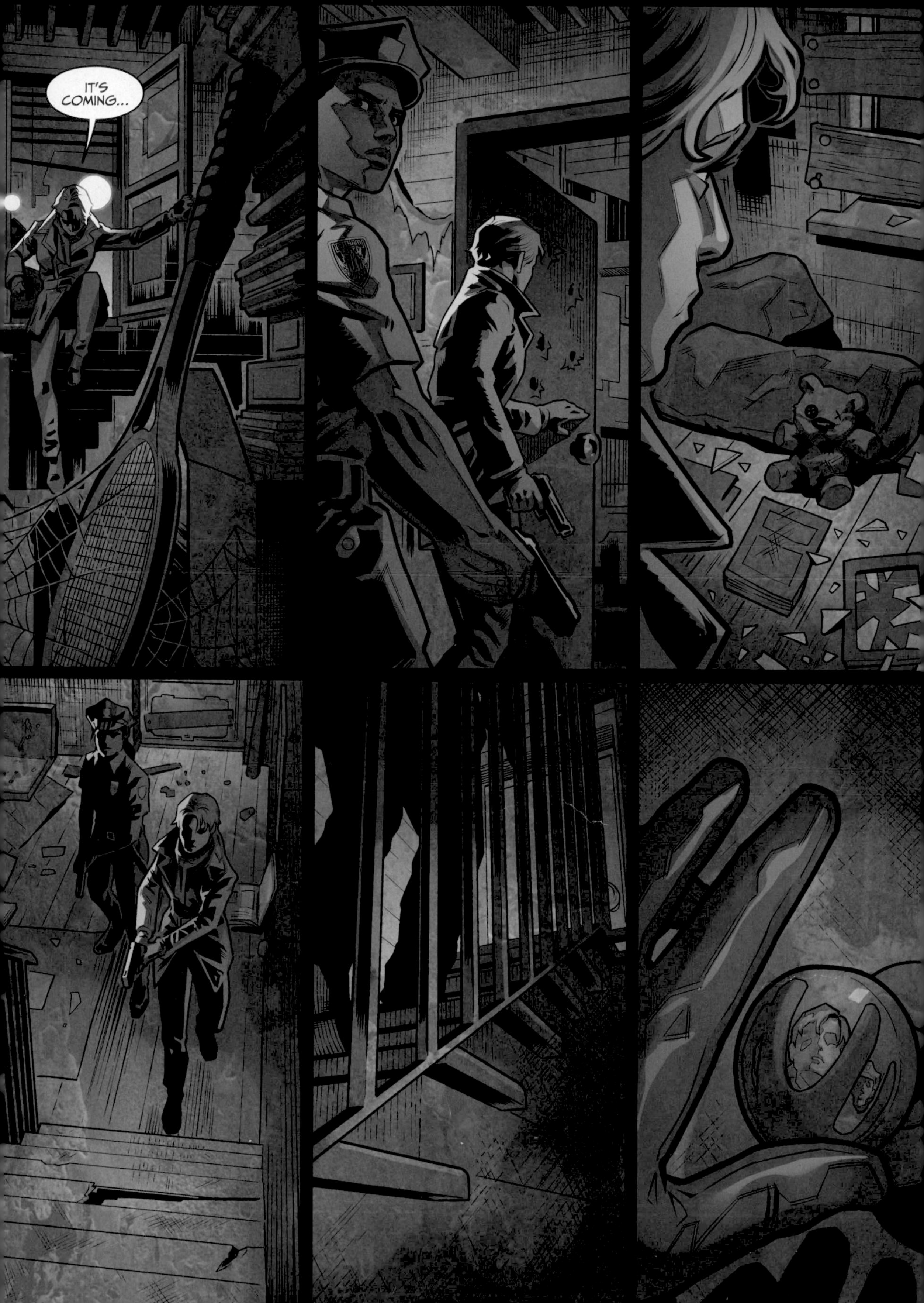
IT'S COMING...

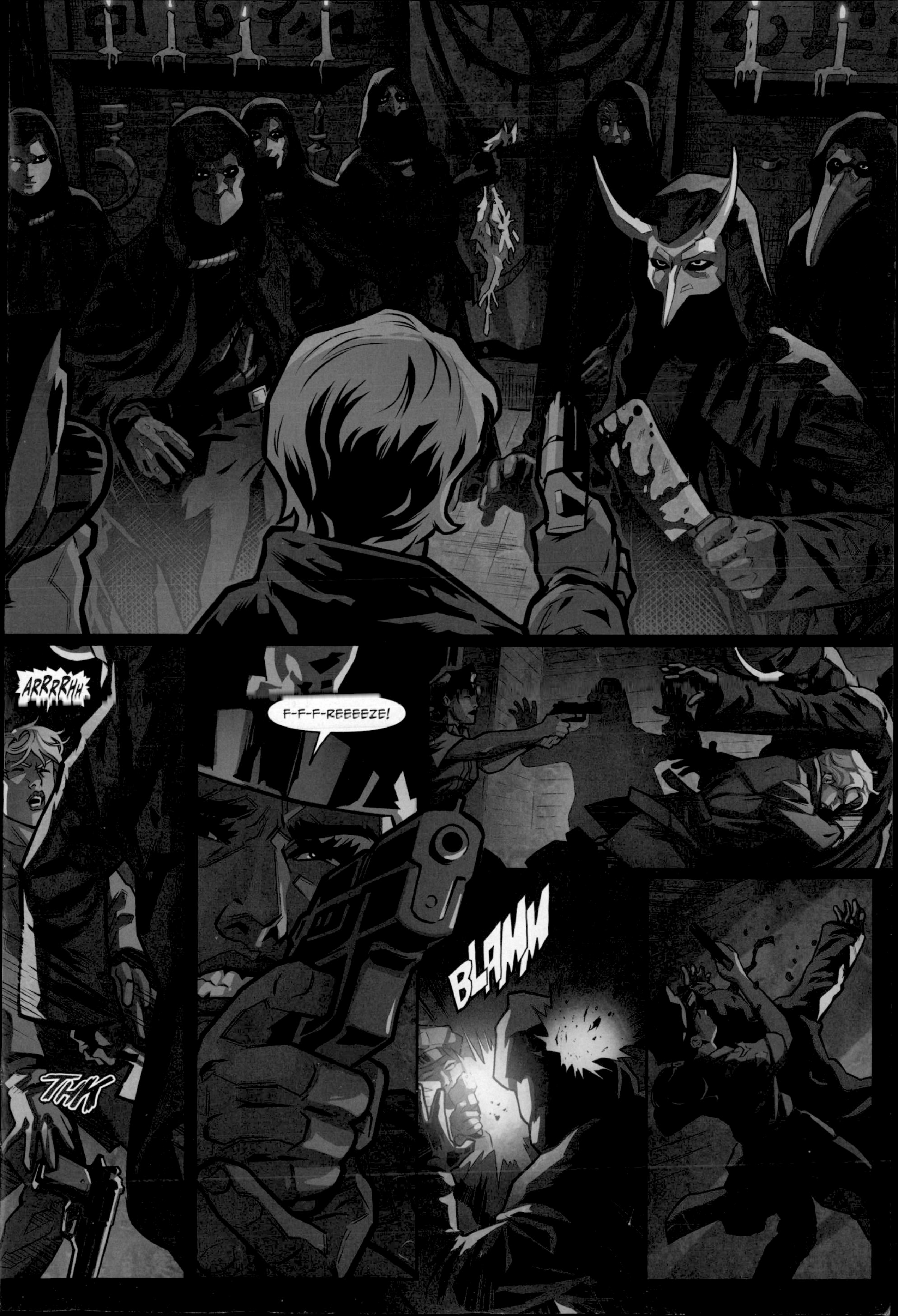
ARRRRHH
F-F-F-REEEEZE!
THK
BLAMM

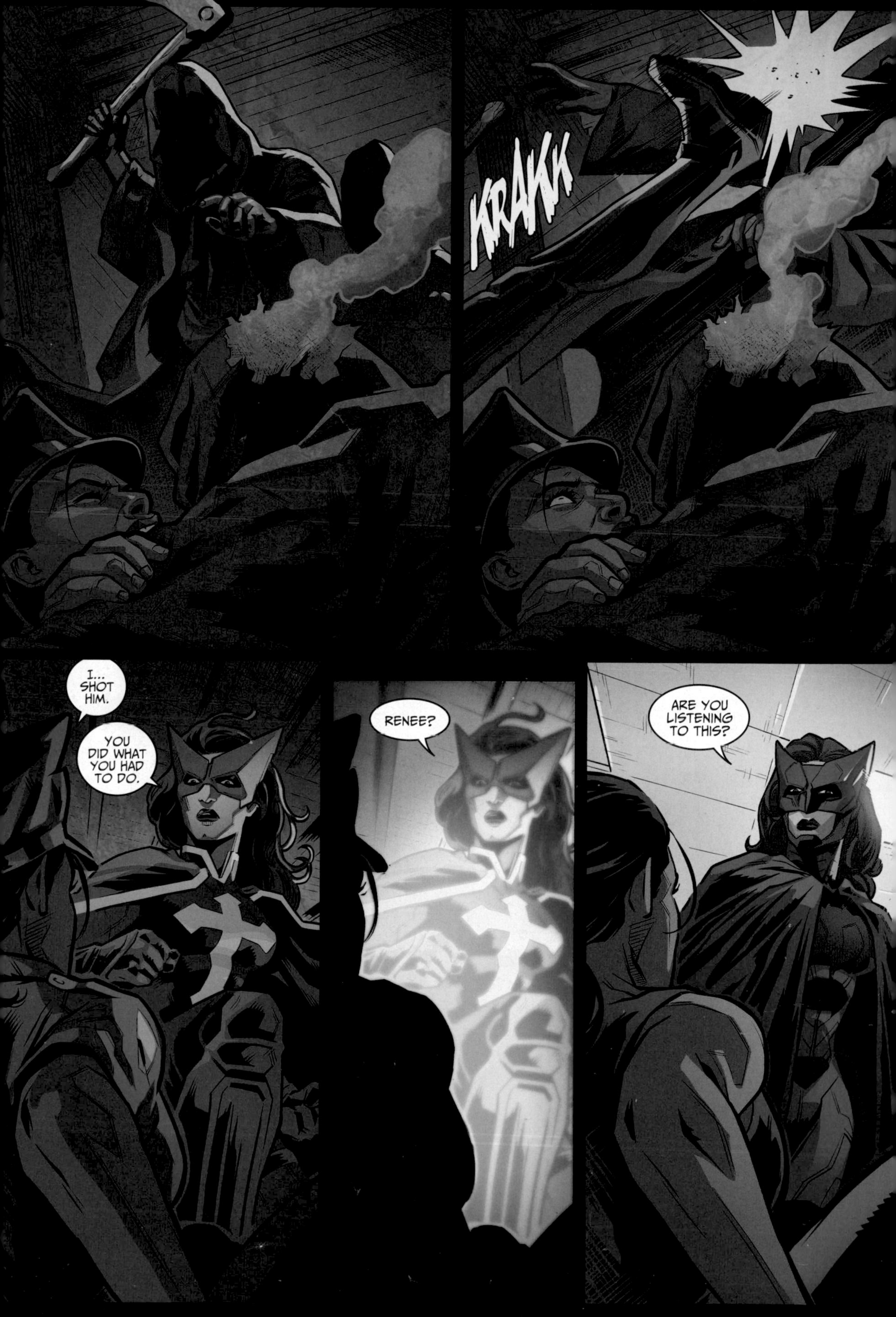
KRAKK
I... SHOT HIM.
YOU DID WHAT YOU HAD TO DO.
RENEE?
ARE YOU LISTENING TO THIS?

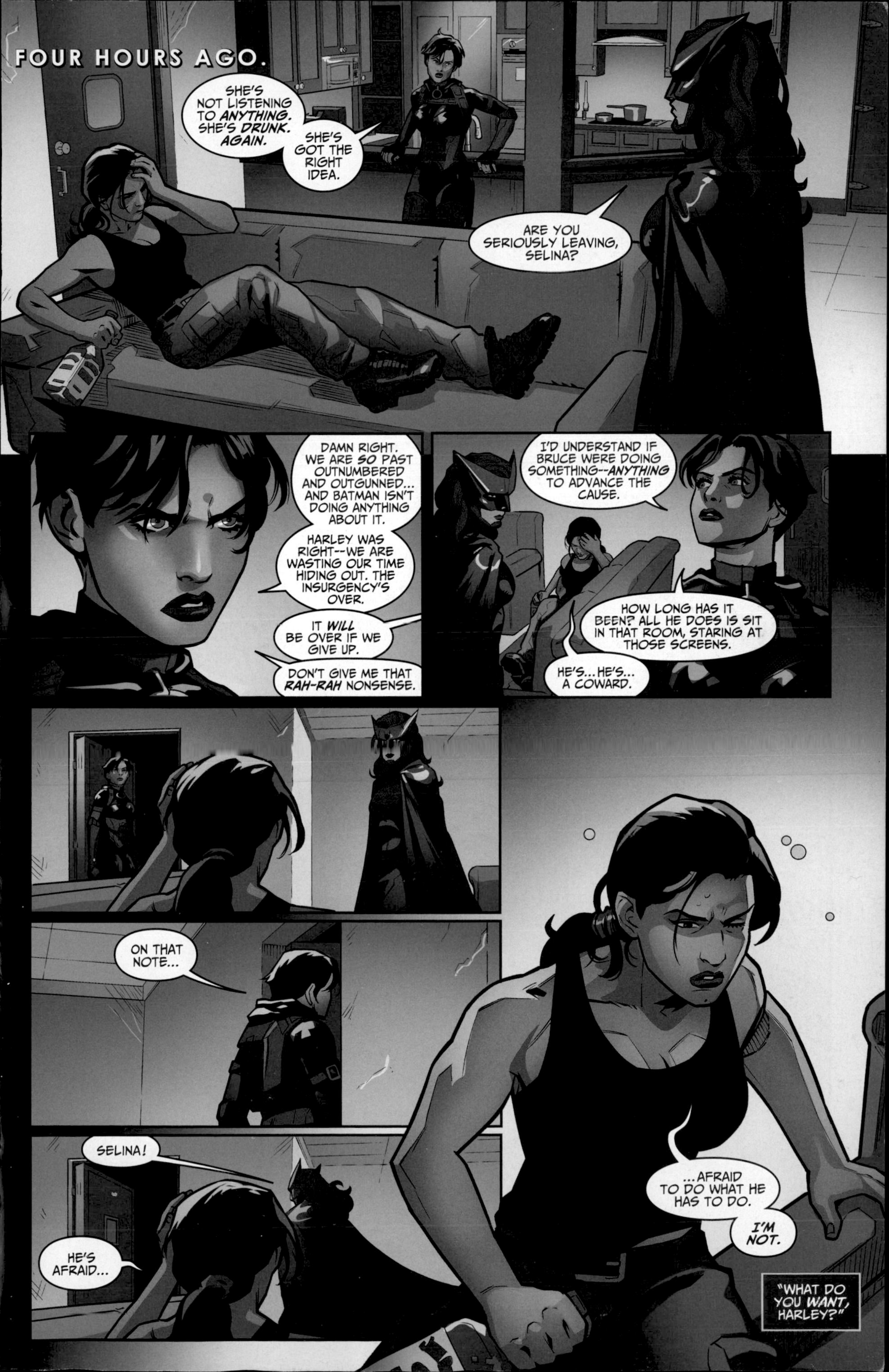
FOUR HOURS AGO.
SHE'S NOT LISTENING TO ANYTHING. SHE'S DRUNK. AGAIN.
SHE'S GOT THE RIGHT IDEA.
ARE YOU SERIOUSLY LEAVING, SELINA?
DAMN RIGHT. WE ARE SO PAST OUTNUMBERED AND OUTGUNNED... AND BATMAN ISN'T DOING ANYTHING ABOUT IT.
HARLEY WAS RIGHT--WE ARE WASTING OUR TIME HIDING OUT. THE INSURGENCY'S OVER.
IT WILL BE OVER IF WE GIVE UP.
DON'T GIVE ME THAT RAH-RAH NONSENSE.
I'D UNDERSTAND IF BRUCE WERE DOING SOMETHING--ANYTHING TO ADVANCE THE CAUSE.
HOW LONG HAS IT BEEN? ALL HE DOES IS SIT IN THAT ROOM, STARING AT THOSE SCREENS.
HE'S... HE'S... A COWARD.
ON THAT NOTE...
SELINA!
HE'S AFRAID...
...AFRAID TO DO WHAT HE HAS TO DO.
I'M NOT.
"WHAT DO YOU WANT, HARLEY?"

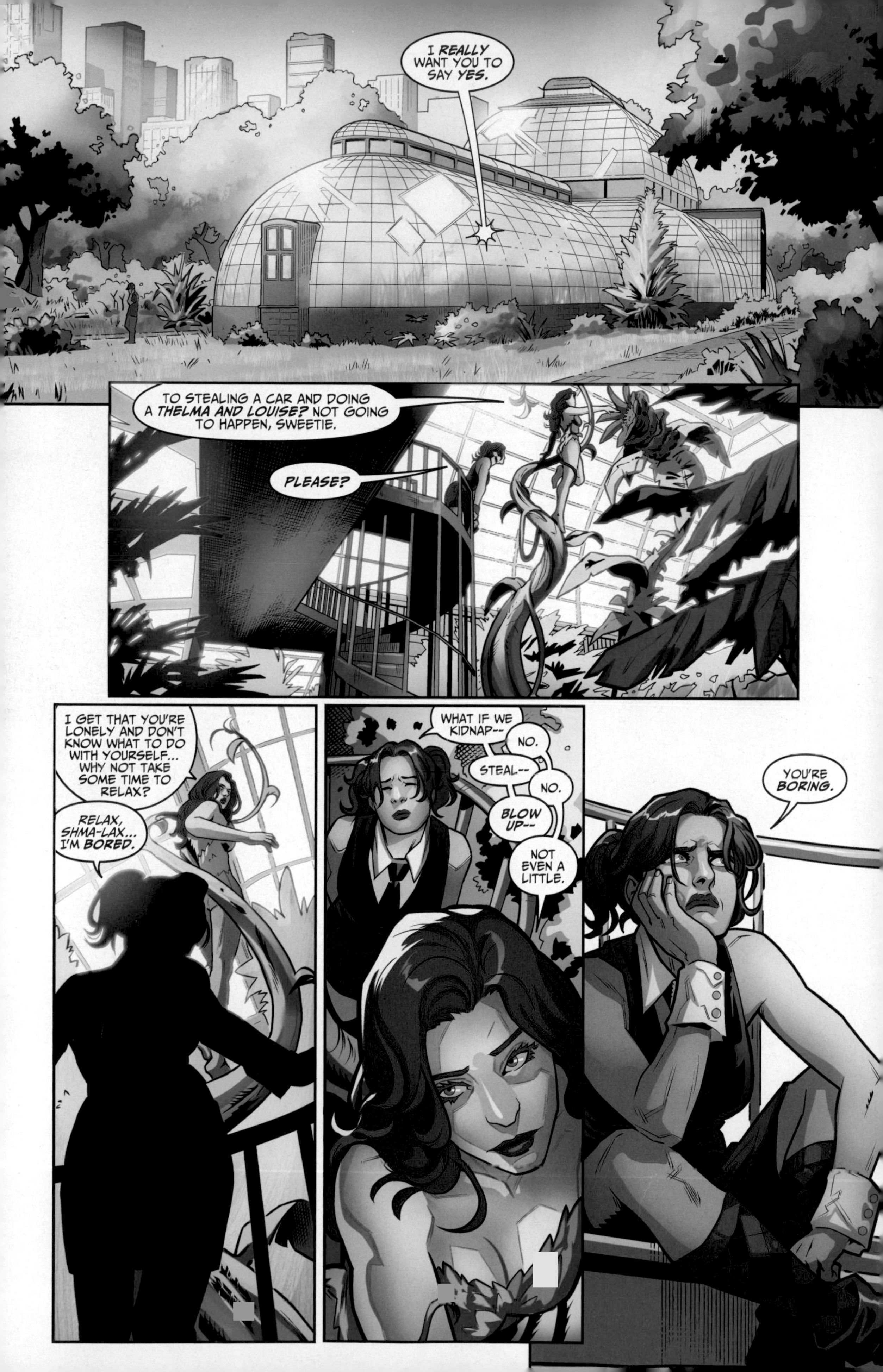
I REALLY WANT YOU TO SAY YES.
TO STEALING A CAR AND DOING A THELMA AND LOUISE? NOT GOING TO HAPPEN, SWEETIE.
PLEASE?
I GET THAT YOU'RE LONELY AND DON'T KNOW WHAT TO DO WITH YOURSELF... WHY NOT TAKE SOME TIME TO RELAX?
RELAX, SHMA-LAX... I'M BORED.
WHAT IF WE KIDNAP--
NO.
STEAL--
NO.
BLOW UP--
NOT EVEN A LITTLE.
YOU'RE BORING.

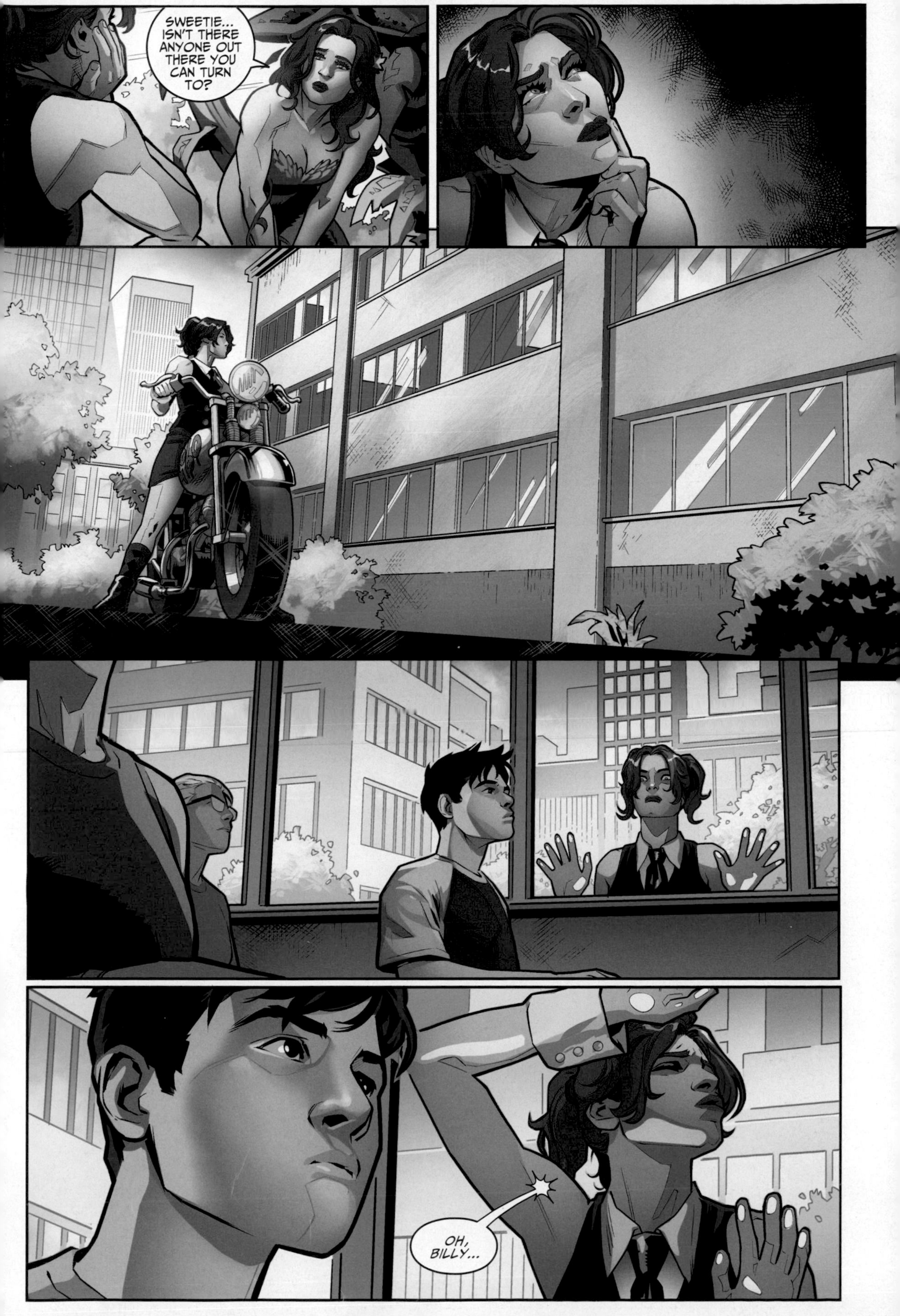
SWEETIE... ISN'T THERE ANYONE OUT THERE YOU CAN TURN TO?
OH, BILLY...

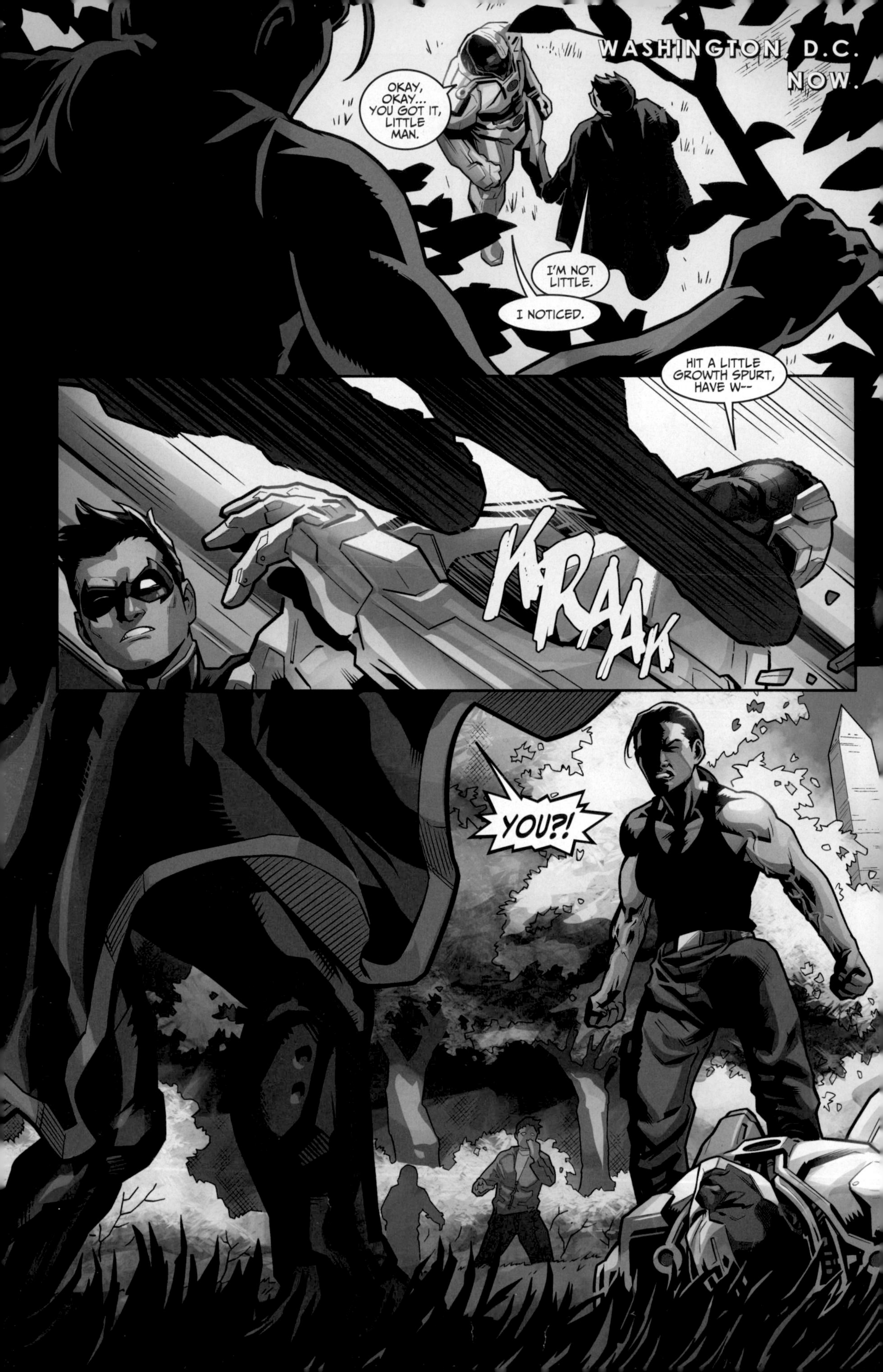
WASHINGTON, D.C. NOW.
OKAY, OKAY... YOU GOT IT, LITTLE MAN.
I'M NOT LITTLE.
I NOTICED.
HIT A LITTLE GROWTH SPURT, HAVE W--
KRAAAK
YOU?!

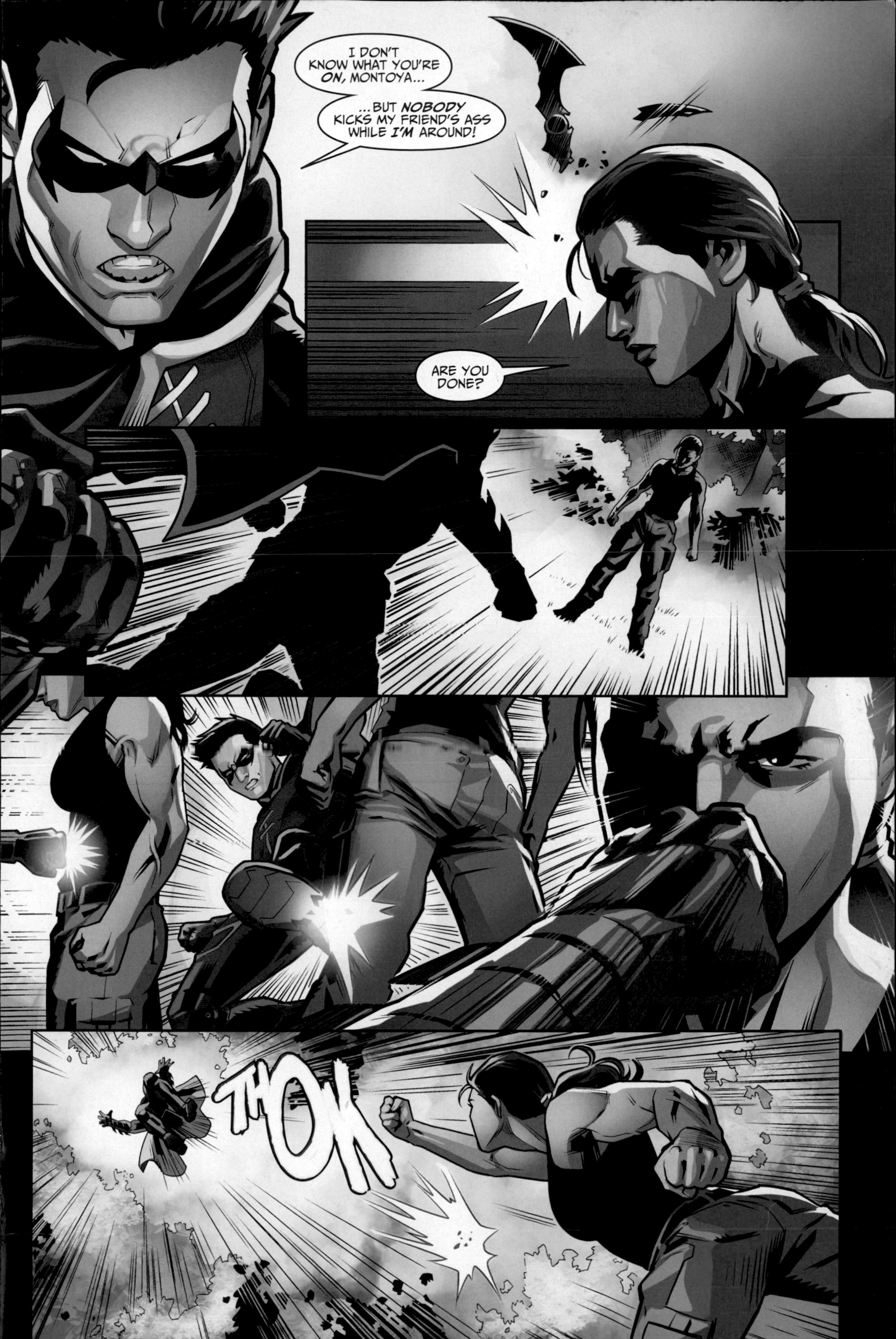

I DON'T KNOW WHAT YOU'RE *ON*, MONTOYA...
...BUT *NOBODY* KICKS MY FRIEND'S ASS WHILE *I'M* AROUND!
ARE YOU DONE?
THOK

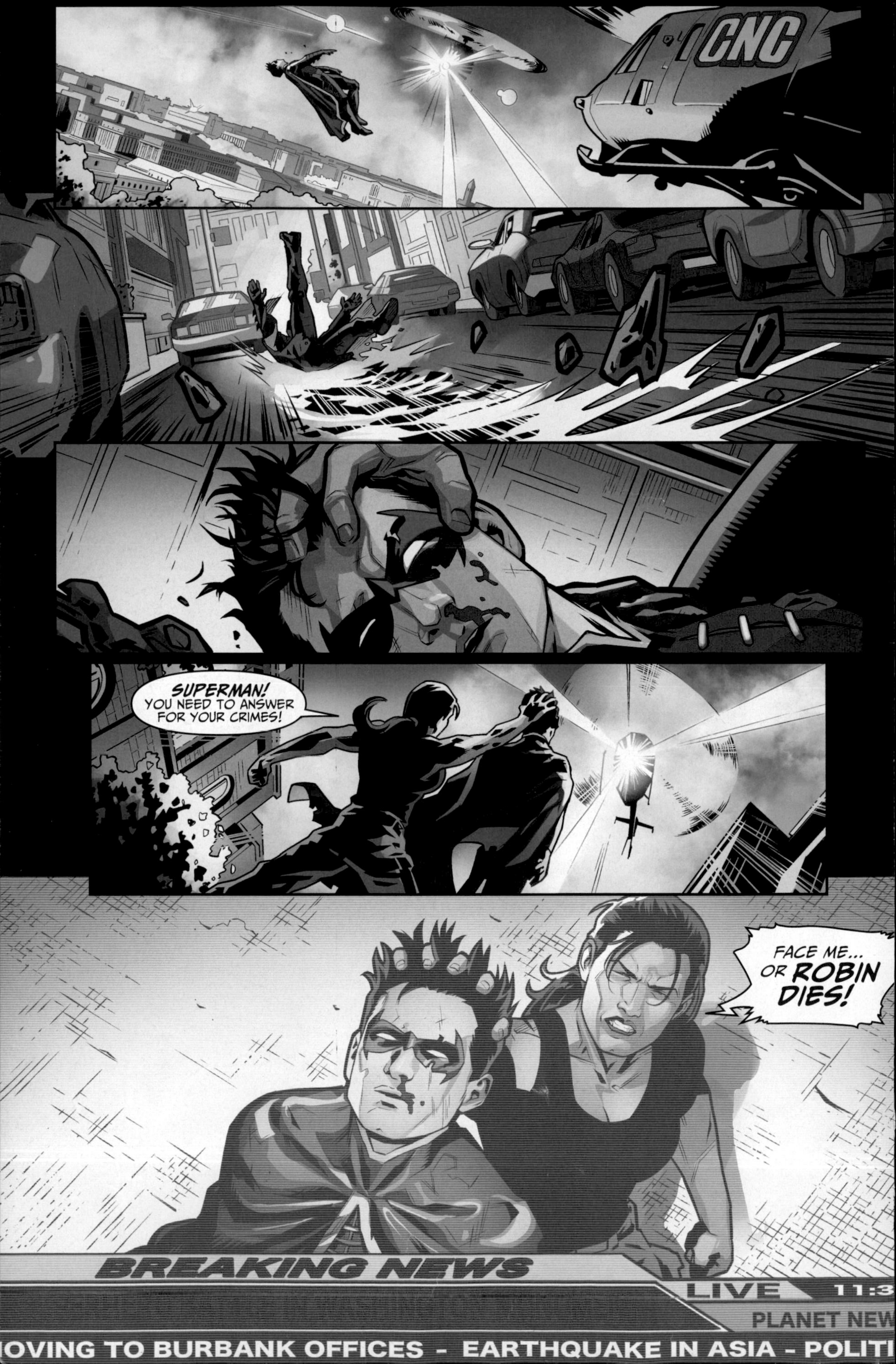
CNC
SUPERMAN! YOU NEED TO ANSWER FOR YOUR CRIMES!
FACE ME... OR ROBIN DIES!
BREAKING NEWS
LIVE
11:3
PLANET NEW
OVING TO BURBANK OFFICES - EARTHQUAKE IN ASIA - POLIT

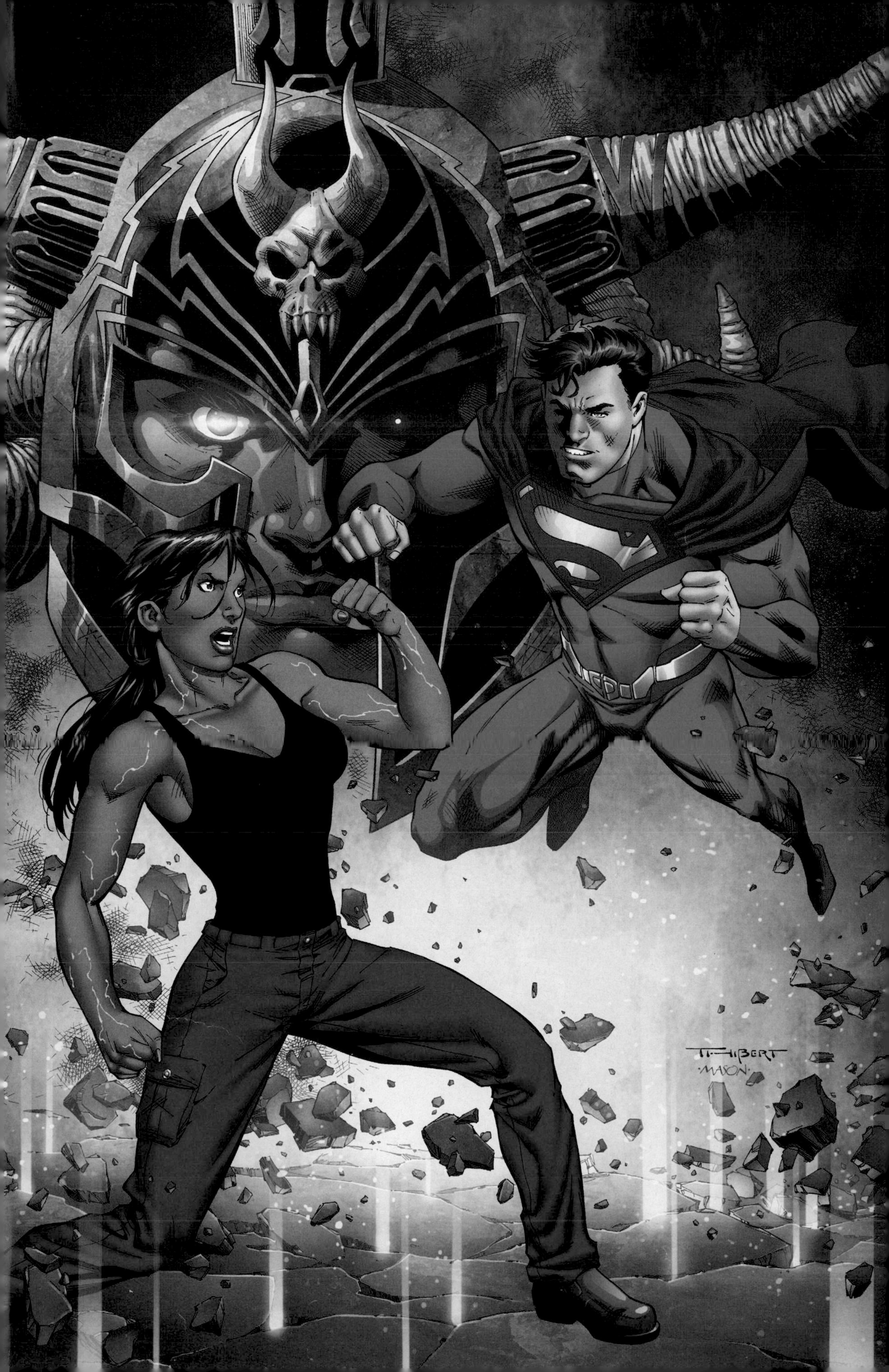

THIBERT
MASON

"Vengeance Is Mine" **Mike S. Miller** Artist **J. Nanjan** Colorist
Cover Art by **Art Thibert & Thomas Mason**

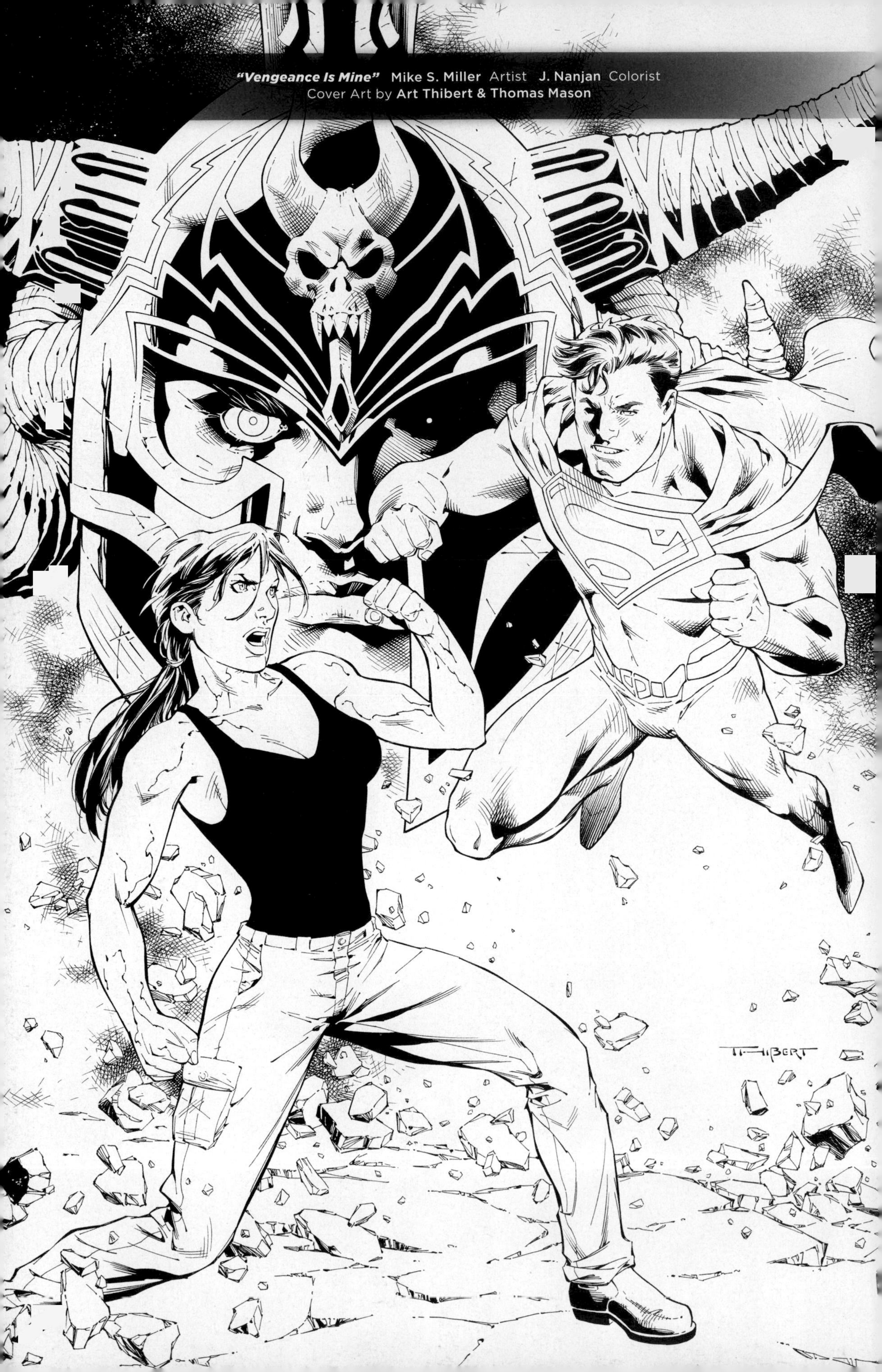

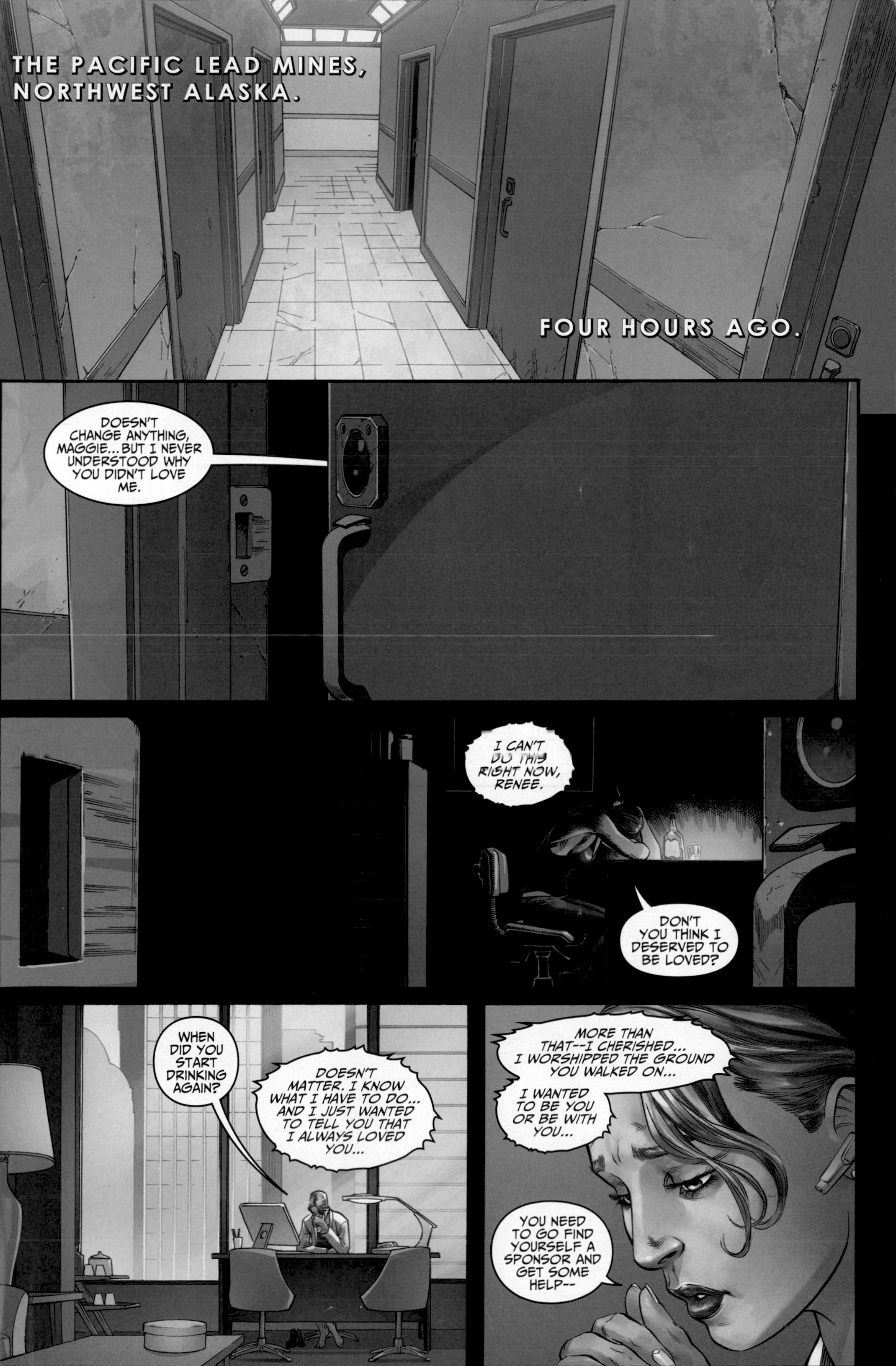
THE PACIFIC LEAD MINES, NORTHWEST ALASKA.
FOUR HOURS AGO.
DOESN'T CHANGE ANYTHING, MAGGIE... BUT I NEVER UNDERSTOOD WHY YOU DIDN'T LOVE ME.
I CAN'T DO THIS RIGHT NOW, RENEE.
DON'T YOU THINK I DESERVED TO BE LOVED?
WHEN DID YOU START DRINKING AGAIN?
DOESN'T MATTER. I KNOW WHAT I HAVE TO DO... AND I JUST WANTED TO TELL YOU THAT I ALWAYS LOVED YOU...
MORE THAN THAT--I CHERISHED... I WORSHIPPED THE GROUND YOU WALKED ON...
I WANTED TO BE YOU OR BE WITH YOU...
YOU NEED TO GO FIND YOURSELF A SPONSOR AND GET SOME HELP--

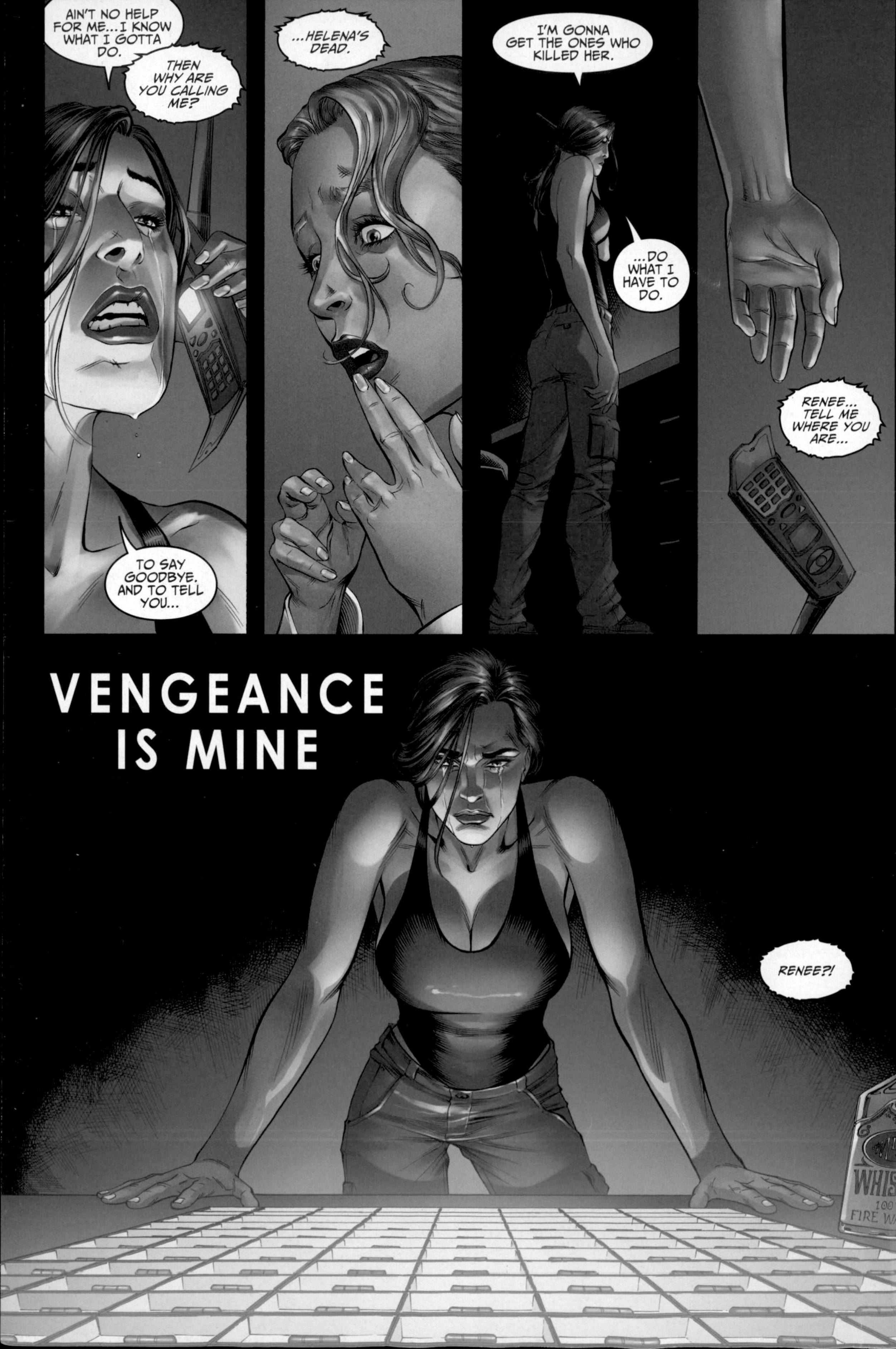
AIN'T NO HELP FOR ME...I KNOW WHAT I GOTTA DO.
THEN WHY ARE YOU CALLING ME?
TO SAY GOODBYE. AND TO TELL YOU...
...HELENA'S DEAD.
I'M GONNA GET THE ONES WHO KILLED HER.
...DO WHAT I HAVE TO DO.
RENEE... TELL ME WHERE YOU ARE...
VENGEANCE IS MINE
RENEE?!

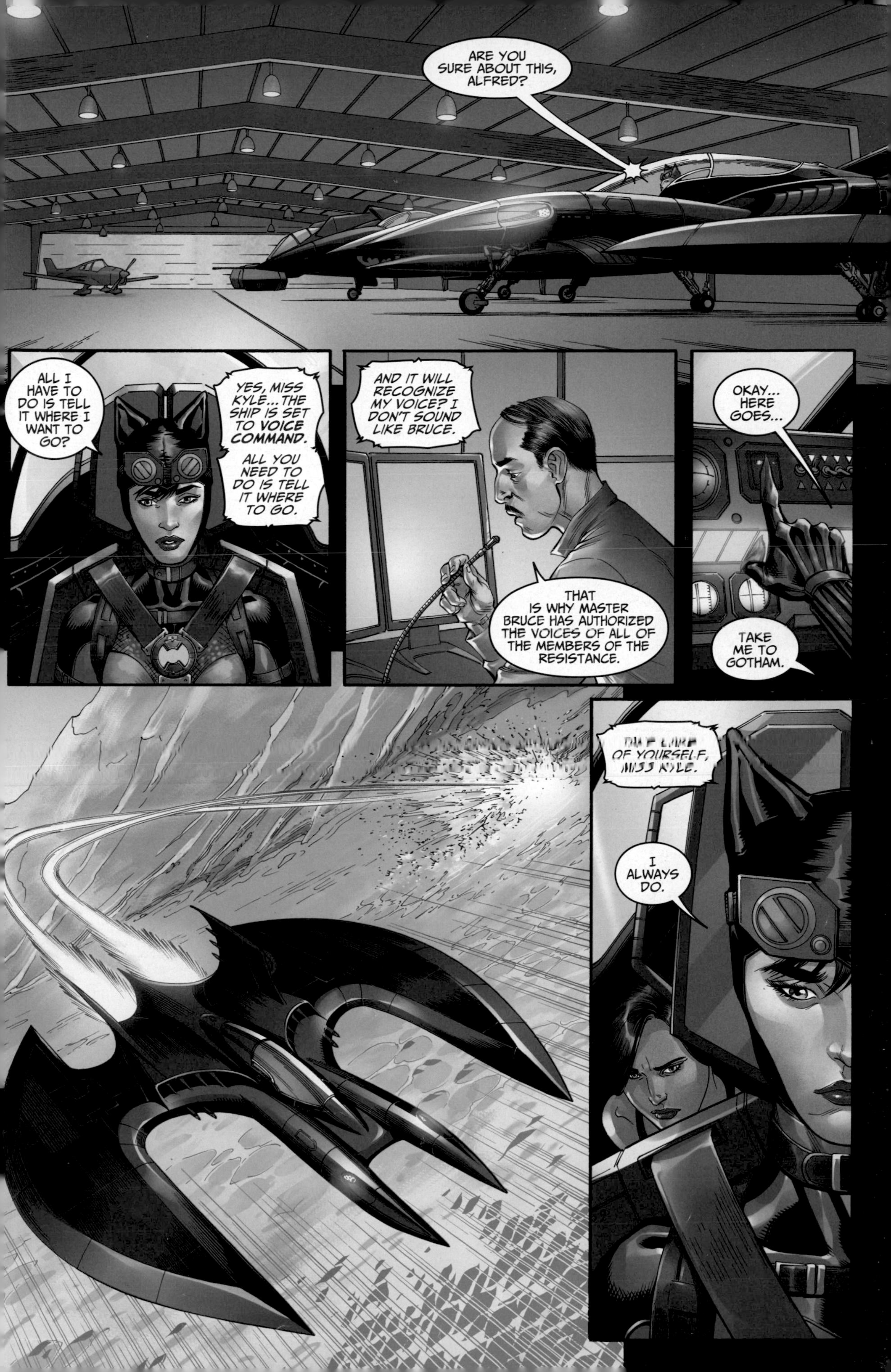
ARE YOU SURE ABOUT THIS, ALFRED?
ALL I HAVE TO DO IS TELL IT WHERE I WANT TO GO?
YES, MISS KYLE...THE SHIP IS SET TO **VOICE COMMAND**.
ALL YOU NEED TO DO IS TELL IT WHERE TO GO.
AND IT WILL RECOGNIZE MY VOICE? I DON'T SOUND LIKE BRUCE.
THAT IS WHY MASTER BRUCE HAS AUTHORIZED THE VOICES OF ALL OF THE MEMBERS OF THE RESISTANCE.
OKAY... HERE GOES...
TAKE ME TO GOTHAM.
OF YOURSELF, MISS KYLE.
I ALWAYS DO.

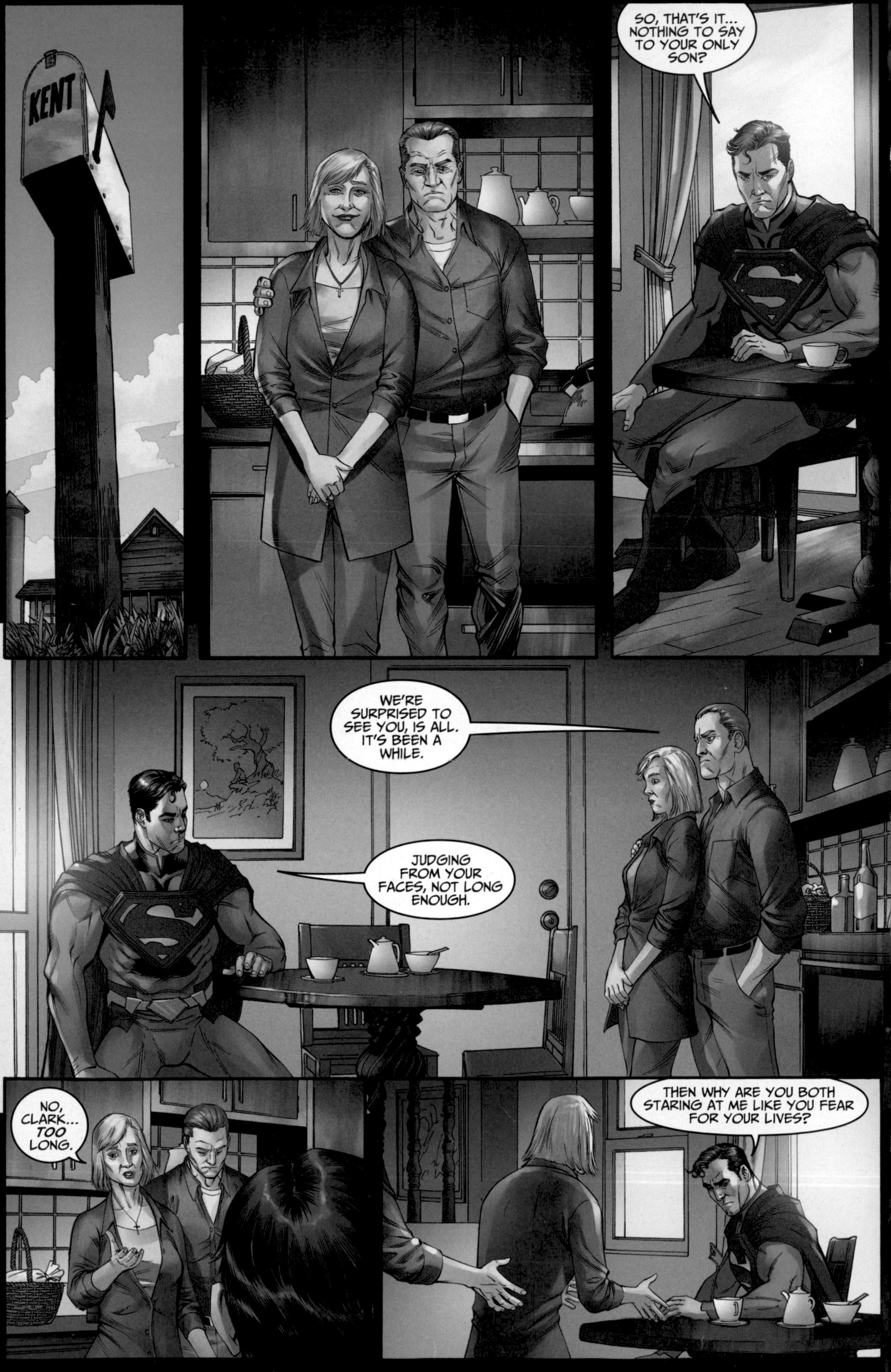
KENT
SO, THAT'S IT... NOTHING TO SAY TO YOUR ONLY SON?
WE'RE SURPRISED TO SEE YOU, IS ALL. IT'S BEEN A WHILE.
JUDGING FROM YOUR FACES, NOT LONG ENOUGH.
NO, CLARK... *TOO* LONG.
THEN WHY ARE YOU BOTH STARING AT ME LIKE YOU FEAR FOR YOUR LIVES?

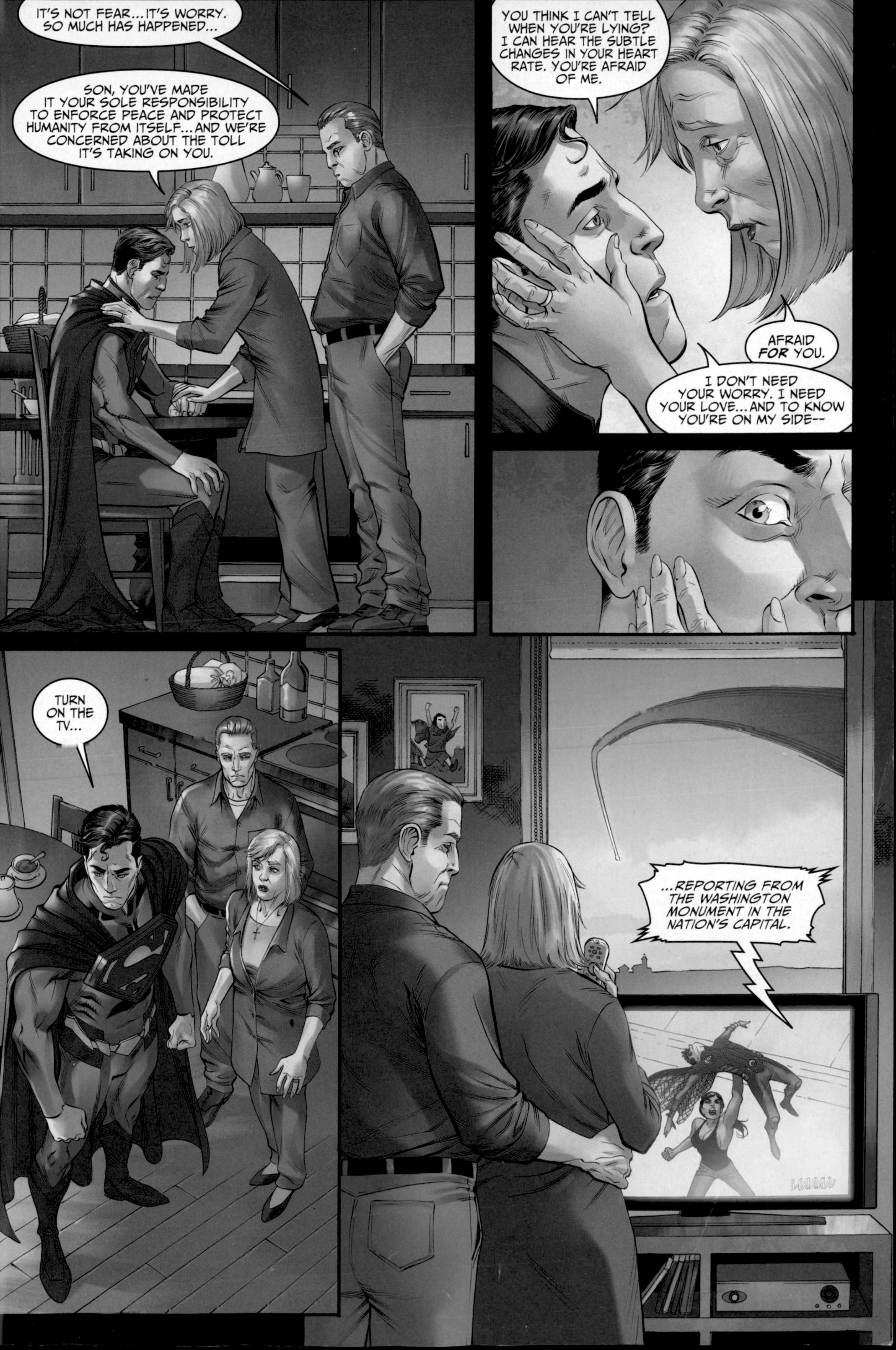
IT'S NOT FEAR...IT'S WORRY. SO MUCH HAS HAPPENED...
SON, YOU'VE MADE IT YOUR SOLE RESPONSIBILITY TO ENFORCE PEACE AND PROTECT HUMANITY FROM ITSELF...AND WE'RE CONCERNED ABOUT THE TOLL IT'S TAKING ON YOU.
YOU THINK I CAN'T TELL WHEN YOU'RE LYING? I CAN HEAR THE SUBTLE CHANGES IN YOUR HEART RATE. YOU'RE AFRAID OF ME.
AFRAID FOR YOU.
I DON'T NEED YOUR WORRY. I NEED YOUR LOVE...AND TO KNOW YOU'RE ON MY SIDE--
TURN ON THE TV...
...REPORTING FROM THE WASHINGTON MONUMENT IN THE NATION'S CAPITAL.

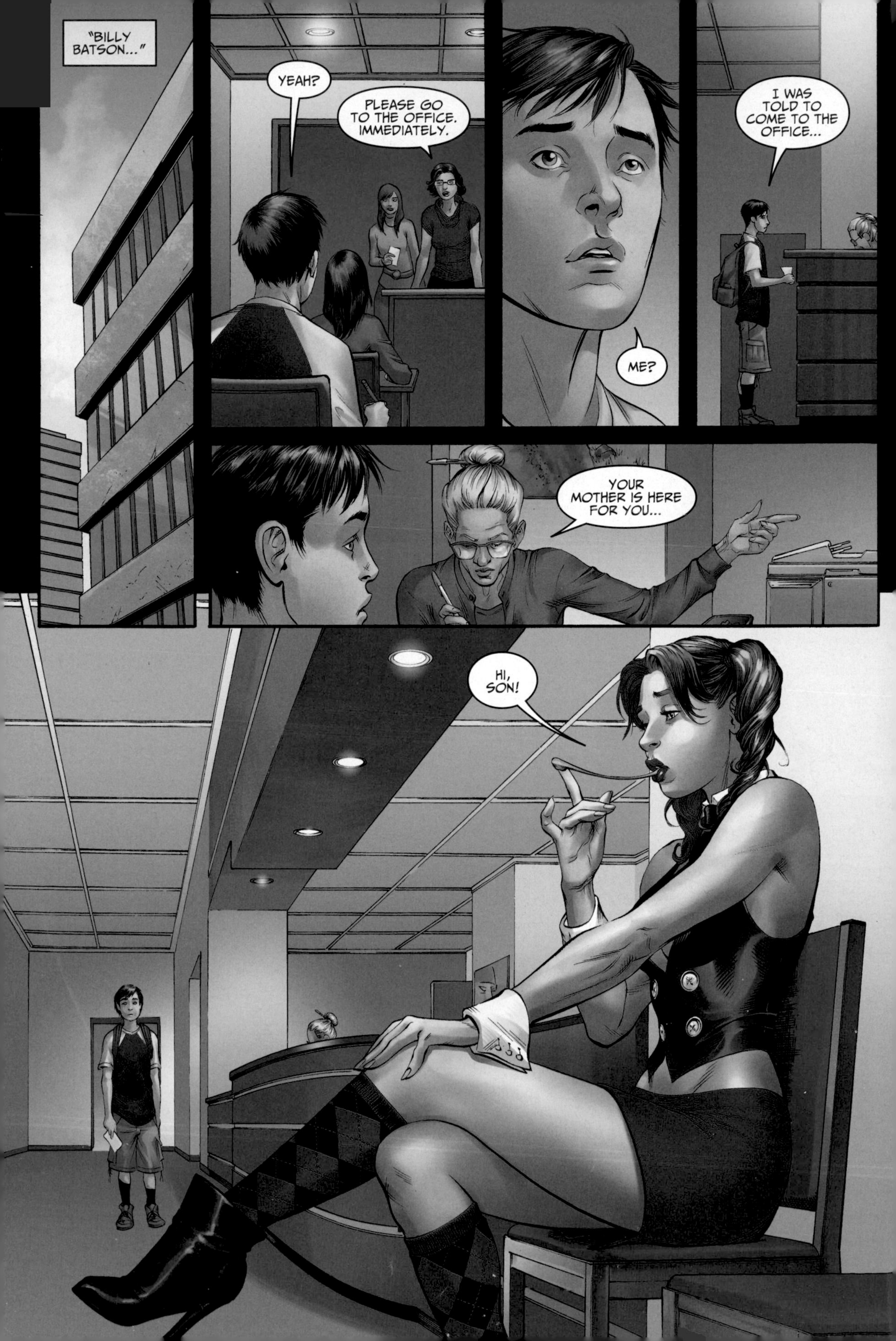

"BILLY BATSON..."
YEAH?
PLEASE GO TO THE OFFICE. IMMEDIATELY.
ME?
I WAS TOLD TO COME TO THE OFFICE...
YOUR MOTHER IS HERE FOR YOU...
HI, SON!

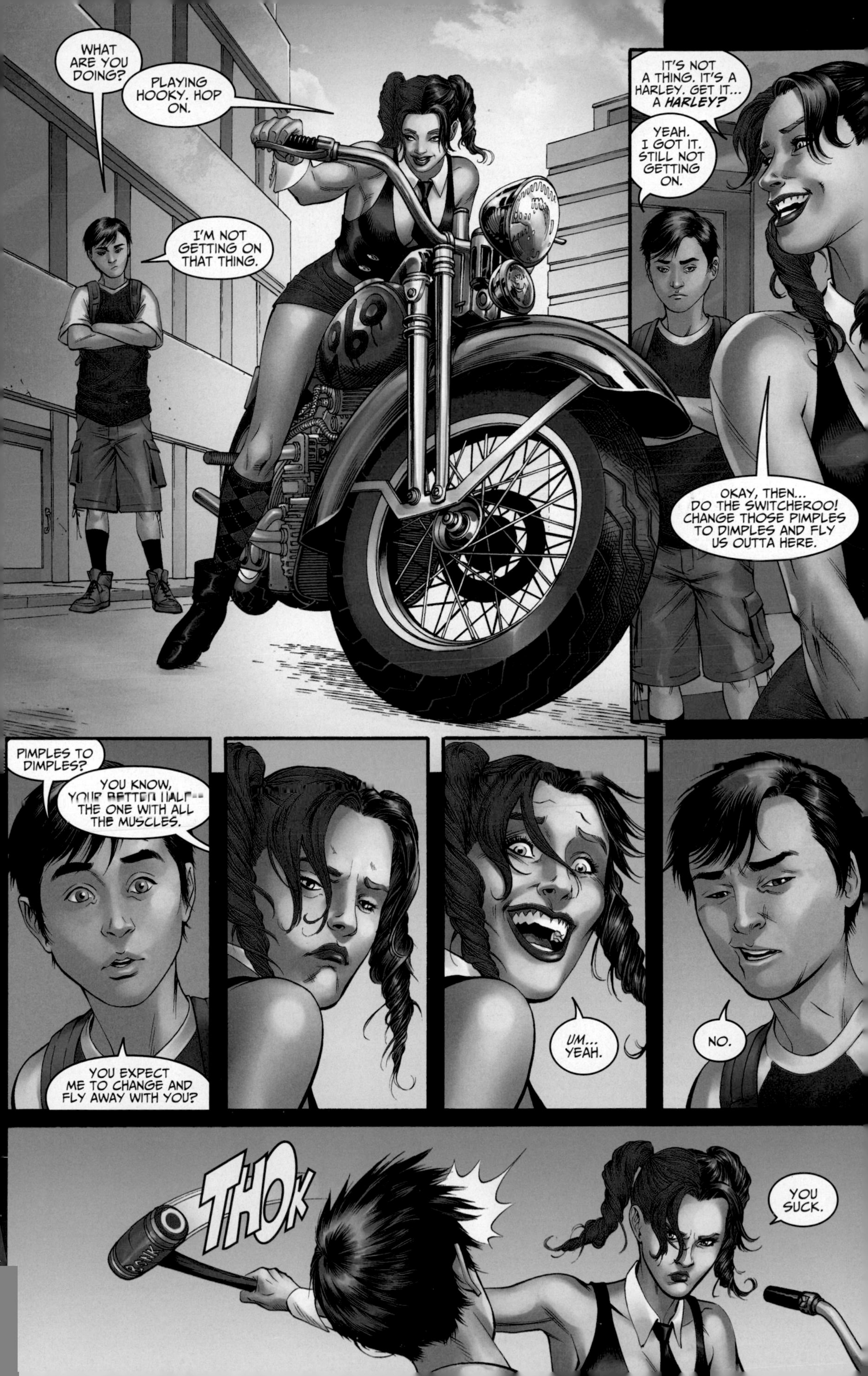
WHAT ARE YOU DOING?
PLAYING HOOKY. HOP ON.
I'M NOT GETTING ON THAT THING.
IT'S NOT A THING. IT'S A HARLEY. GET IT... A *HARLEY?*
YEAH. I GOT IT. STILL NOT GETTING ON.
OKAY, THEN... DO THE SWITCHEROO! CHANGE THOSE PIMPLES TO DIMPLES AND FLY US OUTTA HERE.
PIMPLES TO DIMPLES?
YOU KNOW, YOUR BETTER HALF-- THE ONE WITH ALL THE MUSCLES.
YOU EXPECT ME TO CHANGE AND FLY AWAY WITH YOU?
UM... YEAH.
NO.
THOK
YOU SUCK.

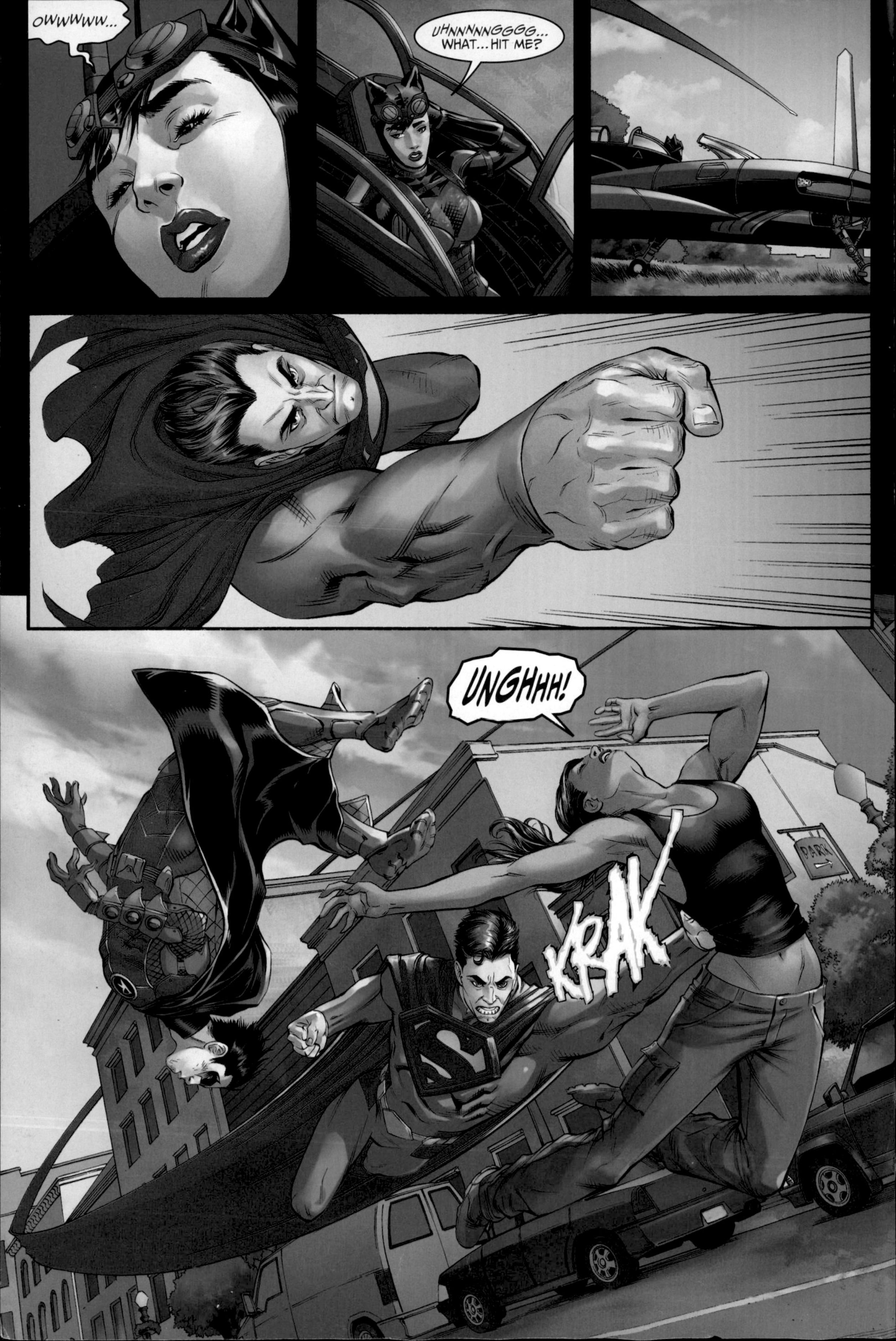
OWWWWW...
UHNNNNNGGGG... WHAT...HIT ME?
UNGHHH!
KRAK
PARK

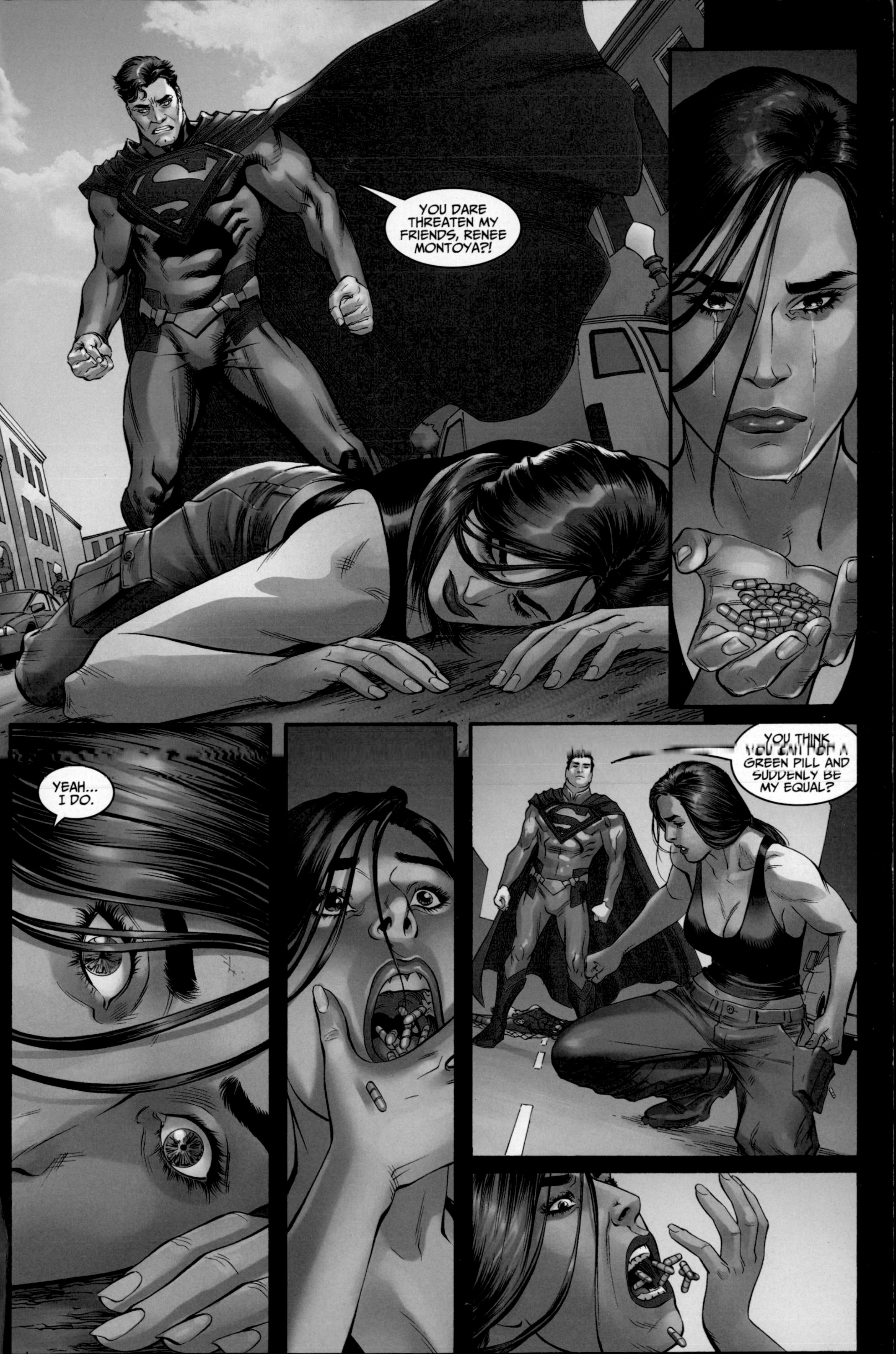
YOU DARE THREATEN MY FRIENDS, RENEE MONTOYA?!
YEAH... I DO.
YOU THINK
GREEN PILL AND SUDDENLY BE MY EQUAL?

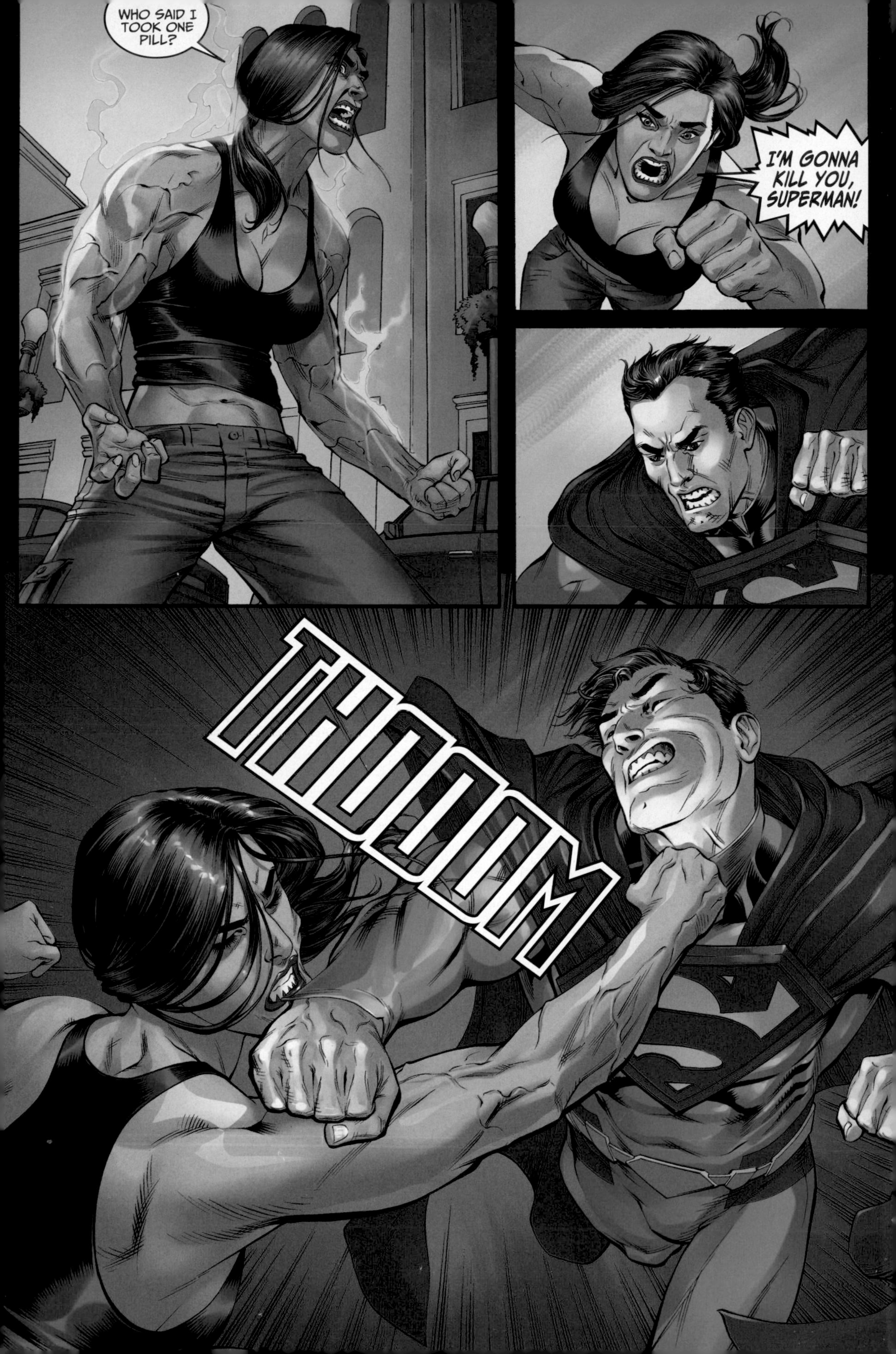
WHO SAID I TOOK ONE PILL?
I'M GONNA KILL YOU, SUPERMAN!
THOOOM

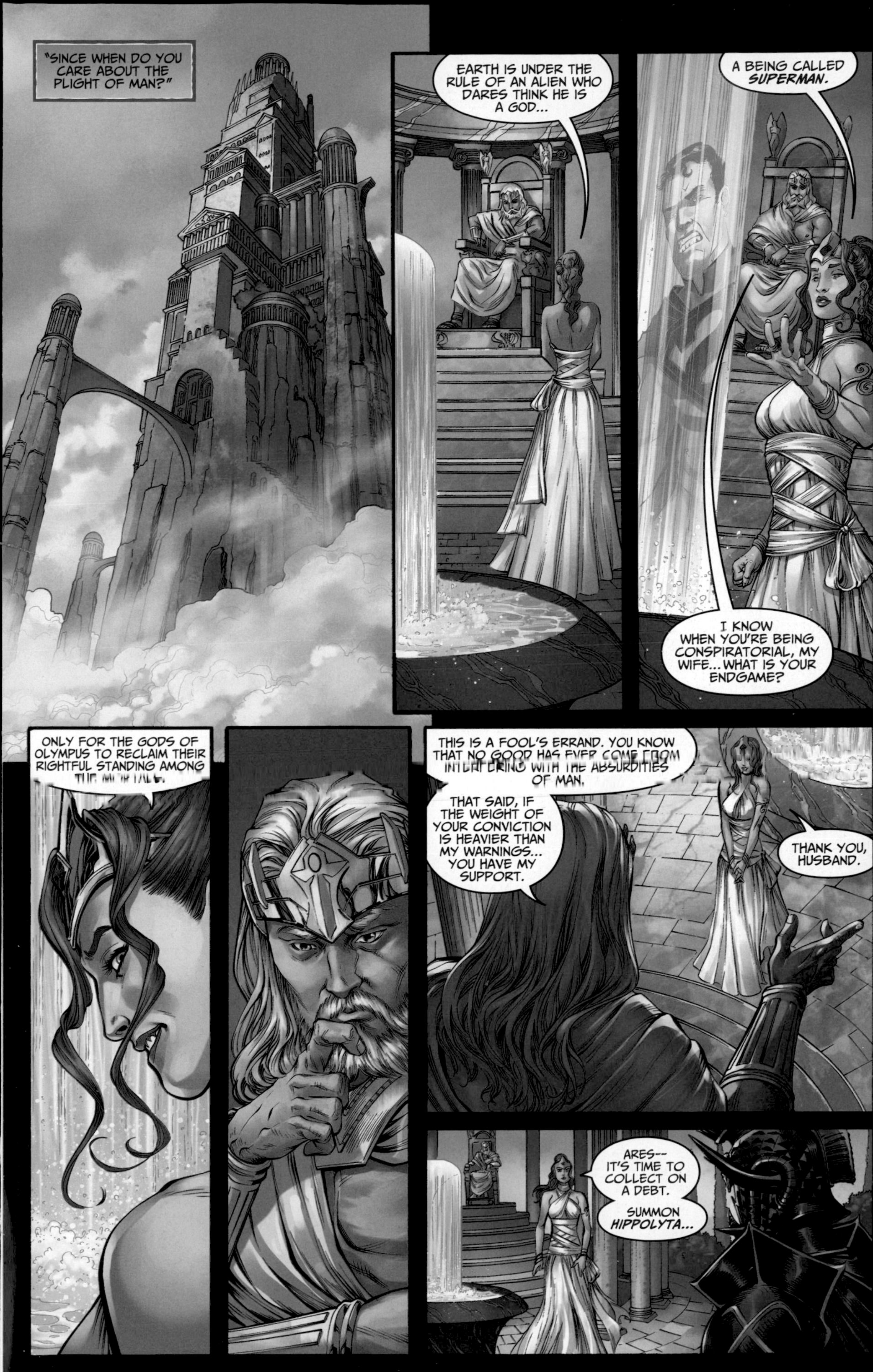

"SINCE WHEN DO YOU CARE ABOUT THE PLIGHT OF MAN?"
EARTH IS UNDER THE RULE OF AN ALIEN WHO DARES THINK HE IS A GOD...
A BEING CALLED *SUPERMAN.*
I KNOW WHEN YOU'RE BEING CONSPIRATORIAL, MY WIFE... WHAT IS YOUR ENDGAME?
ONLY FOR THE GODS OF OLYMPUS TO RECLAIM THEIR RIGHTFUL STANDING AMONG
THIS IS A FOOL'S ERRAND. YOU KNOW THAT NO GOOD HAS EVER COME FROM INTERFERING WITH THE ABSURDITIES OF MAN.
THAT SAID, IF THE WEIGHT OF YOUR CONVICTION IS HEAVIER THAN MY WARNINGS... YOU HAVE MY SUPPORT.
THANK YOU, HUSBAND.
ARES-- IT'S TIME TO COLLECT ON A DEBT.
SUMMON *HIPPOLYTA...*

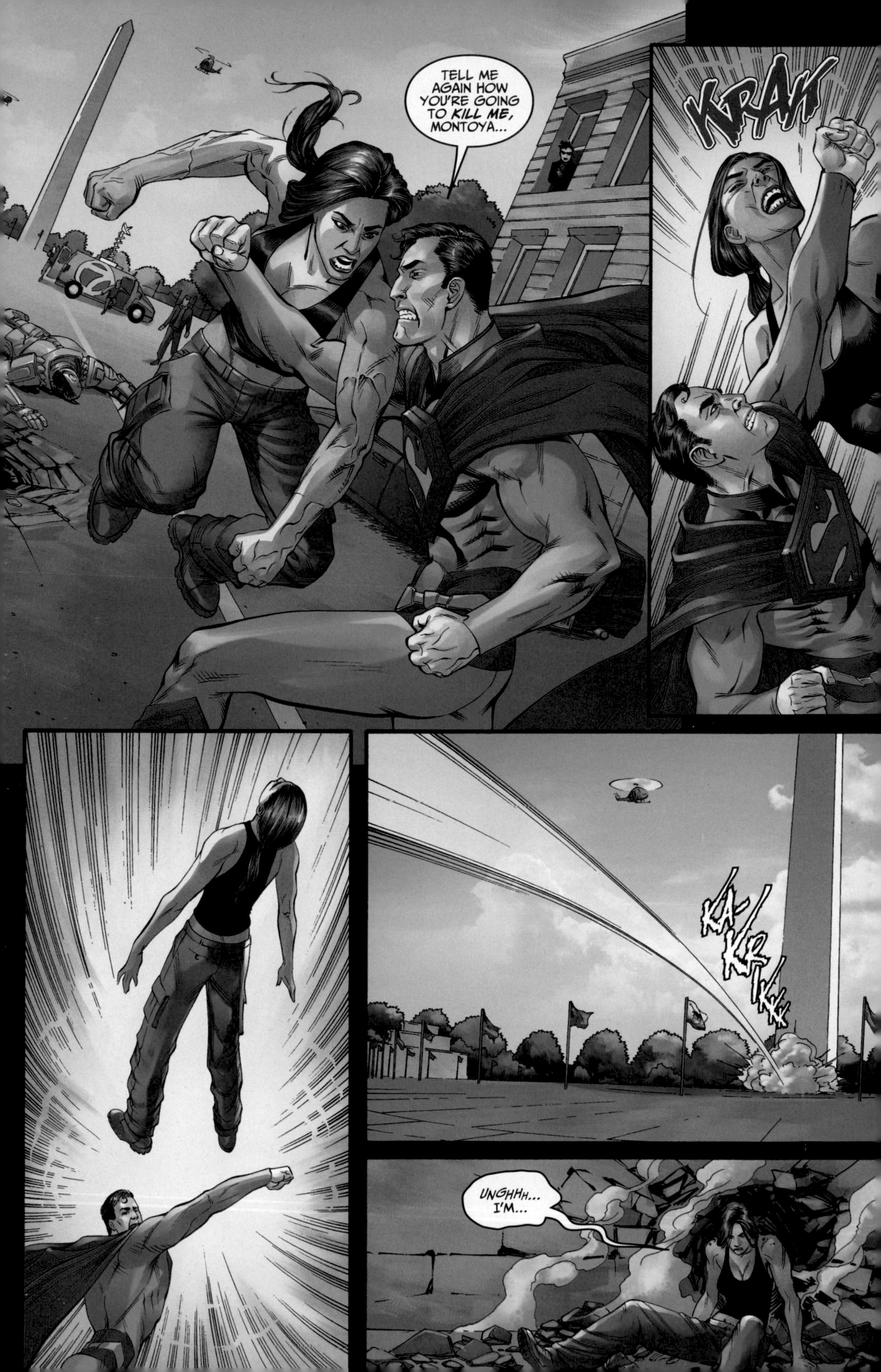
TELL ME AGAIN HOW YOU'RE GOING TO KILL ME, MONTOYA...
KRAK
KA-KR-ISSH
UNGHHH... I'M...

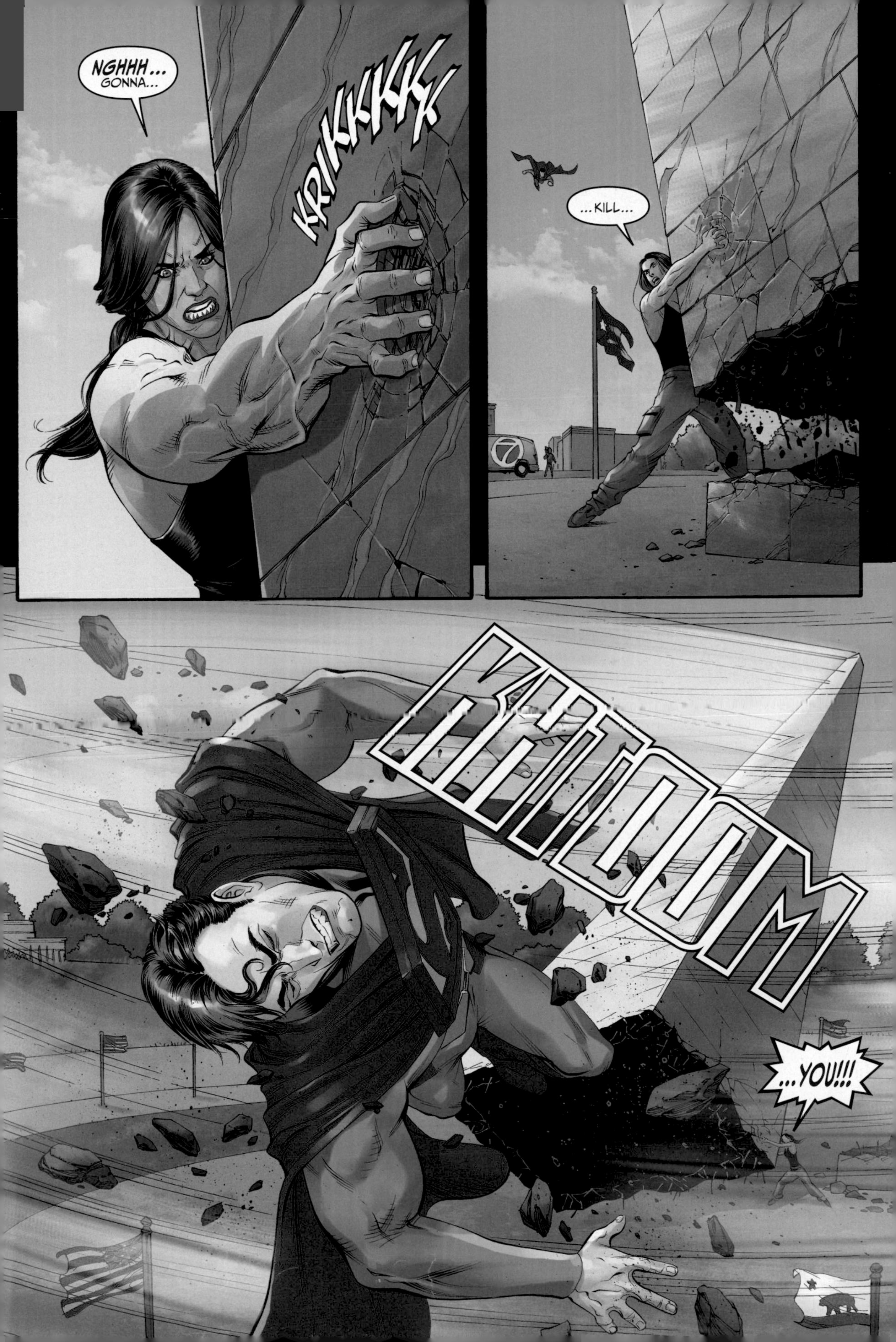
NGHHH... GONNA...
KRIKKKKK
...KILL...
...YOU!!!

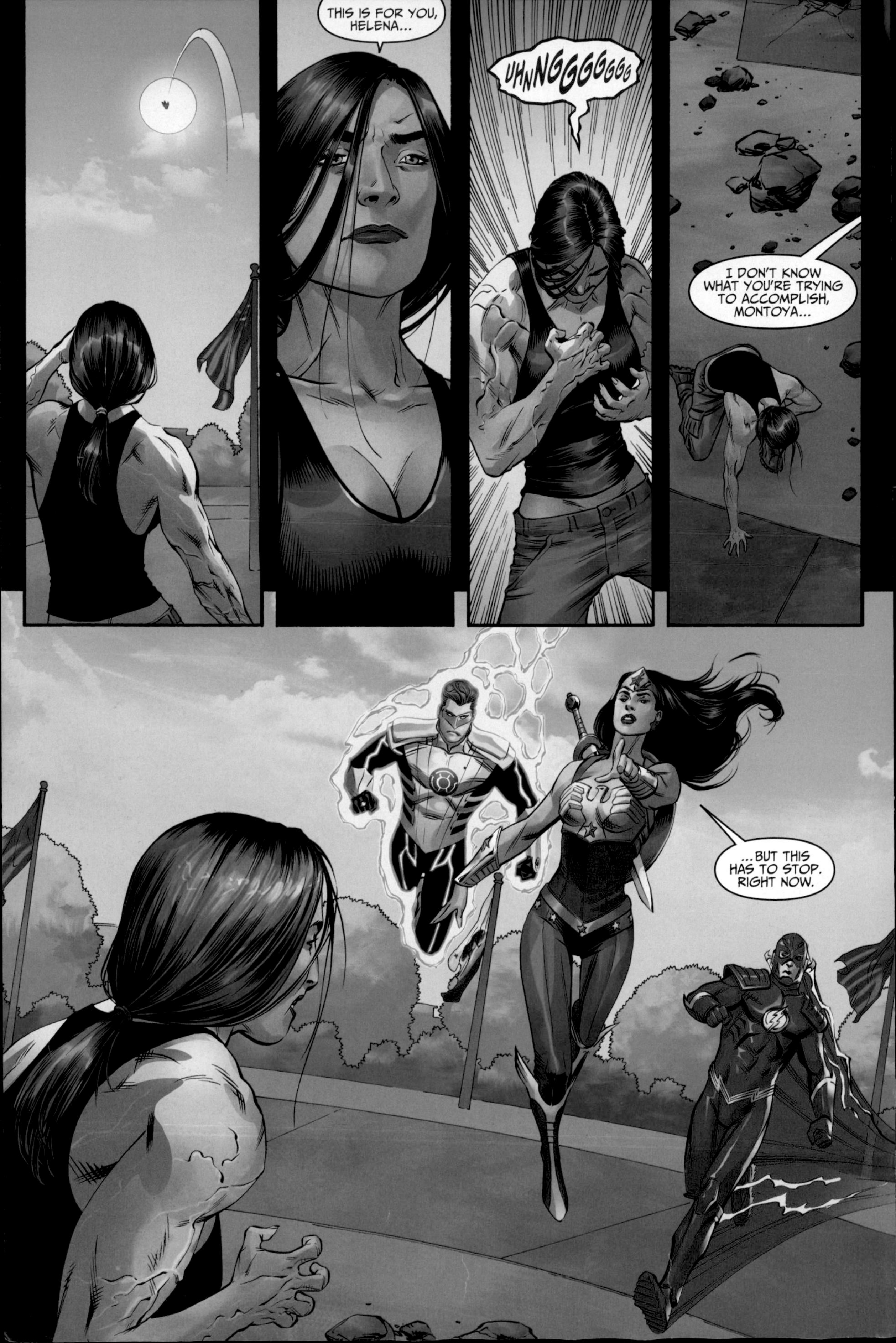
THIS IS FOR YOU, HELENA...
UHNNGGGGGGG
I DON'T KNOW WHAT YOU'RE TRYING TO ACCOMPLISH, MONTOYA...
...BUT THIS HAS TO STOP. RIGHT NOW.

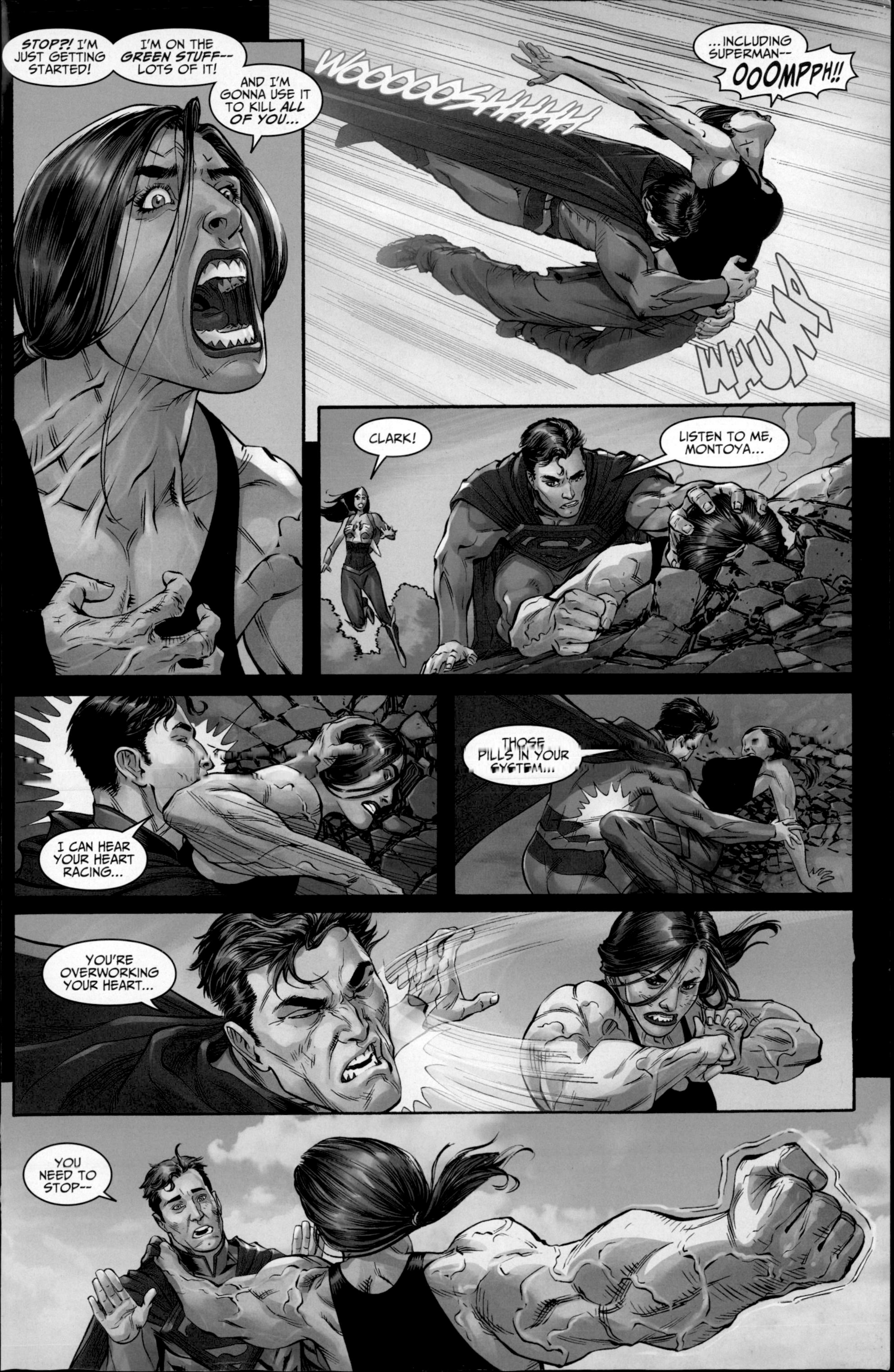
STOP?! I'M JUST GETTING STARTED!
I'M ON THE GREEN STUFF-- LOTS OF IT!
AND I'M GONNA USE IT TO KILL ALL OF YOU...
WOOOOOSHHHH
...INCLUDING SUPERMAN--
OOOMPPH!!
WHUMP
CLARK!
LISTEN TO ME, MONTOYA...
I CAN HEAR YOUR HEART RACING...
THOSE PILLS IN YOUR SYSTEM...
YOU'RE OVERWORKING YOUR HEART...
YOU NEED TO STOP--

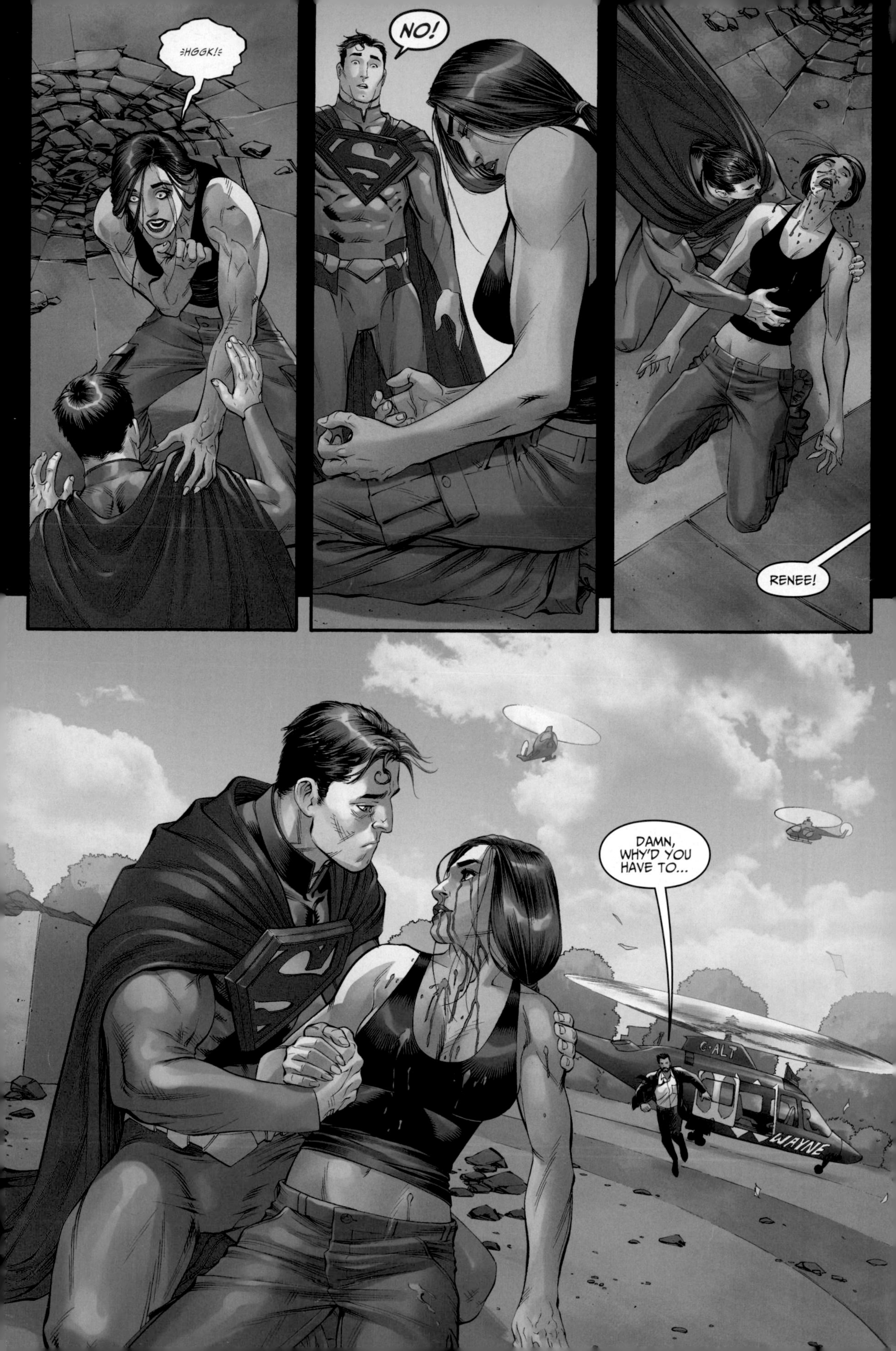
HGGK!
NO!
RENEE!
DAMN, WHY'D YOU HAVE TO...
G-ALT
WAYNE

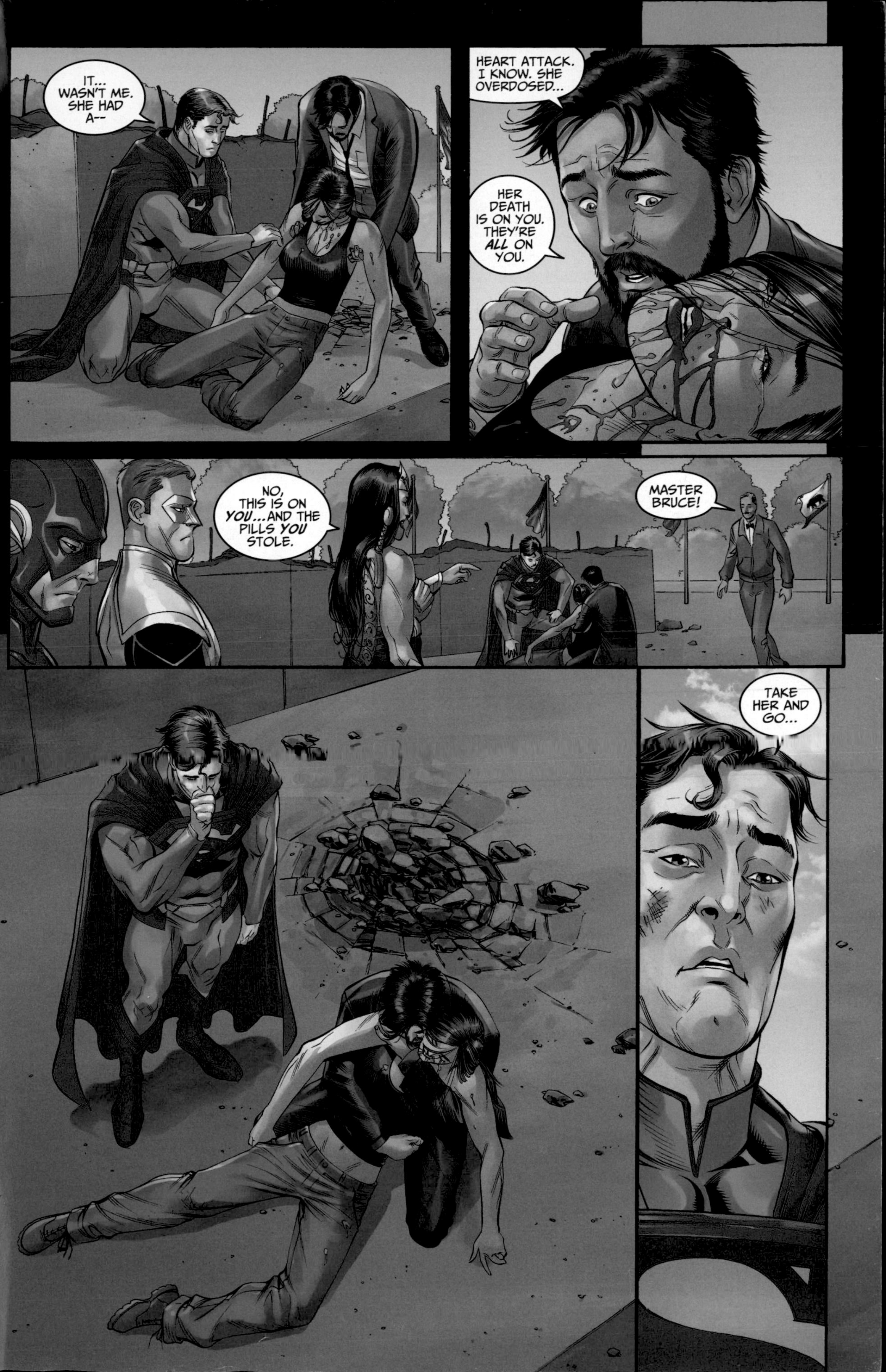
IT... WASN'T ME. SHE HAD A--
HEART ATTACK. I KNOW. SHE OVERDOSED...
HER DEATH IS ON YOU. THEY'RE ALL ON YOU.
NO, THIS IS ON YOU...AND THE PILLS YOU STOLE.
MASTER BRUCE!
TAKE HER AND GO...

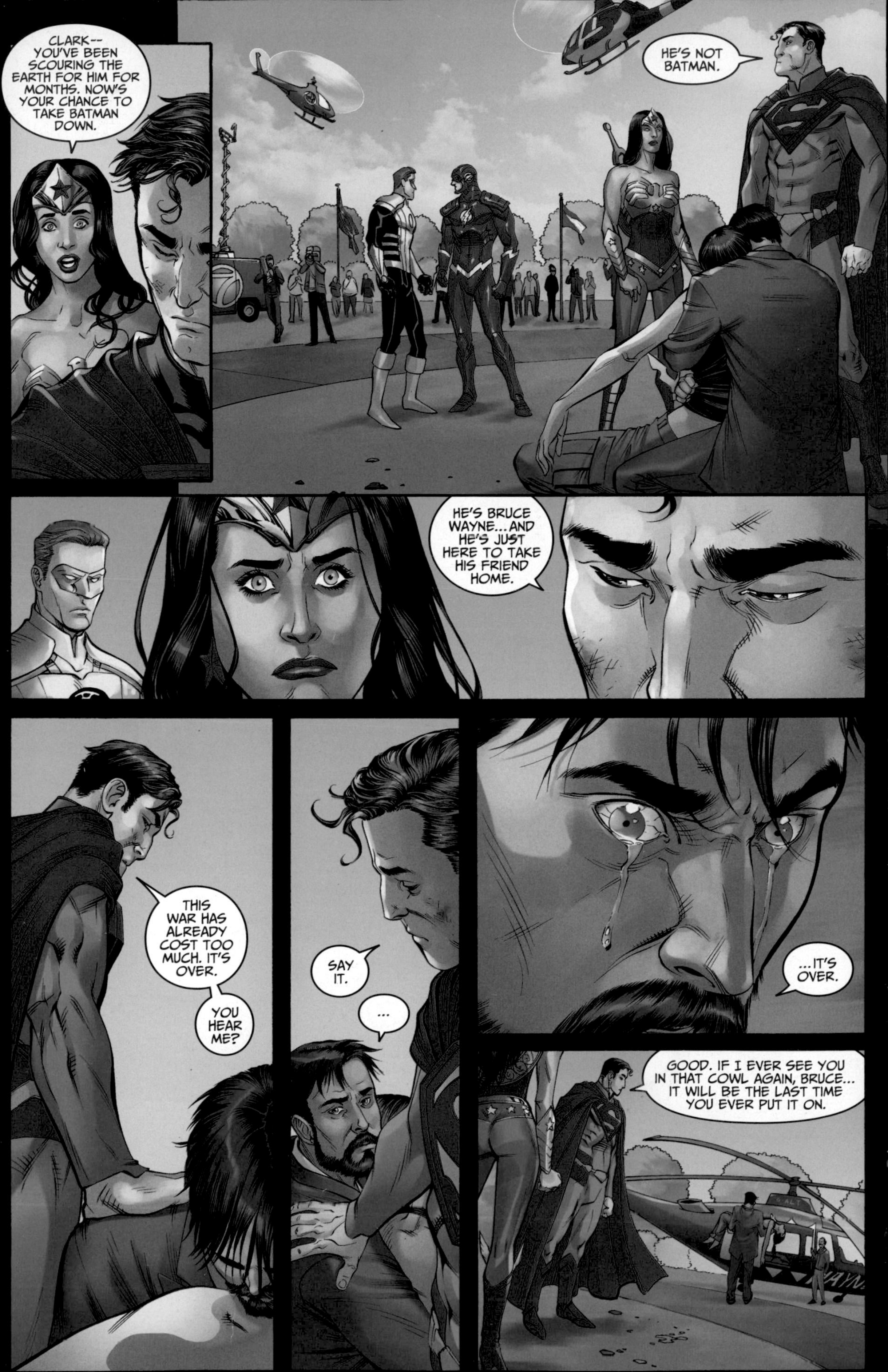
CLARK-- YOU'VE BEEN SCOURING THE EARTH FOR HIM FOR MONTHS. NOW'S YOUR CHANCE TO TAKE BATMAN DOWN.
HE'S NOT BATMAN.
HE'S BRUCE WAYNE... AND HE'S JUST HERE TO TAKE HIS FRIEND HOME.
THIS WAR HAS ALREADY COST TOO MUCH. IT'S OVER.
YOU HEAR ME?
SAY IT.
...
...IT'S OVER.
GOOD. IF I EVER SEE YOU IN THAT COWL AGAIN, BRUCE... IT WILL BE THE LAST TIME YOU EVER PUT IT ON.

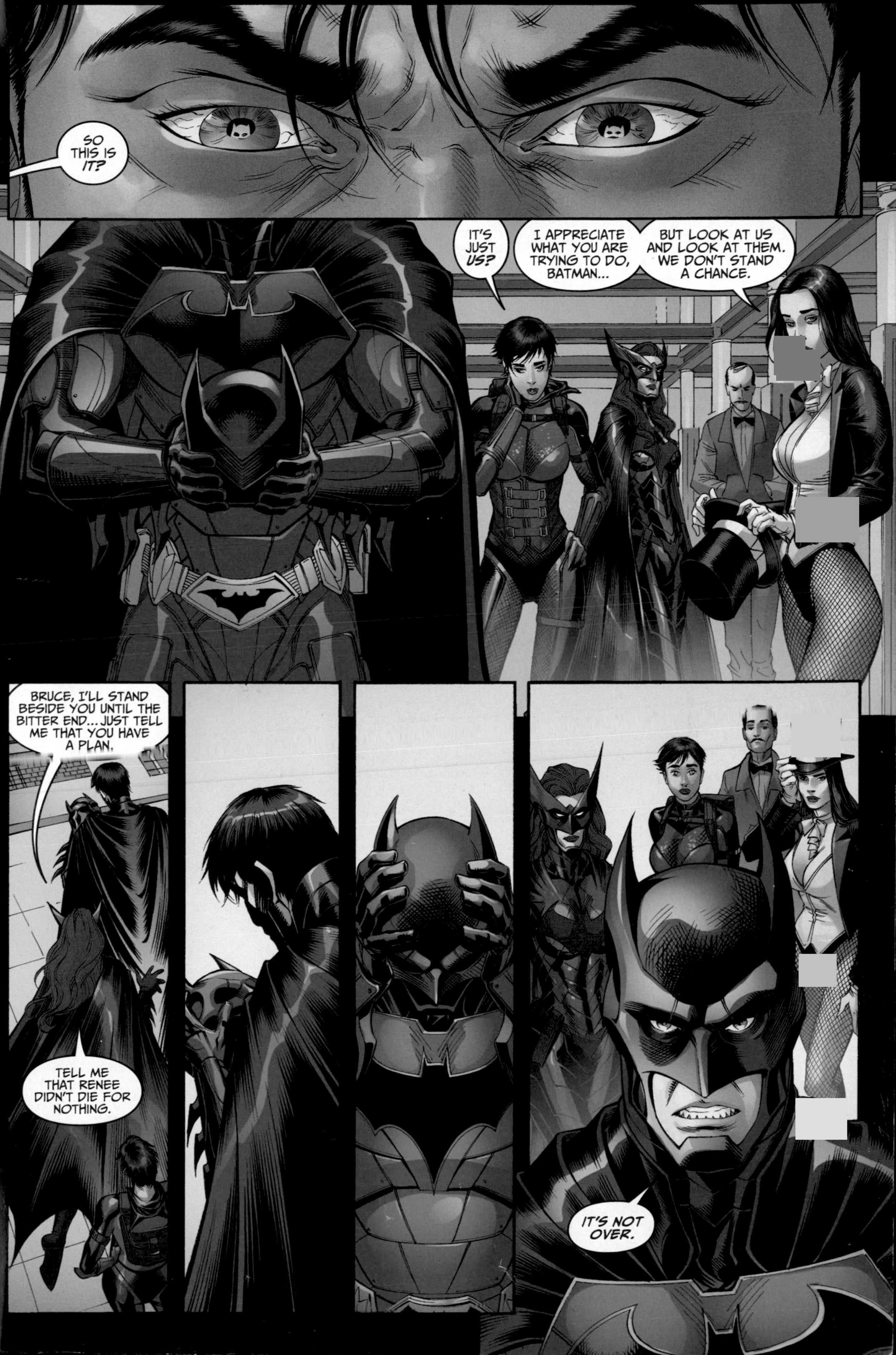
SO THIS IS IT?
IT'S JUST US?
I APPRECIATE WHAT YOU ARE TRYING TO DO, BATMAN...
BUT LOOK AT US AND LOOK AT THEM. WE DON'T STAND A CHANCE.
BRUCE, I'LL STAND BESIDE YOU UNTIL THE BITTER END... JUST TELL ME THAT YOU HAVE A PLAN.
TELL ME THAT RENEE DIDN'T DIE FOR NOTHING.
IT'S NOT OVER.

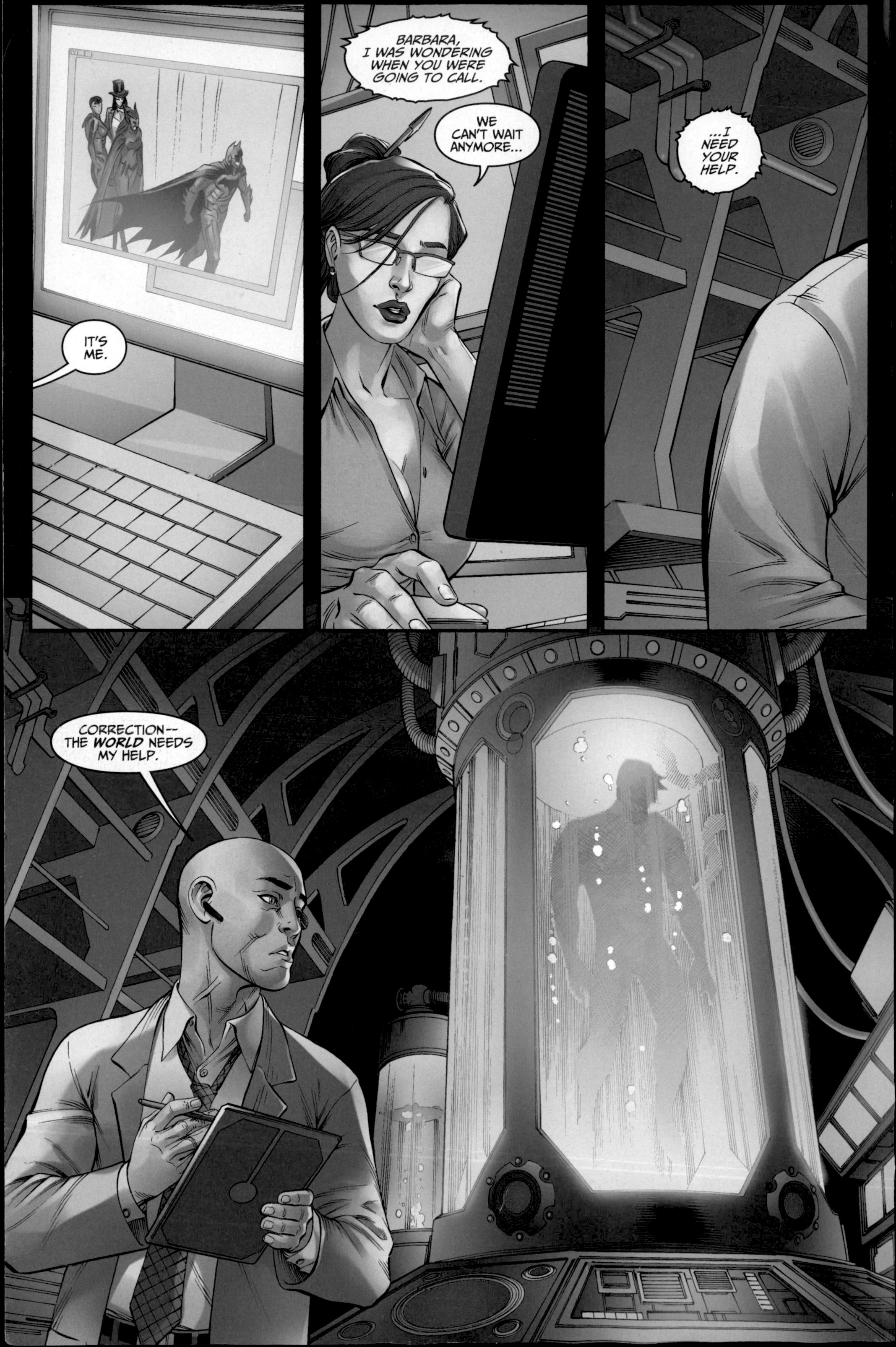
IT'S ME.
BARBARA, I WAS WONDERING WHEN YOU WERE GOING TO CALL.
WE CAN'T WAIT ANYMORE...
...I NEED YOUR HELP.
CORRECTION-- THE WORLD NEEDS MY HELP.

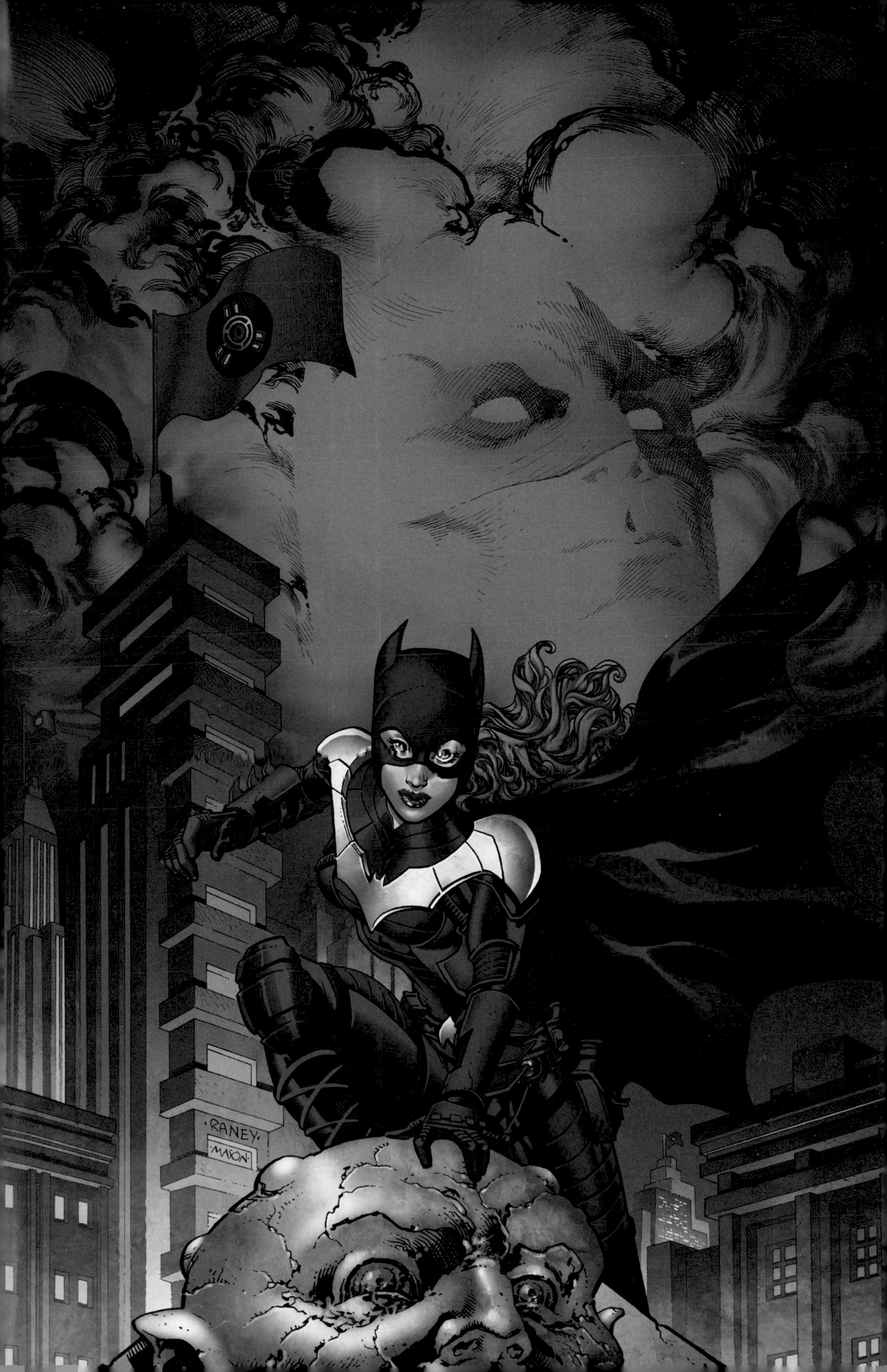
RANEY
MASON

"Choices" **Bruno Redondo** Penciller **Juan Albarran** Inker **Rex Lokus** Colorist
Cover Art by **Tom Raney & Thomas Mason**

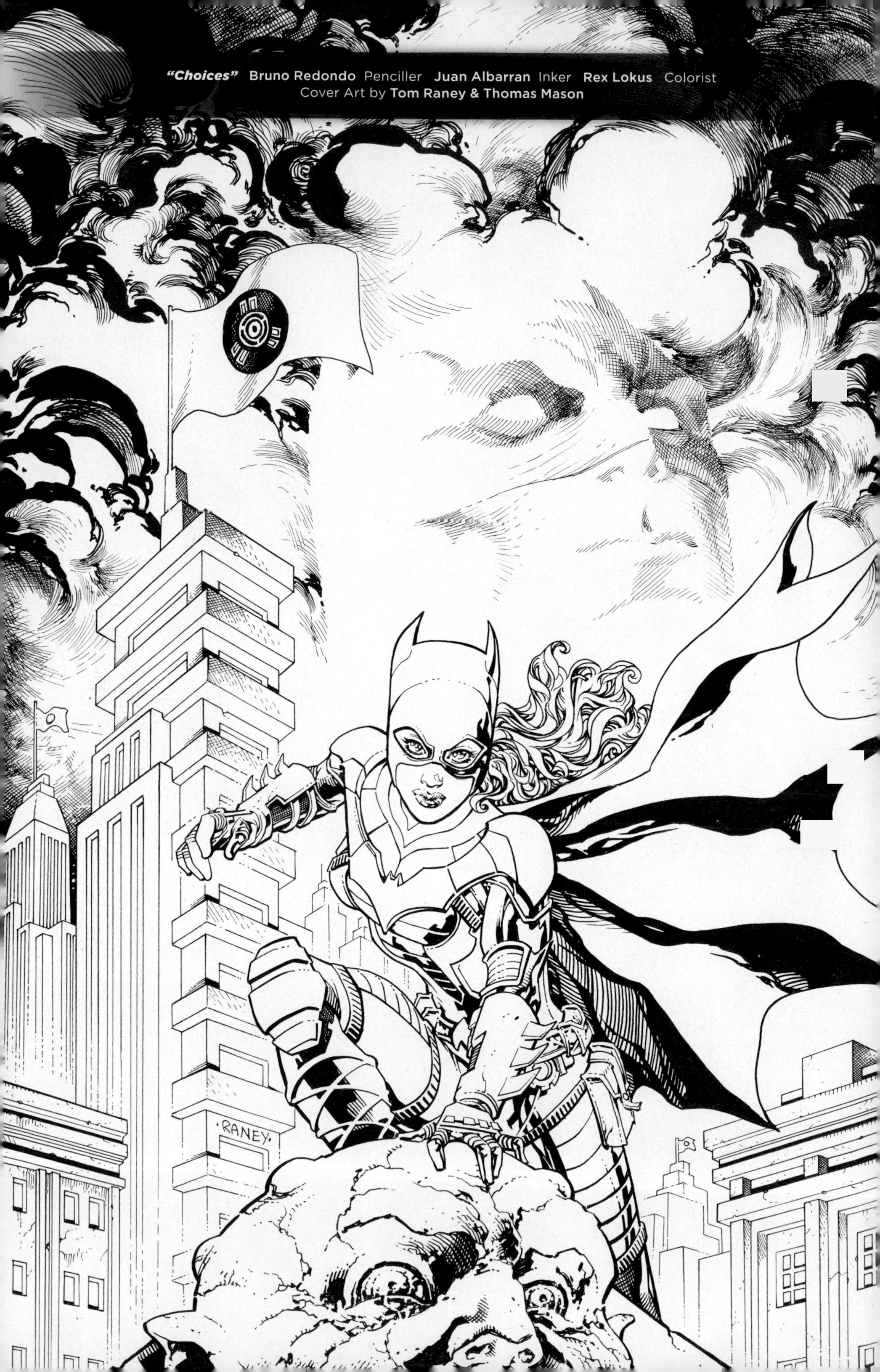
RANEY

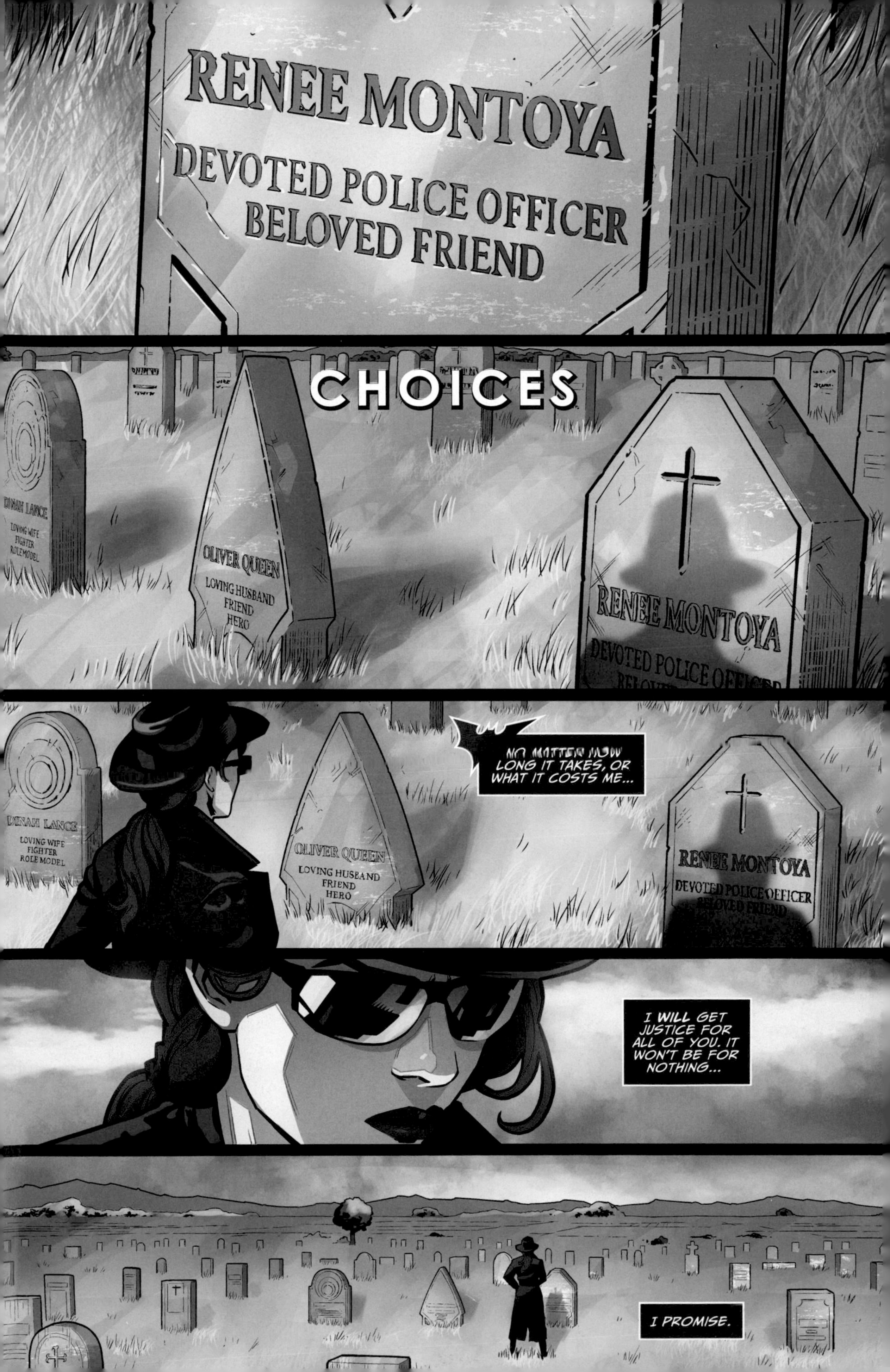
RENEE MONTOYA
DEVOTED POLICE OFFICER
BELOVED FRIEND
CHOICES
DINAH LANCE
LOVING WIFE
FIGHTER
ROLEMODEL
OLIVER QUEEN
LOVING HUSBAND
FRIEND
HERO
RENEE MONTOYA
DEVOTED POLICE OFFICER
NO MATTER HOW LONG IT TAKES, OR WHAT IT COSTS ME...
I WILL GET JUSTICE FOR ALL OF YOU. IT WON'T BE FOR NOTHING...
I PROMISE.

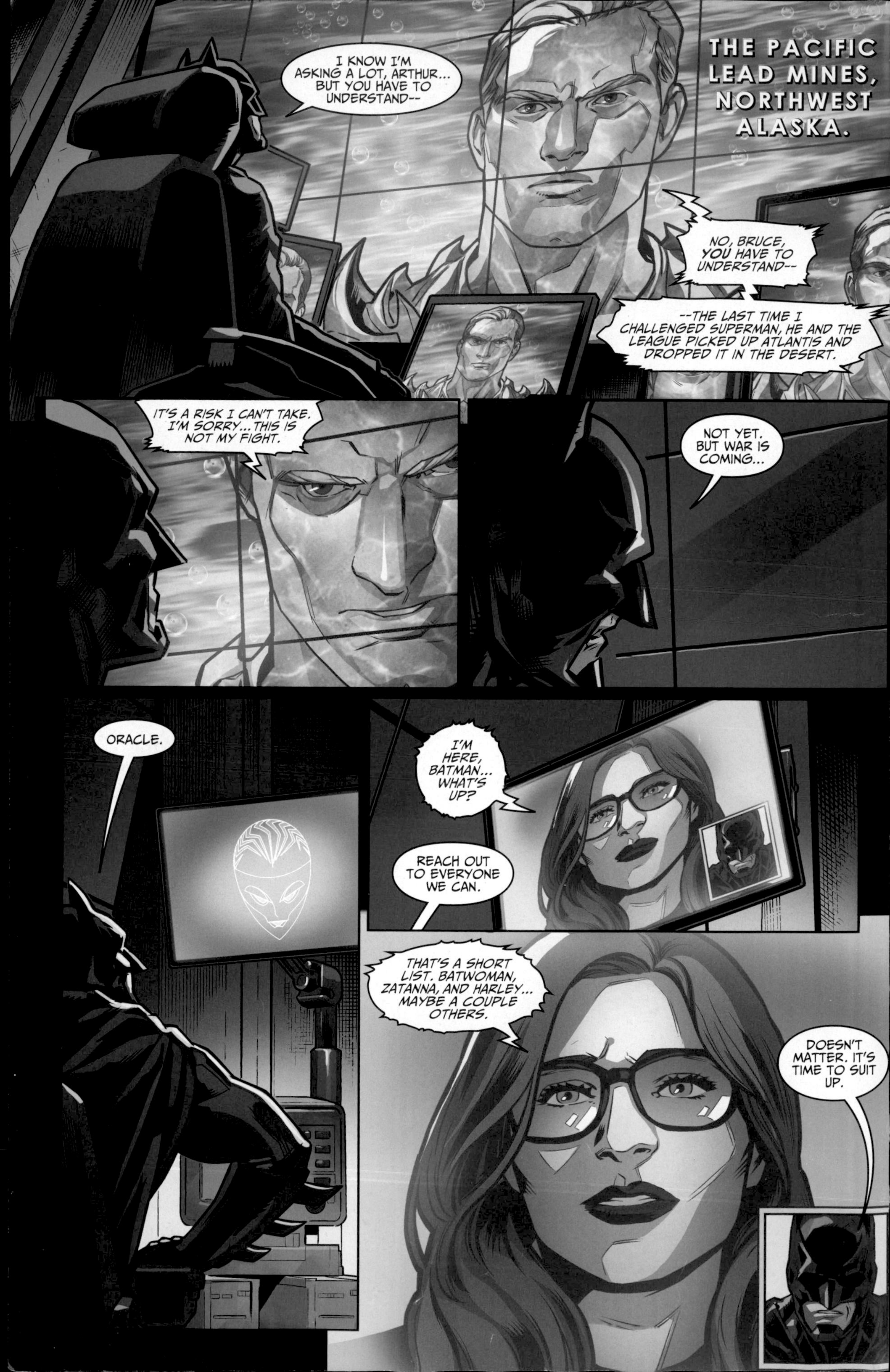
THE PACIFIC LEAD MINES, NORTHWEST ALASKA.
I KNOW I'M ASKING A LOT, ARTHUR... BUT YOU HAVE TO UNDERSTAND--
NO, BRUCE, YOU HAVE TO UNDERSTAND--
--THE LAST TIME I CHALLENGED SUPERMAN, HE AND THE LEAGUE PICKED UP ATLANTIS AND DROPPED IT IN THE DESERT.
IT'S A RISK I CAN'T TAKE. I'M SORRY...THIS IS NOT MY FIGHT.
NOT YET. BUT WAR IS COMING...
ORACLE.
I'M HERE, BATMAN... WHAT'S UP?
REACH OUT TO EVERYONE WE CAN.
THAT'S A SHORT LIST. BATWOMAN, ZATANNA, AND HARLEY... MAYBE A COUPLE OTHERS.
DOESN'T MATTER. IT'S TIME TO SUIT UP.

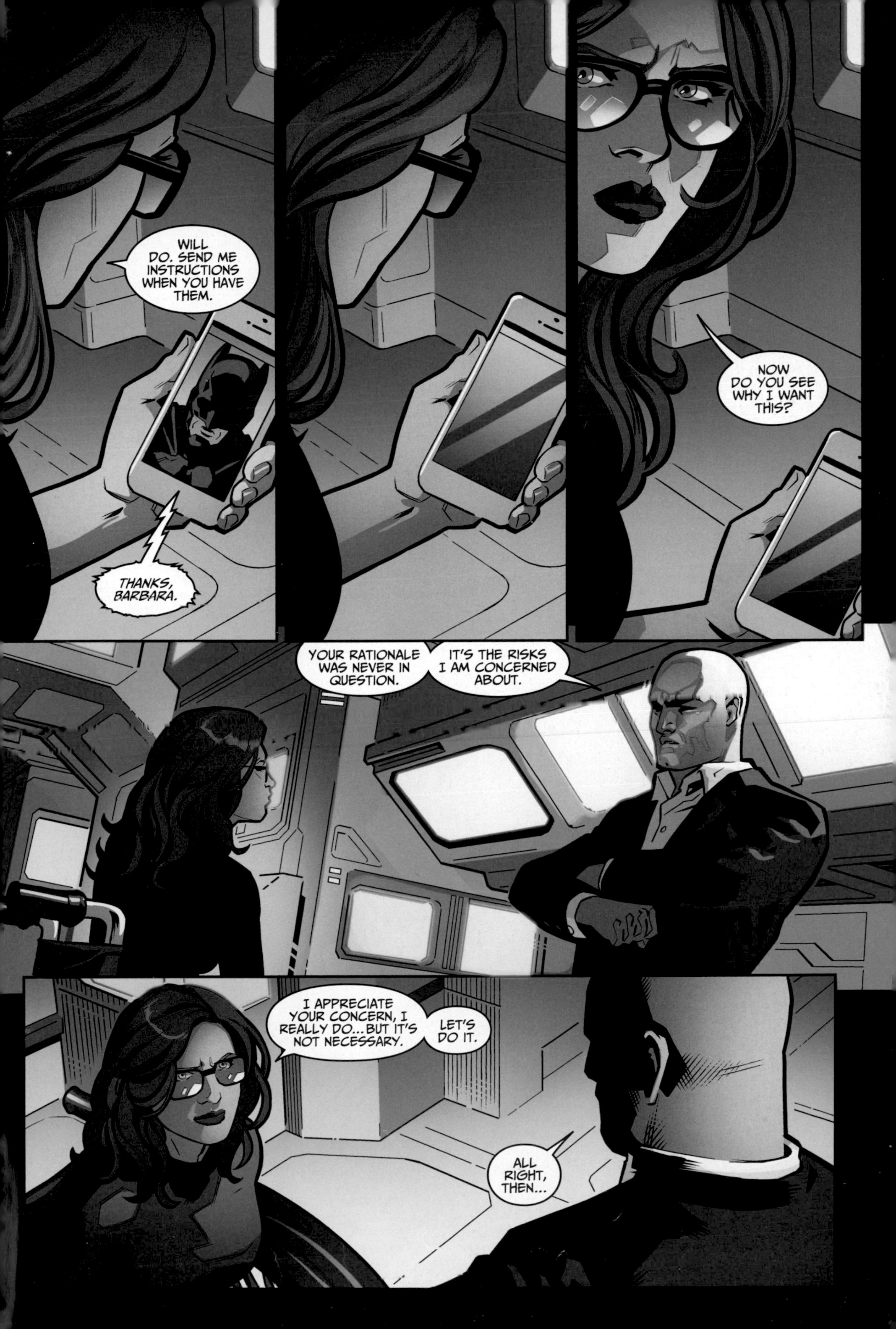
WILL DO. SEND ME INSTRUCTIONS WHEN YOU HAVE THEM.
THANKS, BARBARA.
NOW DO YOU SEE WHY I WANT THIS?
YOUR RATIONALE WAS NEVER IN QUESTION.
IT'S THE RISKS I AM CONCERNED ABOUT.
I APPRECIATE YOUR CONCERN, I REALLY DO...BUT IT'S NOT NECESSARY.
LET'S DO IT.
ALL RIGHT, THEN...

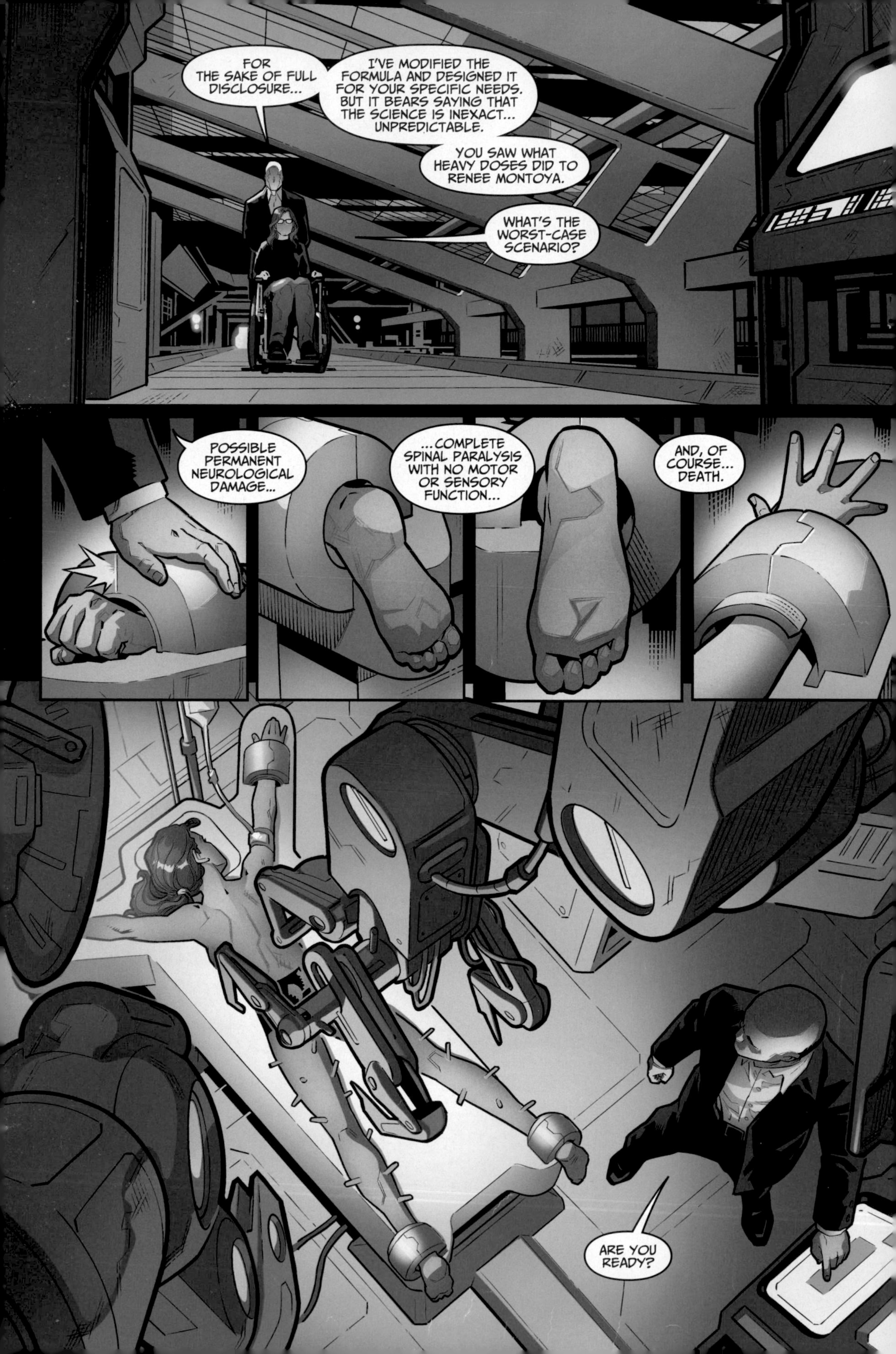
FOR THE SAKE OF FULL DISCLOSURE...
I'VE MODIFIED THE FORMULA AND DESIGNED IT FOR YOUR SPECIFIC NEEDS. BUT IT BEARS SAYING THAT THE SCIENCE IS INEXACT... UNPREDICTABLE.
YOU SAW WHAT HEAVY DOSES DID TO RENEE MONTOYA.
WHAT'S THE WORST-CASE SCENARIO?
POSSIBLE PERMANENT NEUROLOGICAL DAMAGE...
...COMPLETE SPINAL PARALYSIS WITH NO MOTOR OR SENSORY FUNCTION...
AND, OF COURSE... DEATH.
ARE YOU READY?

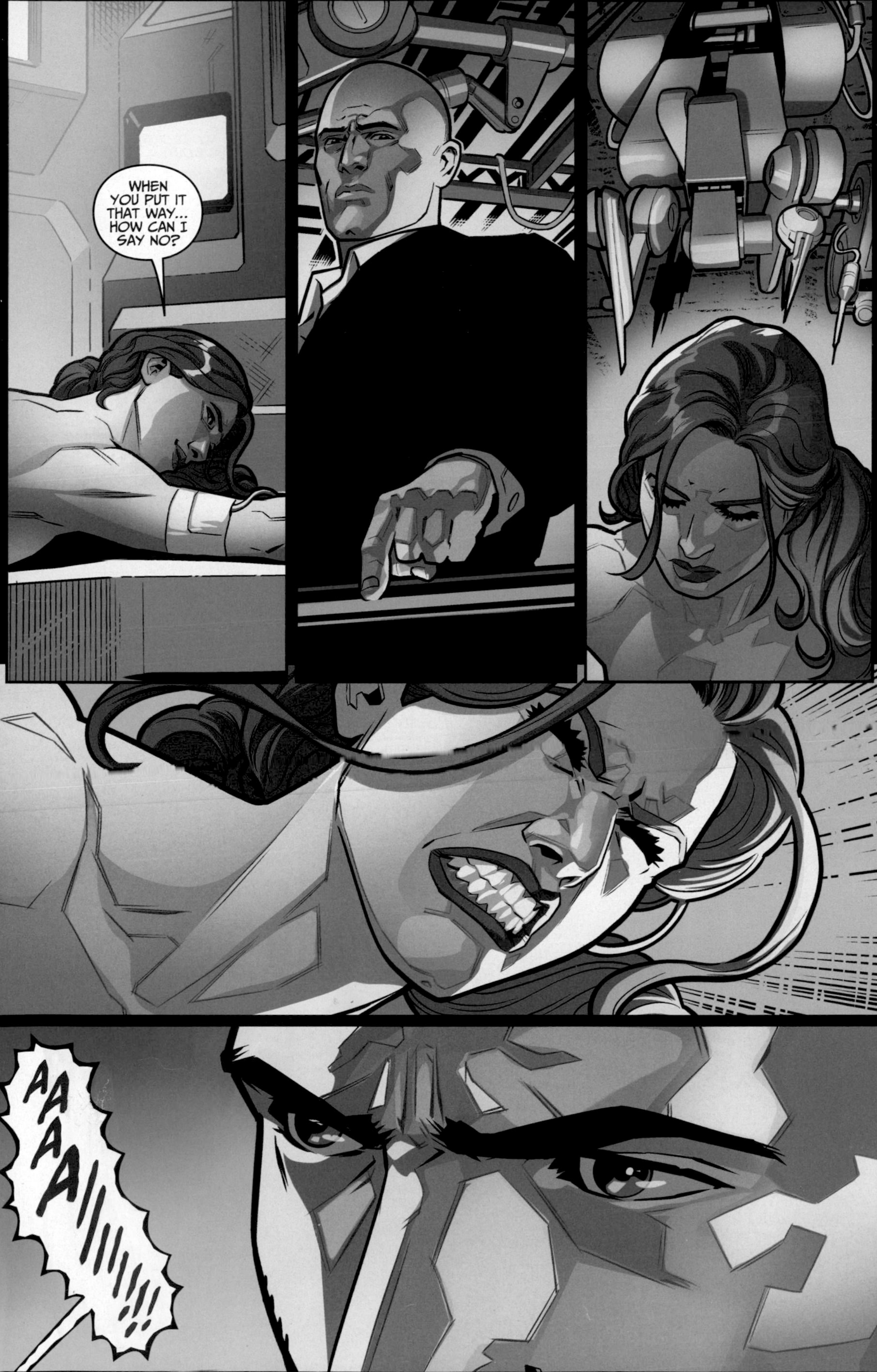
WHEN YOU PUT IT THAT WAY... HOW CAN I SAY NO?
AAAAIIIII!!!!

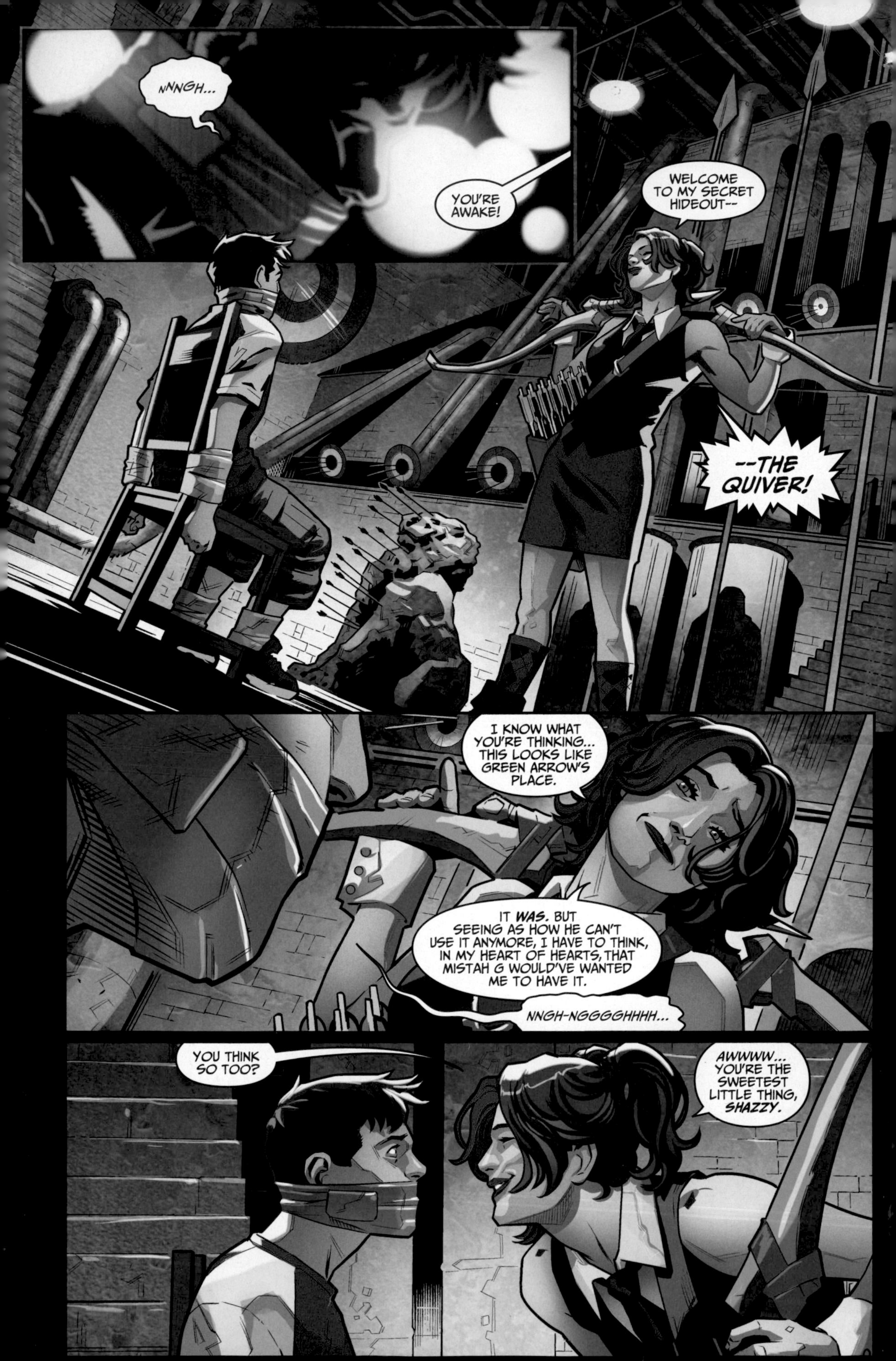
NNNGH...
YOU'RE AWAKE!
WELCOME TO MY SECRET HIDEOUT--
--THE QUIVER!
I KNOW WHAT YOU'RE THINKING... THIS LOOKS LIKE GREEN ARROW'S PLACE.
IT *WAS.* BUT SEEING AS HOW HE CAN'T USE IT ANYMORE, I HAVE TO THINK, IN MY HEART OF HEARTS, THAT MISTAH G WOULD'VE WANTED ME TO HAVE IT.
NNGH-NGGGHHHH...
YOU THINK SO TOO?
AWWWW... YOU'RE THE SWEETEST LITTLE THING, *SHAZZY.*

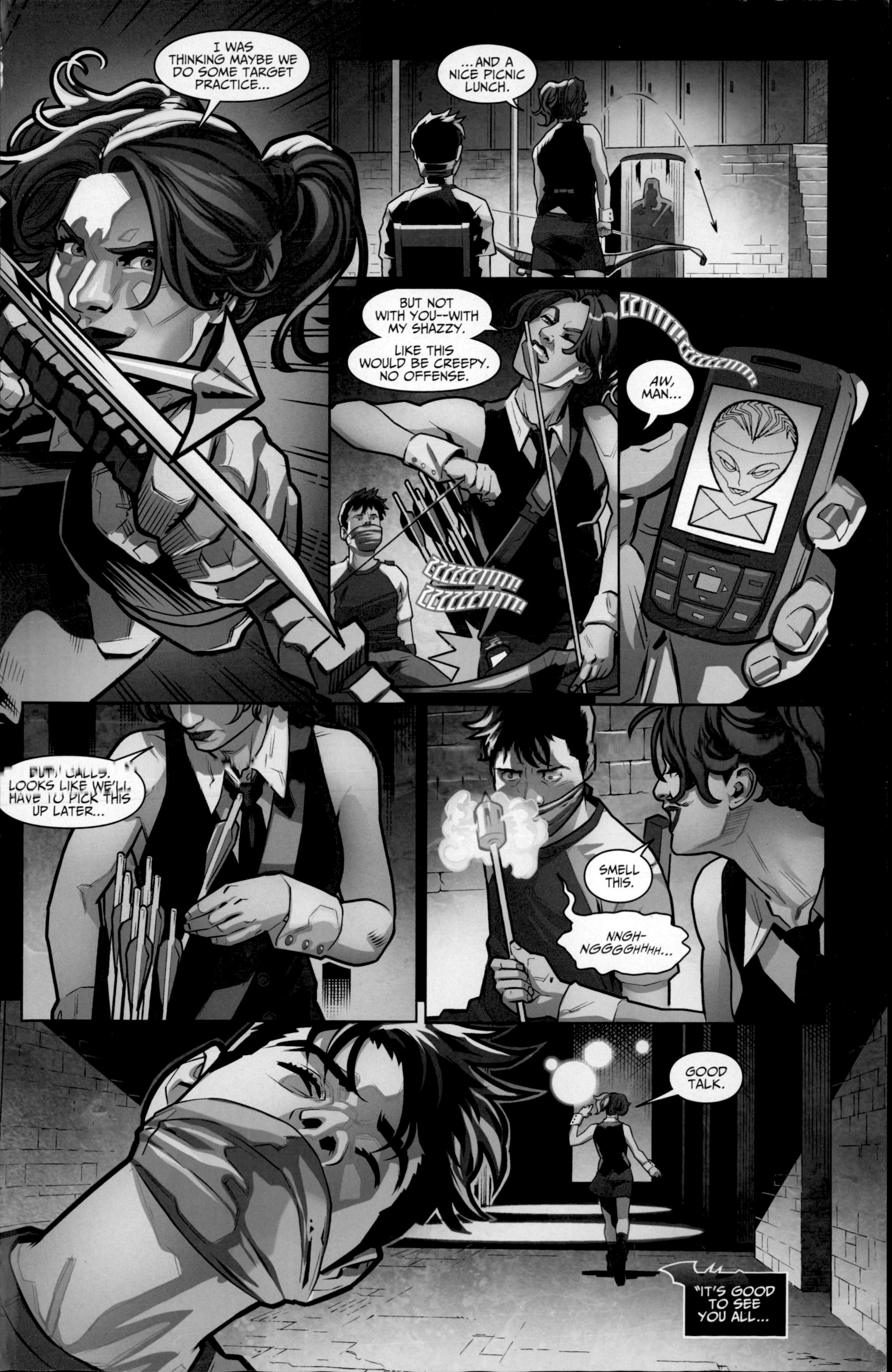
I WAS THINKING MAYBE WE DO SOME TARGET PRACTICE...
...AND A NICE PICNIC LUNCH.
BUT NOT WITH YOU--WITH MY SHAZZY.
LIKE THIS WOULD BE CREEPY. NO OFFENSE.
AW, MAN...
DUTY CALLS. LOOKS LIKE WE'LL HAVE TO PICK THIS UP LATER...
SMELL THIS.
NNGH-NGGGGHHHH...
GOOD TALK.
"IT'S GOOD TO SEE YOU ALL...

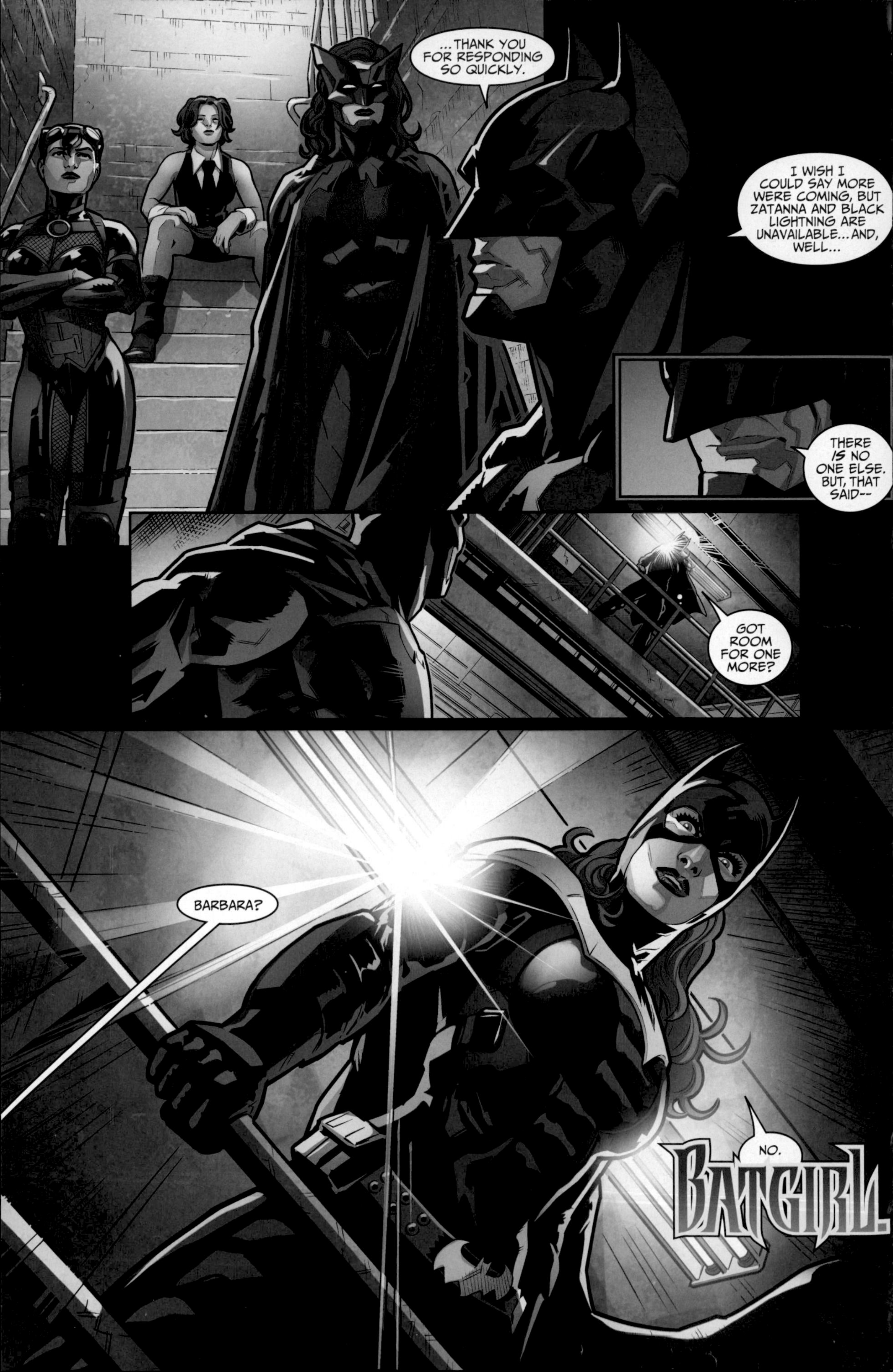
...THANK YOU FOR RESPONDING SO QUICKLY.
I WISH I COULD SAY MORE WERE COMING, BUT ZATANNA AND BLACK LIGHTNING ARE UNAVAILABLE...AND, WELL...
THERE *IS* NO ONE ELSE. BUT, THAT SAID--
GOT ROOM FOR ONE MORE?
BARBARA?
NO.
BATGIRL.

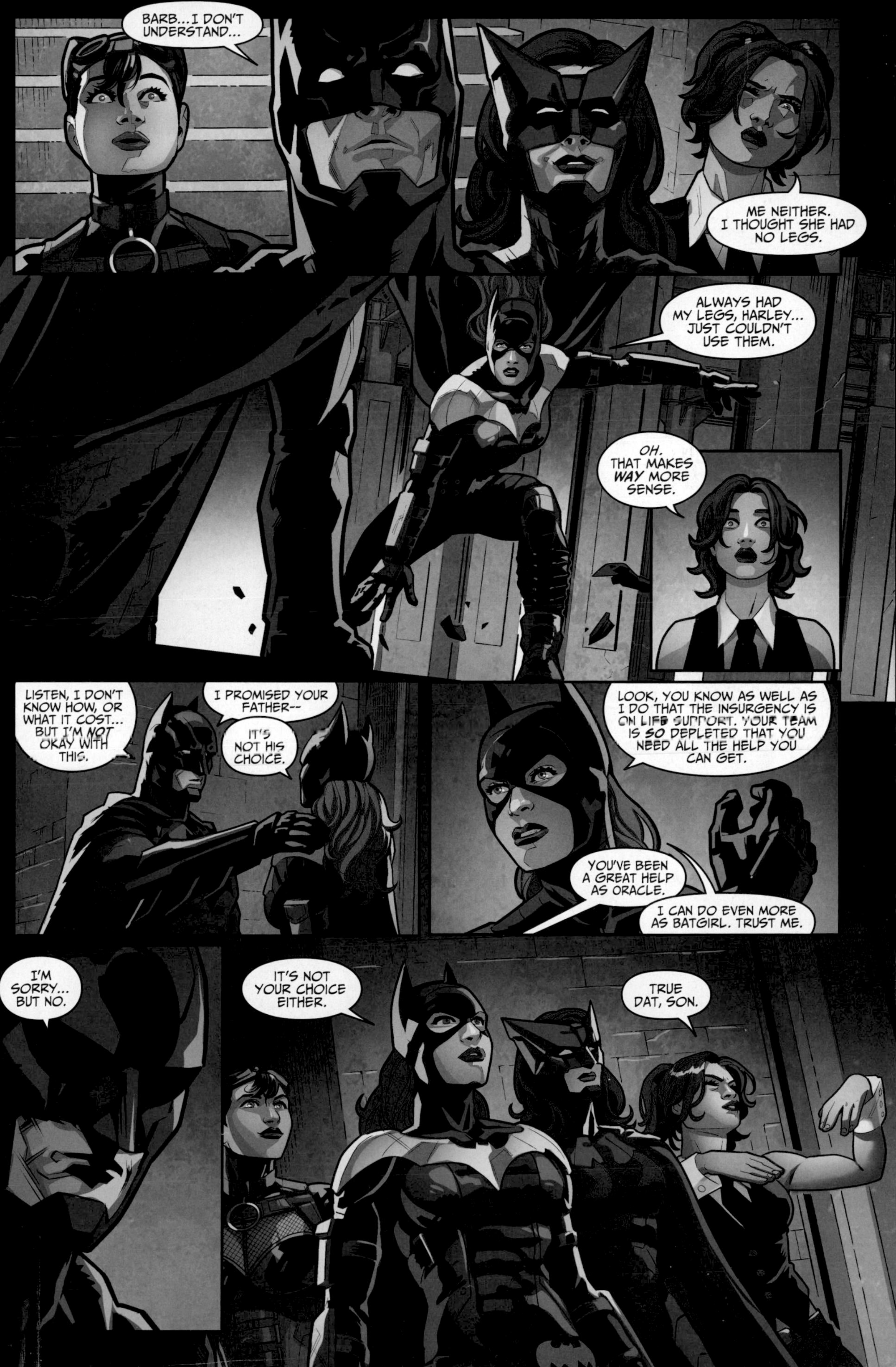
BARB...I DON'T UNDERSTAND...
ME NEITHER. I THOUGHT SHE HAD NO LEGS.
ALWAYS HAD MY LEGS, HARLEY... JUST COULDN'T USE THEM.
OH. THAT MAKES WAY MORE SENSE.
LISTEN, I DON'T KNOW HOW, OR WHAT IT COST... BUT I'M NOT OKAY WITH THIS.
I PROMISED YOUR FATHER--
IT'S NOT HIS CHOICE.
LOOK, YOU KNOW AS WELL AS I DO THAT THE INSURGENCY IS ON LIFE SUPPORT. YOUR TEAM IS SO DEPLETED THAT YOU NEED ALL THE HELP YOU CAN GET.
YOU'VE BEEN A GREAT HELP AS ORACLE.
I CAN DO EVEN MORE AS BATGIRL. TRUST ME.
I'M SORRY... BUT NO.
IT'S NOT YOUR CHOICE EITHER.
TRUE DAT, SON.

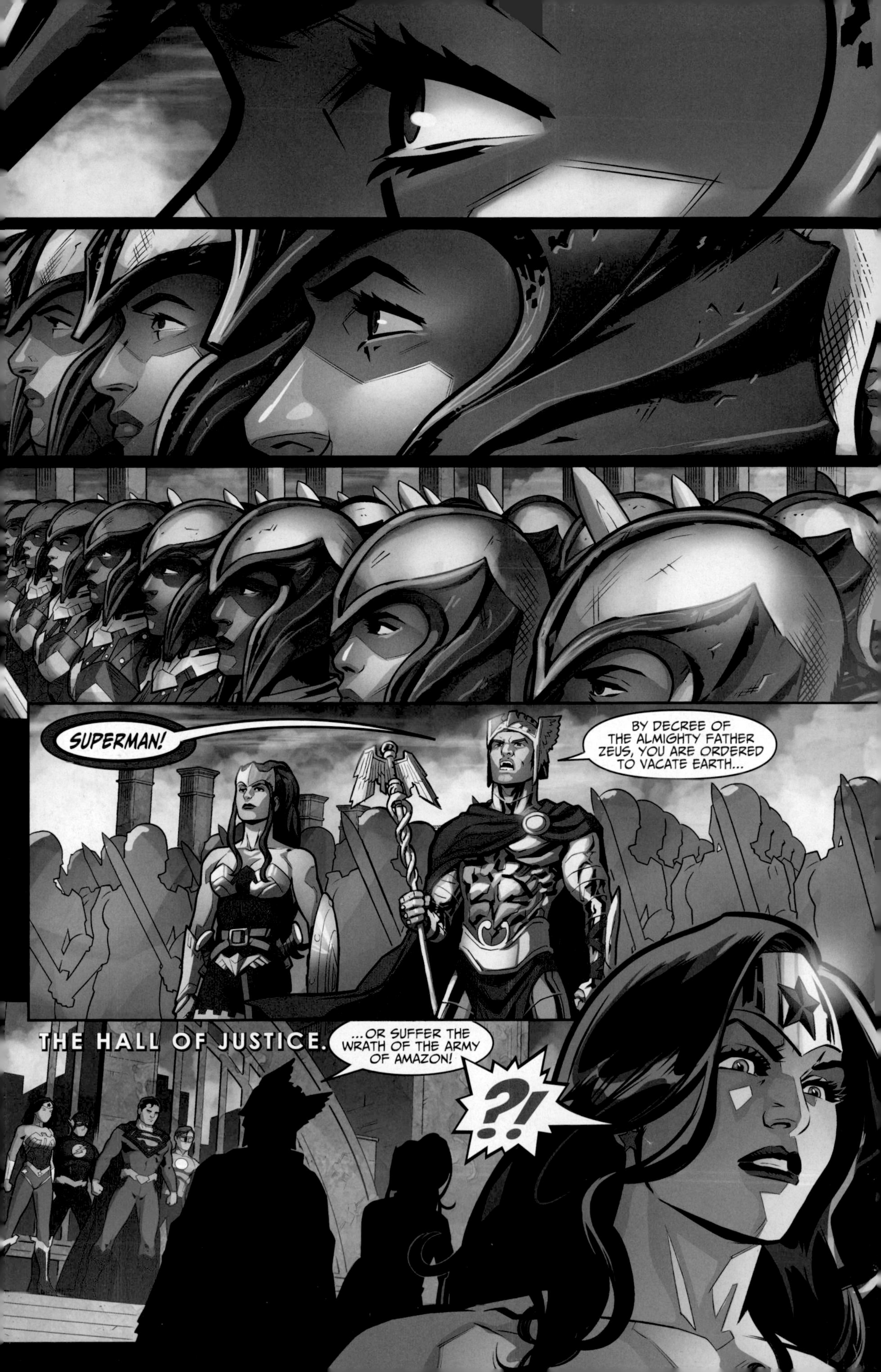
SUPERMAN!
BY DECREE OF THE ALMIGHTY FATHER ZEUS, YOU ARE ORDERED TO VACATE EARTH...
THE HALL OF JUSTICE.
...OR SUFFER THE WRATH OF THE ARMY OF AMAZON!
?!

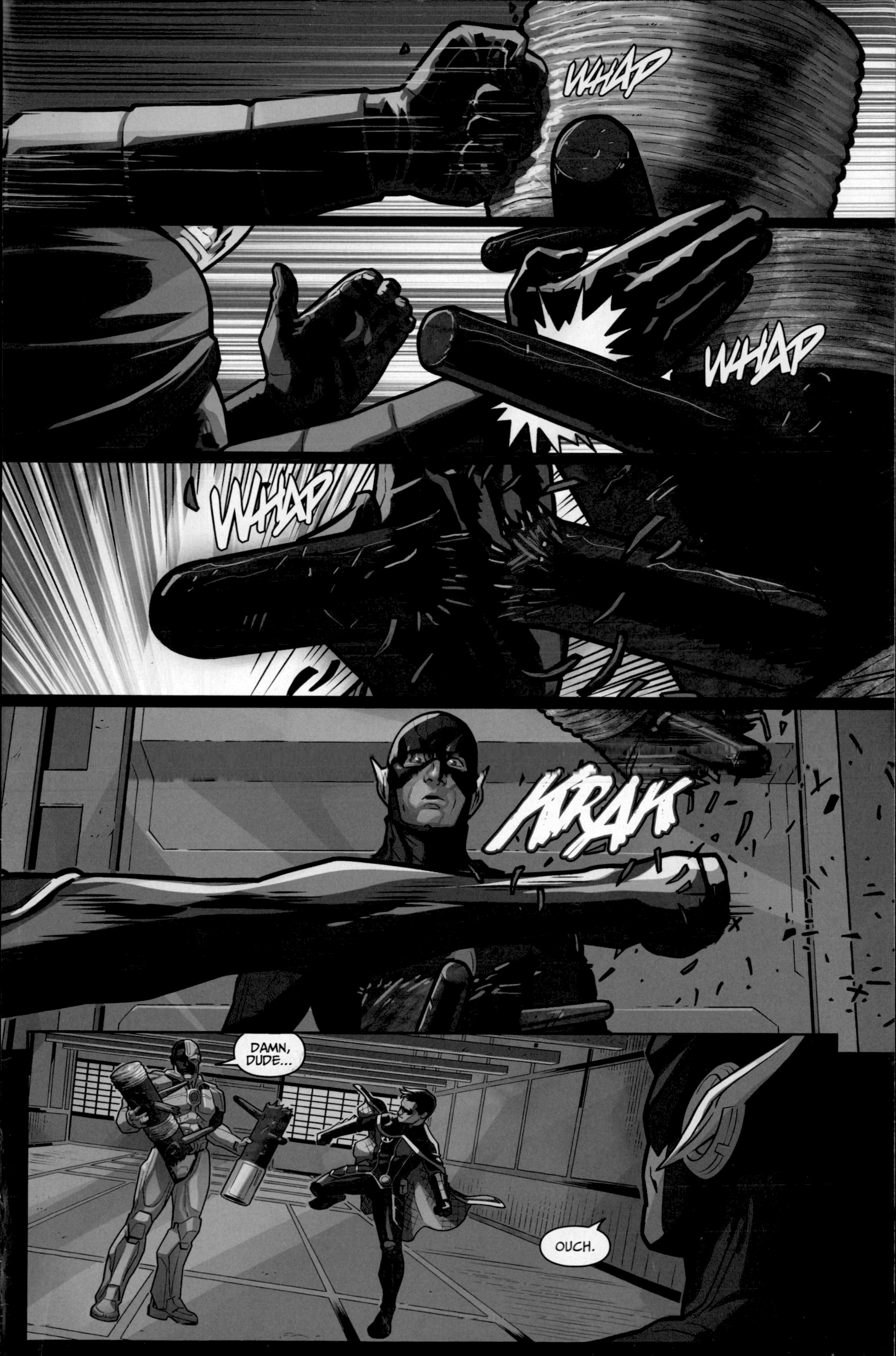
WHAP
WHAP
WHAP
KRAK
DAMN, DUDE...
OUCH.

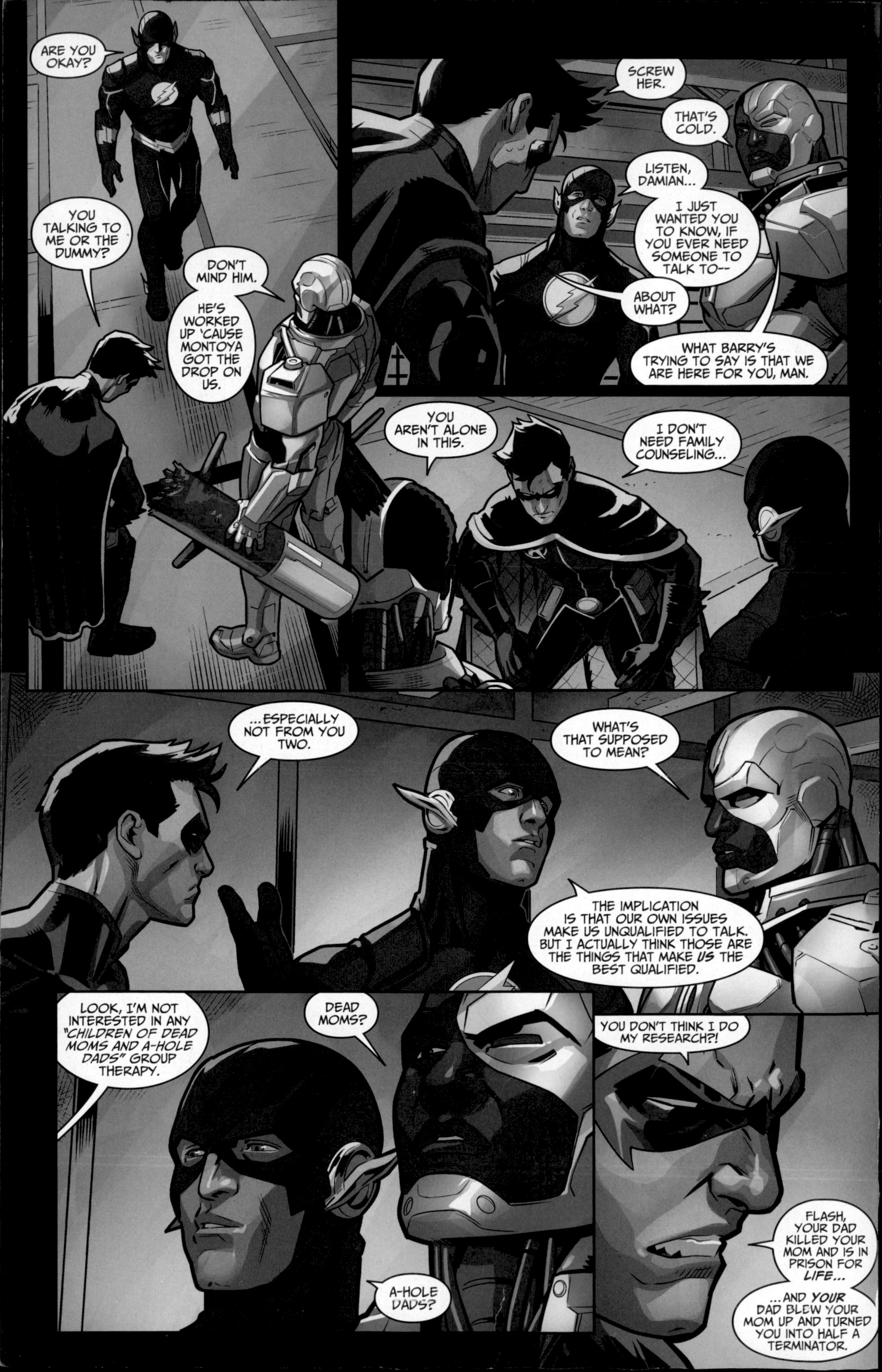
ARE YOU OKAY?
YOU TALKING TO ME OR THE DUMMY?
DON'T MIND HIM.
HE'S WORKED UP 'CAUSE MONTOYA GOT THE DROP ON US.
SCREW HER.
THAT'S COLD.
LISTEN, DAMIAN...
I JUST WANTED YOU TO KNOW, IF YOU EVER NEED SOMEONE TO TALK TO--
ABOUT WHAT?
WHAT BARRY'S TRYING TO SAY IS THAT WE ARE HERE FOR YOU, MAN.
YOU AREN'T ALONE IN THIS.
I DON'T NEED FAMILY COUNSELING...
...ESPECIALLY NOT FROM YOU TWO.
WHAT'S THAT SUPPOSED TO MEAN?
THE IMPLICATION IS THAT OUR OWN ISSUES MAKE US UNQUALIFIED TO TALK. BUT I ACTUALLY THINK THOSE ARE THE THINGS THAT MAKE *US* THE BEST QUALIFIED.
LOOK, I'M NOT INTERESTED IN ANY *"CHILDREN OF DEAD MOMS AND A-HOLE DADS"* GROUP THERAPY.
DEAD MOMS?
A-HOLE DADS?
YOU DON'T THINK I DO MY RESEARCH?!
FLASH, YOUR DAD KILLED YOUR MOM AND IS IN PRISON FOR *LIFE*...
...AND *YOUR* DAD BLEW YOUR MOM UP AND TURNED YOU INTO HALF A TERMINATOR.

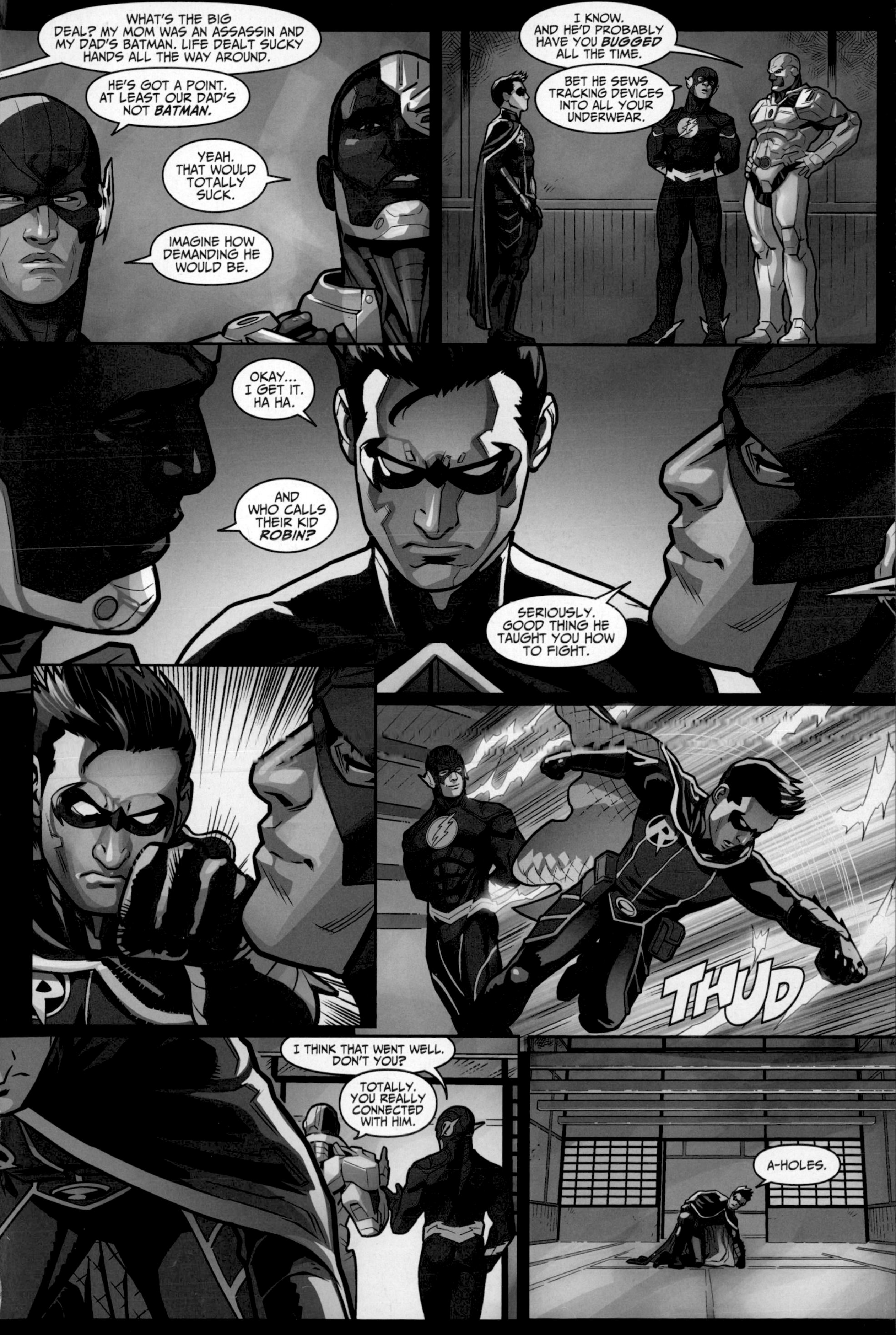
WHAT'S THE BIG DEAL? MY MOM WAS AN ASSASSIN AND MY DAD'S BATMAN. LIFE DEALT SUCKY HANDS ALL THE WAY AROUND.
HE'S GOT A POINT. AT LEAST OUR DAD'S NOT *BATMAN.*
YEAH. THAT WOULD TOTALLY SUCK.
IMAGINE HOW DEMANDING HE WOULD BE.
I KNOW. AND HE'D PROBABLY HAVE YOU *BUGGED* ALL THE TIME.
BET HE SEWS TRACKING DEVICES INTO ALL YOUR UNDERWEAR.
OKAY... I GET IT. HA HA.
AND WHO CALLS THEIR KID *ROBIN?*
SERIOUSLY. GOOD THING HE TAUGHT YOU HOW TO FIGHT.
THUD
I THINK THAT WENT WELL. DON'T YOU?
TOTALLY. YOU REALLY CONNECTED WITH HIM.
A-HOLES.

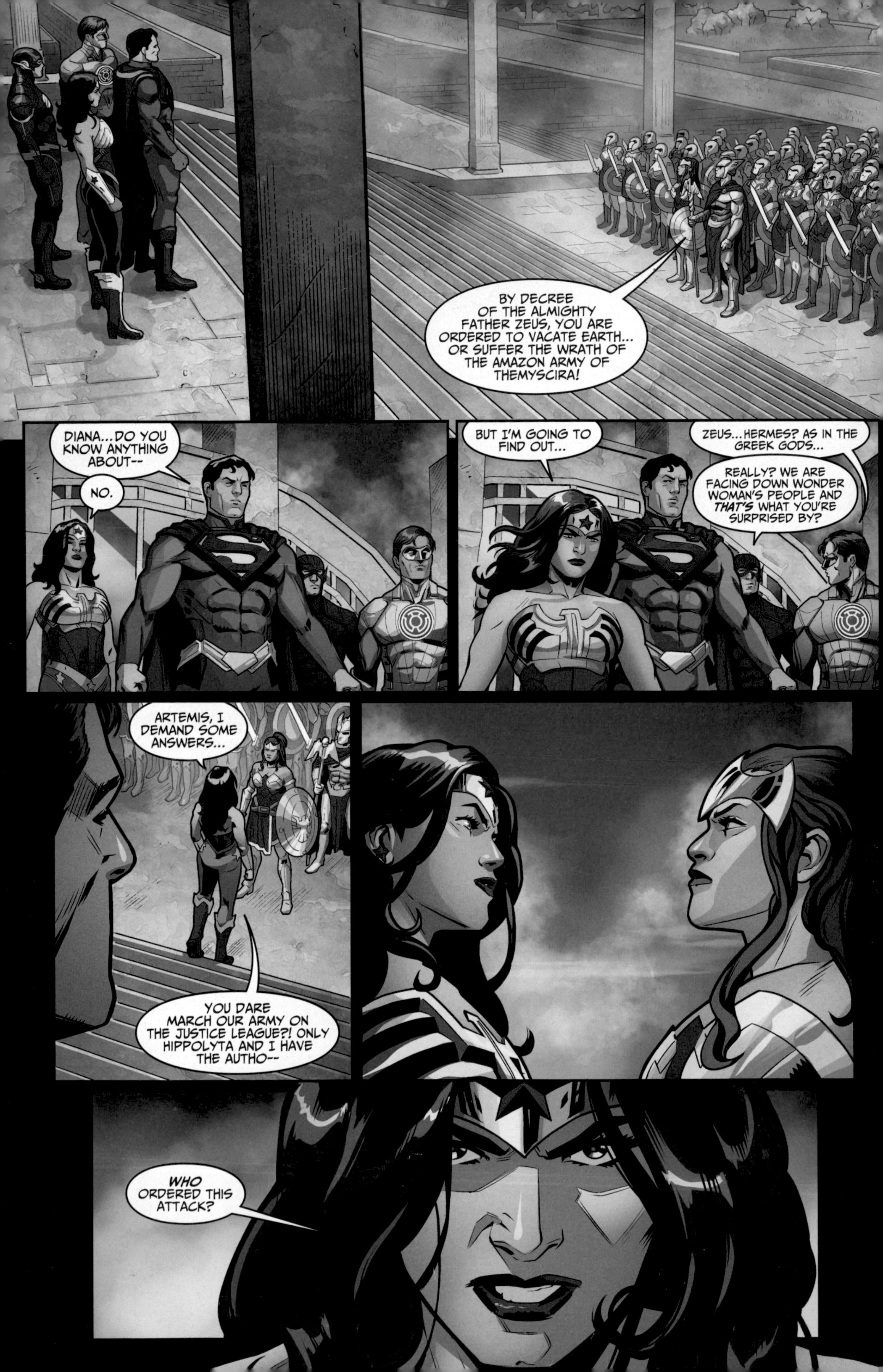
BY DECREE OF THE ALMIGHTY FATHER ZEUS, YOU ARE ORDERED TO VACATE EARTH... OR SUFFER THE WRATH OF THE AMAZON ARMY OF THEMYSCIRA!
DIANA...DO YOU KNOW ANYTHING ABOUT--
NO.
BUT I'M GOING TO FIND OUT...
ZEUS...HERMES? AS IN THE GREEK GODS...
REALLY? WE ARE FACING DOWN WONDER WOMAN'S PEOPLE AND *THAT'S* WHAT YOU'RE SURPRISED BY?
ARTEMIS, I DEMAND SOME ANSWERS...
YOU DARE MARCH OUR ARMY ON THE JUSTICE LEAGUE?! ONLY HIPPOLYTA AND I HAVE THE AUTHO--
WHO ORDERED THIS ATTACK?

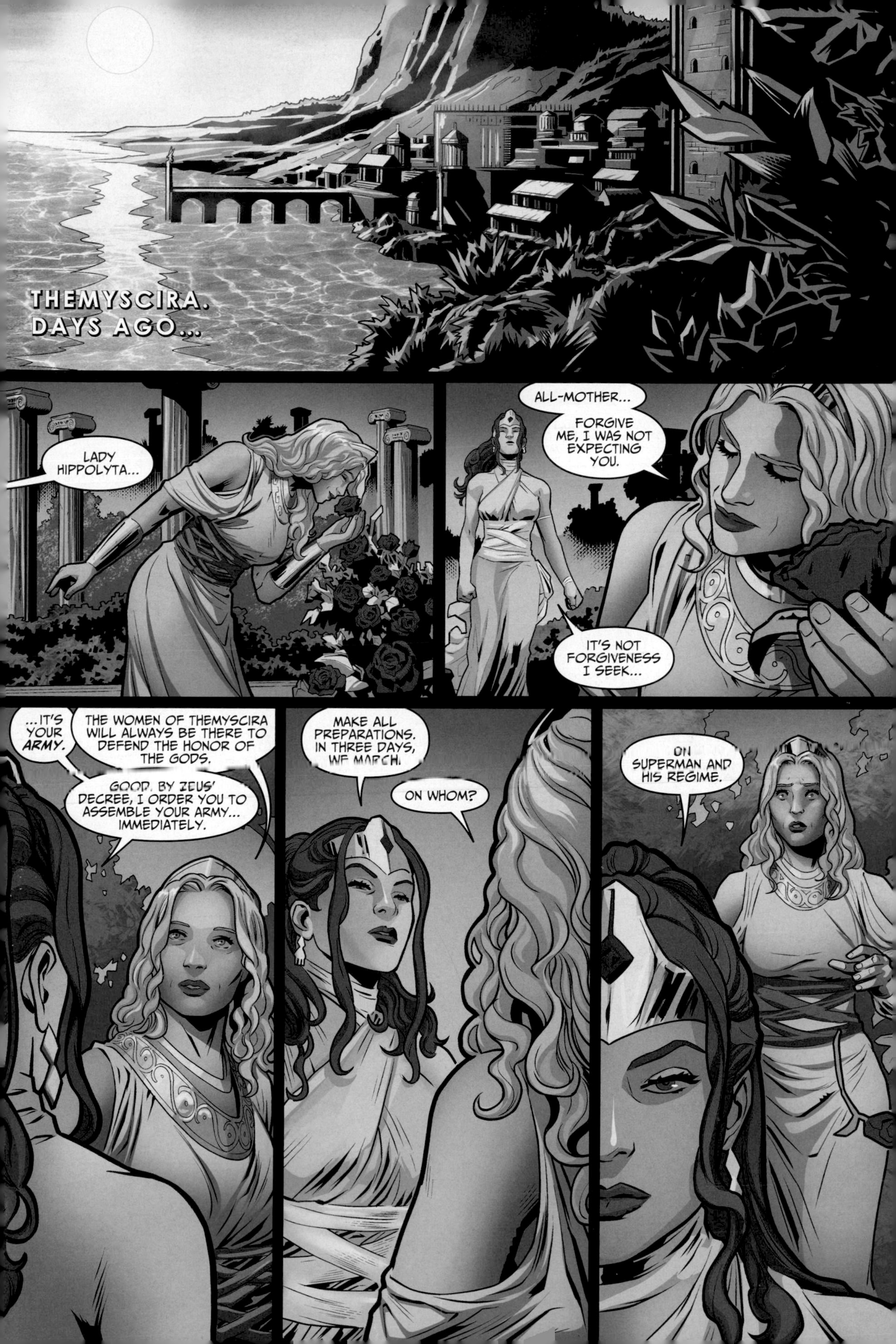
THEMYSCIRA. DAYS AGO...
LADY HIPPOLYTA...
ALL-MOTHER...
FORGIVE ME, I WAS NOT EXPECTING YOU.
IT'S NOT FORGIVENESS I SEEK...
...IT'S YOUR ARMY.
THE WOMEN OF THEMYSCIRA WILL ALWAYS BE THERE TO DEFEND THE HONOR OF THE GODS.
GOOD. BY ZEUS' DECREE, I ORDER YOU TO ASSEMBLE YOUR ARMY... IMMEDIATELY.
MAKE ALL PREPARATIONS. IN THREE DAYS, WE MARCH.
ON WHOM?
ON SUPERMAN AND HIS REGIME.

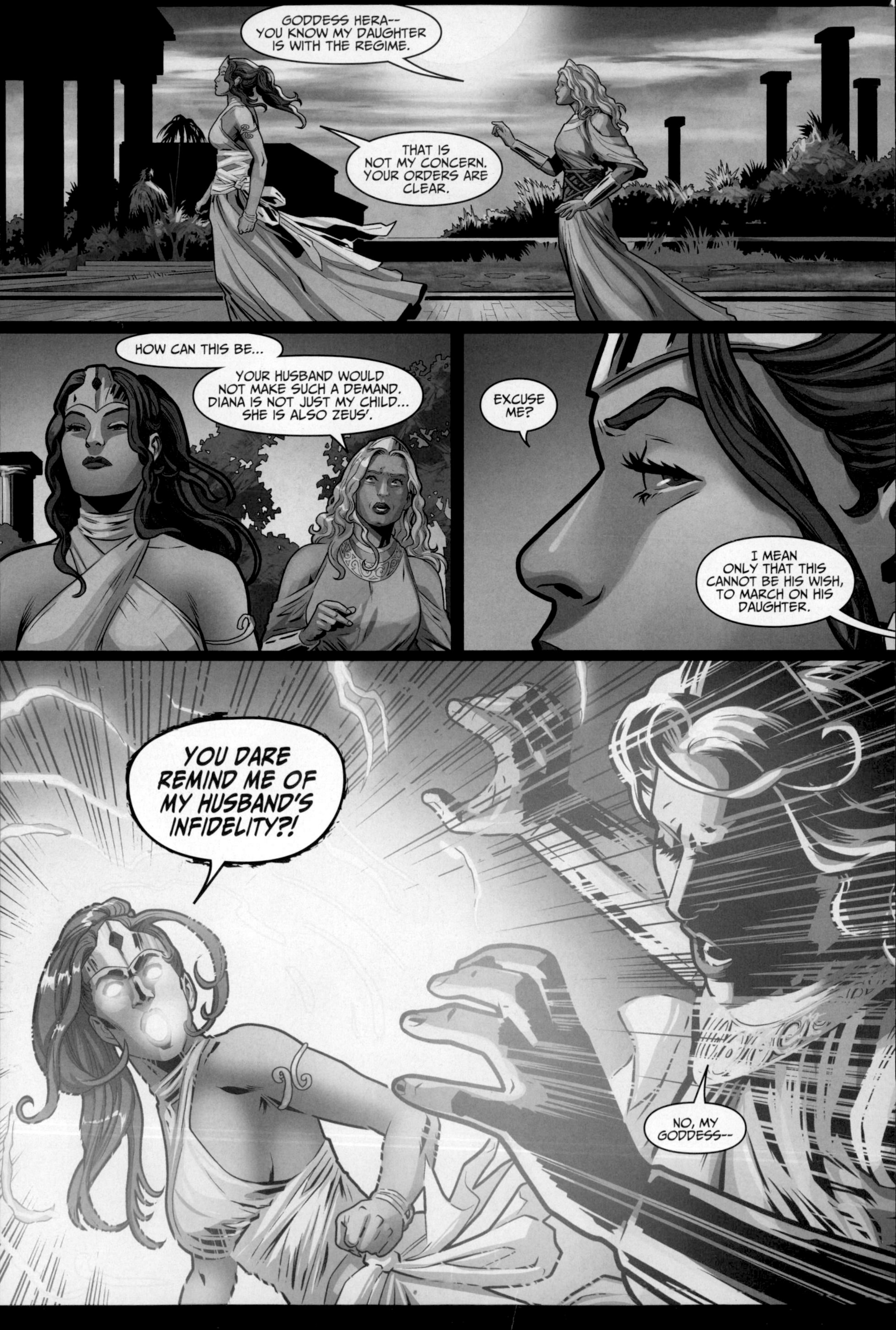
GODDESS HERA-- YOU KNOW MY DAUGHTER IS WITH THE REGIME.
THAT IS NOT MY CONCERN. YOUR ORDERS ARE CLEAR.
HOW CAN THIS BE...
YOUR HUSBAND WOULD NOT MAKE SUCH A DEMAND. DIANA IS NOT JUST MY CHILD... SHE IS ALSO ZEUS'.
EXCUSE ME?
I MEAN ONLY THAT THIS CANNOT BE HIS WISH, TO MARCH ON HIS DAUGHTER.
YOU DARE REMIND ME OF MY HUSBAND'S INFIDELITY?!
NO, MY GODDESS--

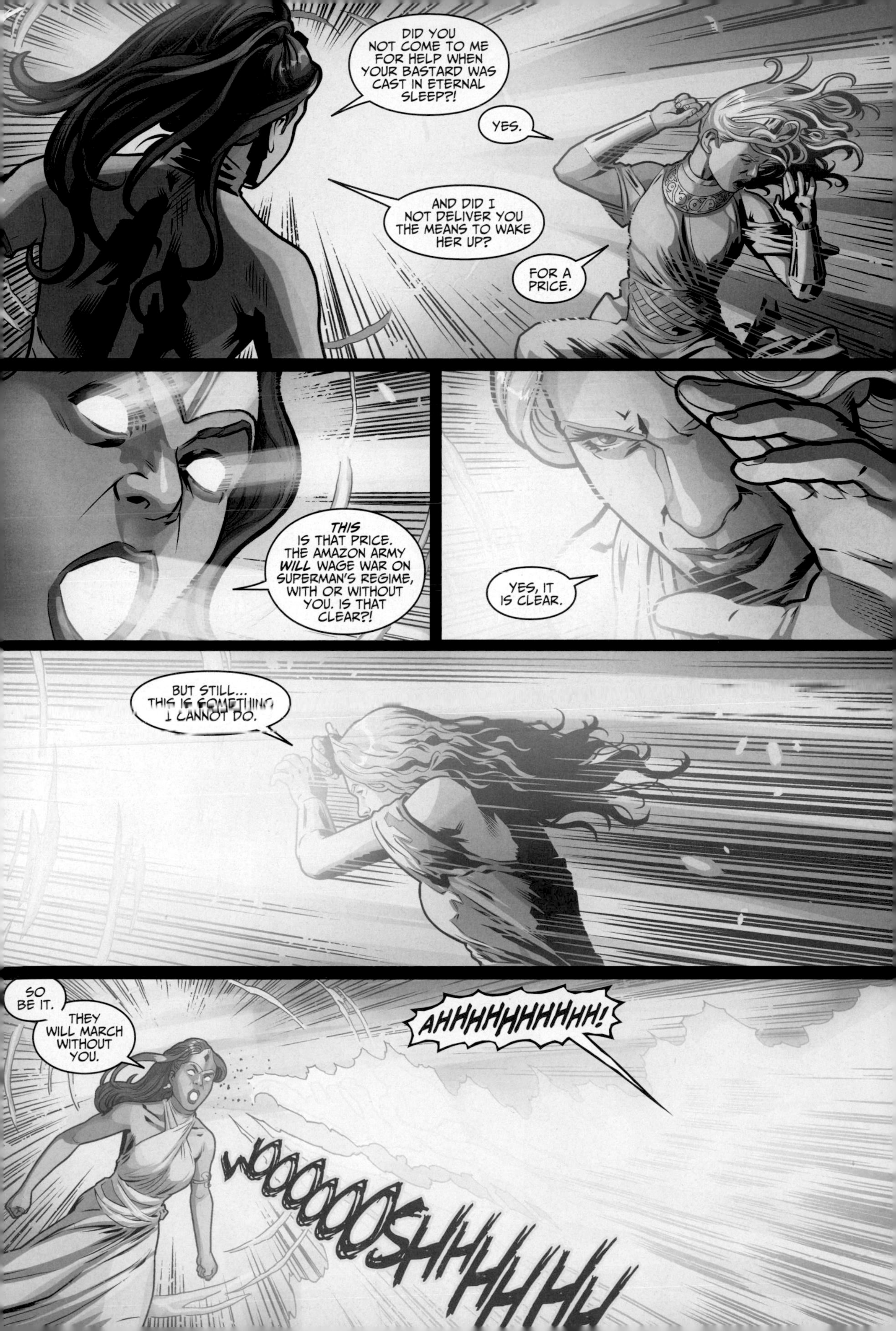

DID YOU NOT COME TO ME FOR HELP WHEN YOUR BASTARD WAS CAST IN ETERNAL SLEEP?!
YES.
AND DID I NOT DELIVER YOU THE MEANS TO WAKE HER UP?
FOR A PRICE.
THIS IS THAT PRICE. THE AMAZON ARMY *WILL* WAGE WAR ON SUPERMAN'S REGIME, WITH OR WITHOUT YOU. IS THAT CLEAR?!
YES, IT IS CLEAR.
BUT STILL... THIS IS SOMETHING I CANNOT DO.
SO BE IT.
THEY WILL MARCH WITHOUT YOU.
AHHHHHHHHH!
WOOOOOOSHHHHHHH

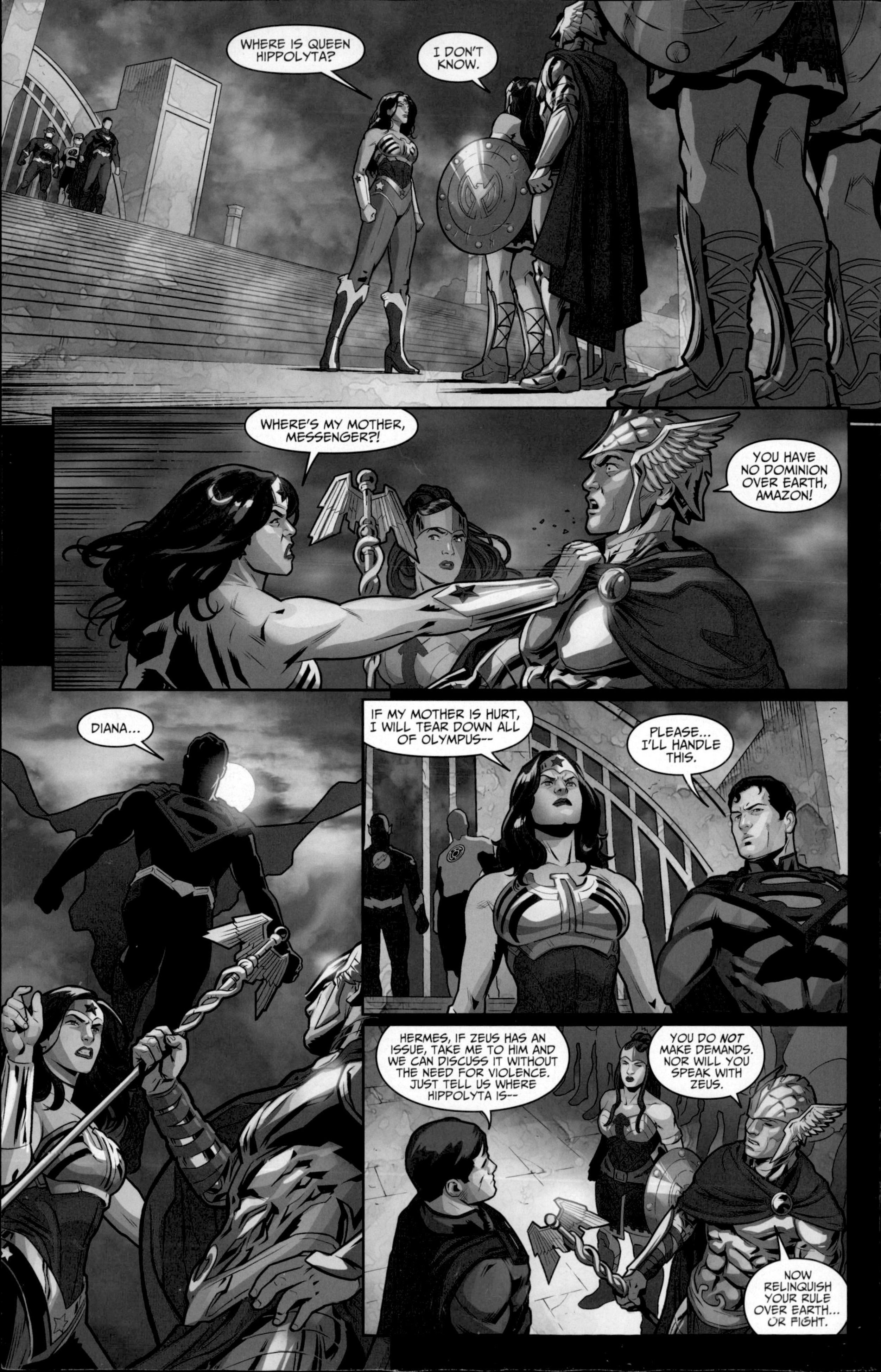
WHERE IS QUEEN HIPPOLYTA?
I DON'T KNOW.
WHERE'S MY MOTHER, MESSENGER?!
YOU HAVE NO DOMINION OVER EARTH, AMAZON!
DIANA...
IF MY MOTHER IS HURT, I WILL TEAR DOWN ALL OF OLYMPUS--
PLEASE... I'LL HANDLE THIS.
HERMES, IF ZEUS HAS AN ISSUE, TAKE ME TO HIM AND WE CAN DISCUSS IT WITHOUT THE NEED FOR VIOLENCE. JUST TELL US WHERE HIPPOLYTA IS--
YOU DO NOT MAKE DEMANDS. NOR WILL YOU SPEAK WITH ZEUS.
NOW RELINQUISH YOUR RULE OVER EARTH... OR FIGHT.

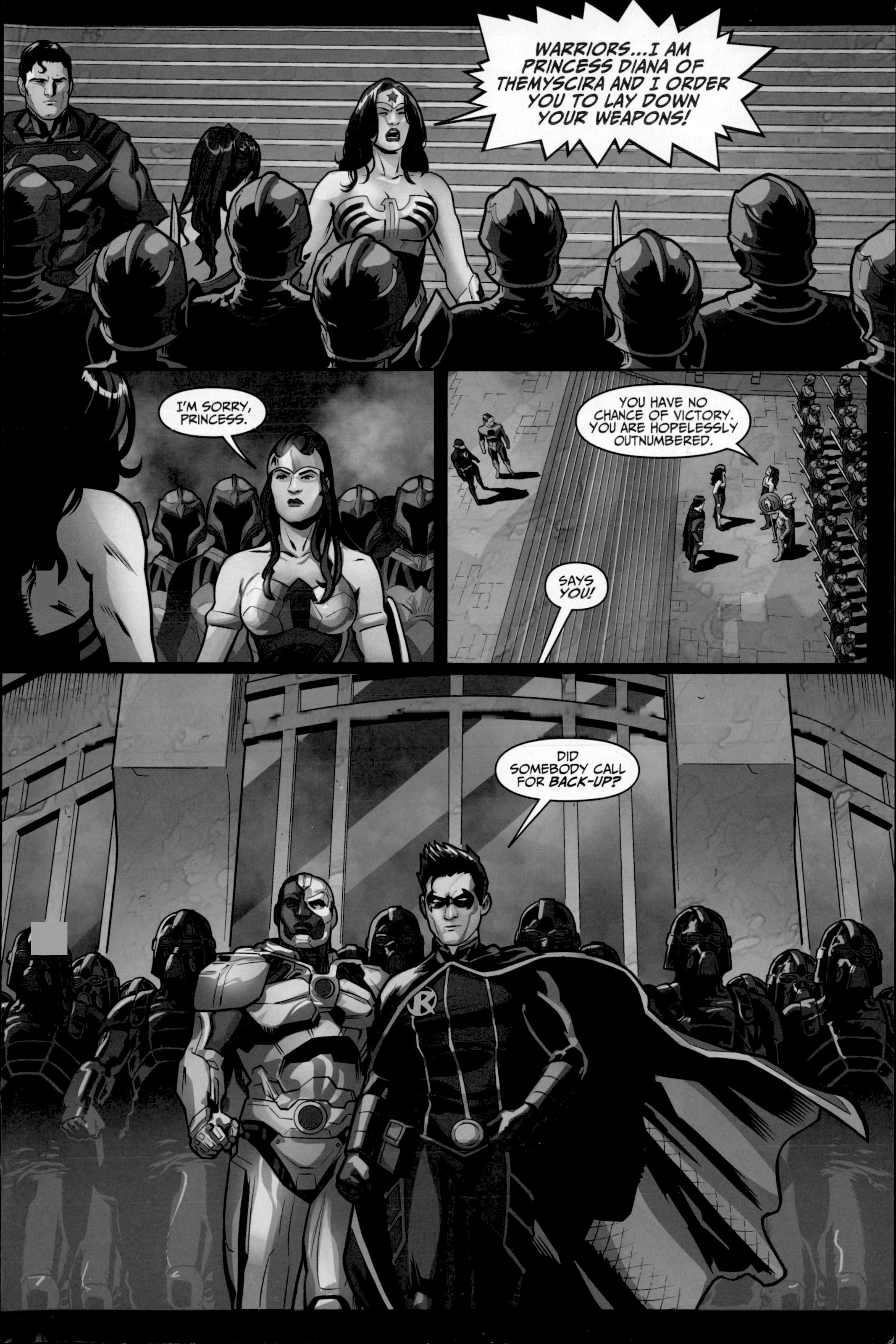
WARRIORS...I AM PRINCESS DIANA OF THEMYSCIRA AND I ORDER YOU TO LAY DOWN YOUR WEAPONS!
I'M SORRY, PRINCESS.
YOU HAVE NO CHANCE OF VICTORY. YOU ARE HOPELESSLY OUTNUMBERED.
SAYS YOU!
DID SOMEBODY CALL FOR BACK-UP?

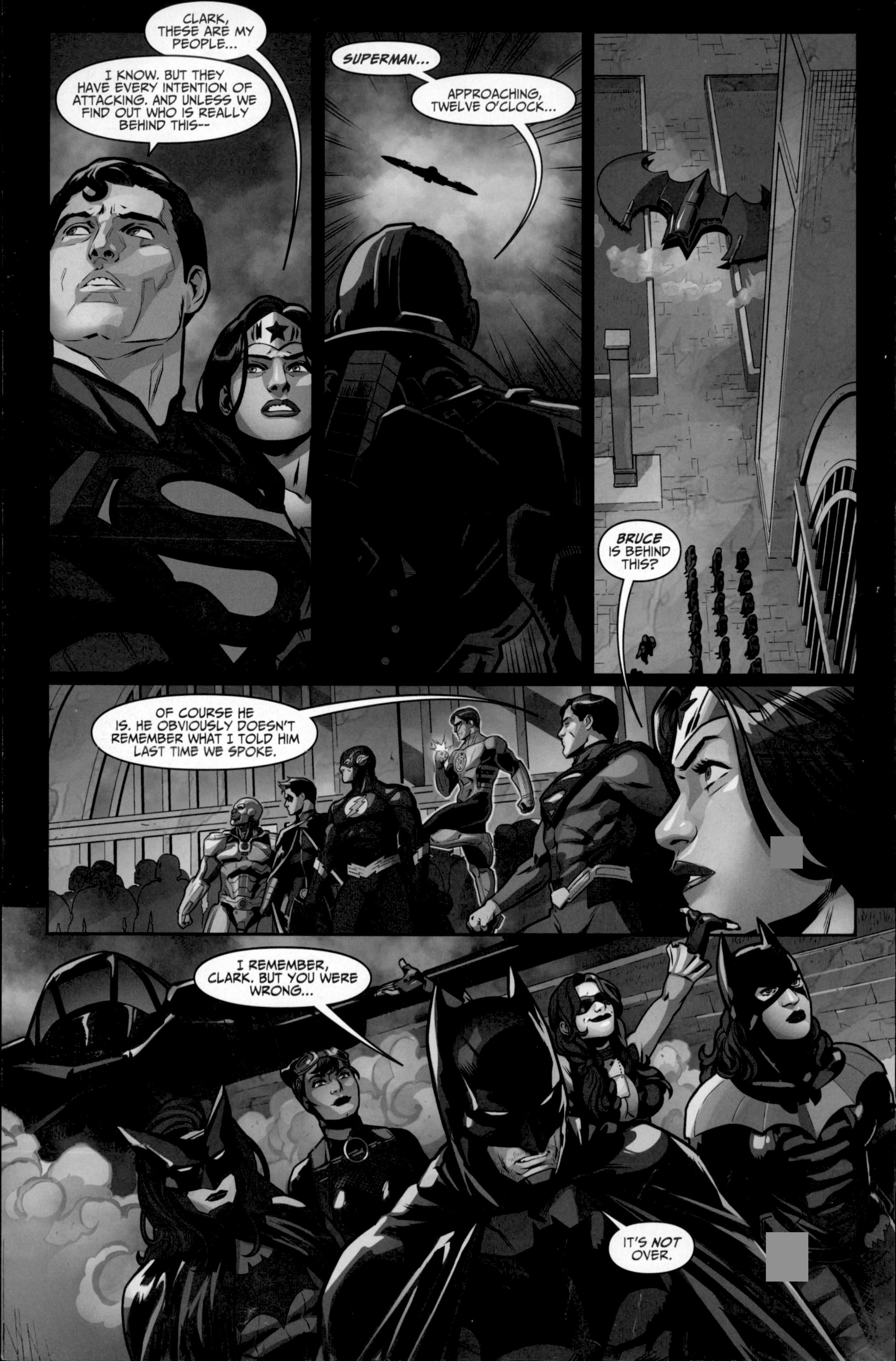
CLARK, THESE ARE MY PEOPLE...
I KNOW. BUT THEY HAVE EVERY INTENTION OF ATTACKING. AND UNLESS WE FIND OUT WHO IS REALLY BEHIND THIS--
SUPERMAN...
APPROACHING, TWELVE O'CLOCK...
BRUCE IS BEHIND THIS?
OF COURSE HE IS. HE OBVIOUSLY DOESN'T REMEMBER WHAT I TOLD HIM LAST TIME WE SPOKE.
I REMEMBER, CLARK. BUT YOU WERE WRONG...
IT'S NOT OVER.

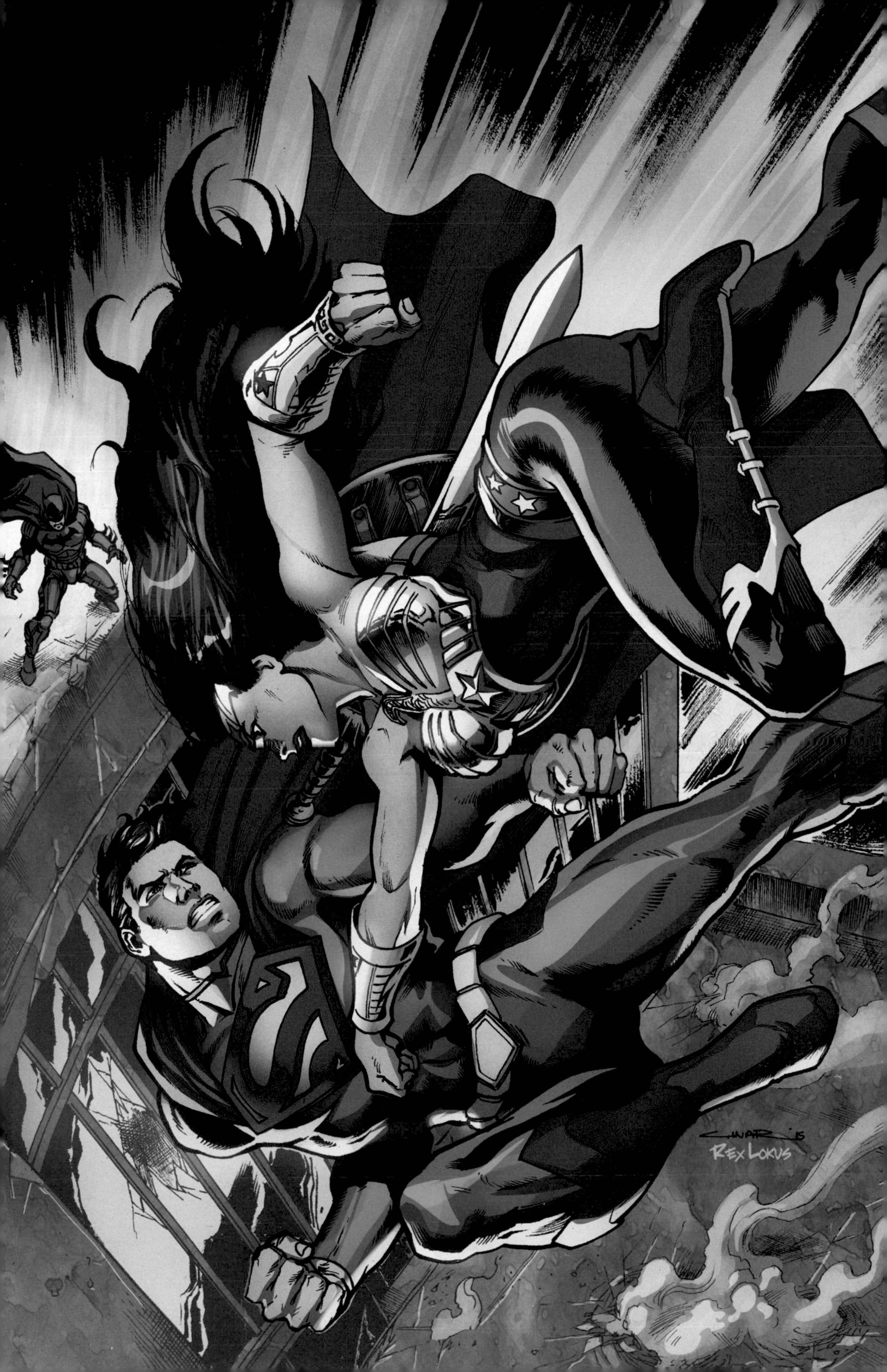
REX LOKUS

"Bargins" **Mike S. Miller** Artist **J. Nanjan** Colorist
Cover Art by **Yildiray Cinar & Rex Lokus**

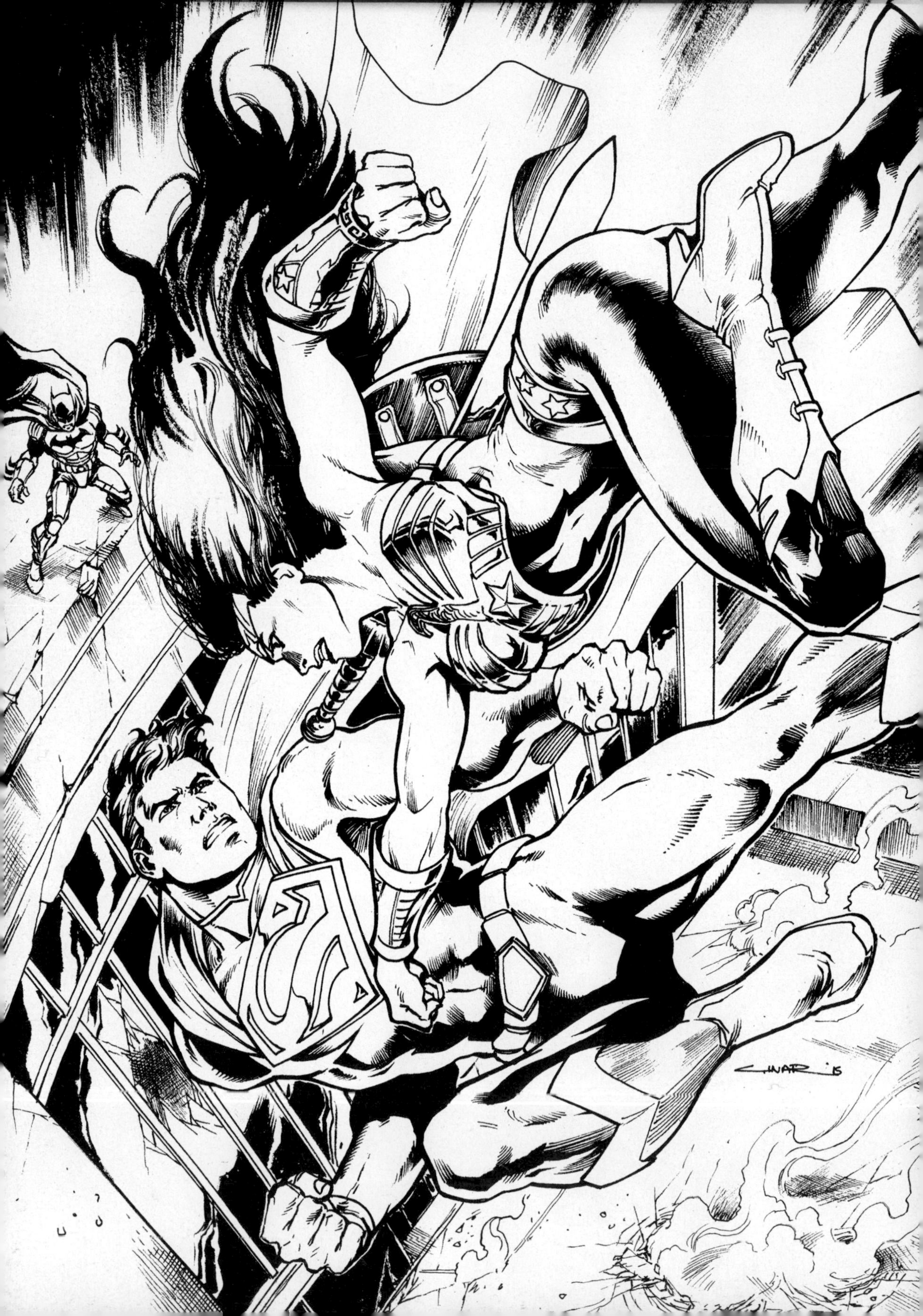

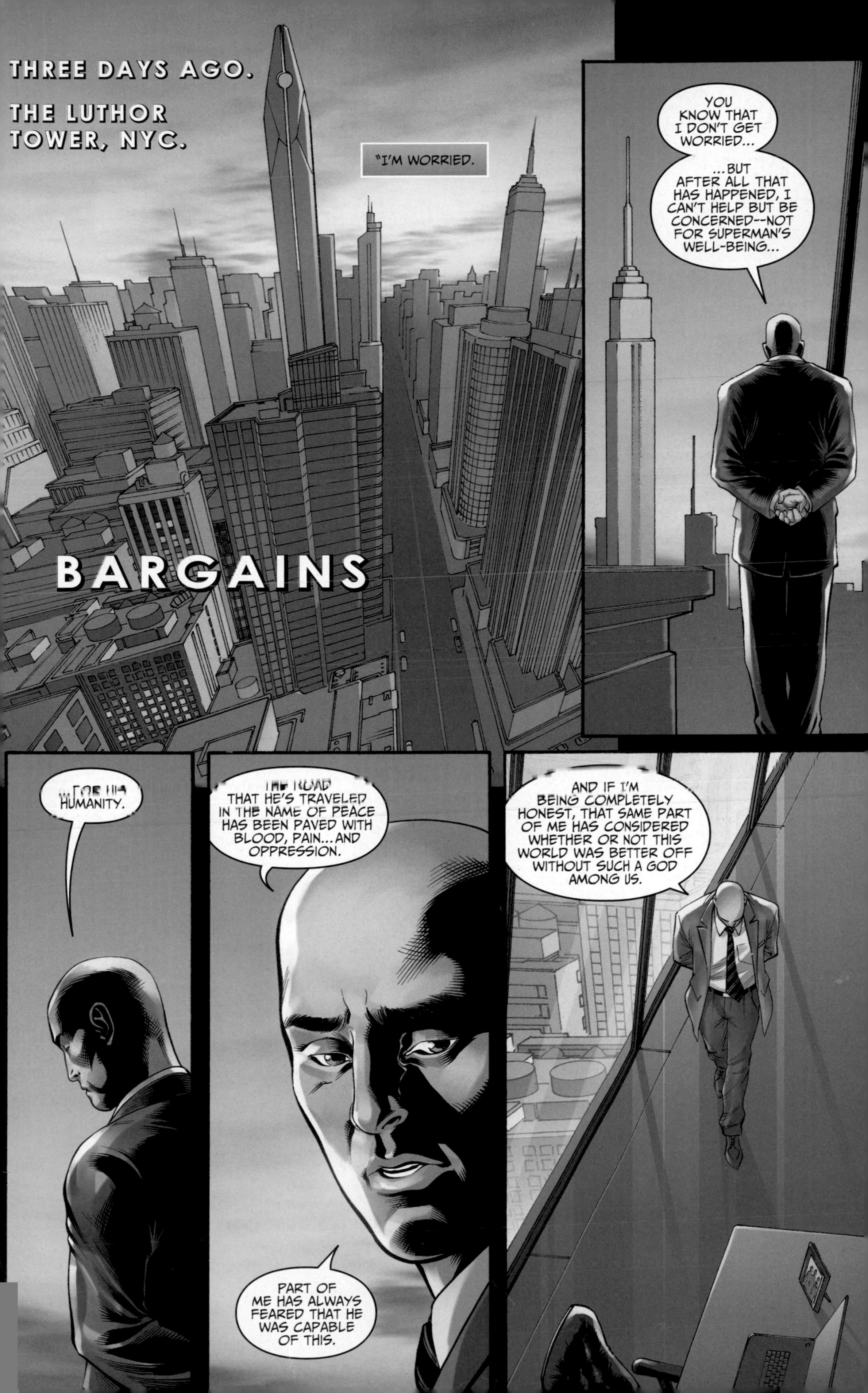
THREE DAYS AGO.
THE LUTHOR TOWER, NYC.
"I'M WORRIED.
BARGAINS
YOU KNOW THAT I DON'T GET WORRIED...
...BUT AFTER ALL THAT HAS HAPPENED, I CAN'T HELP BUT BE CONCERNED--NOT FOR SUPERMAN'S WELL-BEING...
...FOR HIS HUMANITY.
THE ROAD THAT HE'S TRAVELED IN THE NAME OF PEACE HAS BEEN PAVED WITH BLOOD, PAIN...AND OPPRESSION.
PART OF ME HAS ALWAYS FEARED THAT HE WAS CAPABLE OF THIS.
AND IF I'M BEING COMPLETELY HONEST, THAT SAME PART OF ME HAS CONSIDERED WHETHER OR NOT THIS WORLD WAS BETTER OFF WITHOUT SUCH A GOD AMONG US.

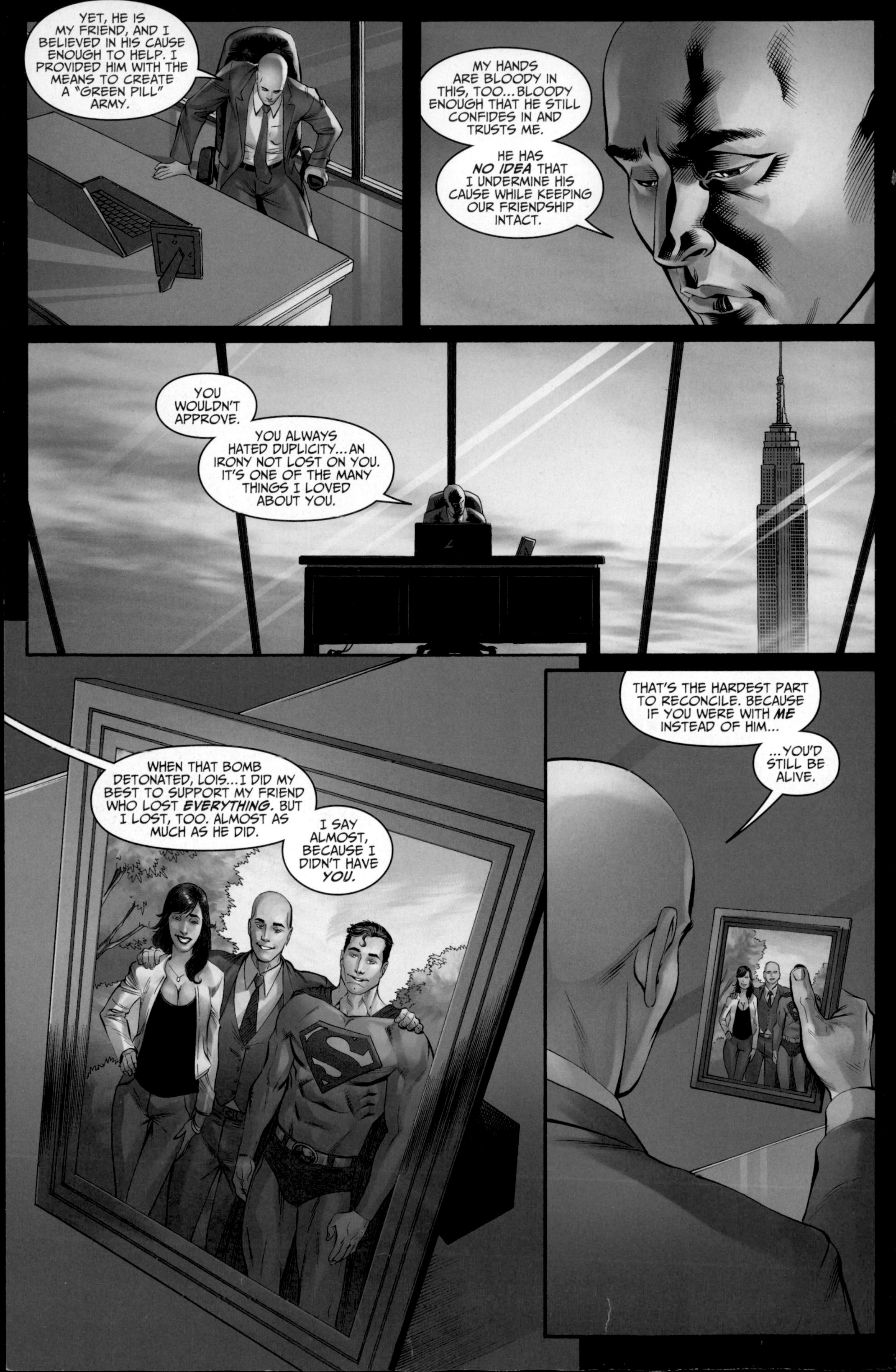

YET, HE IS MY FRIEND, AND I BELIEVED IN HIS CAUSE ENOUGH TO HELP. I PROVIDED HIM WITH THE MEANS TO CREATE A "GREEN PILL" ARMY.
MY HANDS ARE BLOODY IN THIS, TOO...BLOODY ENOUGH THAT HE STILL CONFIDES IN AND TRUSTS ME.
HE HAS NO IDEA THAT I UNDERMINE HIS CAUSE WHILE KEEPING OUR FRIENDSHIP INTACT.
YOU WOULDN'T APPROVE.
YOU ALWAYS HATED DUPLICITY...AN IRONY NOT LOST ON YOU. IT'S ONE OF THE MANY THINGS I LOVED ABOUT YOU.
WHEN THAT BOMB DETONATED, LOIS...I DID MY BEST TO SUPPORT MY FRIEND WHO LOST EVERYTHING. BUT I LOST, TOO. ALMOST AS MUCH AS HE DID.
I SAY ALMOST, BECAUSE I DIDN'T HAVE YOU.
THAT'S THE HARDEST PART TO RECONCILE. BECAUSE IF YOU WERE WITH ME INSTEAD OF HIM...
...YOU'D STILL BE ALIVE.

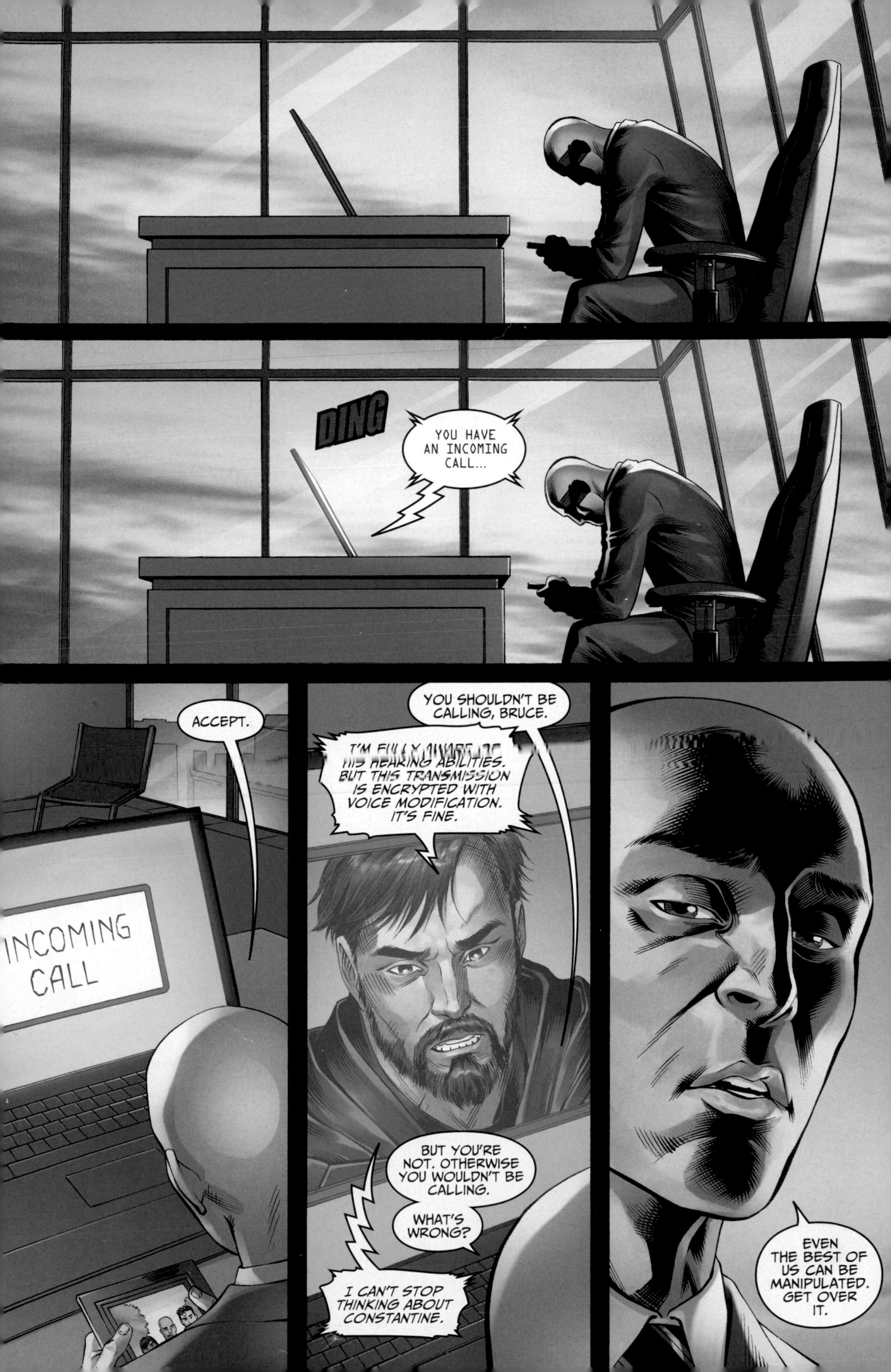
DING
YOU HAVE AN INCOMING CALL...
ACCEPT.
INCOMING CALL
YOU SHOULDN'T BE CALLING, BRUCE.
I'M FULLY HIS HEARING ABILITIES. BUT THIS TRANSMISSION IS ENCRYPTED WITH VOICE MODIFICATION. IT'S FINE.
BUT YOU'RE NOT. OTHERWISE YOU WOULDN'T BE CALLING.
WHAT'S WRONG?
I CAN'T STOP THINKING ABOUT CONSTANTINE.
EVEN THE BEST OF US CAN BE MANIPULATED. GET OVER IT.

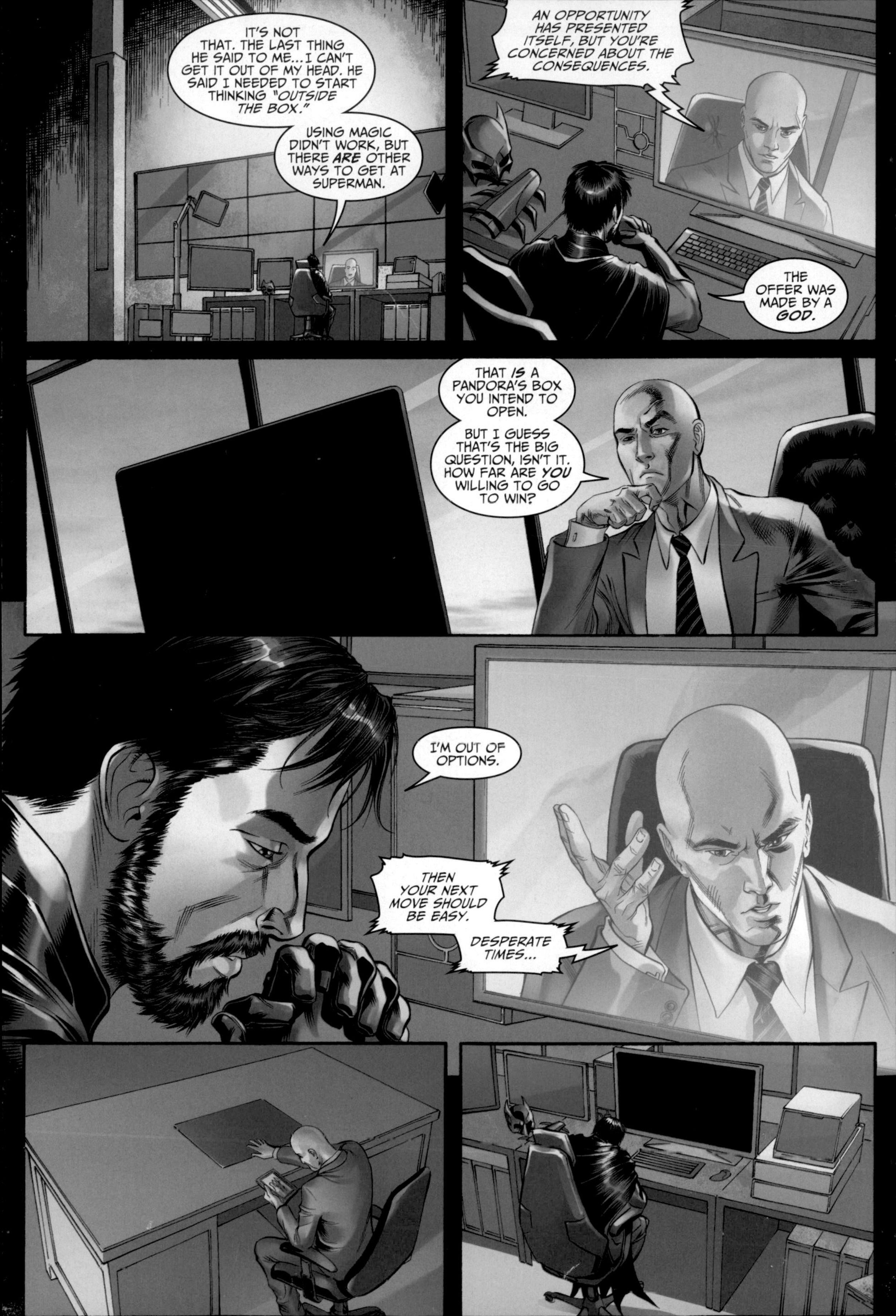

IT'S NOT THAT. THE LAST THING HE SAID TO ME... I CAN'T GET IT OUT OF MY HEAD. HE SAID I NEEDED TO START THINKING "OUTSIDE THE BOX."
USING MAGIC DIDN'T WORK, BUT THERE ARE OTHER WAYS TO GET AT SUPERMAN.
AN OPPORTUNITY HAS PRESENTED ITSELF, BUT YOU'RE CONCERNED ABOUT THE CONSEQUENCES.
THE OFFER WAS MADE BY A GOD.
THAT IS A PANDORA'S BOX YOU INTEND TO OPEN.
BUT I GUESS THAT'S THE BIG QUESTION, ISN'T IT. HOW FAR ARE YOU WILLING TO GO TO WIN?
I'M OUT OF OPTIONS.
THEN YOUR NEXT MOVE SHOULD BE EASY.
DESPERATE TIMES...

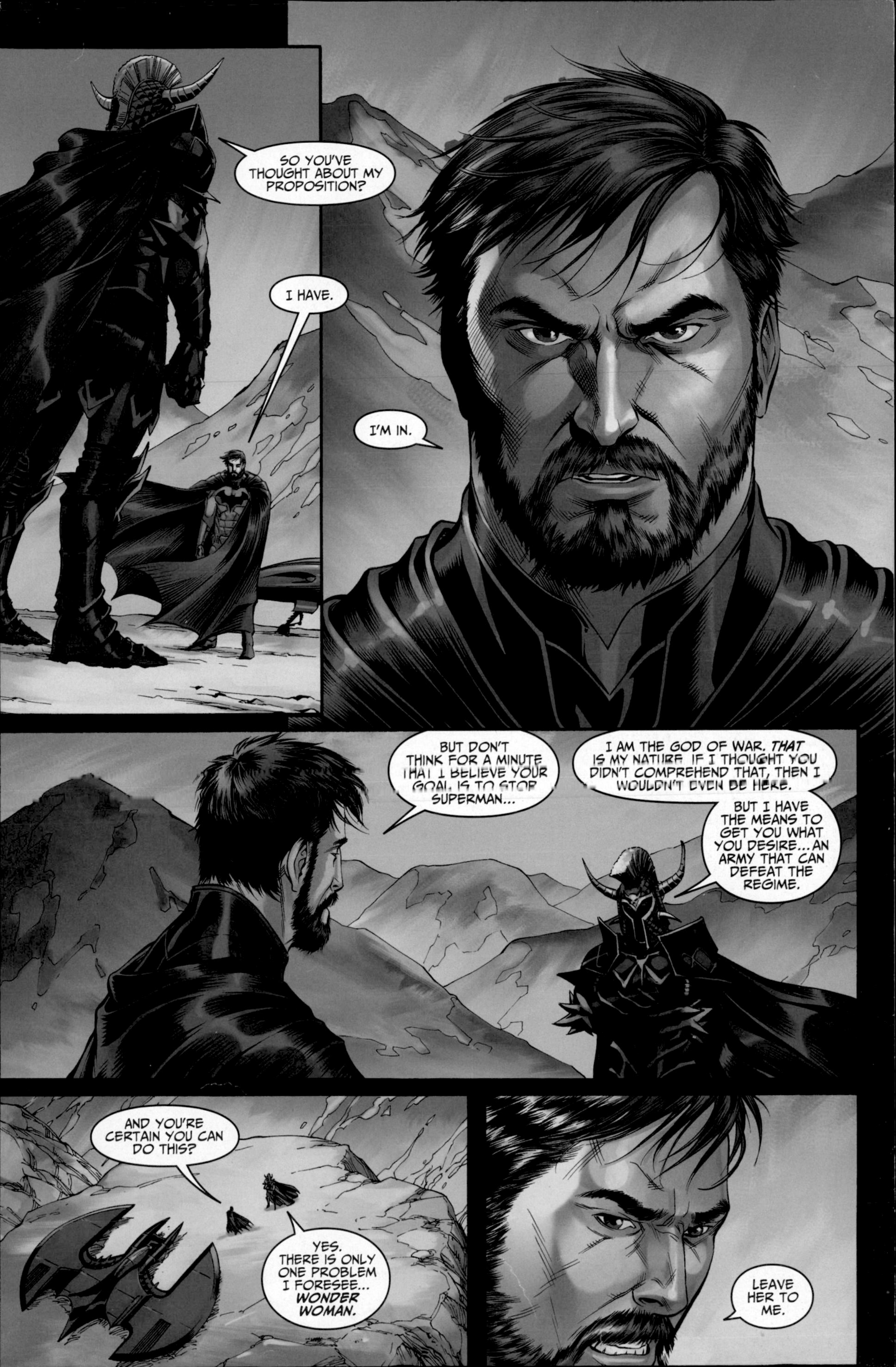
SO YOU'VE THOUGHT ABOUT MY PROPOSITION?
I HAVE.
I'M IN.
BUT DON'T THINK FOR A MINUTE THAT I BELIEVE YOUR GOAL IS TO STOP SUPERMAN...
I AM THE GOD OF WAR. THAT IS MY NATURE. IF I THOUGHT YOU DIDN'T COMPREHEND THAT, THEN I WOULDN'T EVEN BE HERE.
BUT I HAVE THE MEANS TO GET YOU WHAT YOU DESIRE...AN ARMY THAT CAN DEFEAT THE REGIME.
AND YOU'RE CERTAIN YOU CAN DO THIS?
YES. THERE IS ONLY ONE PROBLEM I FORESEE... WONDER WOMAN.
LEAVE HER TO ME.

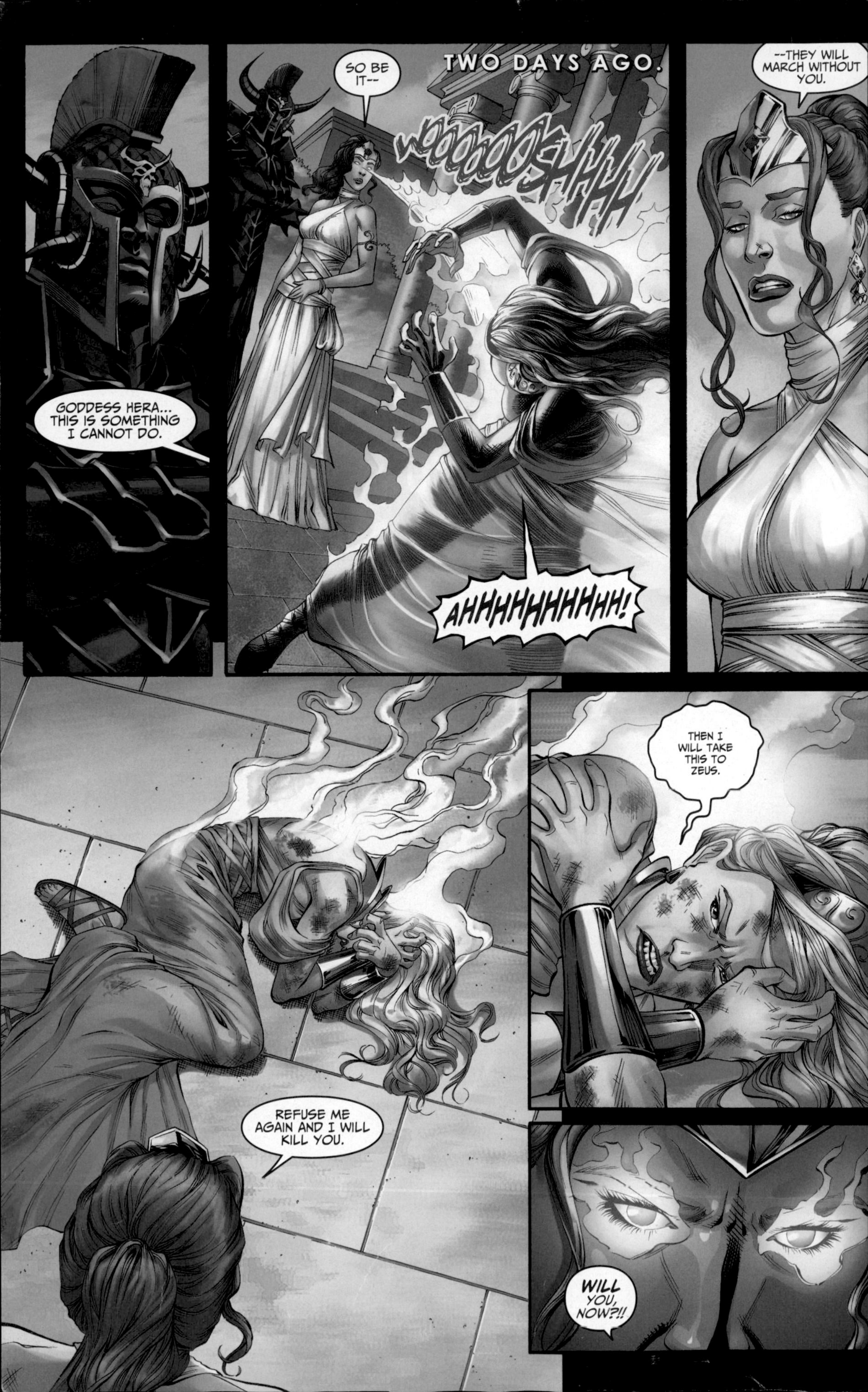

GODDESS HERA... THIS IS SOMETHING I CANNOT DO.
TWO DAYS AGO.
SO BE IT--
WOOOOOOSHHH
AHHHHHHHHHH!
--THEY WILL MARCH WITHOUT YOU.
REFUSE ME AGAIN AND I WILL KILL YOU.
THEN I WILL TAKE THIS TO ZEUS.
WILL YOU, NOW?!!

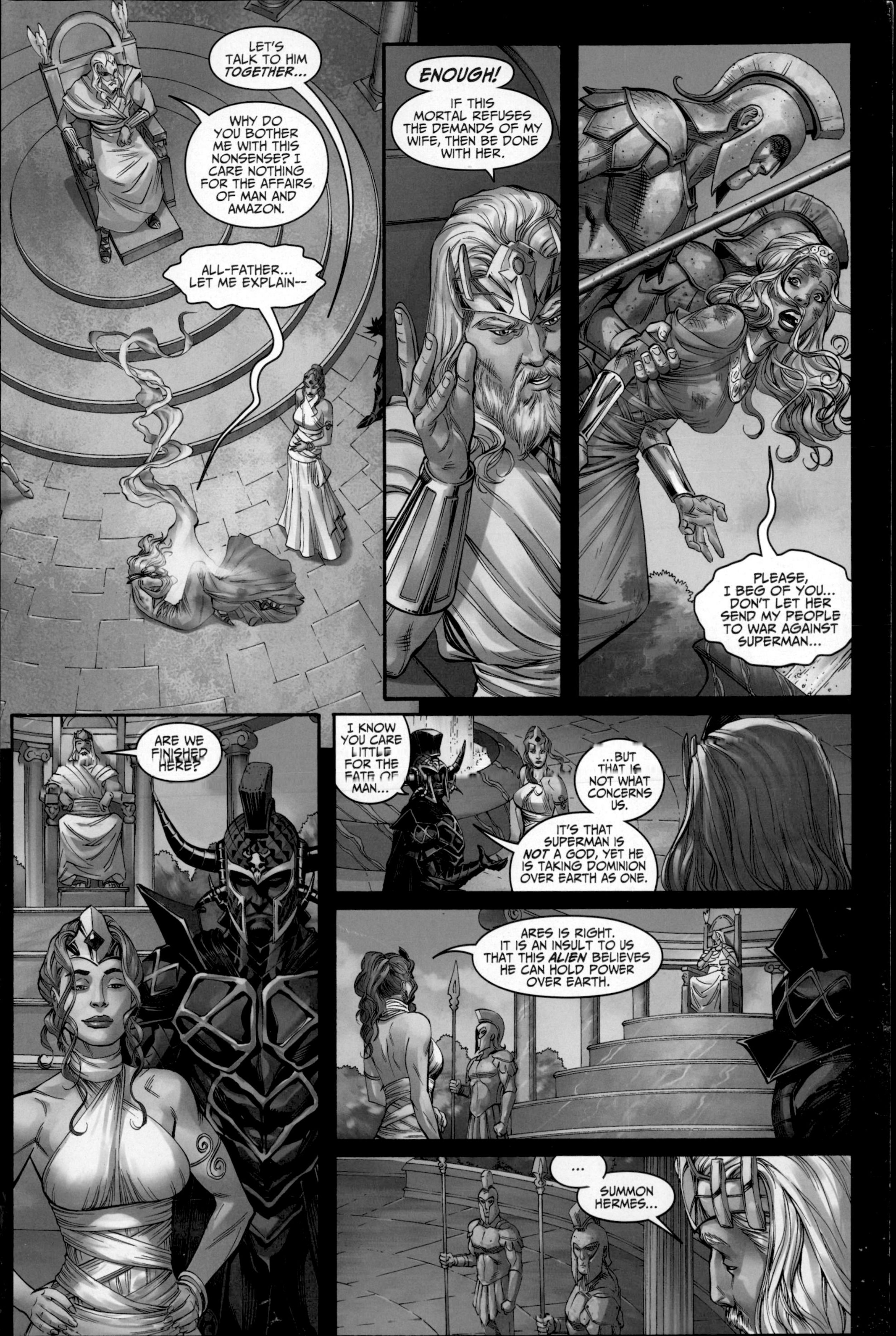
LET'S TALK TO HIM TOGETHER...
WHY DO YOU BOTHER ME WITH THIS NONSENSE? I CARE NOTHING FOR THE AFFAIRS OF MAN AND AMAZON.
ALL-FATHER... LET ME EXPLAIN--
ENOUGH!
IF THIS MORTAL REFUSES THE DEMANDS OF MY WIFE, THEN BE DONE WITH HER.
PLEASE, I BEG OF YOU... DON'T LET HER SEND MY PEOPLE TO WAR AGAINST SUPERMAN...
ARE WE FINISHED HERE?
I KNOW YOU CARE LITTLE FOR THE FATE OF MAN...
...BUT THAT IS NOT WHAT CONCERNS US.
IT'S THAT SUPERMAN IS NOT A GOD, YET HE IS TAKING DOMINION OVER EARTH AS ONE.
ARES IS RIGHT. IT IS AN INSULT TO US THAT THIS ALIEN BELIEVES HE CAN HOLD POWER OVER EARTH.
...
SUMMON HERMES...

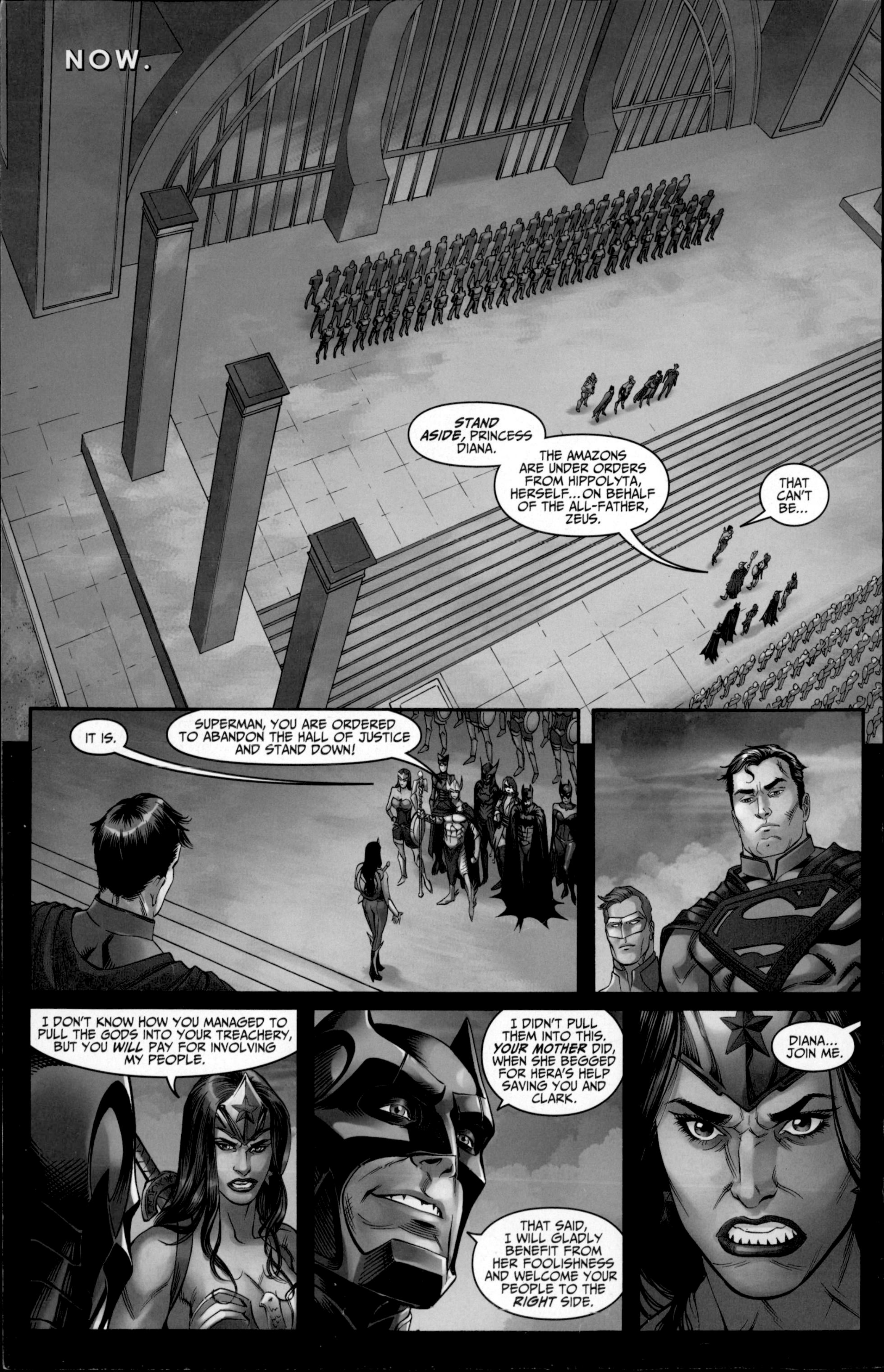
NOW.
STAND ASIDE, PRINCESS DIANA.
THE AMAZONS ARE UNDER ORDERS FROM HIPPOLYTA, HERSELF...ON BEHALF OF THE ALL-FATHER, ZEUS.
THAT CAN'T BE...
IT IS.
SUPERMAN, YOU ARE ORDERED TO ABANDON THE HALL OF JUSTICE AND STAND DOWN!
I DON'T KNOW HOW YOU MANAGED TO PULL THE GODS INTO YOUR TREACHERY, BUT YOU WILL PAY FOR INVOLVING MY PEOPLE.
I DIDN'T PULL THEM INTO THIS. YOUR MOTHER DID, WHEN SHE BEGGED FOR HERA'S HELP SAVING YOU AND CLARK.
THAT SAID, I WILL GLADLY BENEFIT FROM HER FOOLISHNESS AND WELCOME YOUR PEOPLE TO THE RIGHT SIDE.
DIANA... JOIN ME.

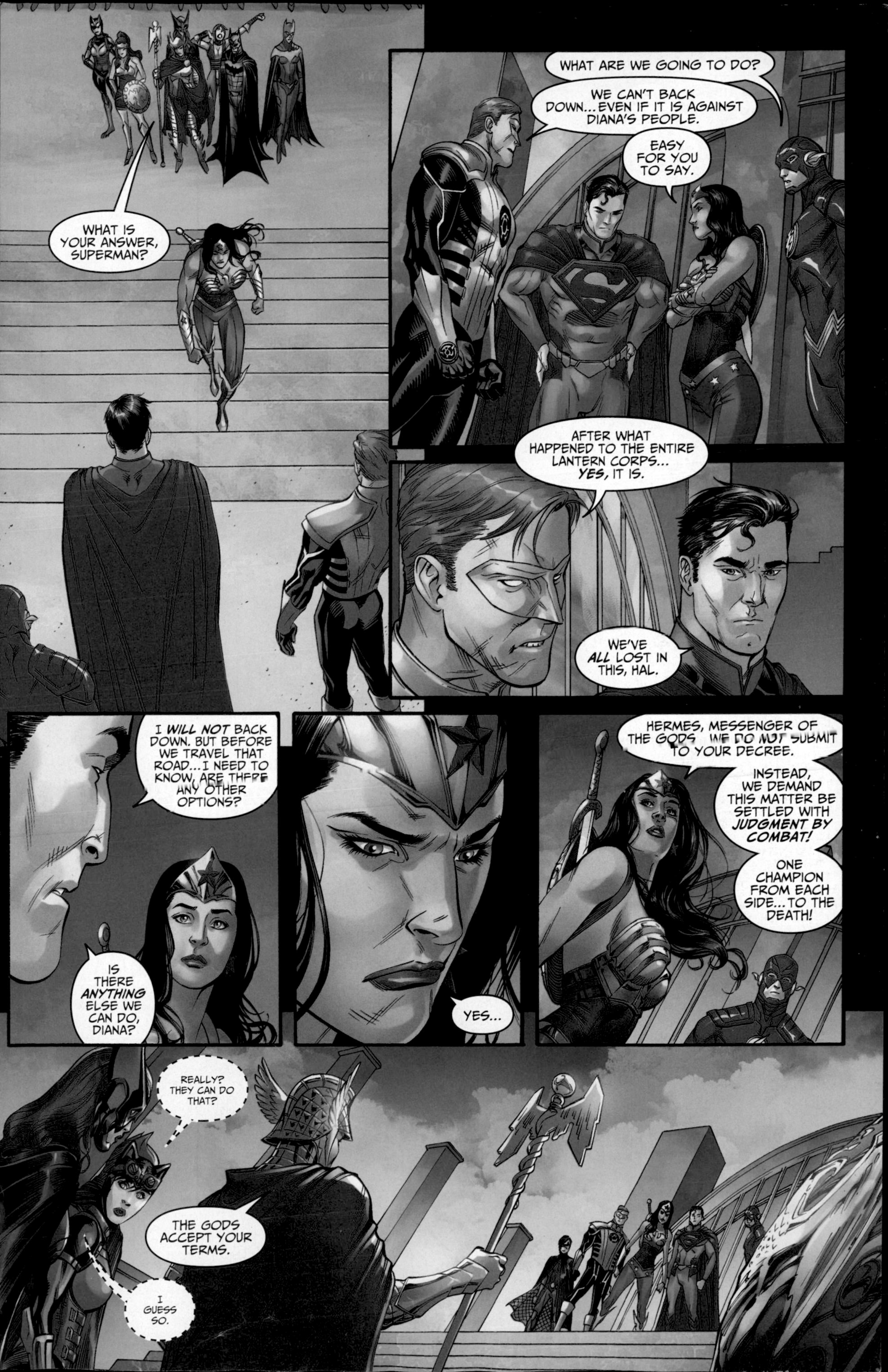
WHAT IS YOUR ANSWER, SUPERMAN?
WHAT ARE WE GOING TO DO?
WE CAN'T BACK DOWN... EVEN IF IT IS AGAINST DIANA'S PEOPLE.
EASY FOR YOU TO SAY.
AFTER WHAT HAPPENED TO THE ENTIRE LANTERN CORPS... YES, IT IS.
WE'VE ALL LOST IN THIS, HAL.
I WILL NOT BACK DOWN. BUT BEFORE WE TRAVEL THAT ROAD... I NEED TO KNOW, ARE THERE ANY OTHER OPTIONS?
IS THERE ANYTHING ELSE WE CAN DO, DIANA?
YES...
HERMES, MESSENGER OF THE GODS... WE DO NOT SUBMIT TO YOUR DECREE.
INSTEAD, WE DEMAND THIS MATTER BE SETTLED WITH JUDGMENT BY COMBAT!
ONE CHAMPION FROM EACH SIDE... TO THE DEATH!
REALLY? THEY CAN DO THAT?
THE GODS ACCEPT YOUR TERMS.
I GUESS SO.

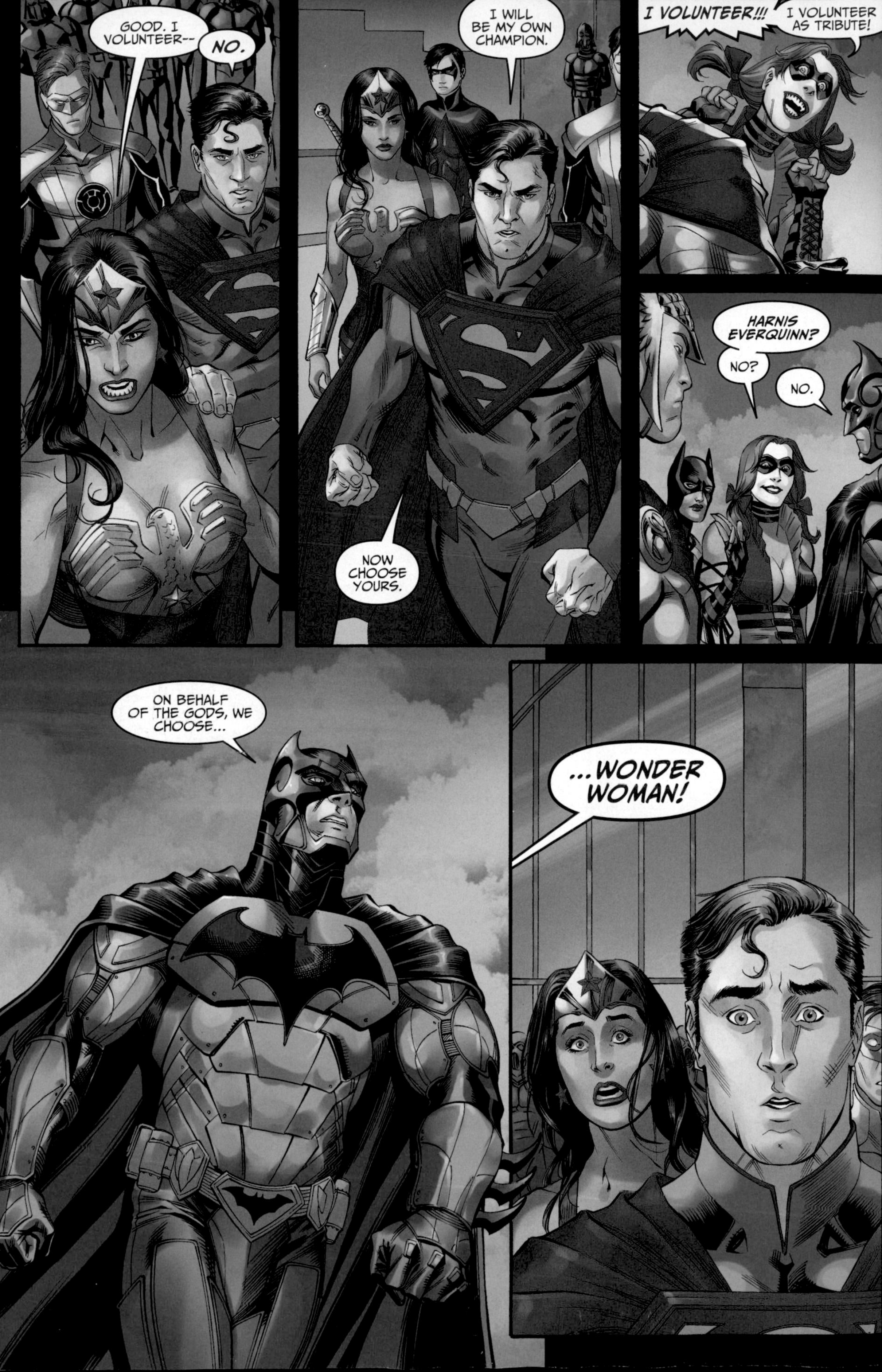
GOOD. I VOLUNTEER--
NO.
I WILL BE MY OWN CHAMPION.
NOW CHOOSE YOURS.
I VOLUNTEER!!!
I VOLUNTEER AS TRIBUTE!
HARNIS EVERQUINN?
NO?
NO.
ON BEHALF OF THE GODS, WE CHOOSE...
...WONDER WOMAN!

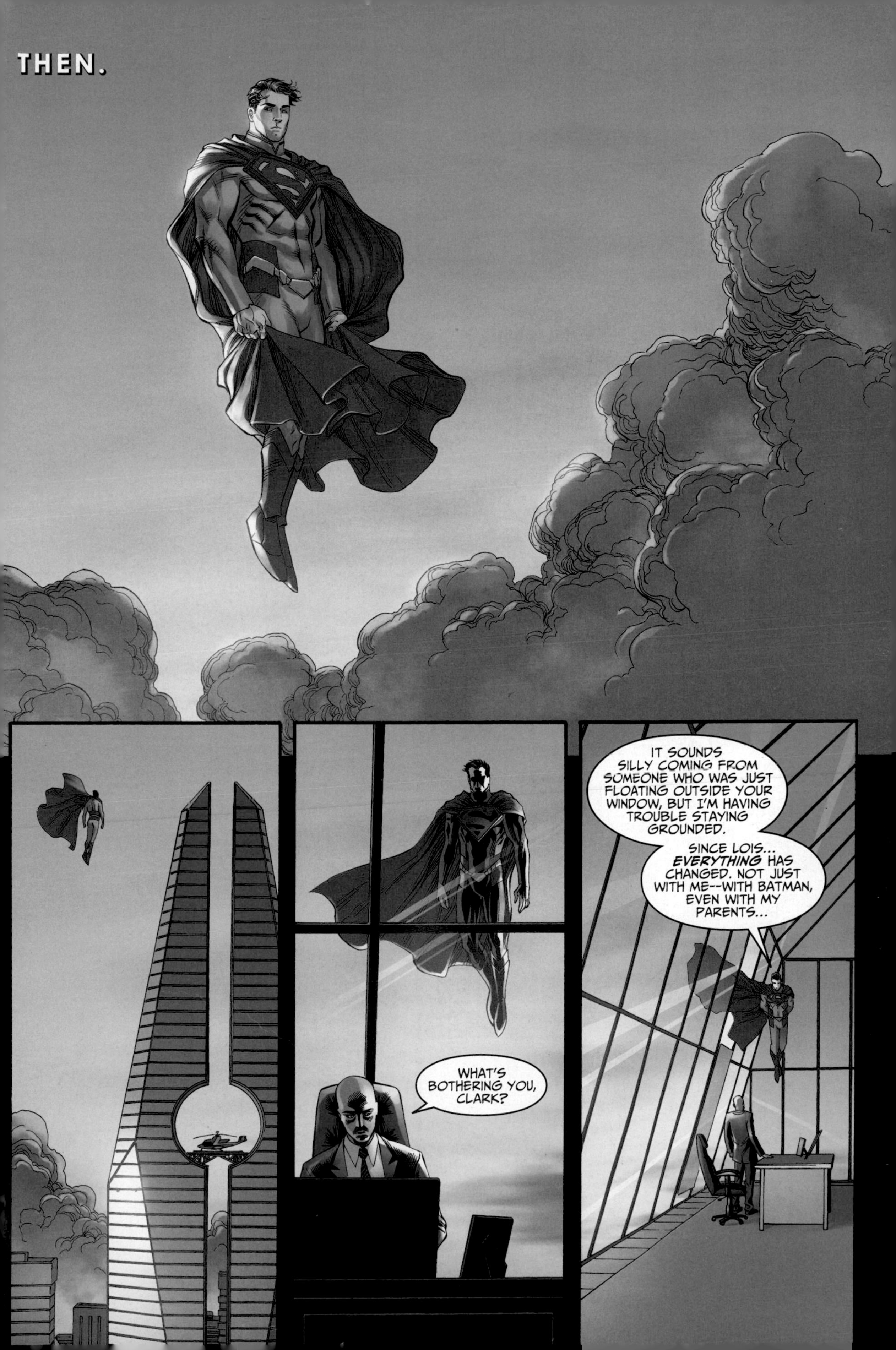
THEN.
WHAT'S BOTHERING YOU, CLARK?
IT SOUNDS SILLY COMING FROM SOMEONE WHO WAS JUST FLOATING OUTSIDE YOUR WINDOW, BUT I'M HAVING TROUBLE STAYING GROUNDED.
SINCE LOIS... EVERYTHING HAS CHANGED. NOT JUST WITH ME--WITH BATMAN, EVEN WITH MY PARENTS...

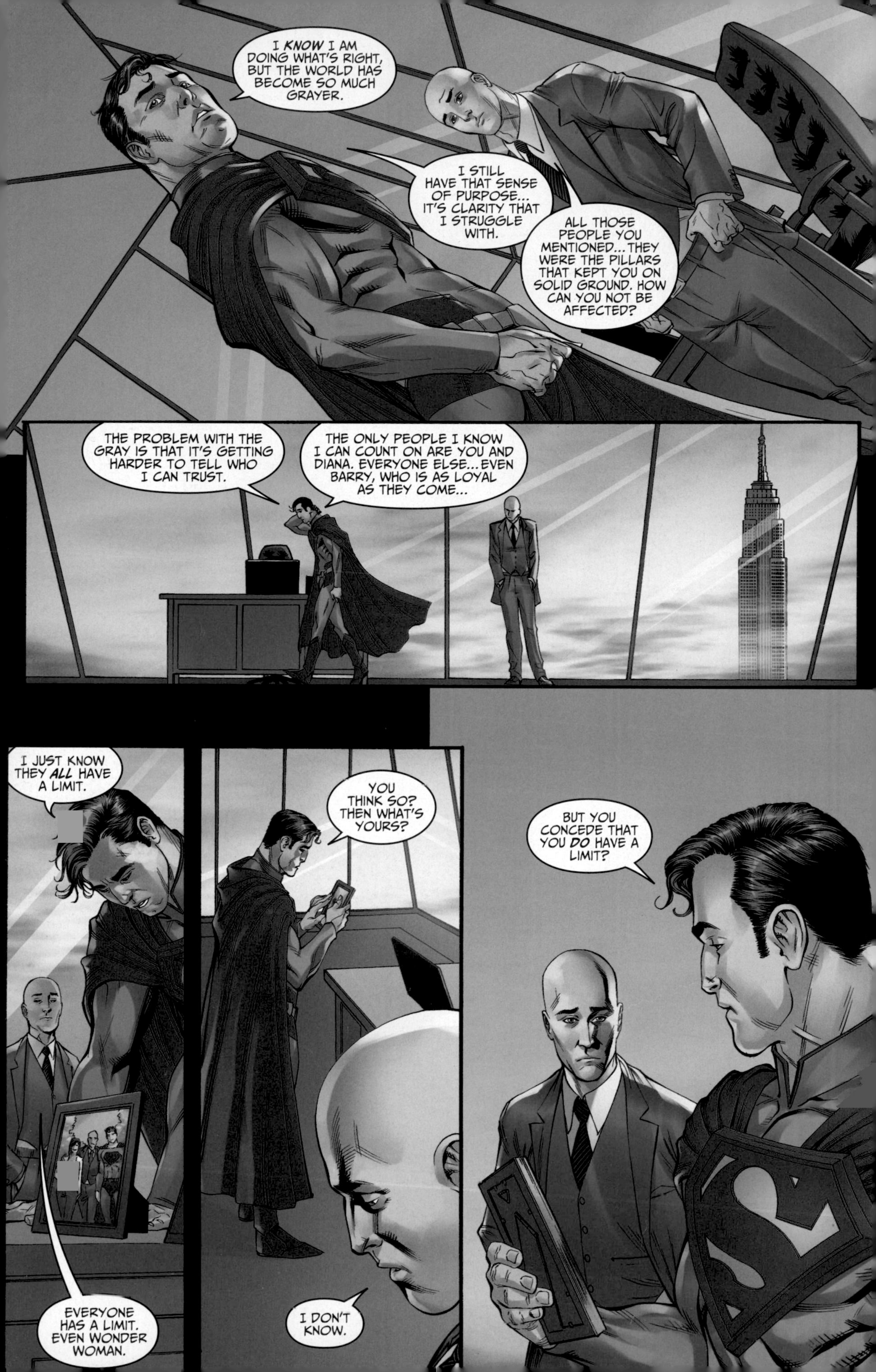
I KNOW I AM DOING WHAT'S RIGHT, BUT THE WORLD HAS BECOME SO MUCH GRAYER.
I STILL HAVE THAT SENSE OF PURPOSE... IT'S CLARITY THAT I STRUGGLE WITH.
ALL THOSE PEOPLE YOU MENTIONED... THEY WERE THE PILLARS THAT KEPT YOU ON SOLID GROUND. HOW CAN YOU NOT BE AFFECTED?
THE PROBLEM WITH THE GRAY IS THAT IT'S GETTING HARDER TO TELL WHO I CAN TRUST.
THE ONLY PEOPLE I KNOW I CAN COUNT ON ARE YOU AND DIANA. EVERYONE ELSE... EVEN BARRY, WHO IS AS LOYAL AS THEY COME...
I JUST KNOW THEY ALL HAVE A LIMIT.
EVERYONE HAS A LIMIT. EVEN WONDER WOMAN.
YOU THINK SO? THEN WHAT'S YOURS?
I DON'T KNOW.
BUT YOU CONCEDE THAT YOU DO HAVE A LIMIT?

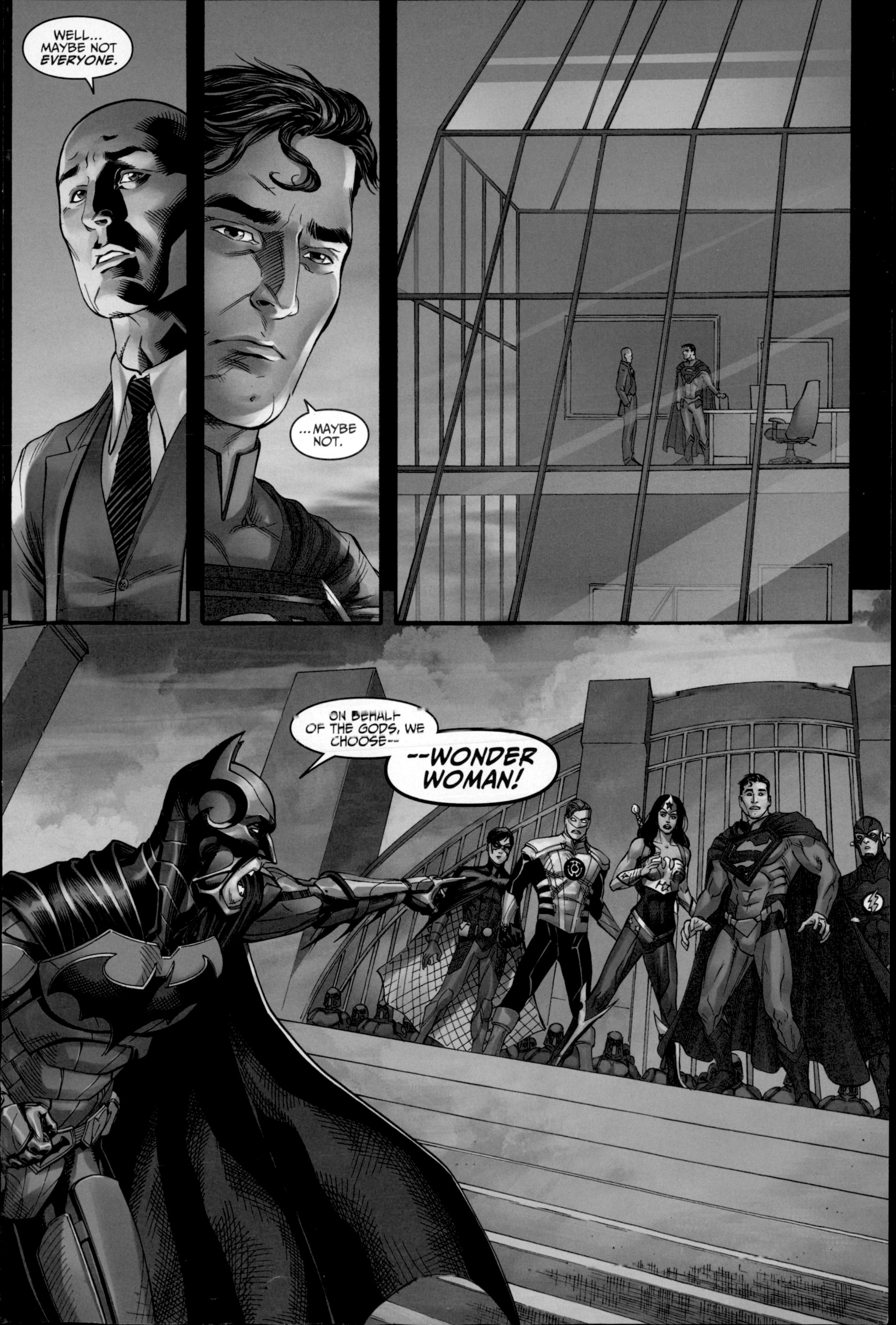
WELL... MAYBE NOT *EVERYONE*.
...MAYBE NOT.
ON BEHALF OF THE GODS, WE CHOOSE--
--WONDER WOMAN!

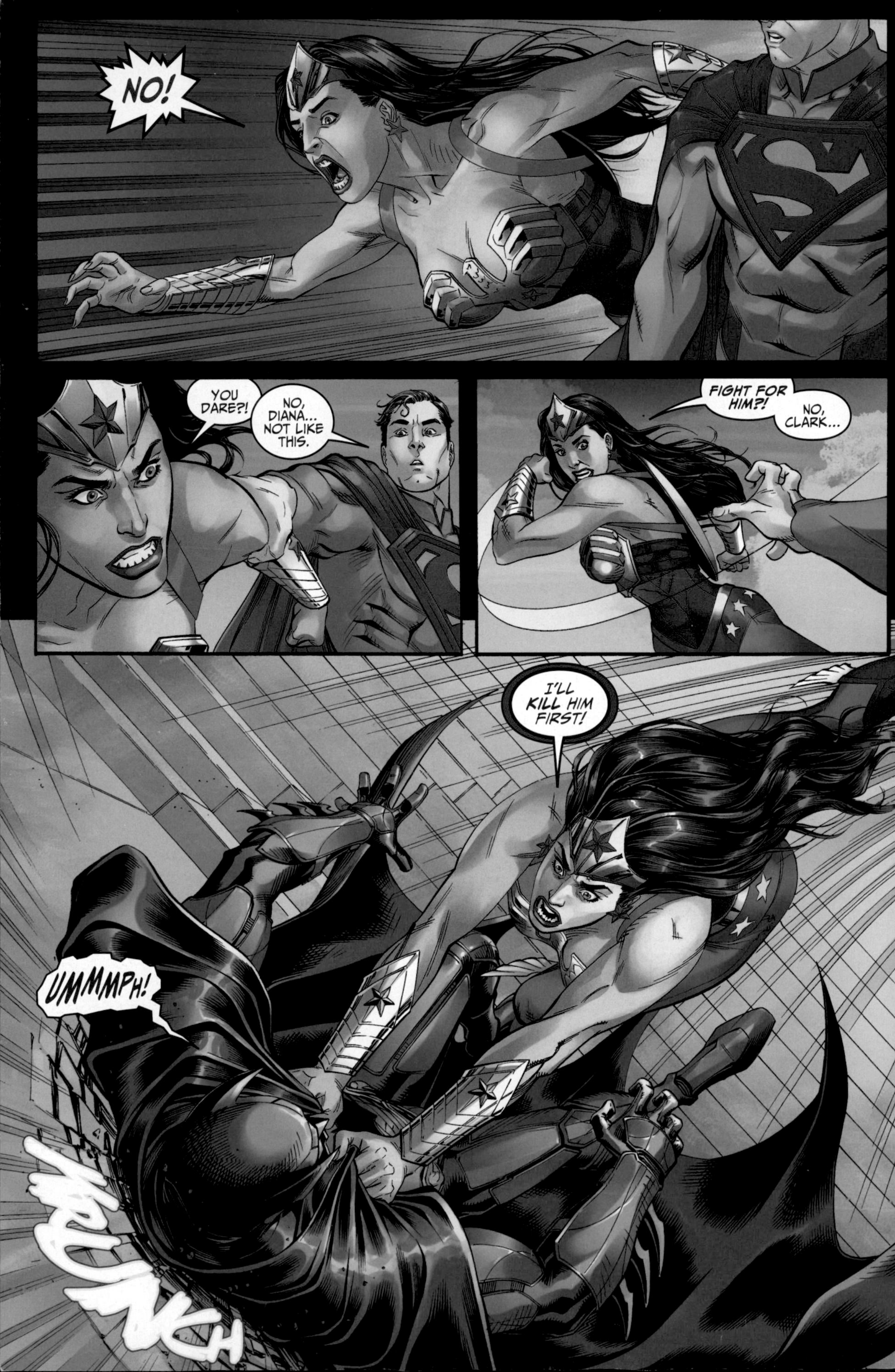
NO!
YOU DARE?!
NO, DIANA... NOT LIKE THIS.
FIGHT FOR HIM?!
NO, CLARK...
I'LL KILL HIM FIRST!
UMMMPH!
KRUNCH

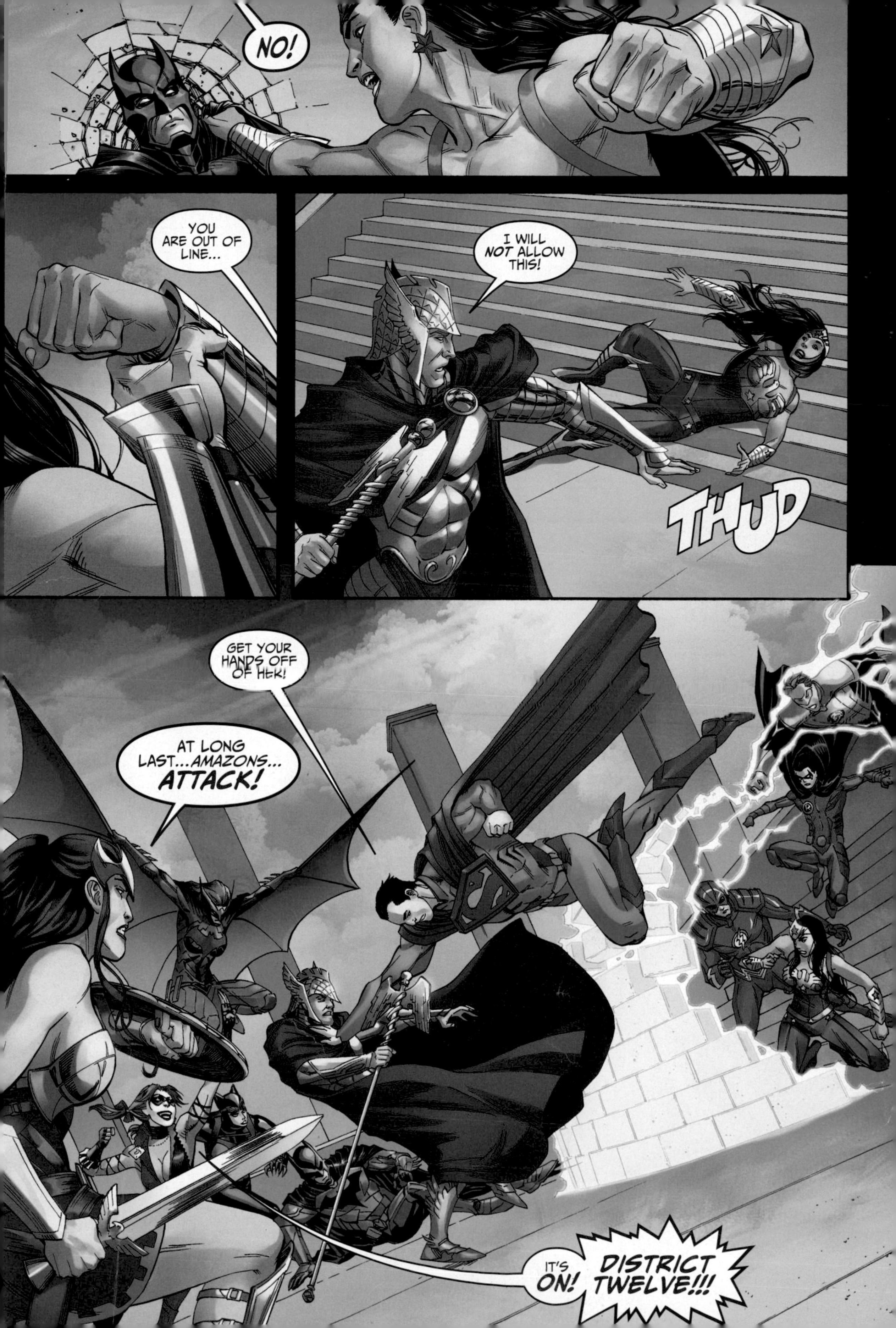
NO!
YOU ARE OUT OF LINE...
I WILL NOT ALLOW THIS!
THUD
GET YOUR HANDS OFF OF HER!
AT LONG LAST...AMAZONS... ATTACK!
IT'S ON!
DISTRICT TWELVE!!!

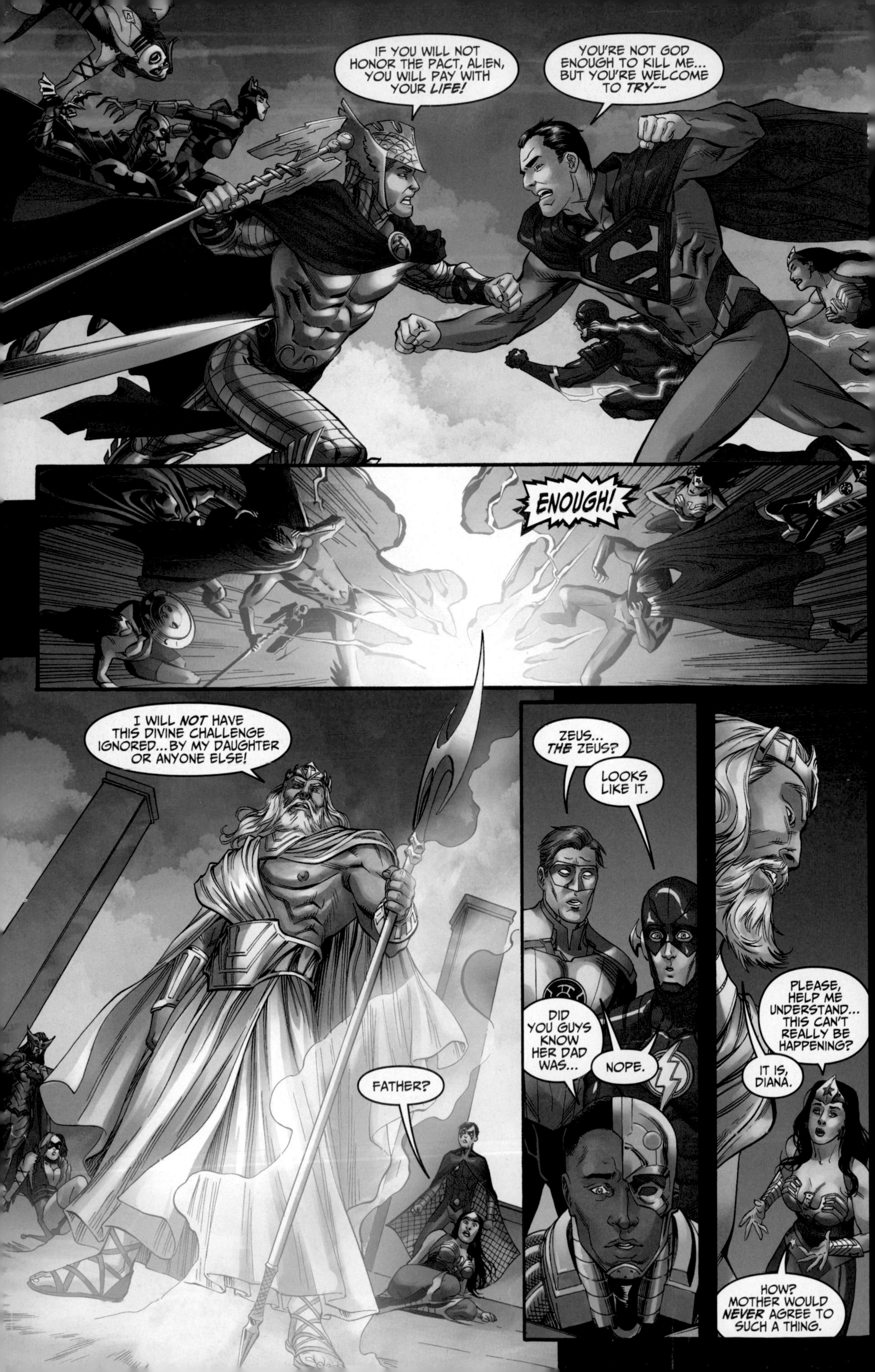
IF YOU WILL NOT HONOR THE PACT, ALIEN, YOU WILL PAY WITH YOUR LIFE!
YOU'RE NOT GOD ENOUGH TO KILL ME... BUT YOU'RE WELCOME TO TRY--
ENOUGH!
I WILL NOT HAVE THIS DIVINE CHALLENGE IGNORED...BY MY DAUGHTER OR ANYONE ELSE!
FATHER?
ZEUS... THE ZEUS?
LOOKS LIKE IT.
DID YOU GUYS KNOW HER DAD WAS...
NOPE.
PLEASE, HELP ME UNDERSTAND... THIS CAN'T REALLY BE HAPPENING?
IT IS, DIANA.
HOW? MOTHER WOULD NEVER AGREE TO SUCH A THING.

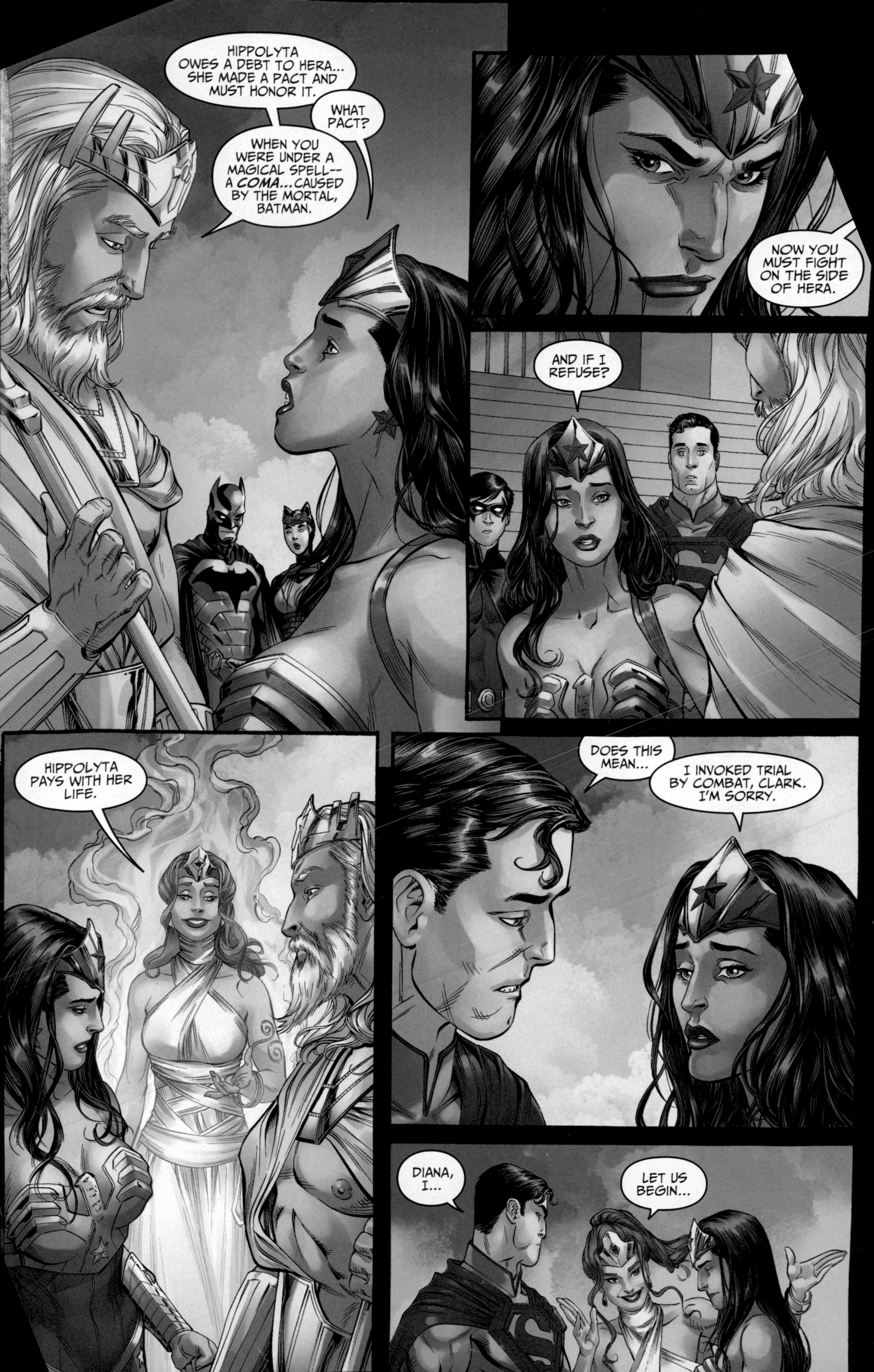

HIPPOLYTA OWES A DEBT TO HERA... SHE MADE A PACT AND MUST HONOR IT.
WHAT PACT?
WHEN YOU WERE UNDER A MAGICAL SPELL-- A COMA...CAUSED BY THE MORTAL, BATMAN.
NOW YOU MUST FIGHT ON THE SIDE OF HERA.
AND IF I REFUSE?
HIPPOLYTA PAYS WITH HER LIFE.
DOES THIS MEAN...
I INVOKED TRIAL BY COMBAT, CLARK. I'M SORRY.
DIANA, I...
LET US BEGIN...

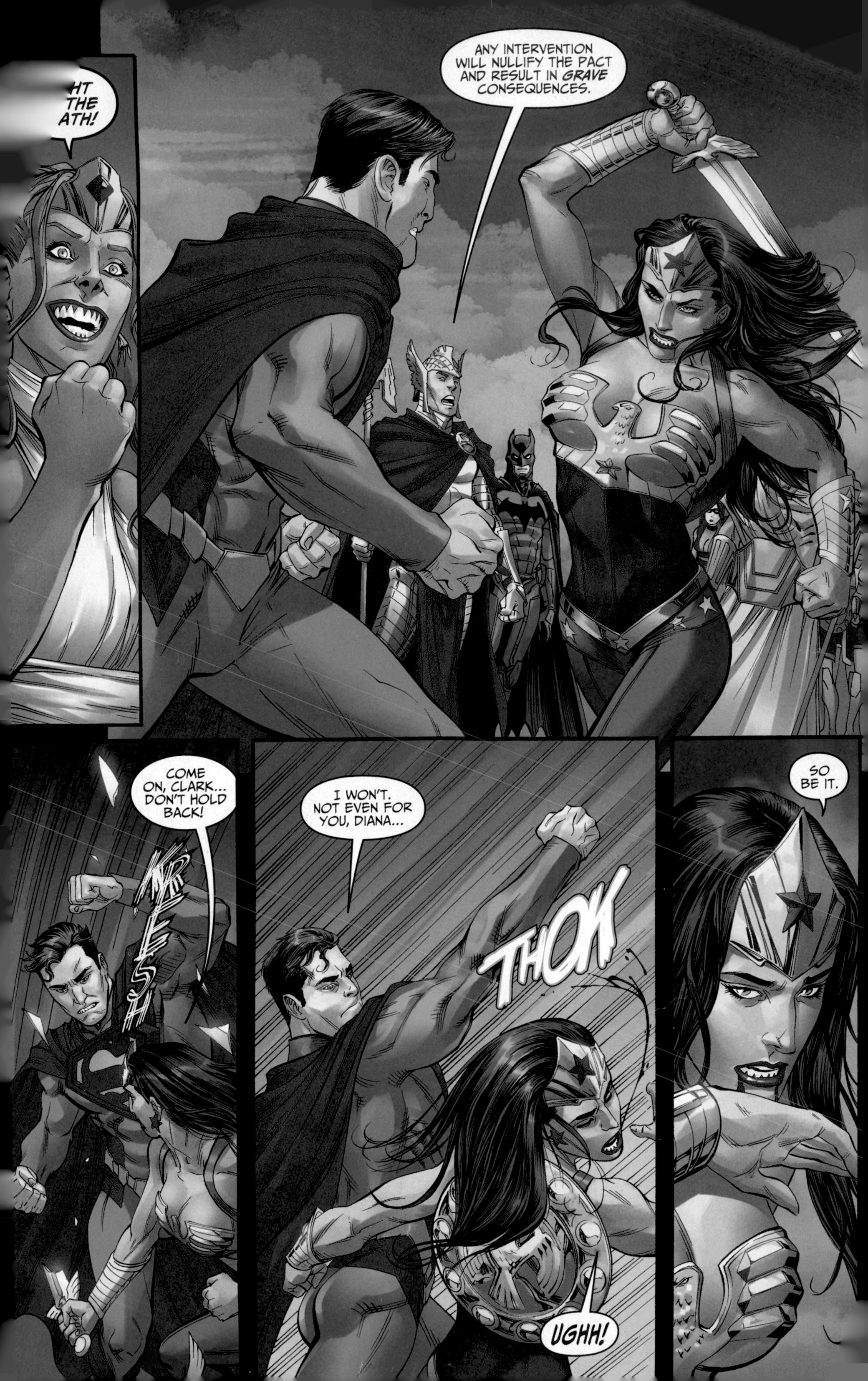
HT THE ATH!
ANY INTERVENTION WILL NULLIFY THE PACT AND RESULT IN GRAVE CONSEQUENCES.
COME ON, CLARK... DON'T HOLD BACK!
I WON'T. NOT EVEN FOR YOU, DIANA...
THOK
UGHH!
SO BE IT.

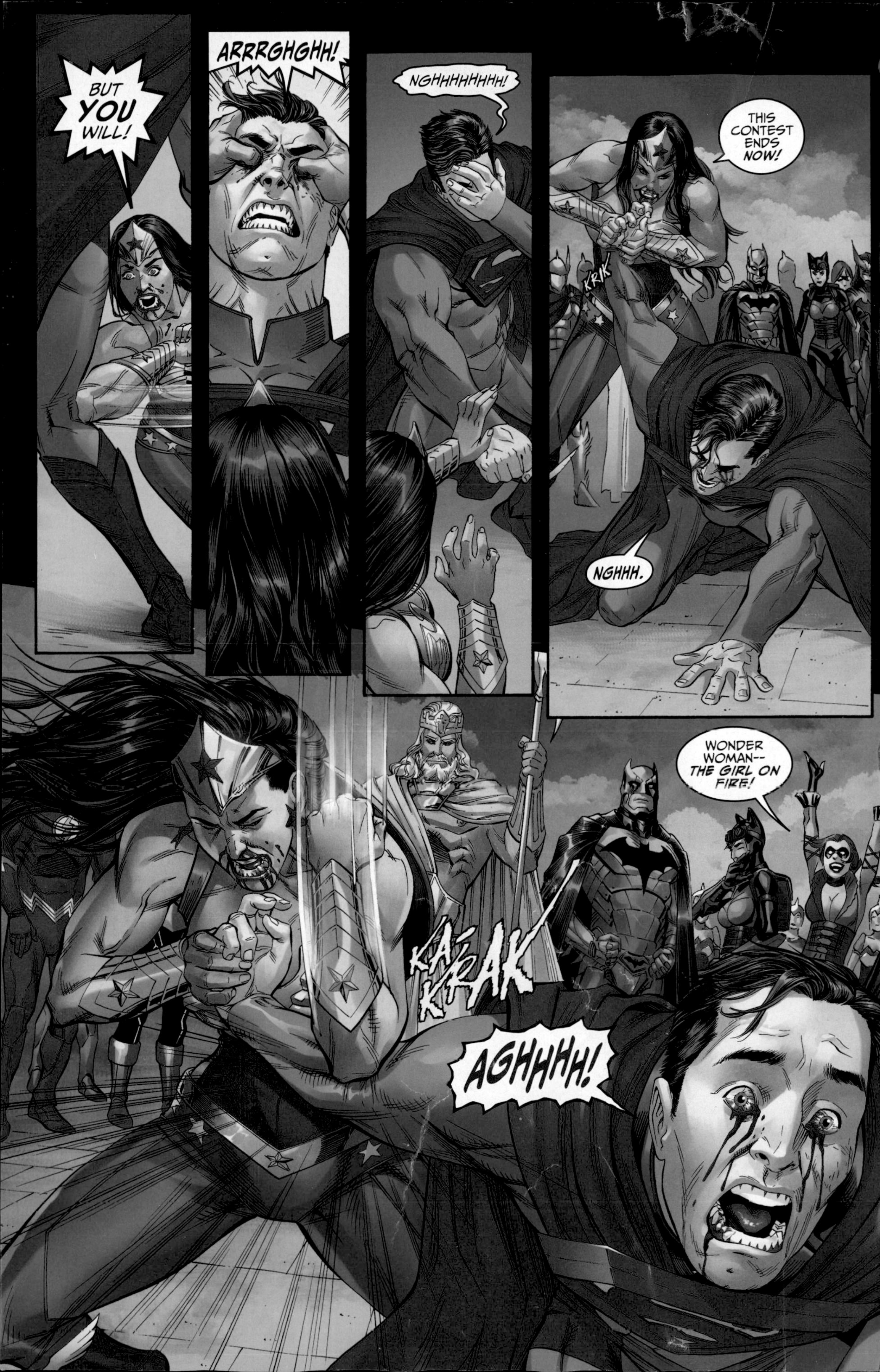
BUT YOU WILL!
ARRRGHGHH!
NGHHHHHHHH!
THIS CONTEST ENDS NOW!
KRIK
NGHHH.
WONDER WOMAN-- THE GIRL ON FIRE!
KA-KRAK
AGHHHH!

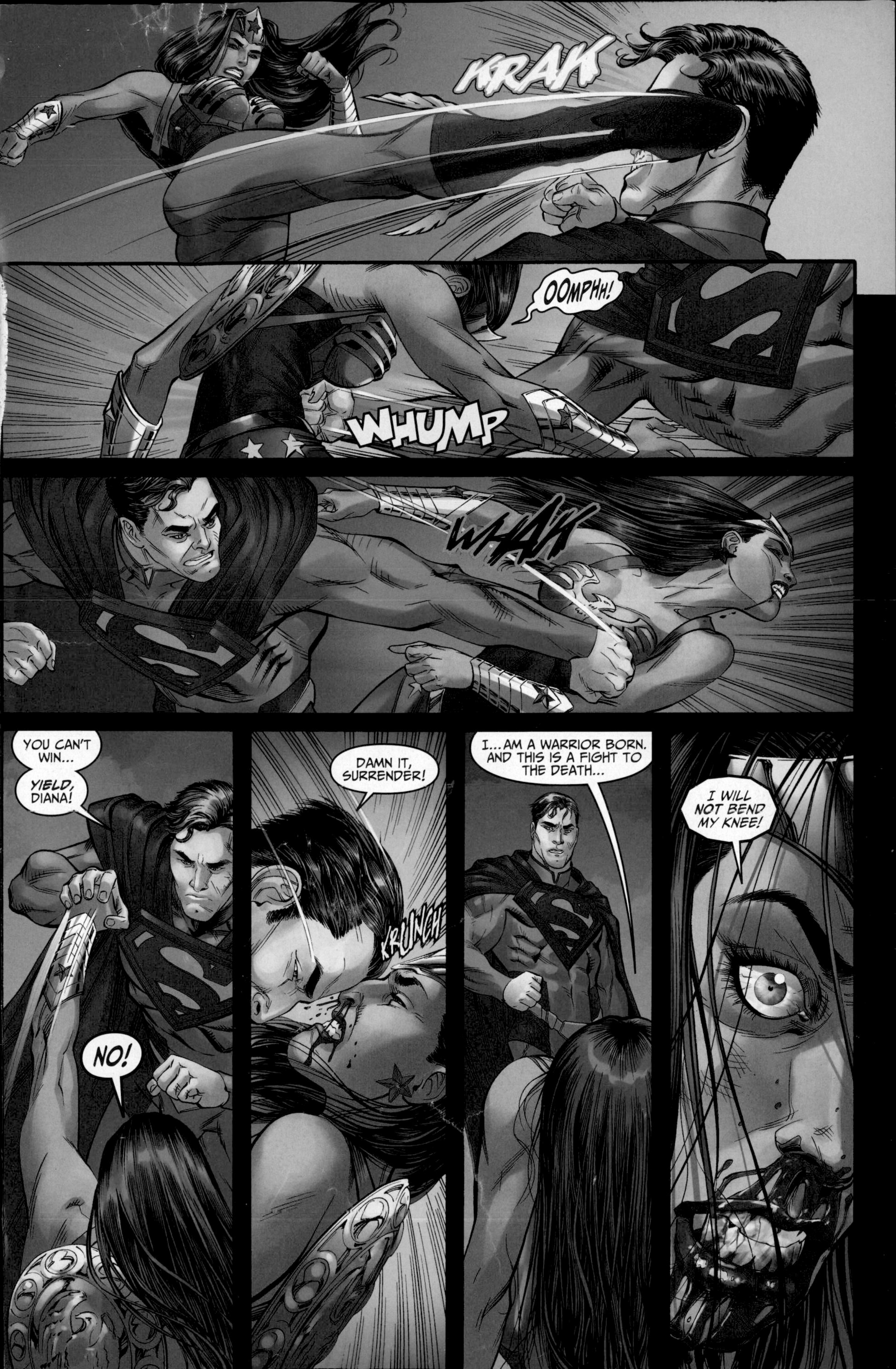
KRAK
OOMPHH!
WHUMP
WHAK
YOU CAN'T WIN...
YIELD, DIANA!
NO!
DAMN IT, SURRENDER!
KRUNCH
I...AM A WARRIOR BORN. AND THIS IS A FIGHT TO THE DEATH...
I WILL NOT BEND MY KNEE!

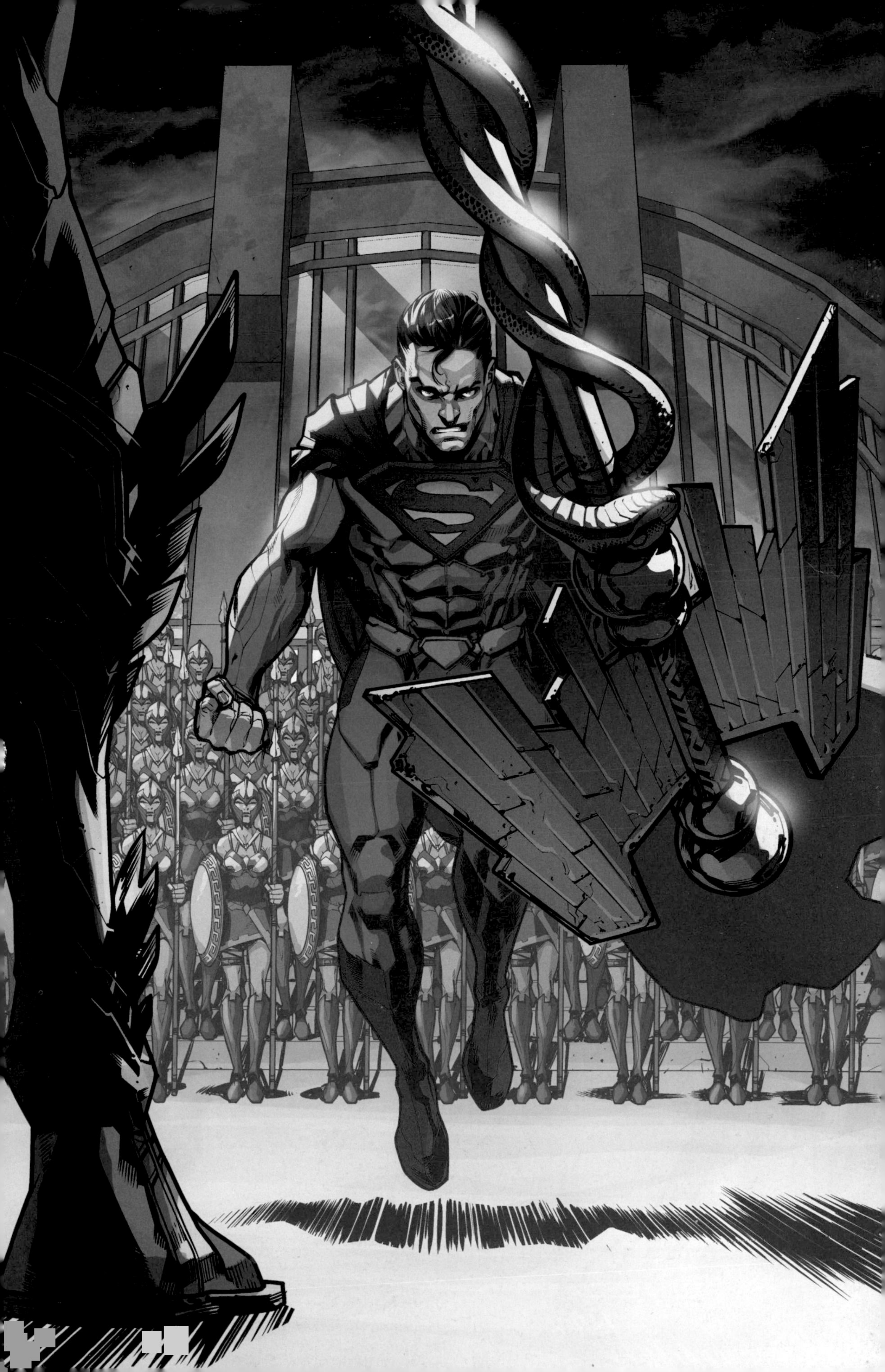

"Willpower" **Bruno Redondo** Penciller **Juan Albarran** Inker **Rex Lokus** Colorist
"Mayhem" **Xermanico** Artist **Rex Lokus** Colorist
Cover Art by **Neil Googe & Rex Lokus**

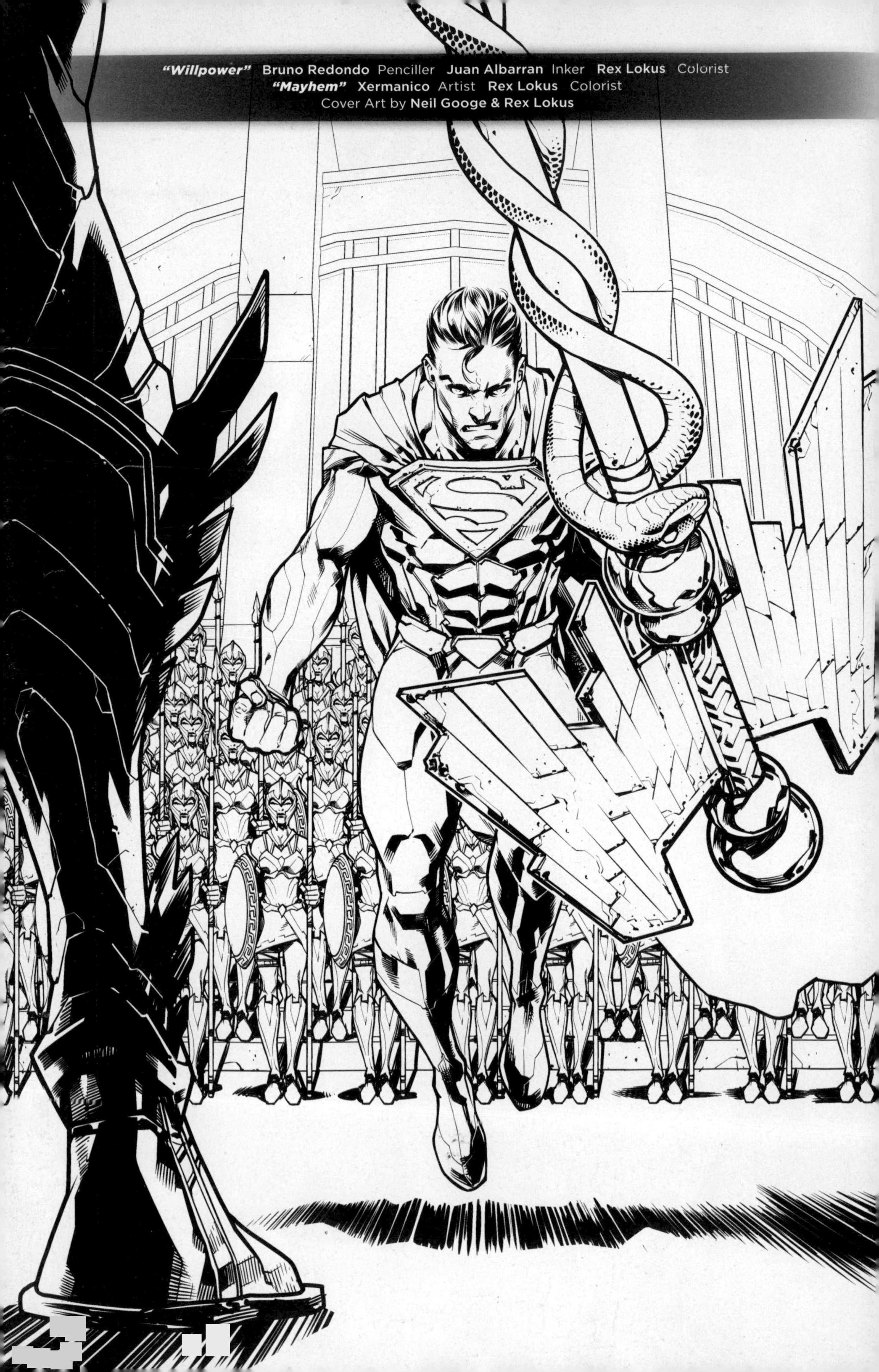

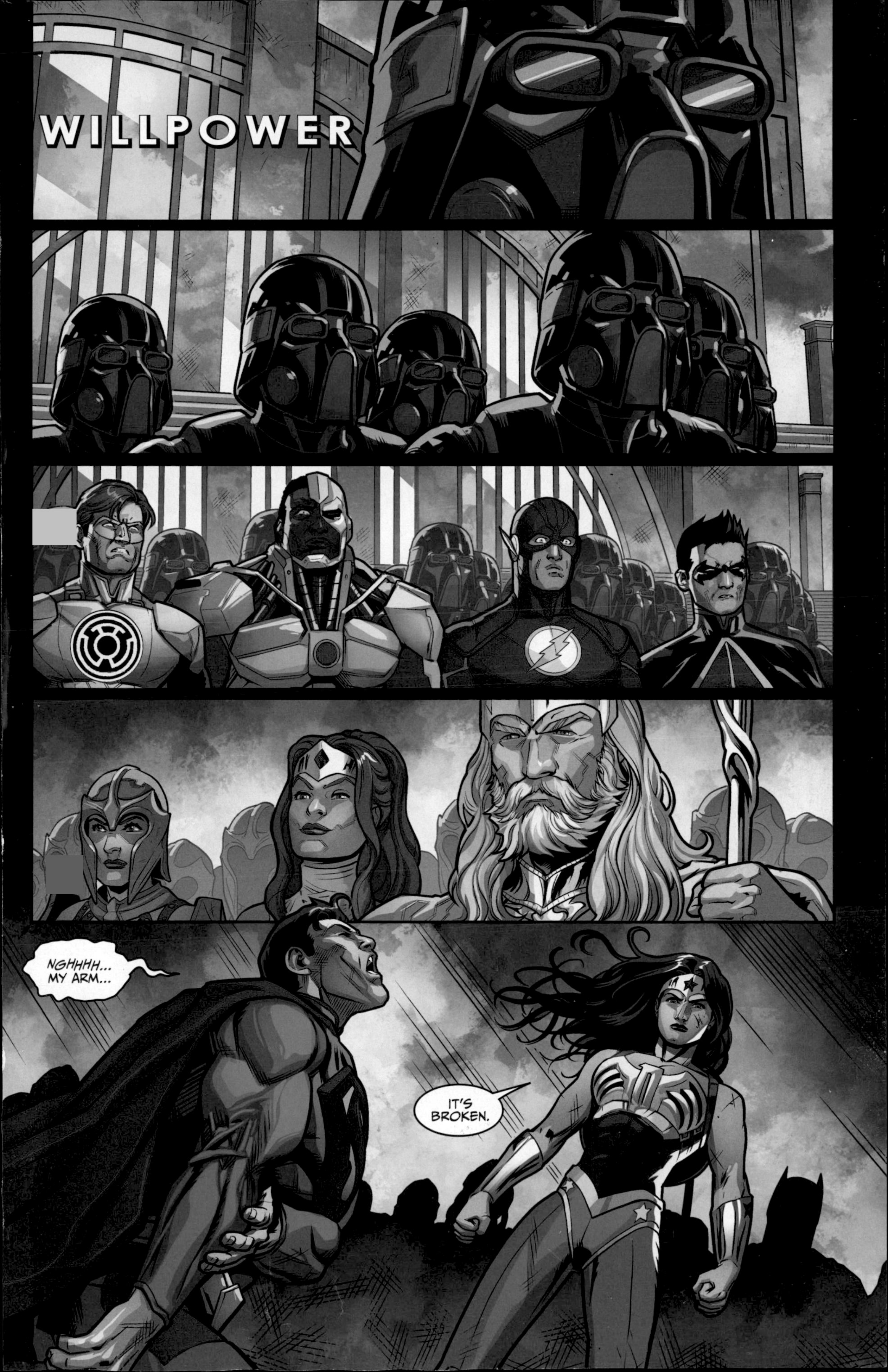
WILLPOWER
NGHHHH... MY ARM...
IT'S BROKEN.

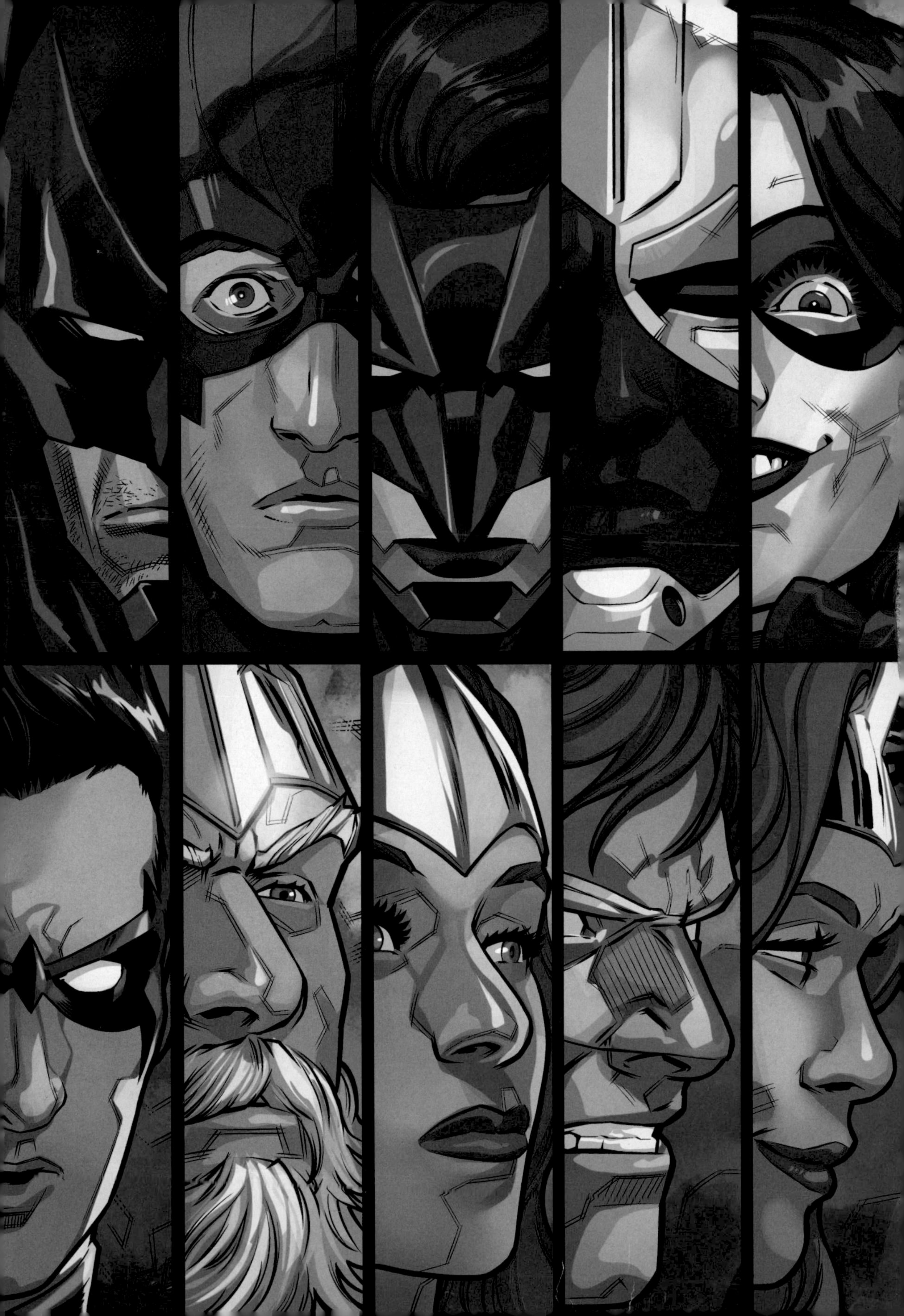

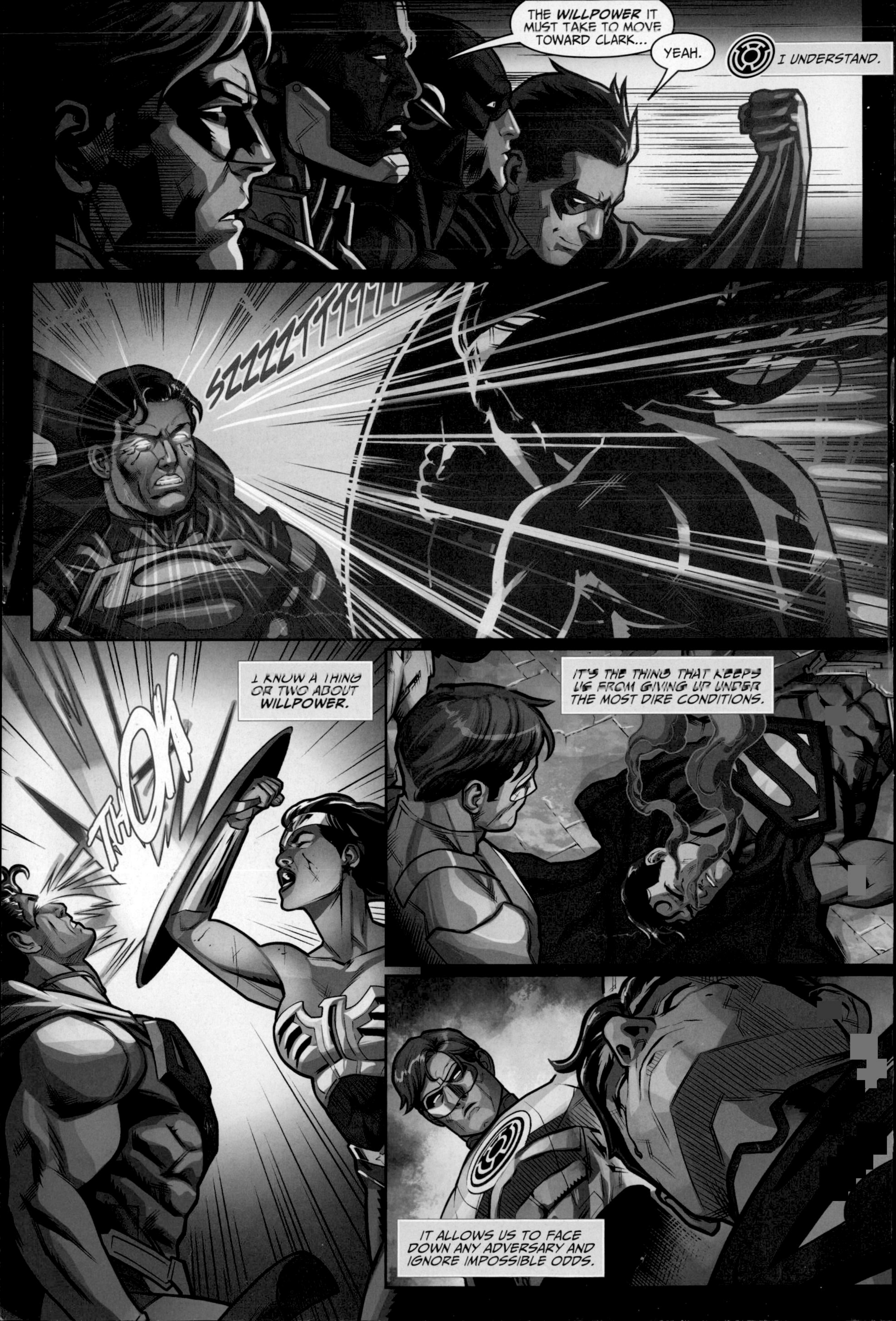

THE WILLPOWER IT MUST TAKE TO MOVE TOWARD CLARK...
YEAH.
I UNDERSTAND.
SZZZZTTTTTTT
I KNOW A THING OR TWO ABOUT WILLPOWER.
THOK
IT'S THE THING THAT KEEPS US FROM GIVING UP UNDER THE MOST DIRE CONDITIONS.
IT ALLOWS US TO FACE DOWN ANY ADVERSARY AND IGNORE IMPOSSIBLE ODDS.

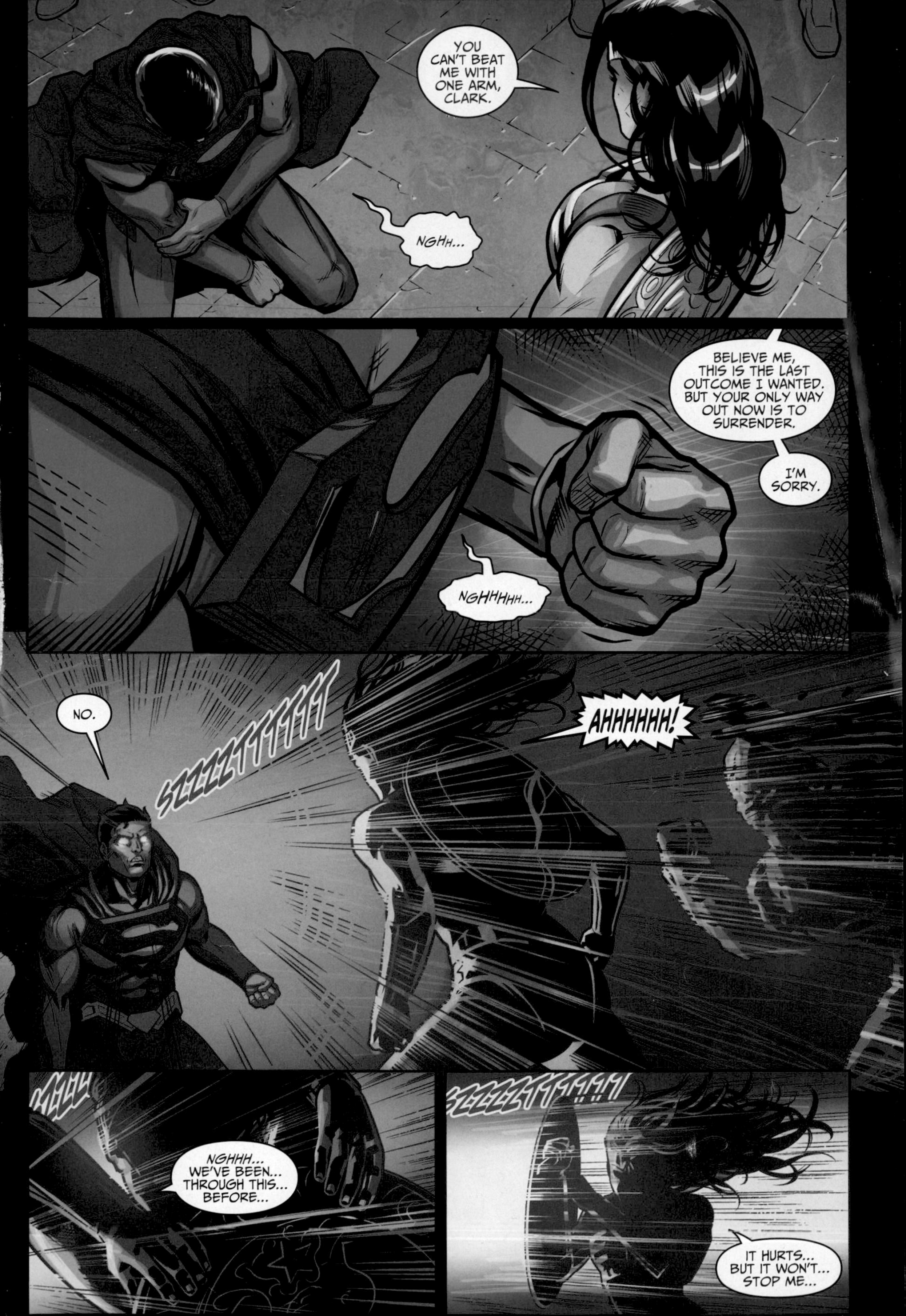
YOU CAN'T BEAT ME WITH ONE ARM, CLARK.
NGHH...
BELIEVE ME, THIS IS THE LAST OUTCOME I WANTED. BUT YOUR ONLY WAY OUT NOW IS TO SURRENDER.
I'M SORRY.
NGHHHHH...
NO.
SZZZZTTTTTTTT
AHHHHHH!
NGHHH... WE'VE BEEN... THROUGH THIS... BEFORE...
SZZZZZTTTTTTT
IT HURTS... BUT IT WON'T... STOP ME...

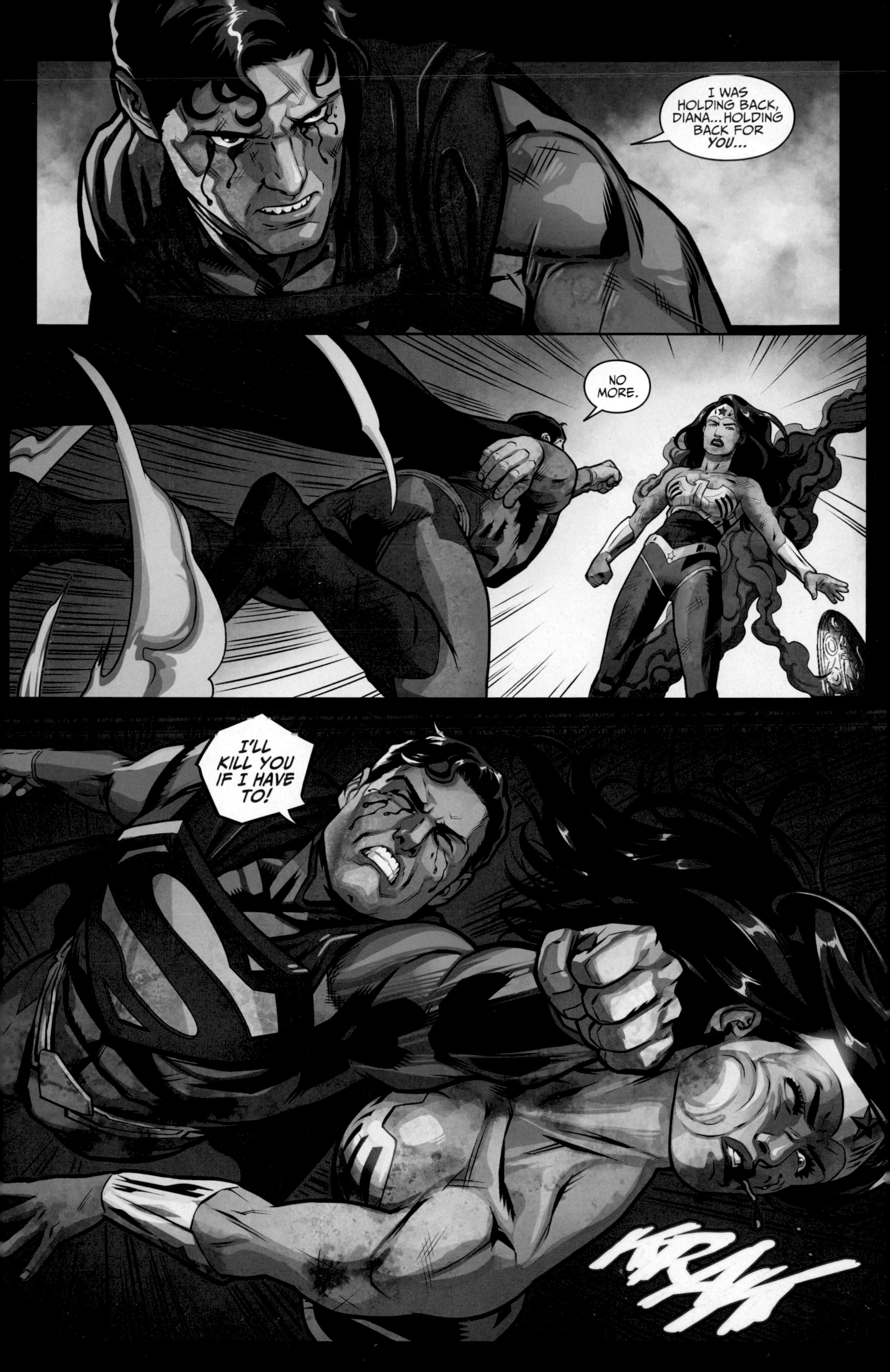
I WAS HOLDING BACK, DIANA...HOLDING BACK FOR YOU...
NO MORE.
I'LL KILL YOU IF I HAVE TO!
KRAK

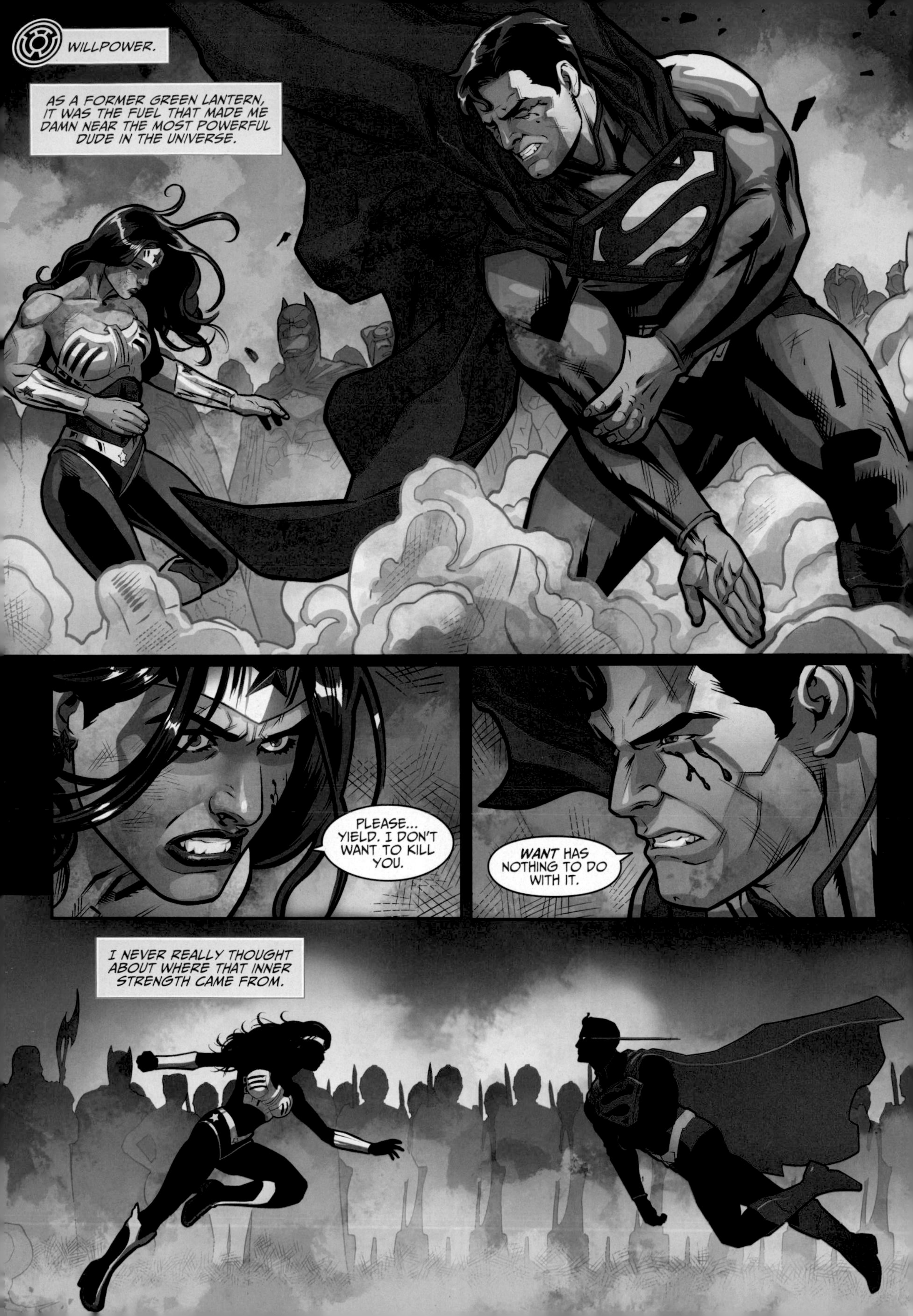
WILLPOWER.
AS A FORMER GREEN LANTERN, IT WAS THE FUEL THAT MADE ME DAMN NEAR THE MOST POWERFUL DUDE IN THE UNIVERSE.
PLEASE... YIELD. I DON'T WANT TO KILL YOU.
WANT HAS NOTHING TO DO WITH IT.
I NEVER REALLY THOUGHT ABOUT WHERE THAT INNER STRENGTH CAME FROM.

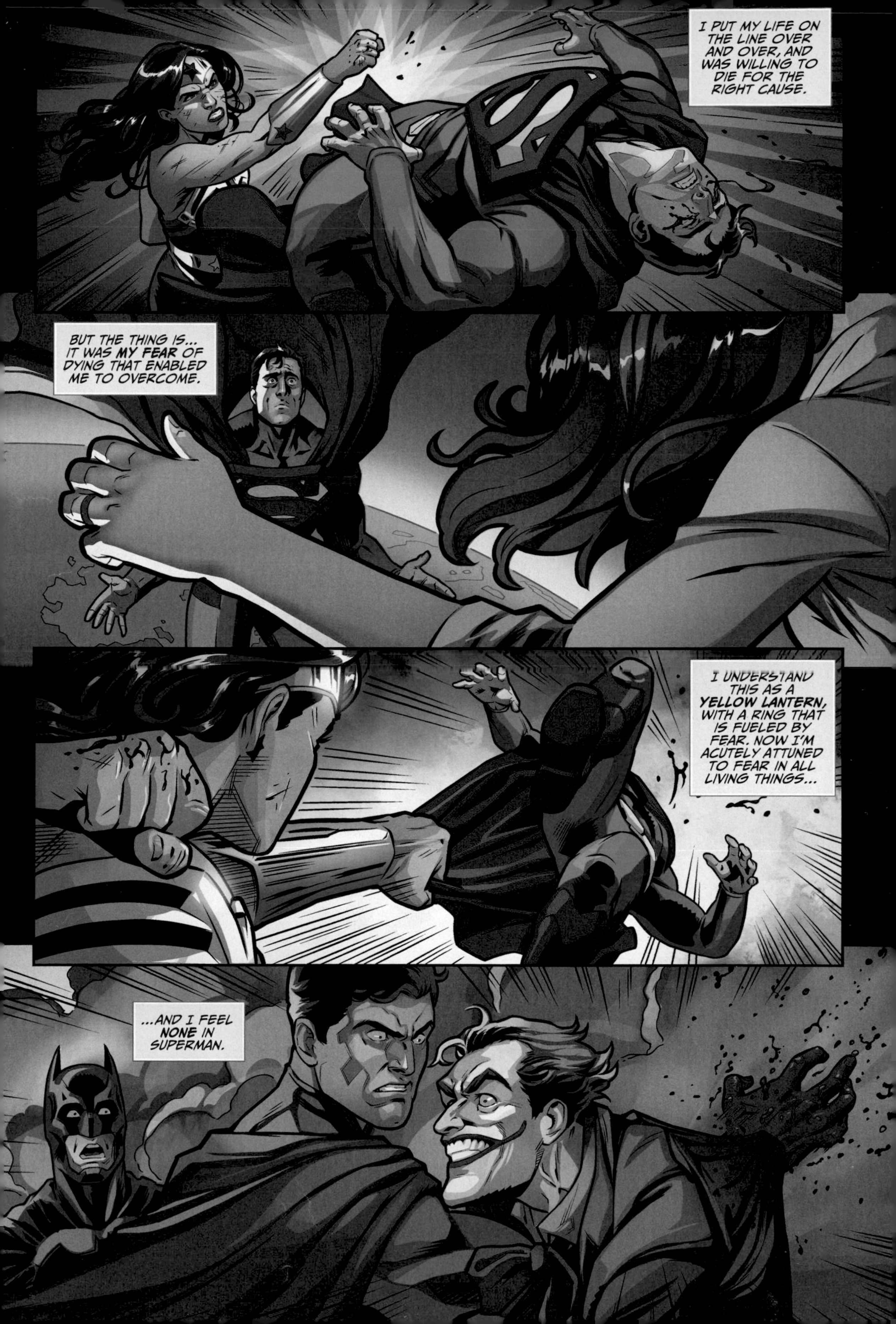
I PUT MY LIFE ON THE LINE OVER AND OVER, AND WAS WILLING TO DIE FOR THE RIGHT CAUSE.
BUT THE THING IS... IT WAS **MY FEAR** OF DYING THAT ENABLED ME TO OVERCOME.
I UNDERSTAND THIS AS A **YELLOW LANTERN,** WITH A RING THAT IS FUELED BY FEAR. NOW I'M ACUTELY ATTUNED TO FEAR IN ALL LIVING THINGS...
...AND I FEEL **NONE** IN SUPERMAN.

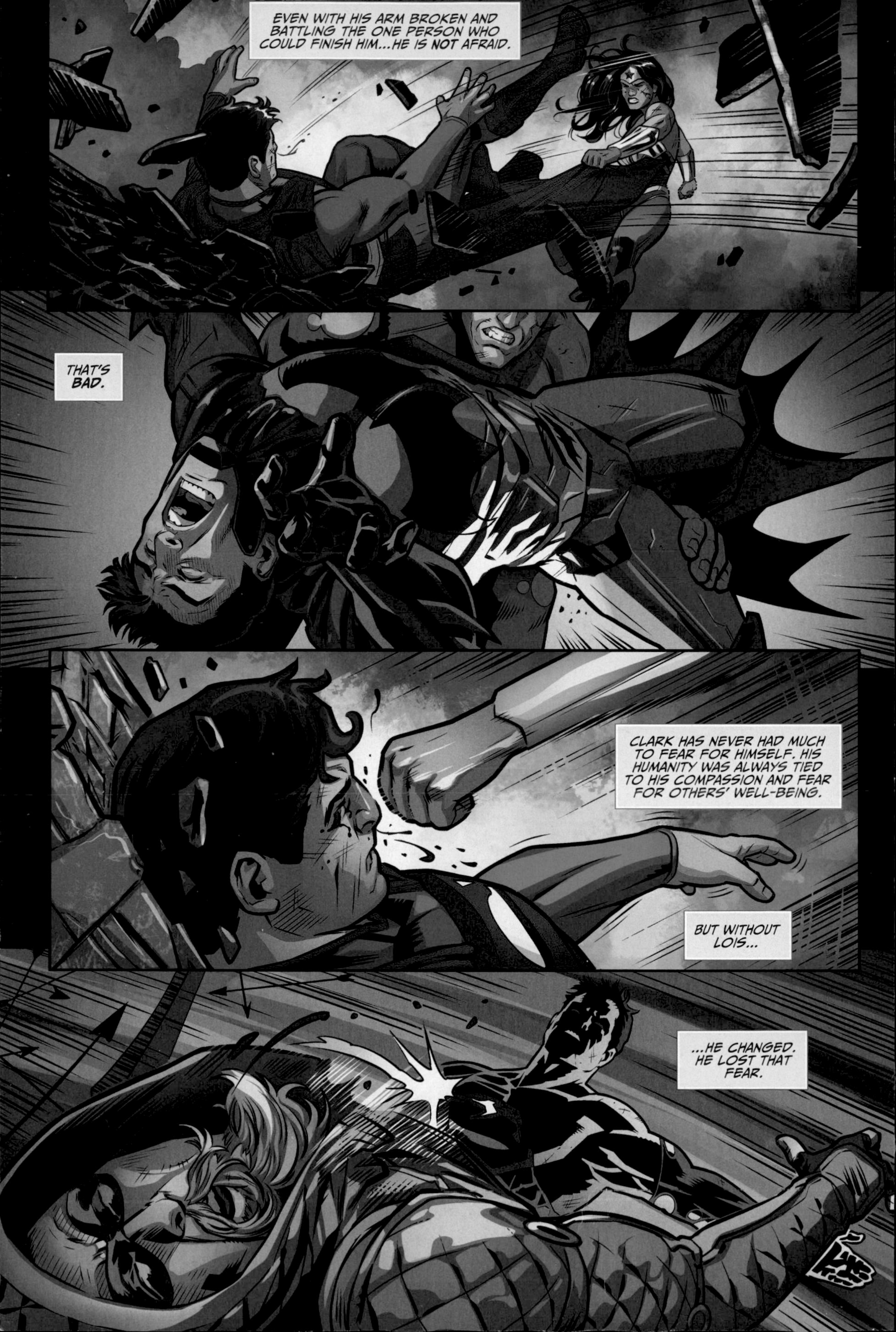
EVEN WITH HIS ARM BROKEN AND BATTLING THE ONE PERSON WHO COULD FINISH HIM...HE IS NOT AFRAID.
THAT'S BAD.
CLARK HAS NEVER HAD MUCH TO FEAR FOR HIMSELF. HIS HUMANITY WAS ALWAYS TIED TO HIS COMPASSION AND FEAR FOR OTHERS' WELL-BEING.
BUT WITHOUT LOIS...
...HE CHANGED. HE LOST THAT FEAR.

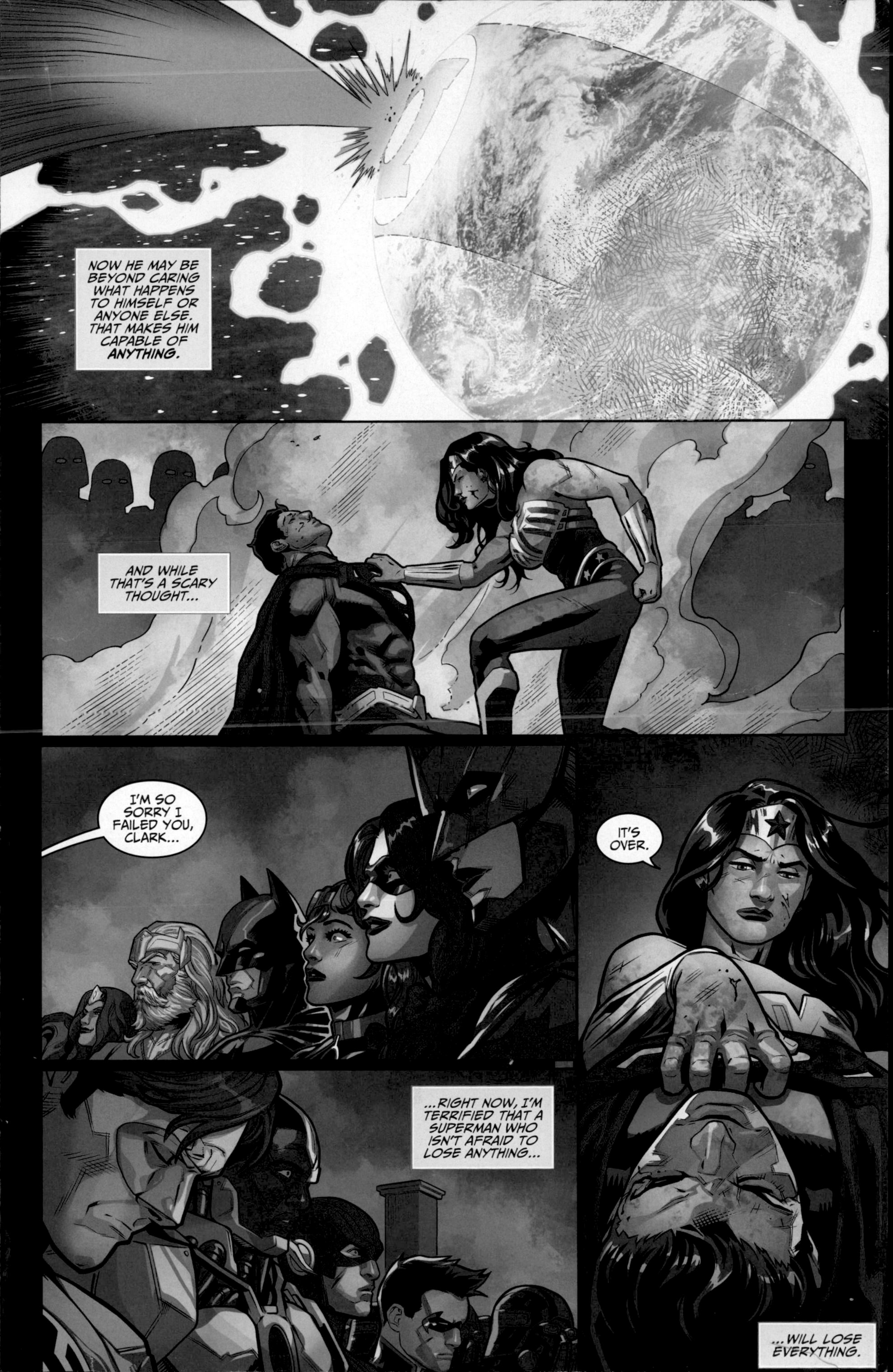
NOW HE MAY BE BEYOND CARING WHAT HAPPENS TO HIMSELF OR ANYONE ELSE. THAT MAKES HIM CAPABLE OF ANYTHING.
AND WHILE THAT'S A SCARY THOUGHT...
I'M SO SORRY I FAILED YOU, CLARK...
IT'S OVER.
...RIGHT NOW, I'M TERRIFIED THAT A SUPERMAN WHO ISN'T AFRAID TO LOSE ANYTHING...
...WILL LOSE EVERYTHING.

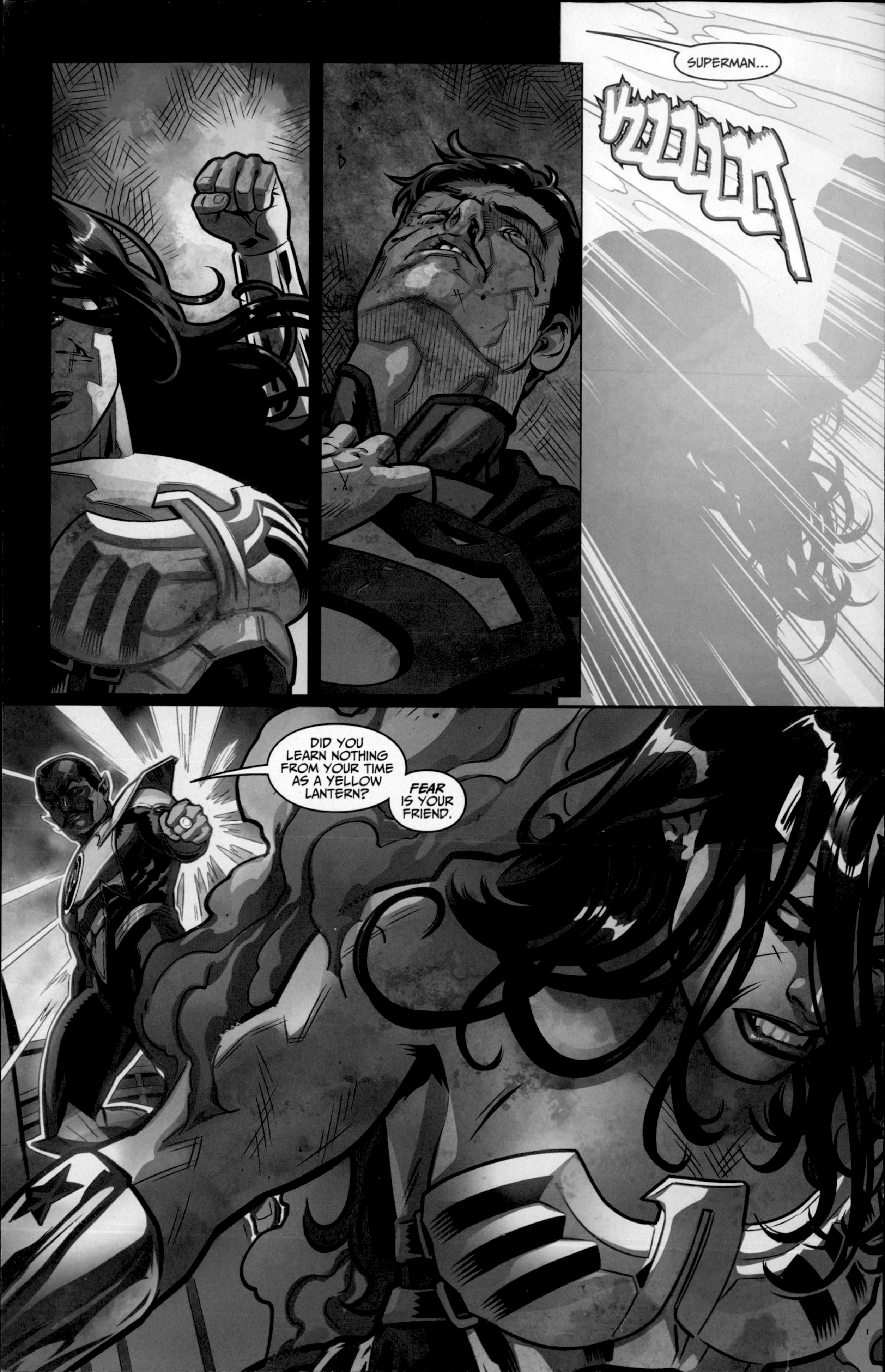
SUPERMAN...
DID YOU LEARN NOTHING FROM YOUR TIME AS A YELLOW LANTERN?
FEAR IS YOUR FRIEND.

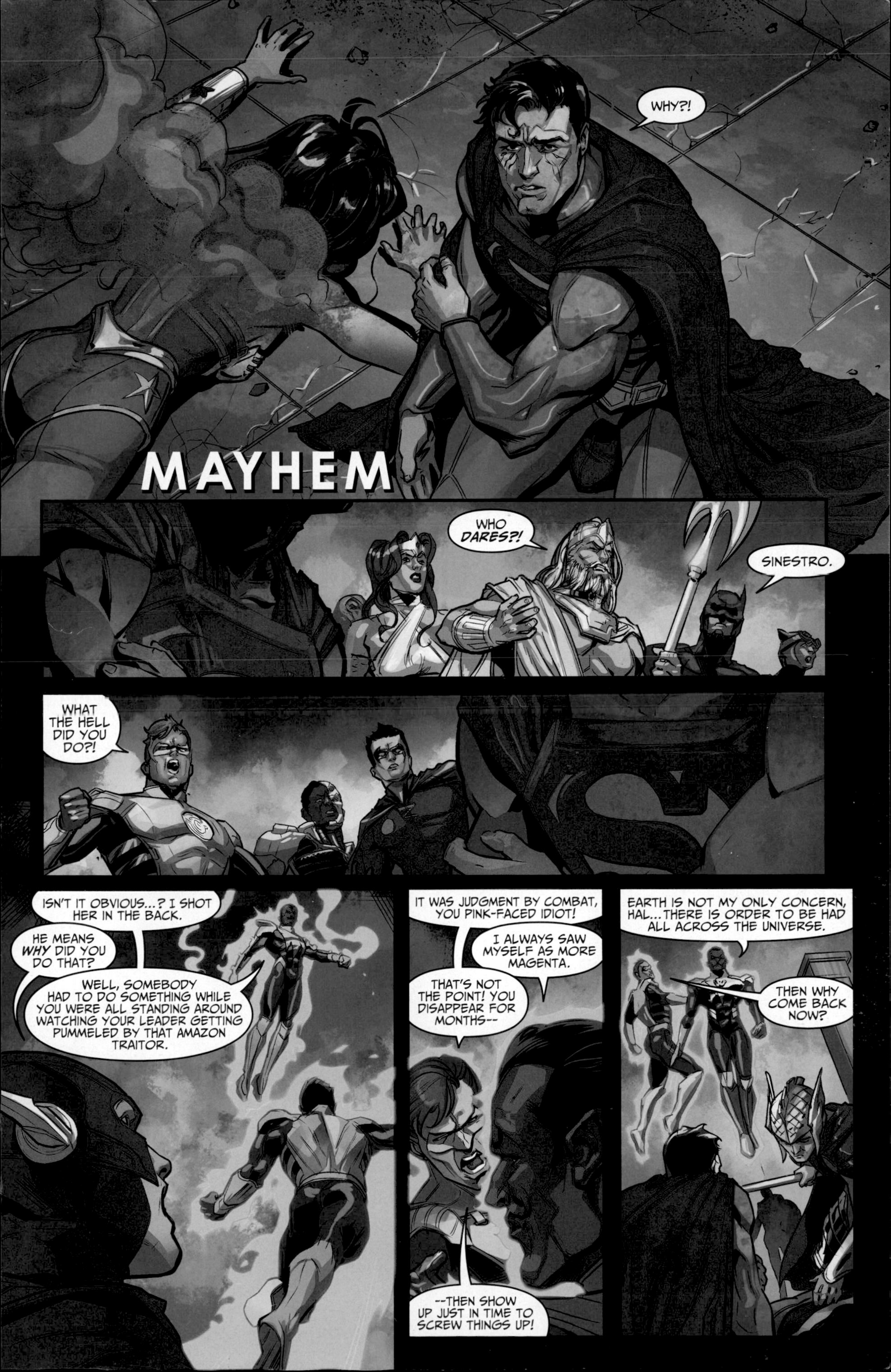
WHY?!
MAYHEM
WHO DARES?!
SINESTRO.
WHAT THE HELL DID YOU DO?!
ISN'T IT OBVIOUS...? I SHOT HER IN THE BACK.
HE MEANS WHY DID YOU DO THAT?
WELL, SOMEBODY HAD TO DO SOMETHING WHILE YOU WERE ALL STANDING AROUND WATCHING YOUR LEADER GETTING PUMMELED BY THAT AMAZON TRAITOR.
IT WAS JUDGMENT BY COMBAT, YOU PINK-FACED IDIOT!
I ALWAYS SAW MYSELF AS MORE MAGENTA.
THAT'S NOT THE POINT! YOU DISAPPEAR FOR MONTHS--
--THEN SHOW UP JUST IN TIME TO SCREW THINGS UP!
EARTH IS NOT MY ONLY CONCERN, HAL...THERE IS ORDER TO BE HAD ALL ACROSS THE UNIVERSE.
THEN WHY COME BACK NOW?

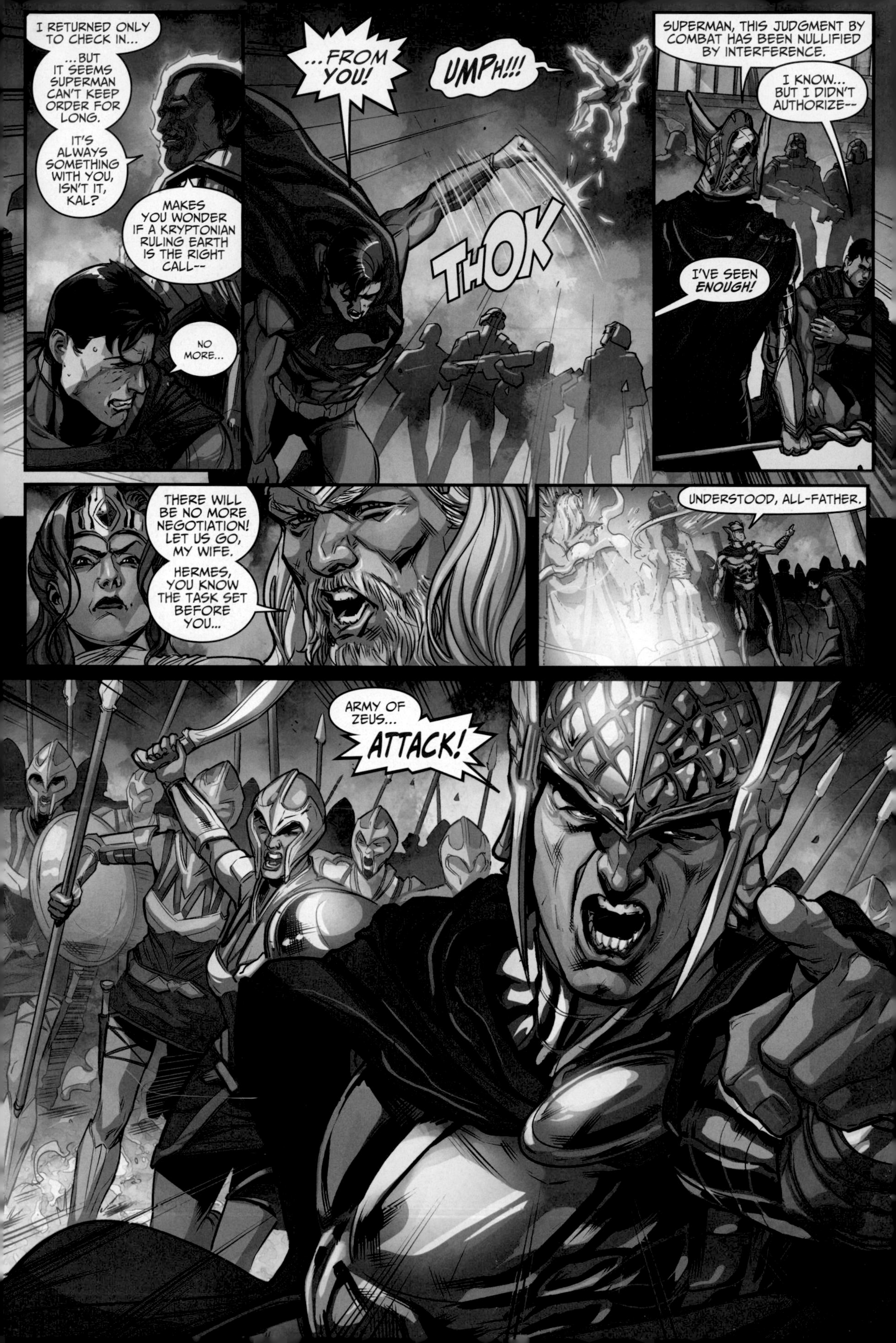
I RETURNED ONLY TO CHECK IN...
...BUT IT SEEMS SUPERMAN CAN'T KEEP ORDER FOR LONG.
IT'S ALWAYS SOMETHING WITH YOU, ISN'T IT, KAL?
MAKES YOU WONDER IF A KRYPTONIAN RULING EARTH IS THE RIGHT CALL--
NO MORE...
...FROM YOU!
UMPH!!!
THOK
SUPERMAN, THIS JUDGMENT BY COMBAT HAS BEEN NULLIFIED BY INTERFERENCE.
I KNOW... BUT I DIDN'T AUTHORIZE--
I'VE SEEN ENOUGH!
THERE WILL BE NO MORE NEGOTIATION! LET US GO, MY WIFE.
HERMES, YOU KNOW THE TASK SET BEFORE YOU...
UNDERSTOOD, ALL-FATHER.
ARMY OF ZEUS...
ATTACK!

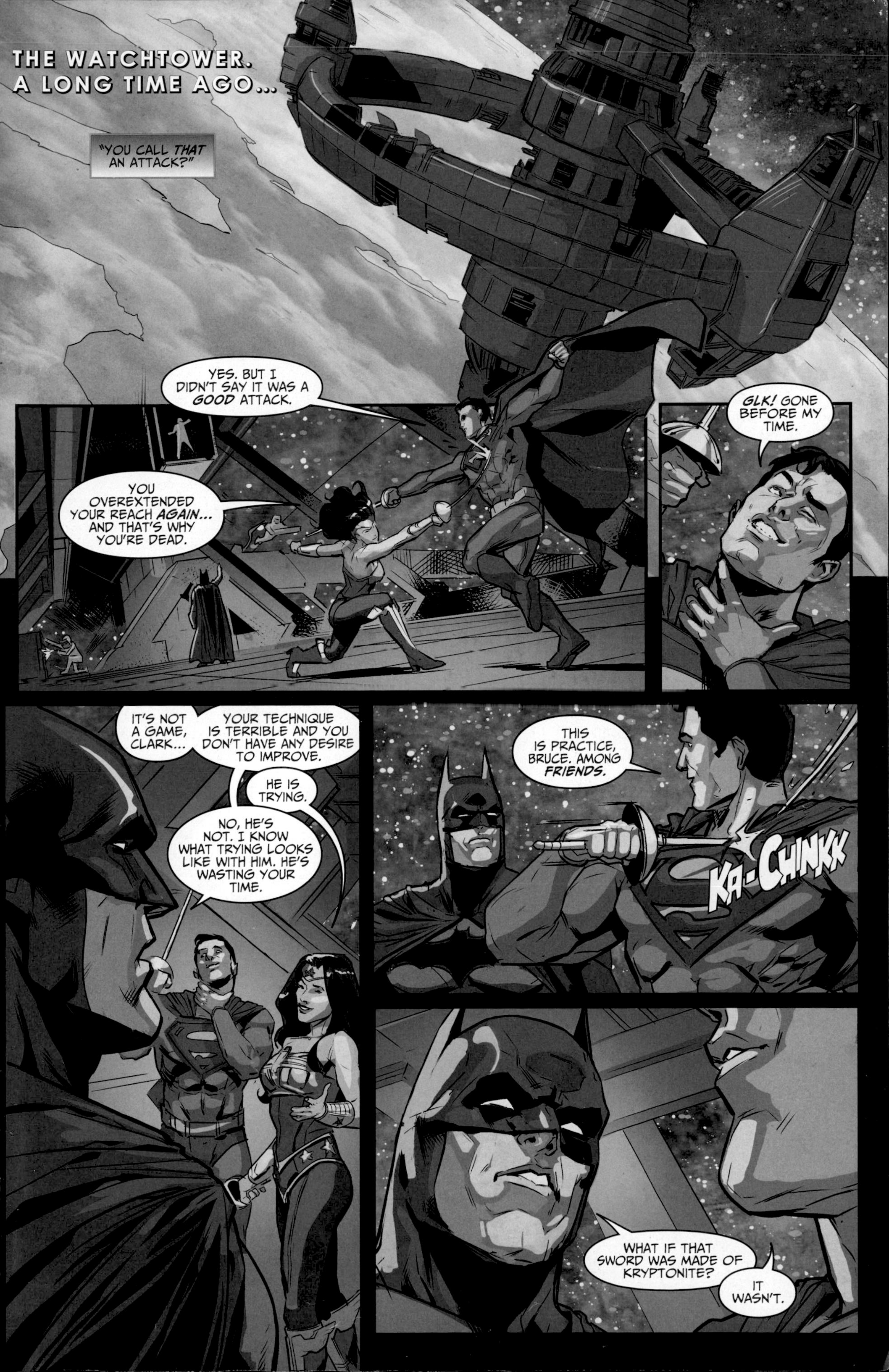
THE WATCHTOWER.
A LONG TIME AGO...
"YOU CALL THAT AN ATTACK?"
YES. BUT I DIDN'T SAY IT WAS A GOOD ATTACK.
YOU OVEREXTENDED YOUR REACH AGAIN... AND THAT'S WHY YOU'RE DEAD.
GLK! GONE BEFORE MY TIME.
IT'S NOT A GAME, CLARK...
YOUR TECHNIQUE IS TERRIBLE AND YOU DON'T HAVE ANY DESIRE TO IMPROVE.
HE IS TRYING.
NO, HE'S NOT. I KNOW WHAT TRYING LOOKS LIKE WITH HIM. HE'S WASTING YOUR TIME.
THIS IS PRACTICE, BRUCE. AMONG FRIENDS.
KA-CHINKK
WHAT IF THAT SWORD WAS MADE OF KRYPTONITE?
IT WASN'T.

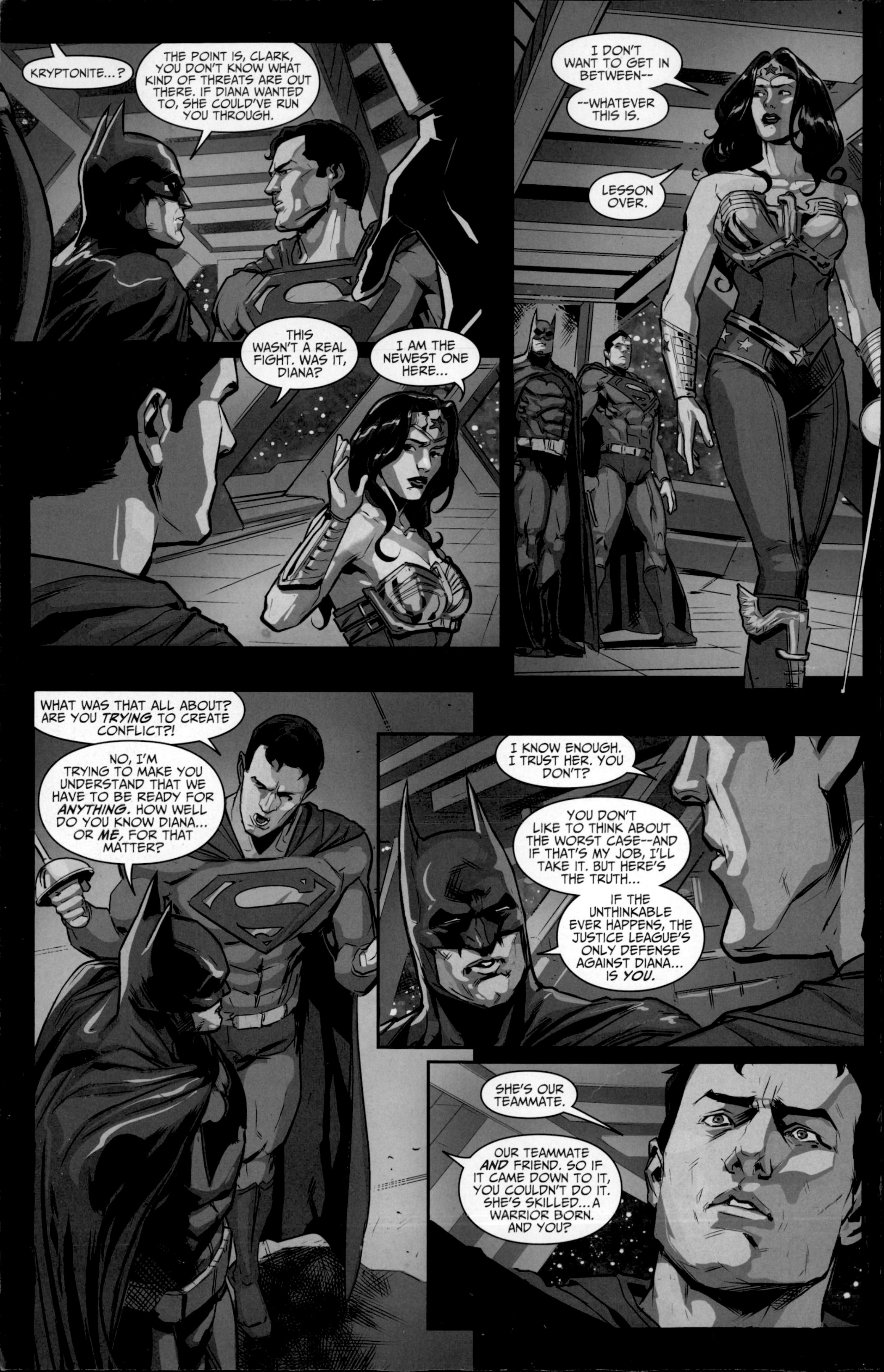
KRYPTONITE...?
THE POINT IS, CLARK, YOU DON'T KNOW WHAT KIND OF THREATS ARE OUT THERE. IF DIANA WANTED TO, SHE COULD'VE RUN YOU THROUGH.
THIS WASN'T A REAL FIGHT. WAS IT, DIANA?
I AM THE NEWEST ONE HERE...
I DON'T WANT TO GET IN BETWEEN--
--WHATEVER THIS IS.
LESSON OVER.
WHAT WAS THAT ALL ABOUT? ARE YOU *TRYING* TO CREATE CONFLICT?!
NO, I'M TRYING TO MAKE YOU UNDERSTAND THAT WE HAVE TO BE READY FOR *ANYTHING*. HOW WELL DO YOU KNOW DIANA... OR *ME*, FOR THAT MATTER?
I KNOW ENOUGH. I TRUST HER. YOU DON'T?
YOU DON'T LIKE TO THINK ABOUT THE WORST CASE--AND IF THAT'S MY JOB, I'LL TAKE IT. BUT HERE'S THE TRUTH...
IF THE UNTHINKABLE EVER HAPPENS, THE JUSTICE LEAGUE'S ONLY DEFENSE AGAINST DIANA... IS *YOU.*
SHE'S OUR TEAMMATE.
OUR TEAMMATE *AND* FRIEND. SO IF IT CAME DOWN TO IT, YOU COULDN'T DO IT. SHE'S SKILLED... A WARRIOR BORN. AND YOU?

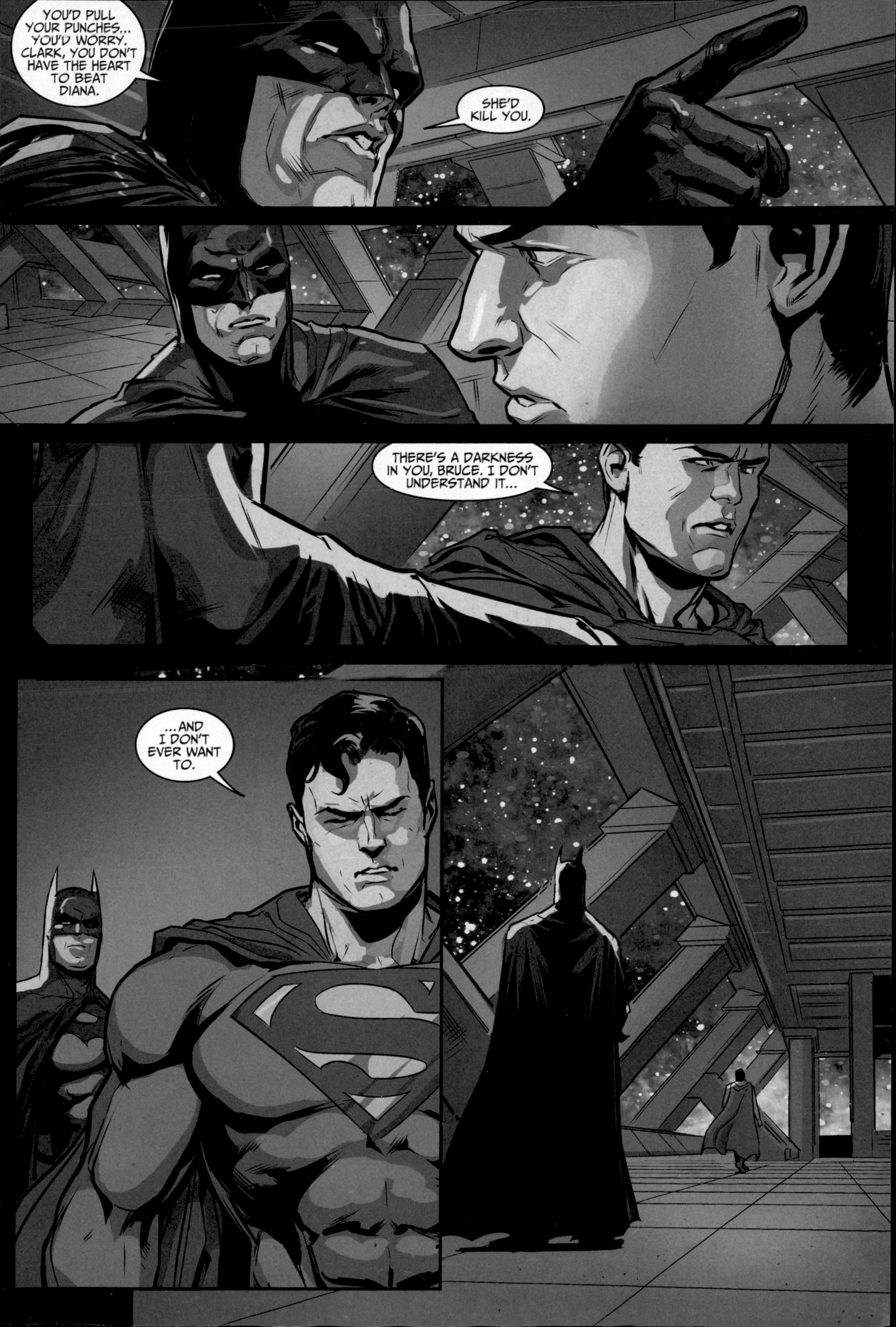
YOU'D PULL YOUR PUNCHES... YOU'D WORRY. CLARK, YOU DON'T HAVE THE HEART TO BEAT DIANA.
SHE'D KILL YOU.
THERE'S A DARKNESS IN YOU, BRUCE. I DON'T UNDERSTAND IT...
...AND I DON'T EVER WANT TO.

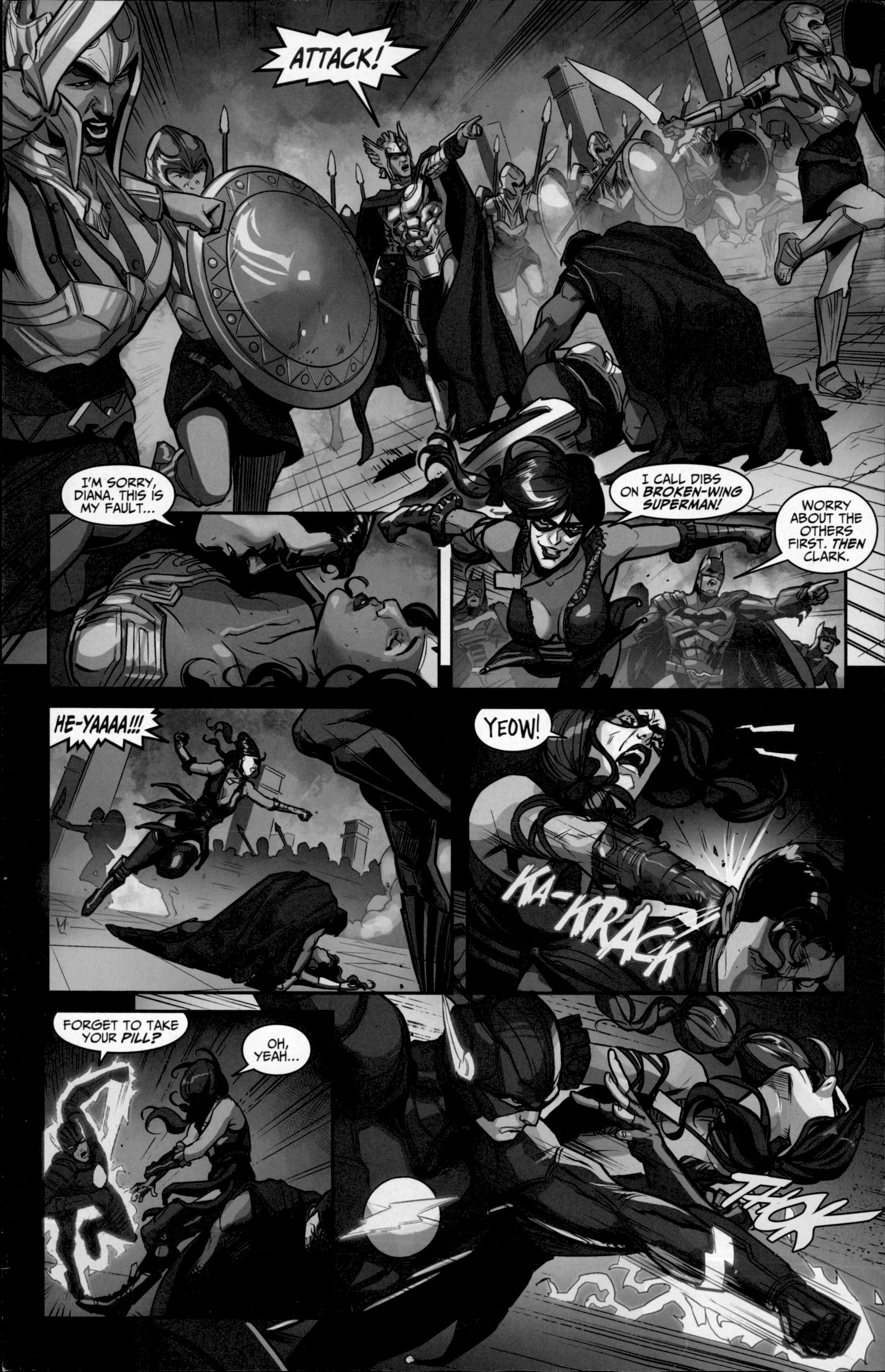
ATTACK!
I'M SORRY, DIANA. THIS IS MY FAULT...
I CALL DIBS ON BROKEN-WING SUPERMAN!
WORRY ABOUT THE OTHERS FIRST. THEN CLARK.
HE-YAAAA!!!
YEOW!
KA-KRACK
FORGET TO TAKE YOUR PILL?
OH, YEAH...
THOK

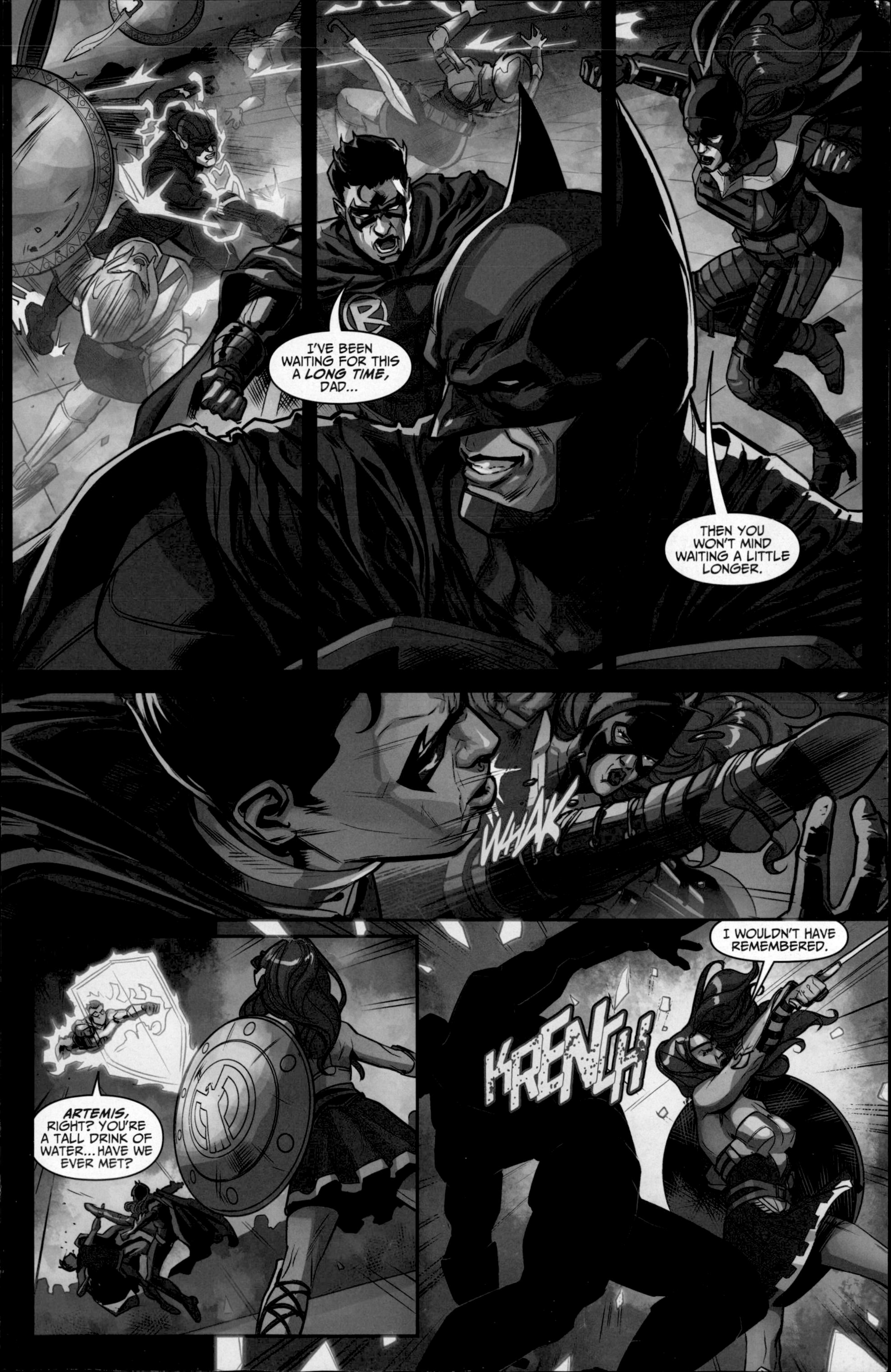
I'VE BEEN WAITING FOR THIS A LONG TIME, DAD...
THEN YOU WON'T MIND WAITING A LITTLE LONGER.
WHAK
ARTEMIS, RIGHT? YOU'RE A TALL DRINK OF WATER... HAVE WE EVER MET?
I WOULDN'T HAVE REMEMBERED.
KRENCH

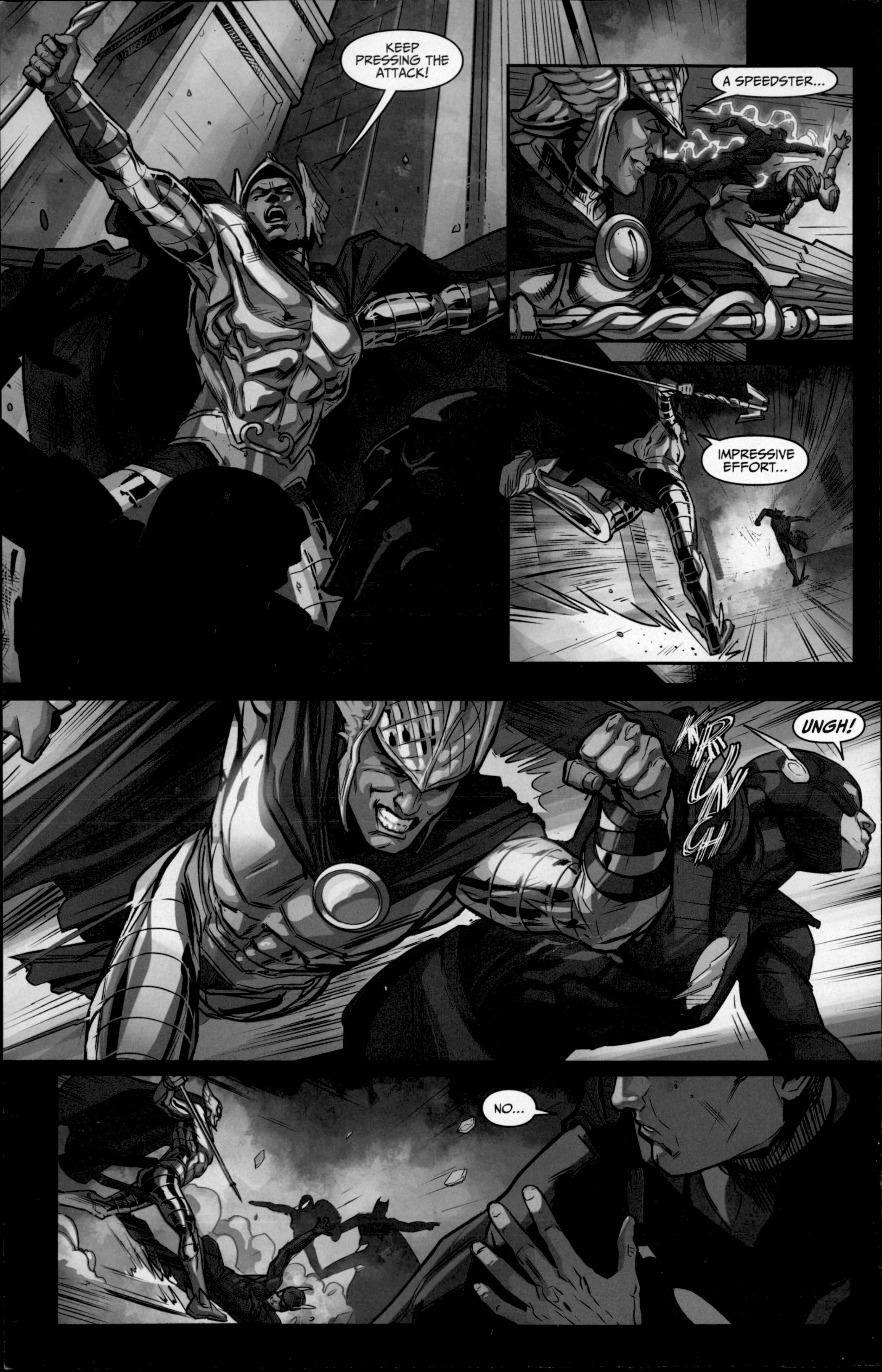
KEEP PRESSING THE ATTACK!
A SPEEDSTER...
IMPRESSIVE EFFORT...
KRUNCH
UNGH!
NO...

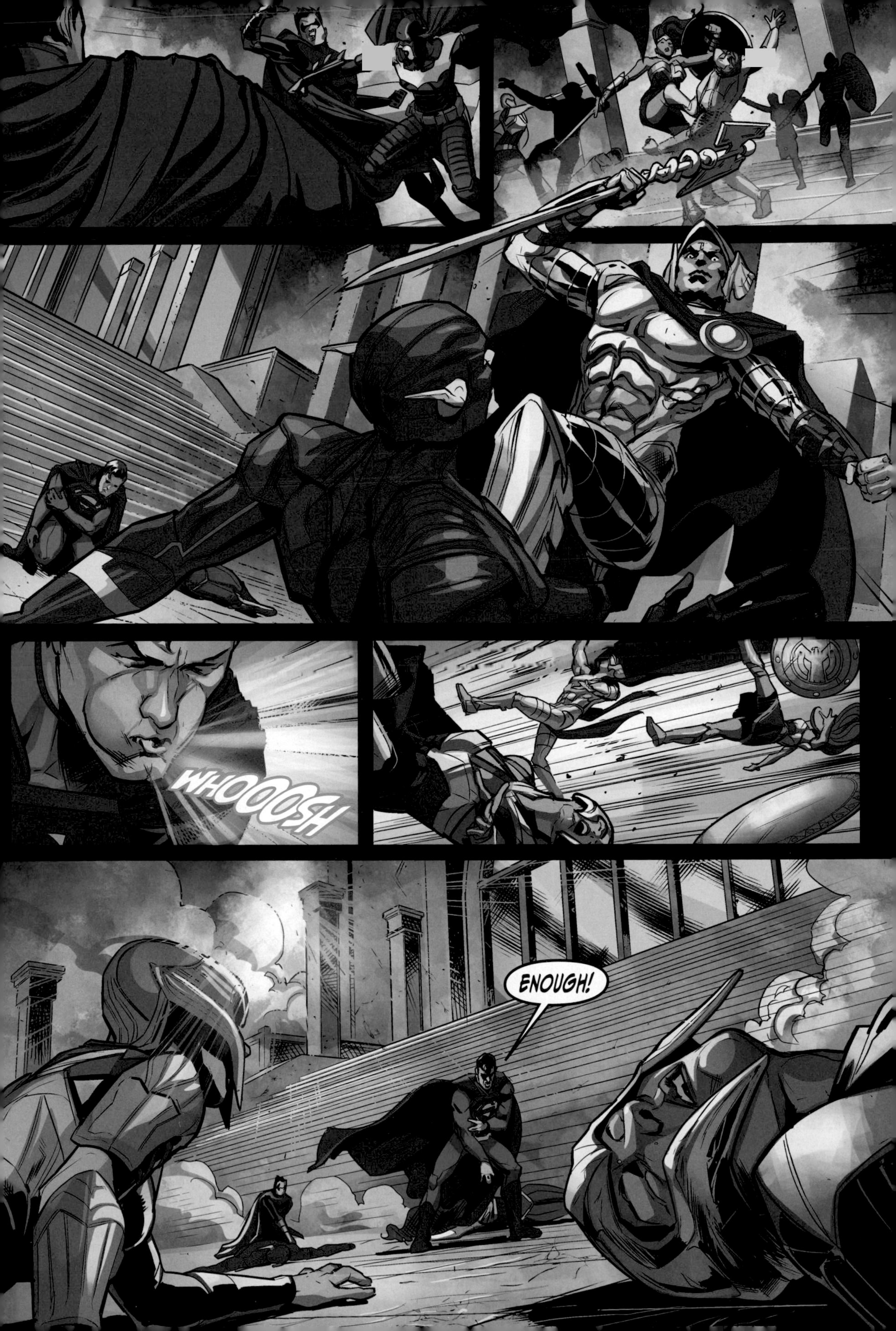
WHOOOSH
ENOUGH!

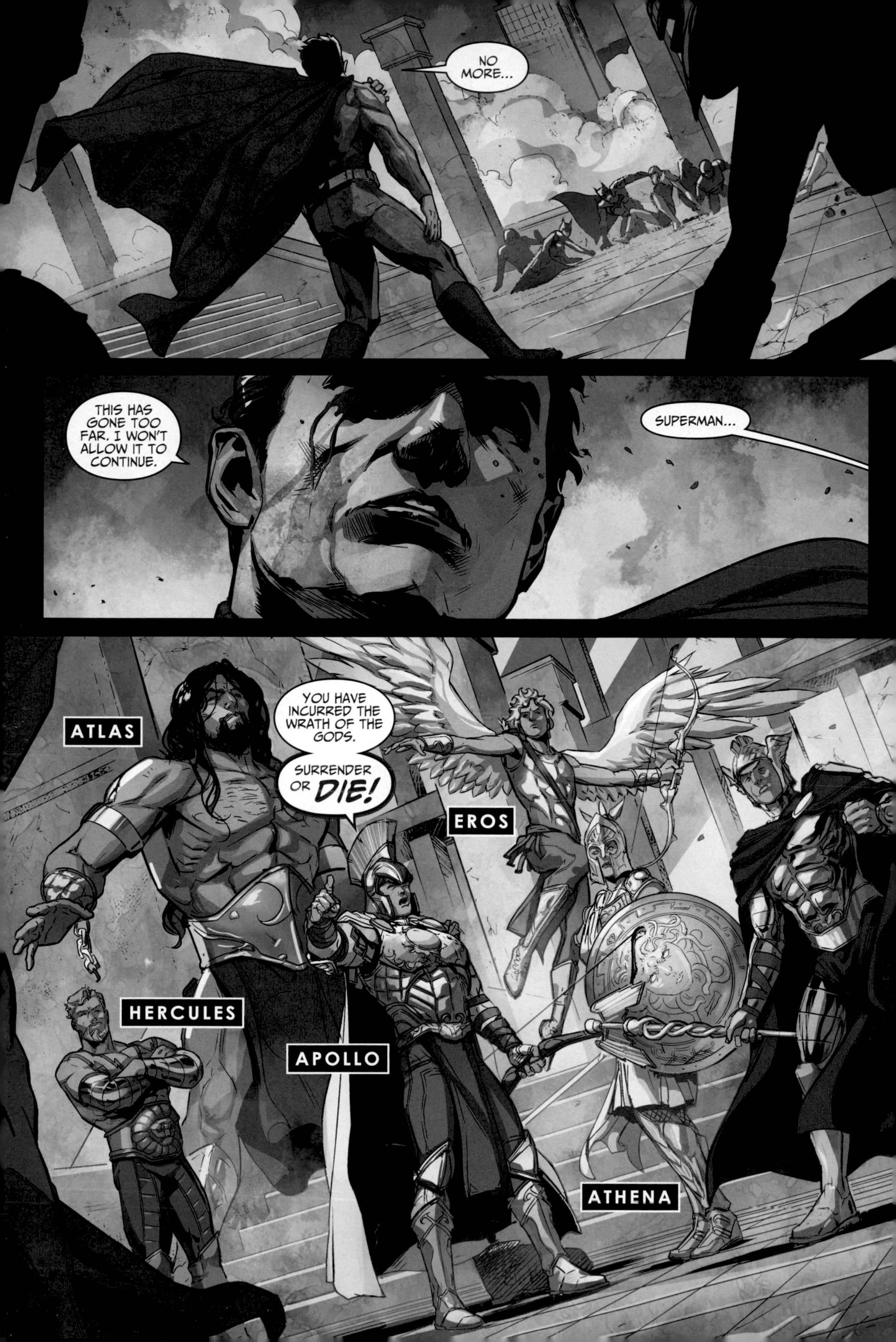

NO MORE...
THIS HAS GONE TOO FAR. I WON'T ALLOW IT TO CONTINUE.
SUPERMAN...
ATLAS
YOU HAVE INCURRED THE WRATH OF THE GODS.
SURRENDER OR DIE!
EROS
HERCULES
APOLLO
ATHENA

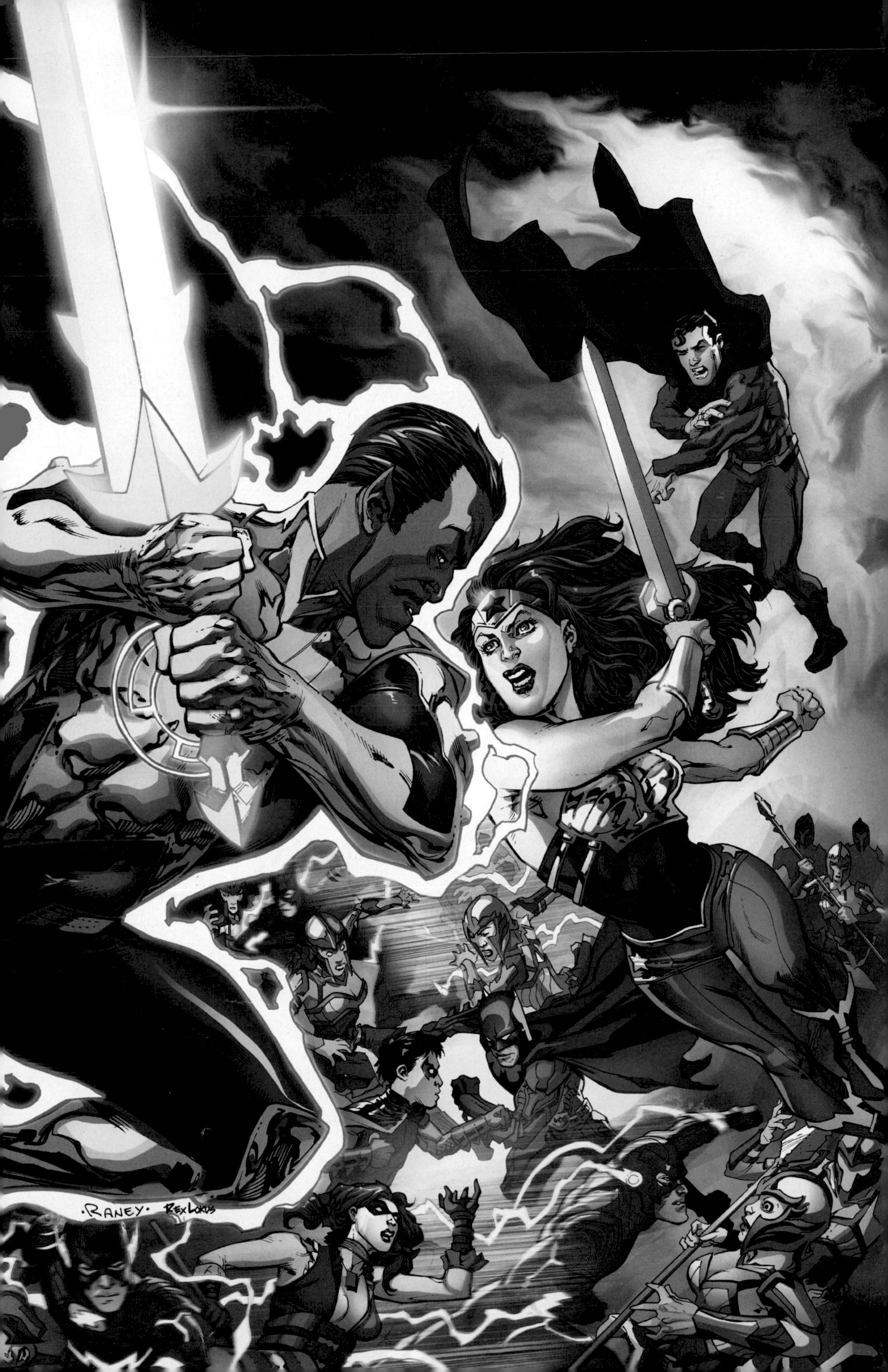
·RANEY·
REX LOKUS

"Ultimatums" **Mike S. Miller** Artist **J. Nanjan** Colorist
Cover Art by **Tom Raney & Rex Lokus**

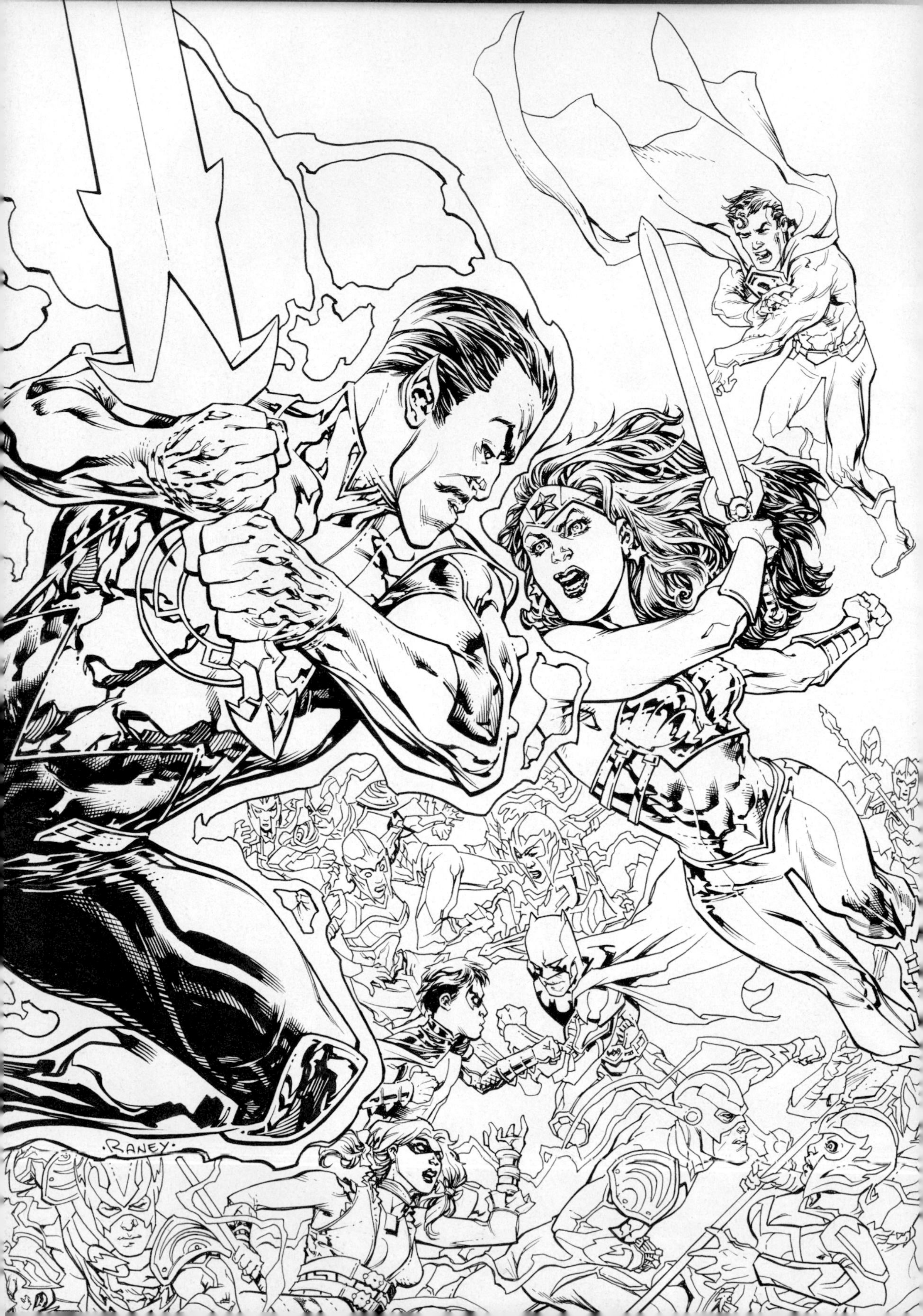
RANEY

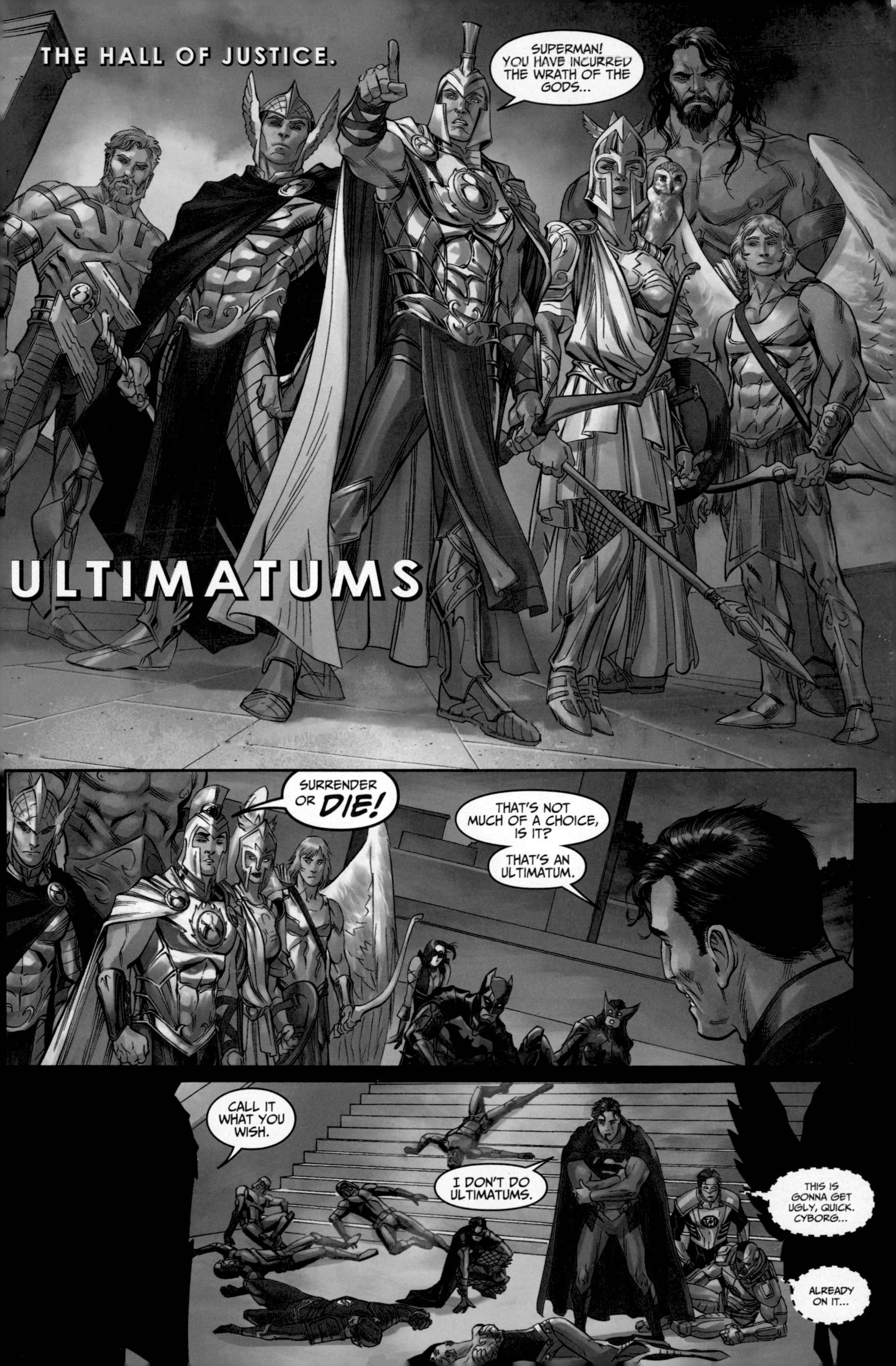
THE HALL OF JUSTICE.
SUPERMAN! YOU HAVE INCURRED THE WRATH OF THE GODS...
ULTIMATUMS
SURRENDER OR DIE!
THAT'S NOT MUCH OF A CHOICE, IS IT?
THAT'S AN ULTIMATUM.
CALL IT WHAT YOU WISH.
I DON'T DO ULTIMATUMS.
THIS IS GONNA GET UGLY, QUICK. CYBORG...
ALREADY ON IT...

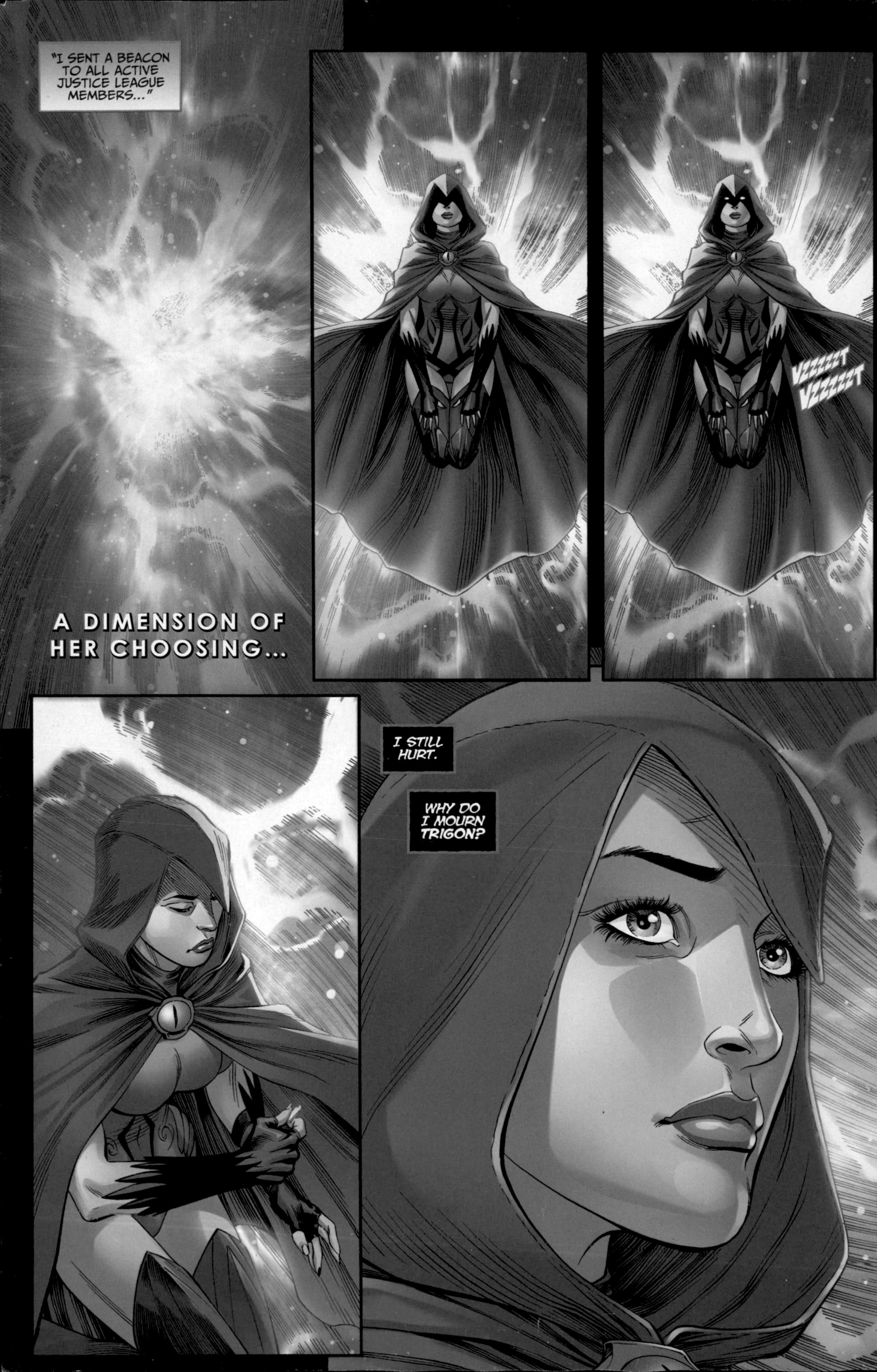
"I SENT A BEACON TO ALL ACTIVE JUSTICE LEAGUE MEMBERS..."
A DIMENSION OF HER CHOOSING...
VZZZZZT VZZZZZT
I STILL HURT.
WHY DO I MOURN TRIGON?

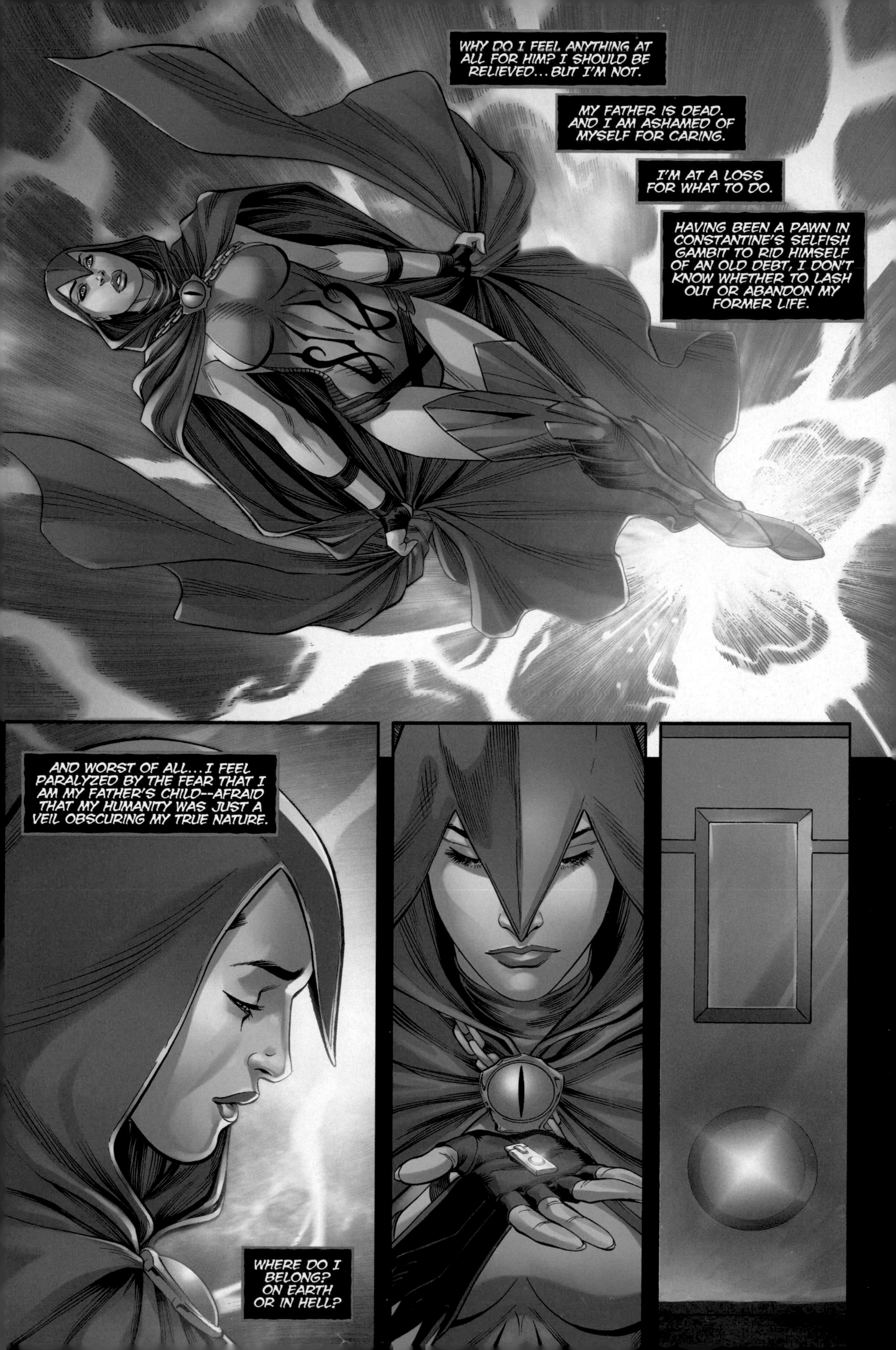
WHY DO I FEEL ANYTHING AT ALL FOR HIM? I SHOULD BE RELIEVED... BUT I'M NOT.
MY FATHER IS DEAD. AND I AM ASHAMED OF MYSELF FOR CARING.
I'M AT A LOSS FOR WHAT TO DO.
HAVING BEEN A PAWN IN CONSTANTINE'S SELFISH GAMBIT TO RID HIMSELF OF AN OLD DEBT, I DON'T KNOW WHETHER TO LASH OUT OR ABANDON MY FORMER LIFE.
AND WORST OF ALL... I FEEL PARALYZED BY THE FEAR THAT I AM MY FATHER'S CHILD--AFRAID THAT MY HUMANITY WAS JUST A VEIL OBSCURING MY TRUE NATURE.
WHERE DO I BELONG? ON EARTH OR IN HELL?

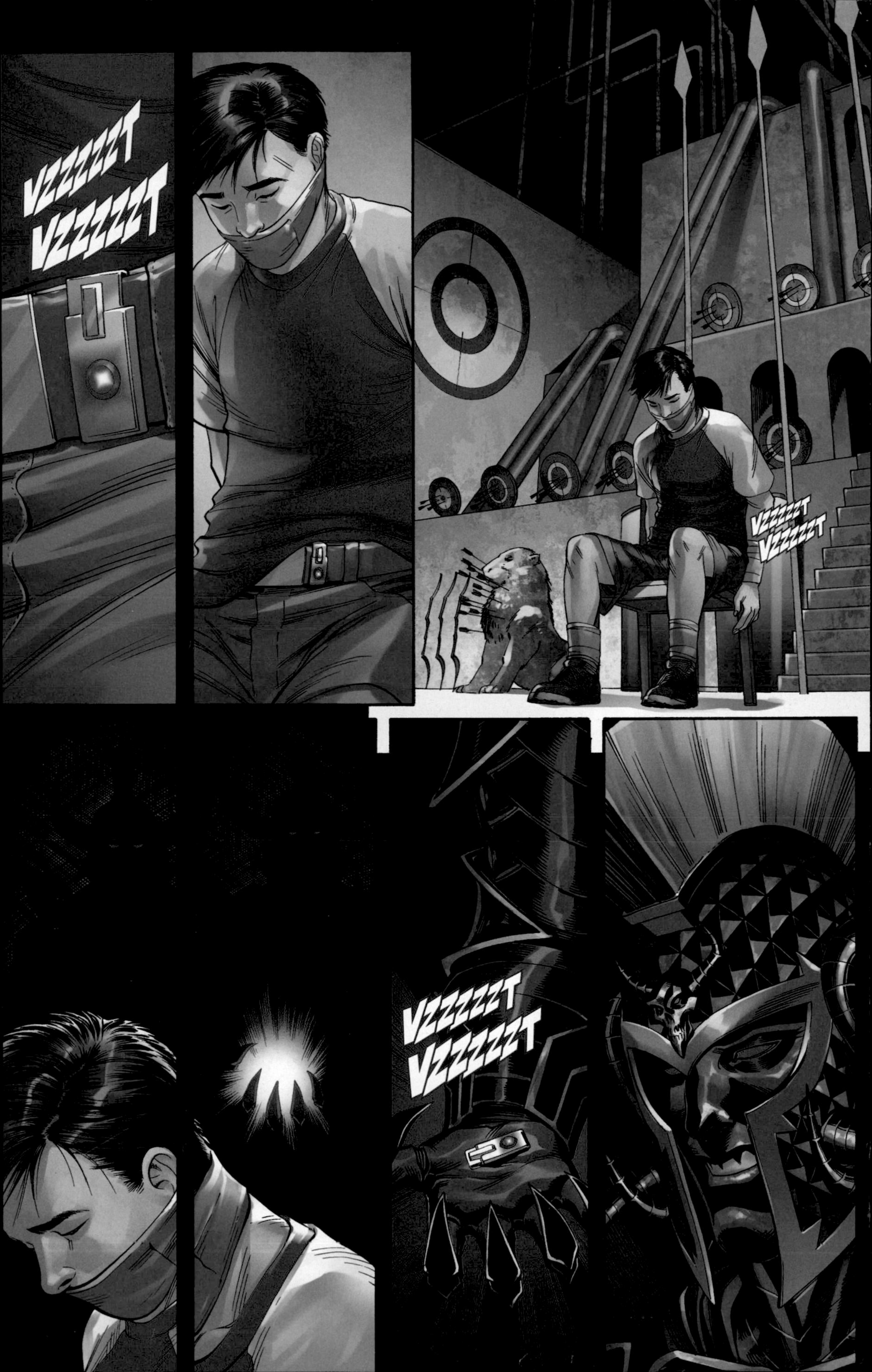
VZZZZZT
VZZZZZT
VZZZZZT
VZZZZZT
VZZZZZT
VZZZZZT

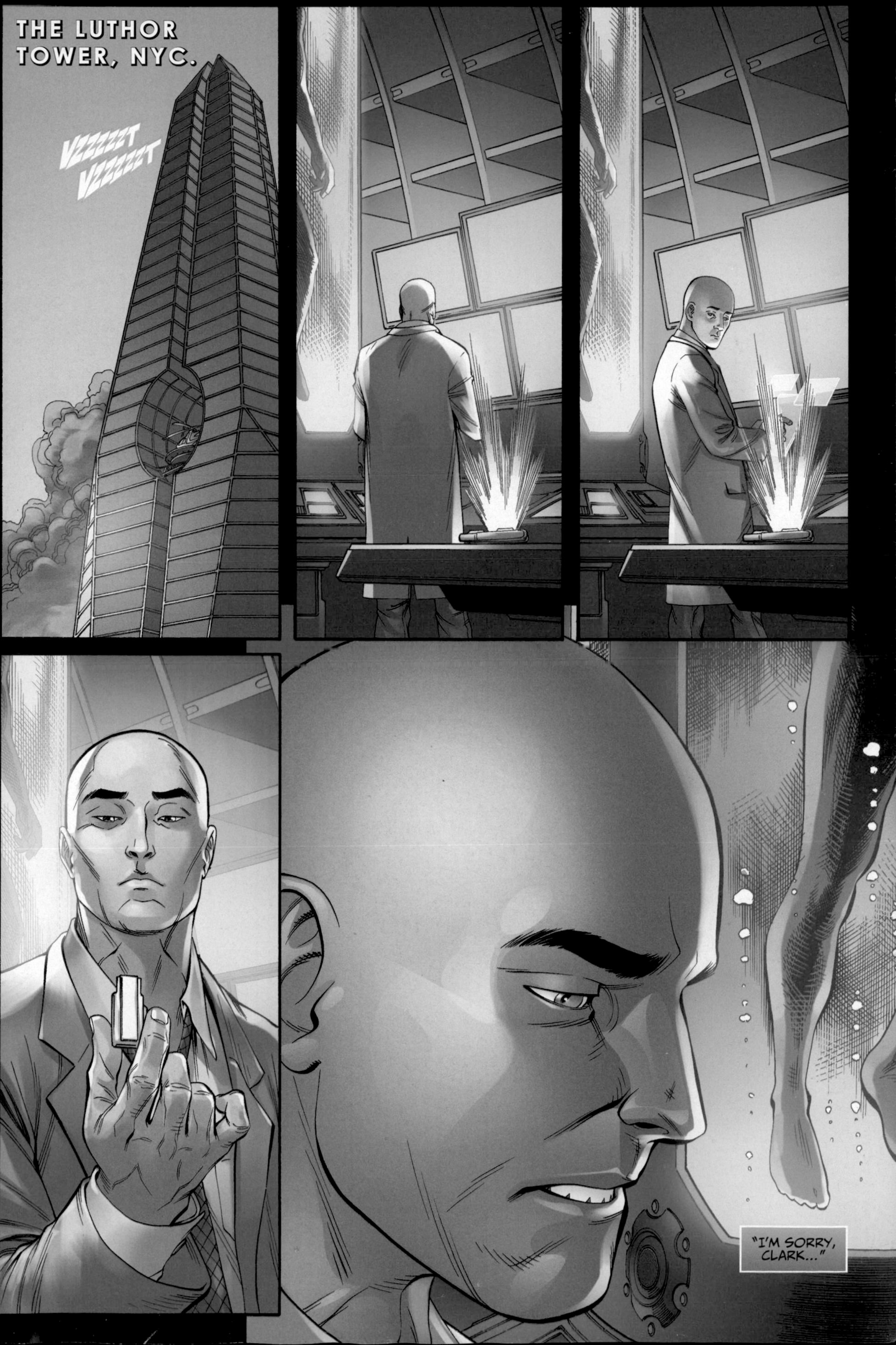
THE LUTHOR TOWER, NYC.
VZZZZZT
VZZZZZT
"I'M SORRY, CLARK..."

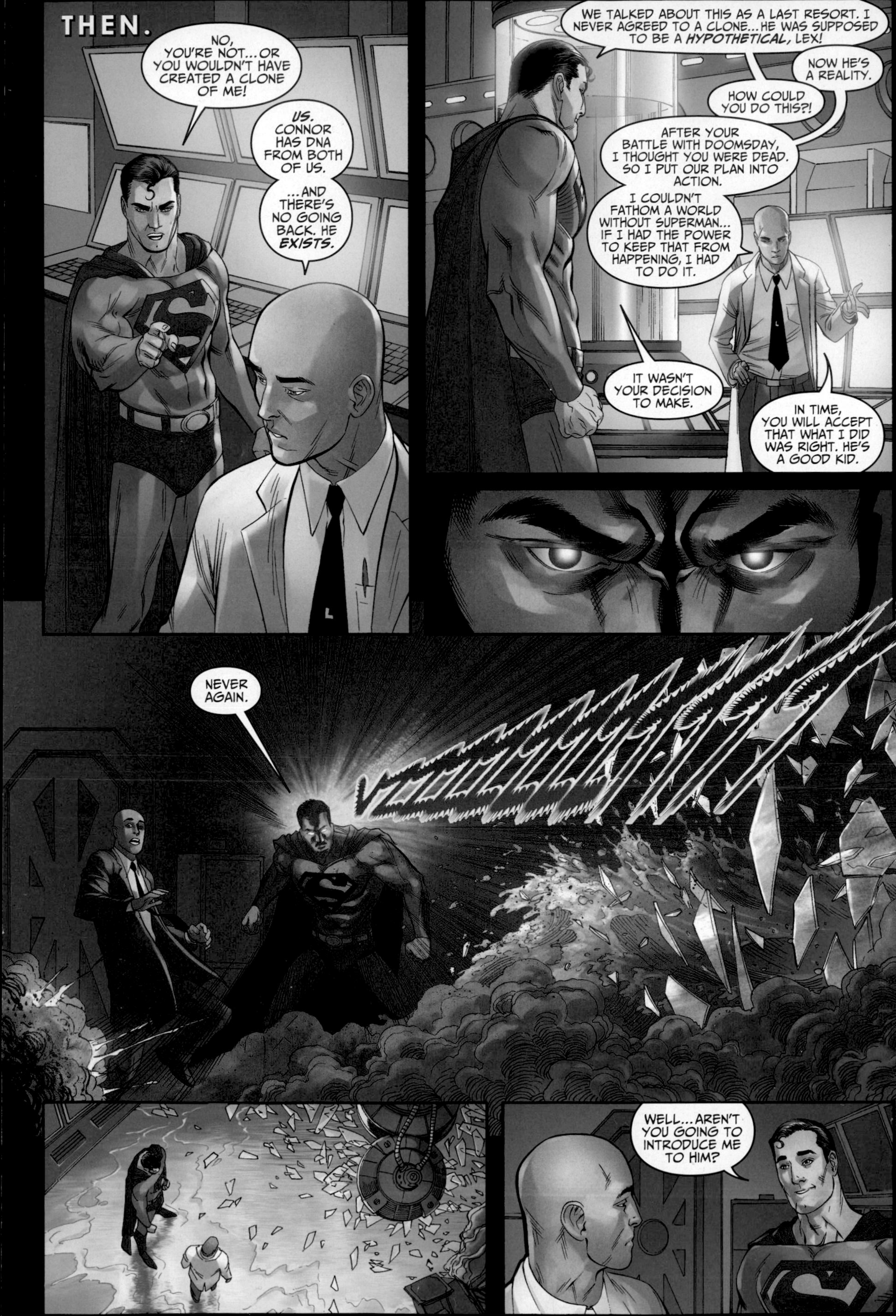

THEN.
NO, YOU'RE NOT...OR YOU WOULDN'T HAVE CREATED A CLONE OF ME!
US. CONNOR HAS DNA FROM BOTH OF US.
...AND THERE'S NO GOING BACK. HE EXISTS.
WE TALKED ABOUT THIS AS A LAST RESORT. I NEVER AGREED TO A CLONE...HE WAS SUPPOSED TO BE A HYPOTHETICAL, LEX!
NOW HE'S A REALITY.
HOW COULD YOU DO THIS?!
AFTER YOUR BATTLE WITH DOOMSDAY, I THOUGHT YOU WERE DEAD. SO I PUT OUR PLAN INTO ACTION.
I COULDN'T FATHOM A WORLD WITHOUT SUPERMAN... IF I HAD THE POWER TO KEEP THAT FROM HAPPENING, I HAD TO DO IT.
IT WASN'T YOUR DECISION TO MAKE.
IN TIME, YOU WILL ACCEPT THAT WHAT I DID WAS RIGHT. HE'S A GOOD KID.
NEVER AGAIN.
VZOOOMMMM
WELL...AREN'T YOU GOING TO INTRODUCE ME TO HIM?

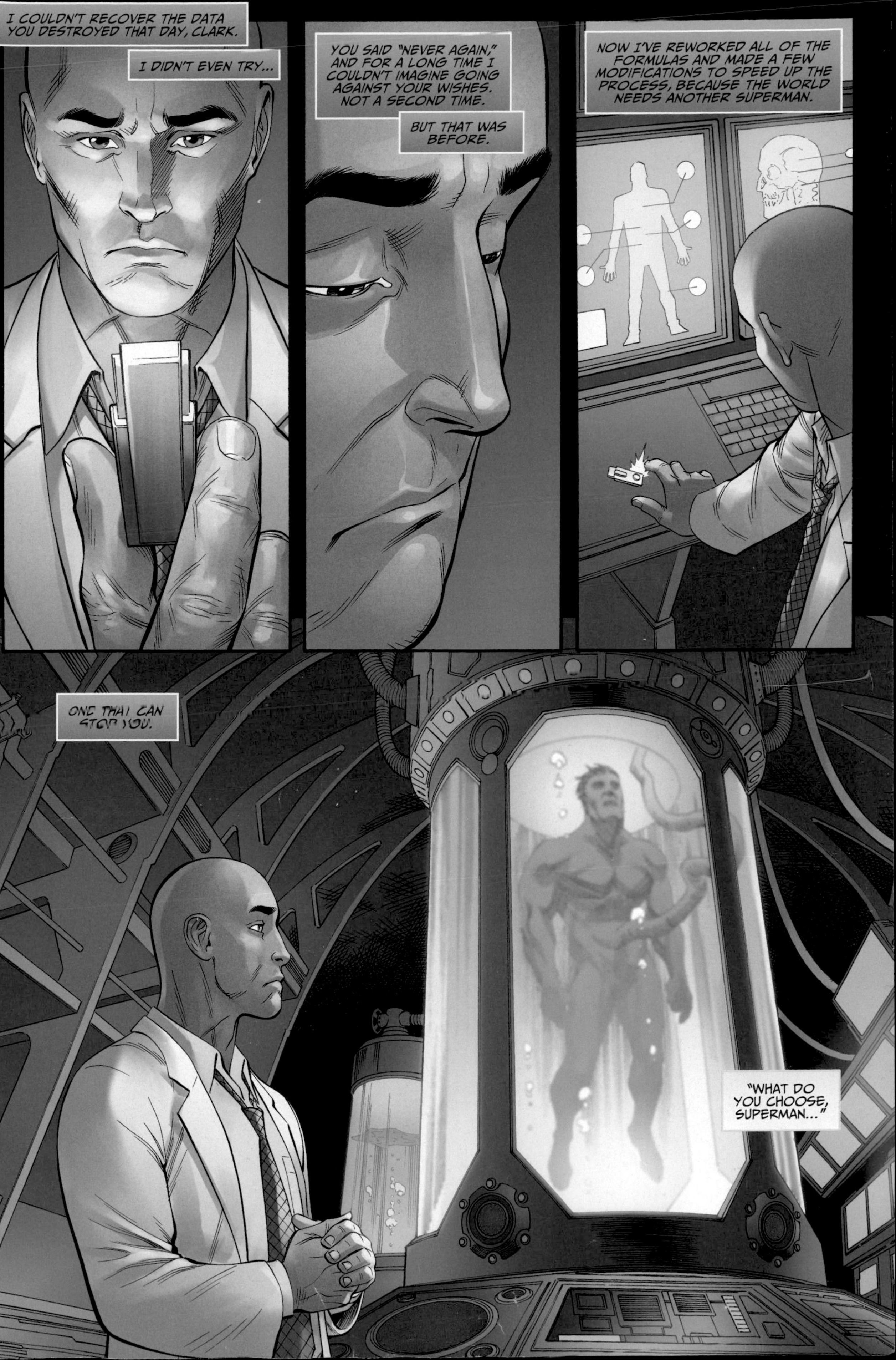
I COULDN'T RECOVER THE DATA YOU DESTROYED THAT DAY, CLARK.
I DIDN'T EVEN TRY...
YOU SAID "NEVER AGAIN," AND FOR A LONG TIME I COULDN'T IMAGINE GOING AGAINST YOUR WISHES. NOT A SECOND TIME.
BUT THAT WAS BEFORE.
NOW I'VE REWORKED ALL OF THE FORMULAS AND MADE A FEW MODIFICATIONS TO SPEED UP THE PROCESS, BECAUSE THE WORLD NEEDS ANOTHER SUPERMAN.
ONE THAT CAN STOP YOU.
"WHAT DO YOU CHOOSE, SUPERMAN..."

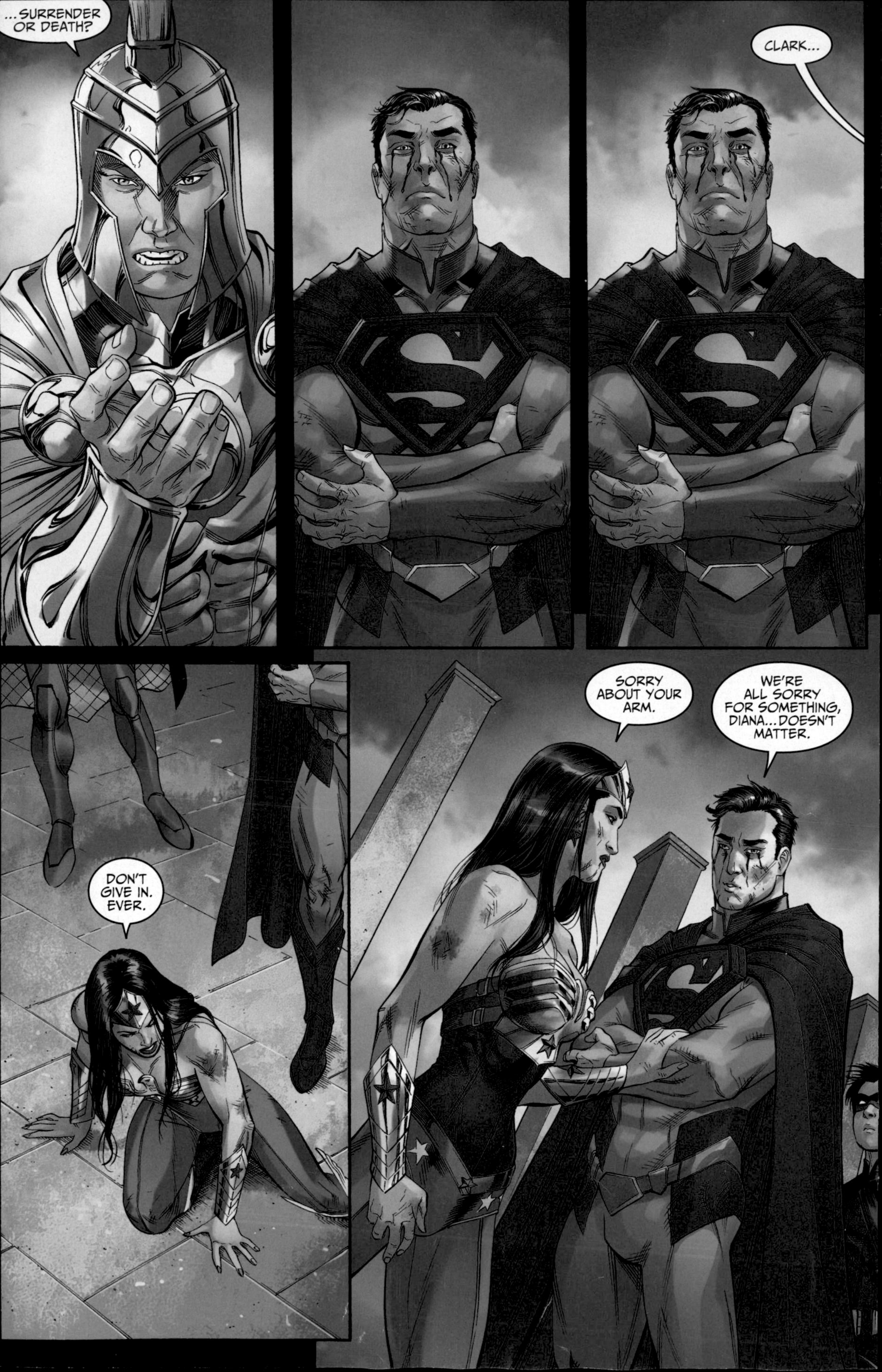
...SURRENDER OR DEATH?
CLARK...
DON'T GIVE IN. EVER.
SORRY ABOUT YOUR ARM.
WE'RE ALL SORRY FOR SOMETHING, DIANA...DOESN'T MATTER.

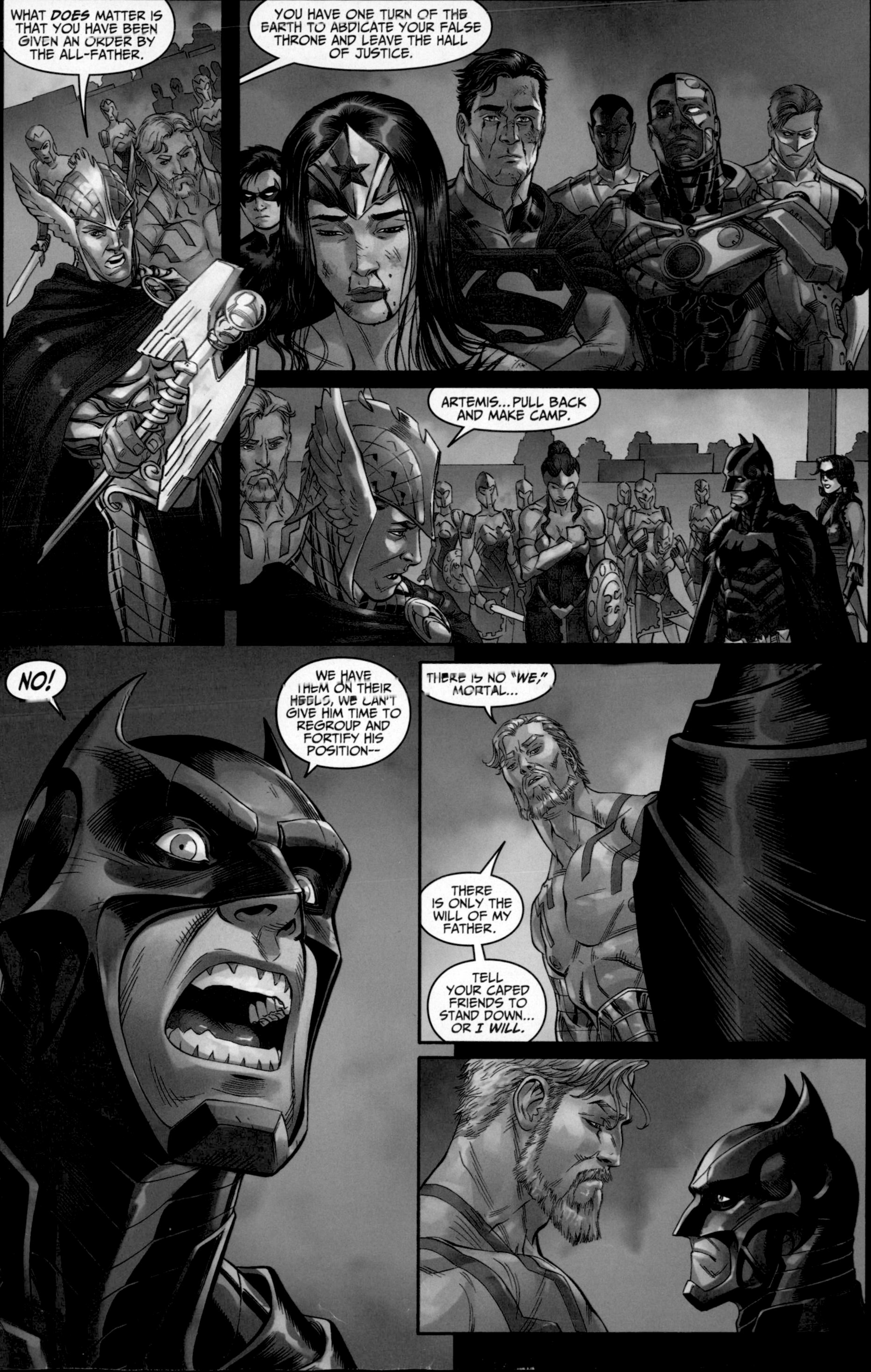

WHAT **DOES** MATTER IS THAT YOU HAVE BEEN GIVEN AN ORDER BY THE ALL-FATHER.
YOU HAVE ONE TURN OF THE EARTH TO ABDICATE YOUR FALSE THRONE AND LEAVE THE HALL OF JUSTICE.
ARTEMIS...PULL BACK AND MAKE CAMP.
NO!
WE HAVE THEM ON THEIR HEELS, WE CAN'T GIVE HIM TIME TO REGROUP AND FORTIFY HIS POSITION--
THERE IS NO "WE," MORTAL...
THERE IS ONLY THE WILL OF MY FATHER.
TELL YOUR CAPED FRIENDS TO STAND DOWN... OR **I WILL.**

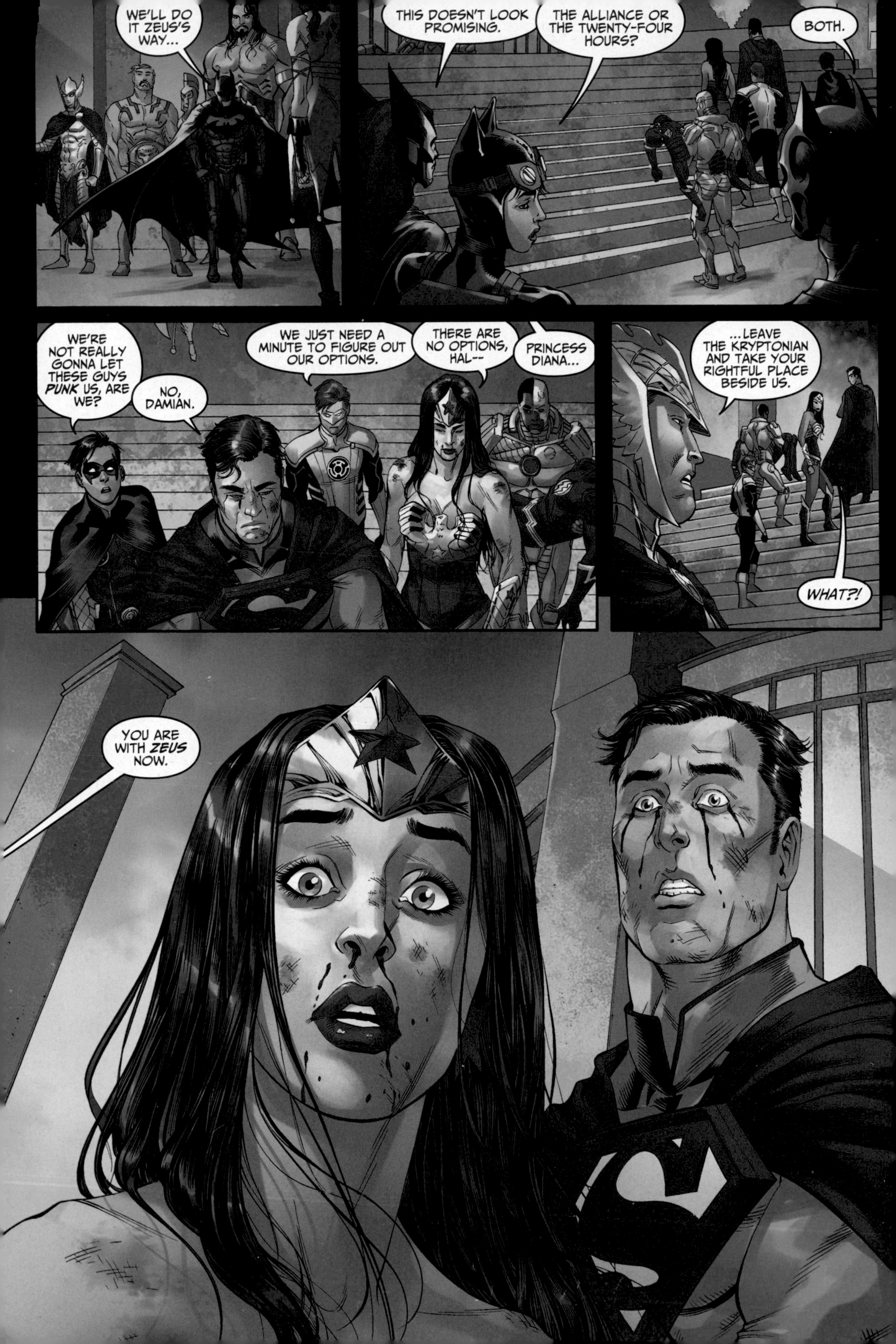
WE'LL DO IT ZEUS'S WAY...
THIS DOESN'T LOOK PROMISING.
THE ALLIANCE OR THE TWENTY-FOUR HOURS?
BOTH.
WE'RE NOT REALLY GONNA LET THESE GUYS PUNK US, ARE WE?
NO, DAMIAN.
WE JUST NEED A MINUTE TO FIGURE OUT OUR OPTIONS.
THERE ARE NO OPTIONS, HAL--
PRINCESS DIANA...
...LEAVE THE KRYPTONIAN AND TAKE YOUR RIGHTFUL PLACE BESIDE US.
WHAT?!
YOU ARE WITH ZEUS NOW.

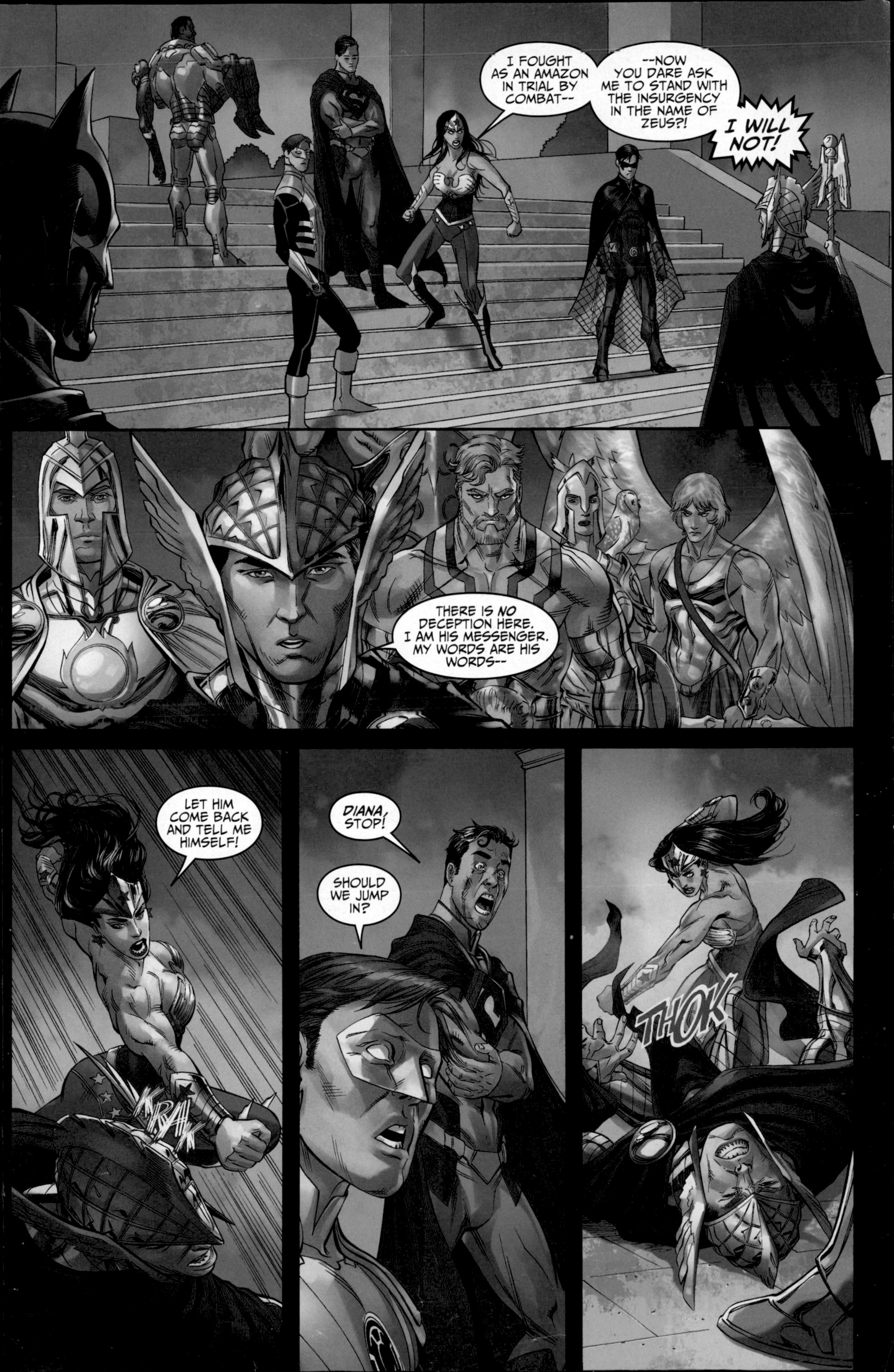
I FOUGHT AS AN AMAZON IN TRIAL BY COMBAT--
--NOW YOU DARE ASK ME TO STAND WITH THE INSURGENCY IN THE NAME OF ZEUS?!
I WILL NOT!
THERE IS NO DECEPTION HERE. I AM HIS MESSENGER. MY WORDS ARE HIS WORDS--
LET HIM COME BACK AND TELL ME HIMSELF!
KRAK
DIANA, STOP!
SHOULD WE JUMP IN?
THOK

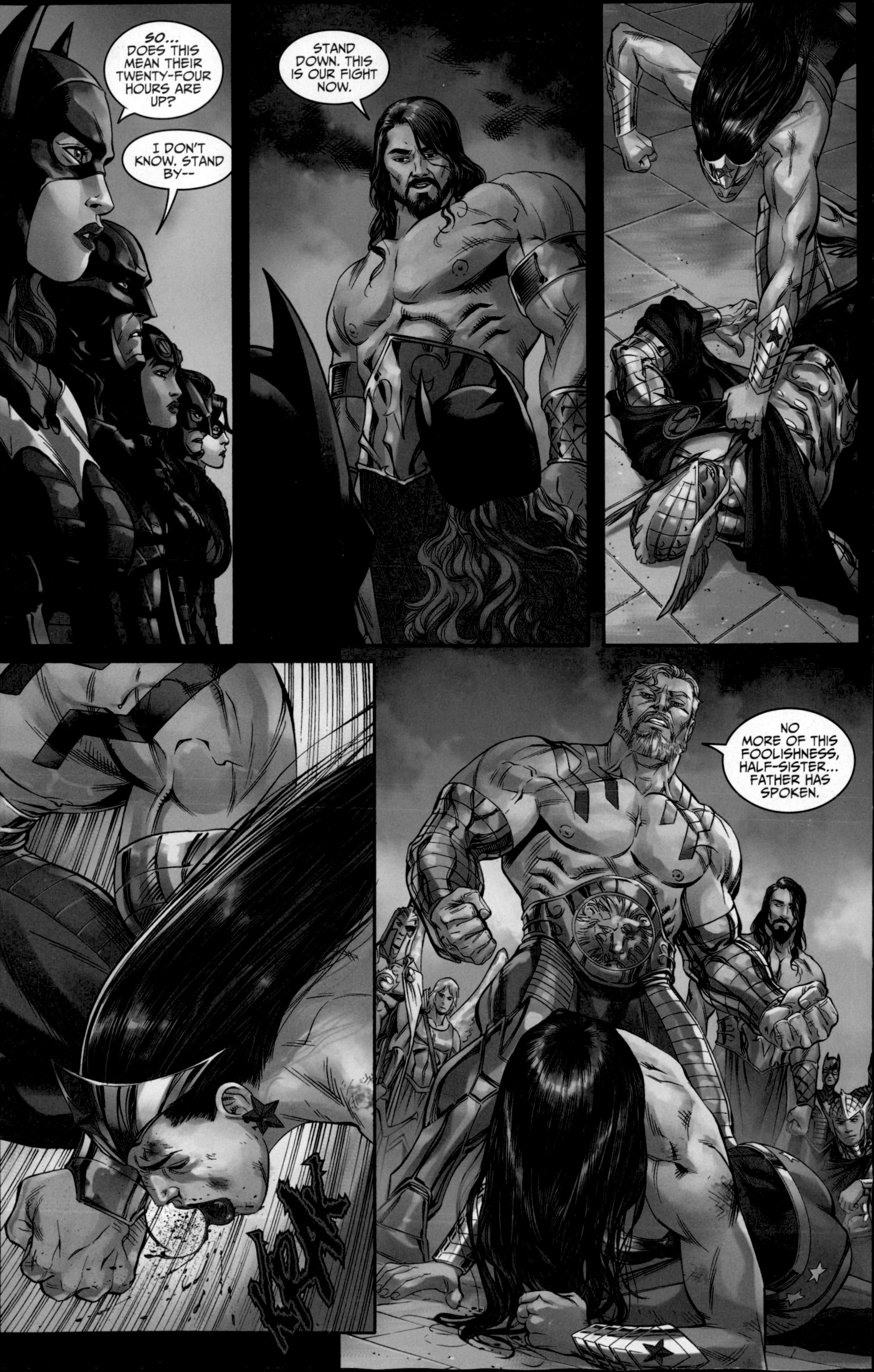
SO... DOES THIS MEAN THEIR TWENTY-FOUR HOURS ARE UP?
I DON'T KNOW. STAND BY--
STAND DOWN. THIS IS OUR FIGHT NOW.
KOF
NO MORE OF THIS FOOLISHNESS, HALF-SISTER... FATHER HAS SPOKEN.

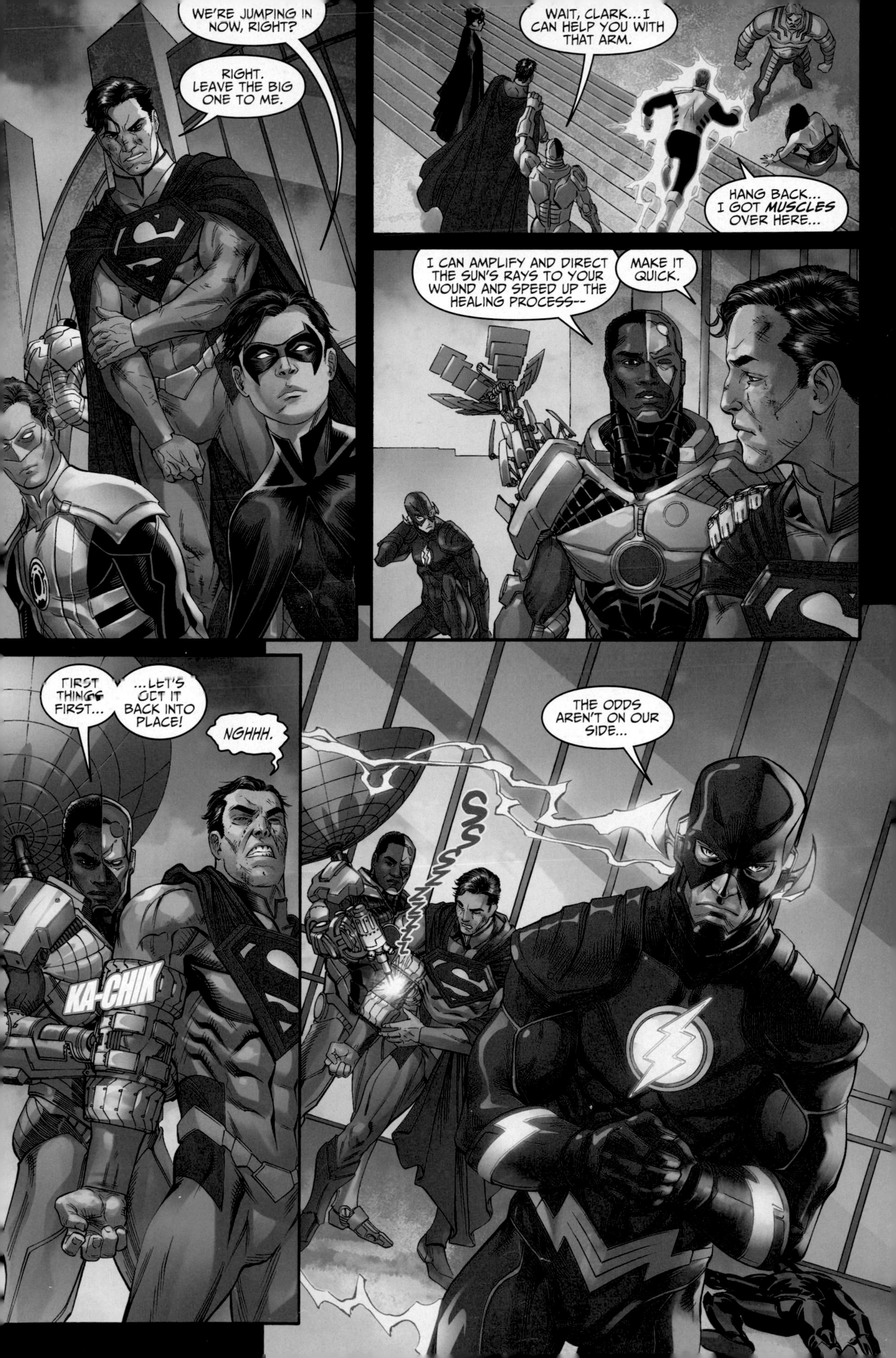
WE'RE JUMPING IN NOW, RIGHT?
RIGHT. LEAVE THE BIG ONE TO ME.
WAIT, CLARK...I CAN HELP YOU WITH THAT ARM.
HANG BACK... I GOT *MUSCLES* OVER HERE...
I CAN AMPLIFY AND DIRECT THE SUN'S RAYS TO YOUR WOUND AND SPEED UP THE HEALING PROCESS--
MAKE IT QUICK.
FIRST THINGS FIRST...
...LET'S GET IT BACK INTO PLACE!
NGHHH.
KA-CHIK
THE ODDS AREN'T ON OUR SIDE...

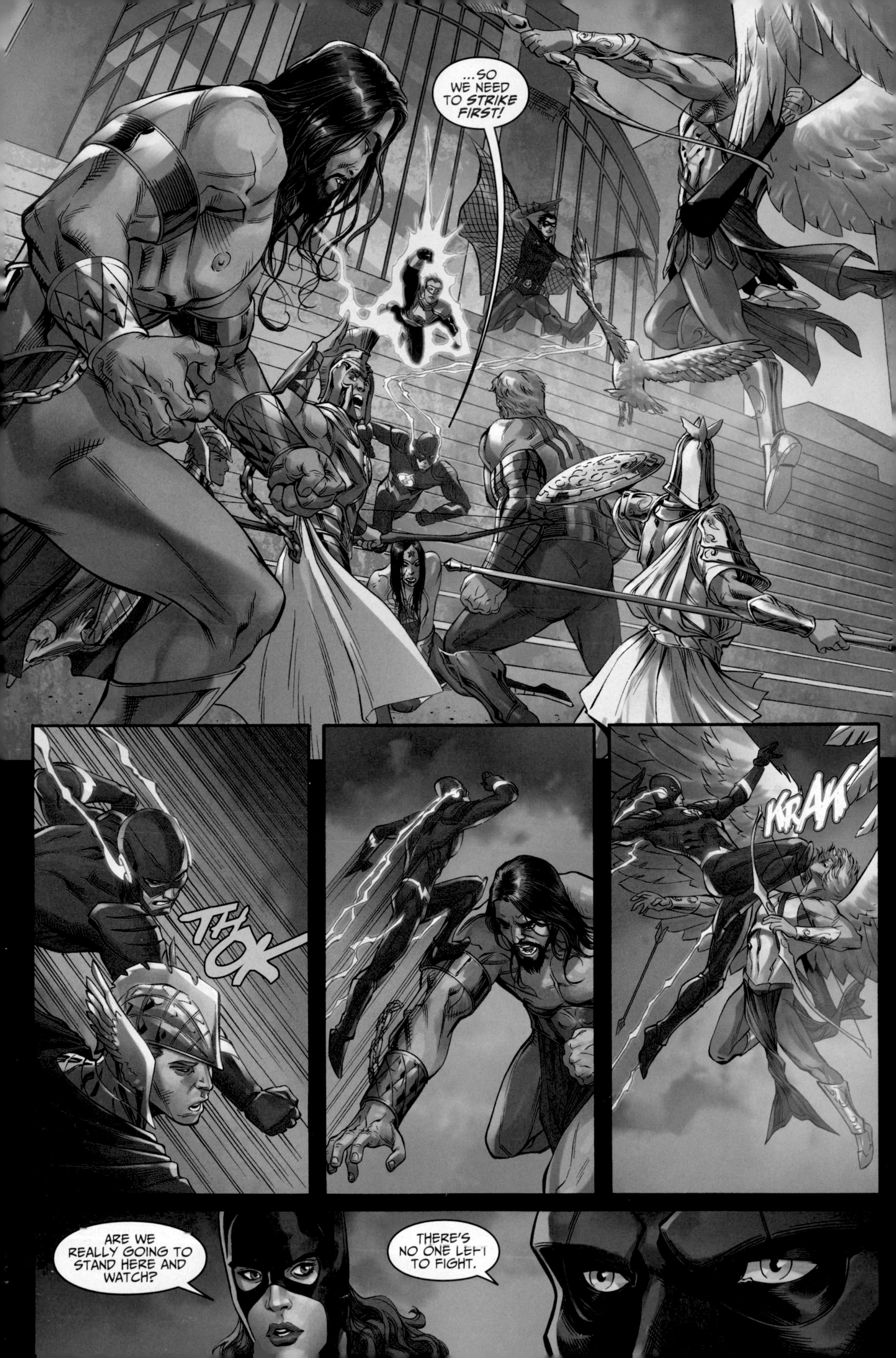
...SO WE NEED TO STRIKE FIRST!
THOK
KRAK
ARE WE REALLY GOING TO STAND HERE AND WATCH?
THERE'S NO ONE LEFT TO FIGHT.

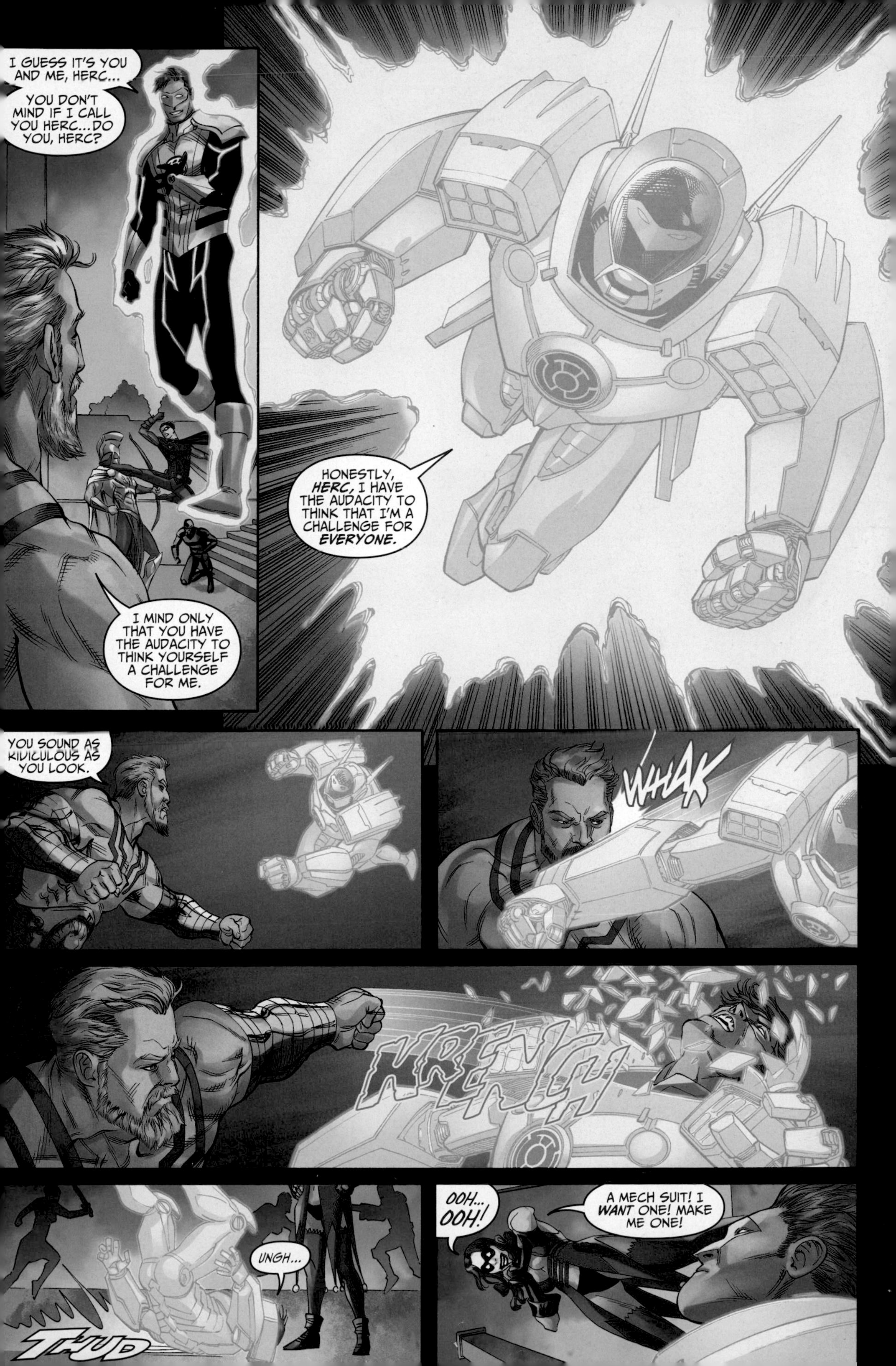
I GUESS IT'S YOU AND ME, HERC...
YOU DON'T MIND IF I CALL YOU HERC...DO YOU, HERC?
I MIND ONLY THAT YOU HAVE THE AUDACITY TO THINK YOURSELF A CHALLENGE FOR ME.
HONESTLY, HERC, I HAVE THE AUDACITY TO THINK THAT I'M A CHALLENGE FOR EVERYONE.
YOU SOUND AS RIDICULOUS AS YOU LOOK.
WHAK
KRENCH
UNGH...
THUD
OOH... OOH!
A MECH SUIT! I WANT ONE! MAKE ME ONE!

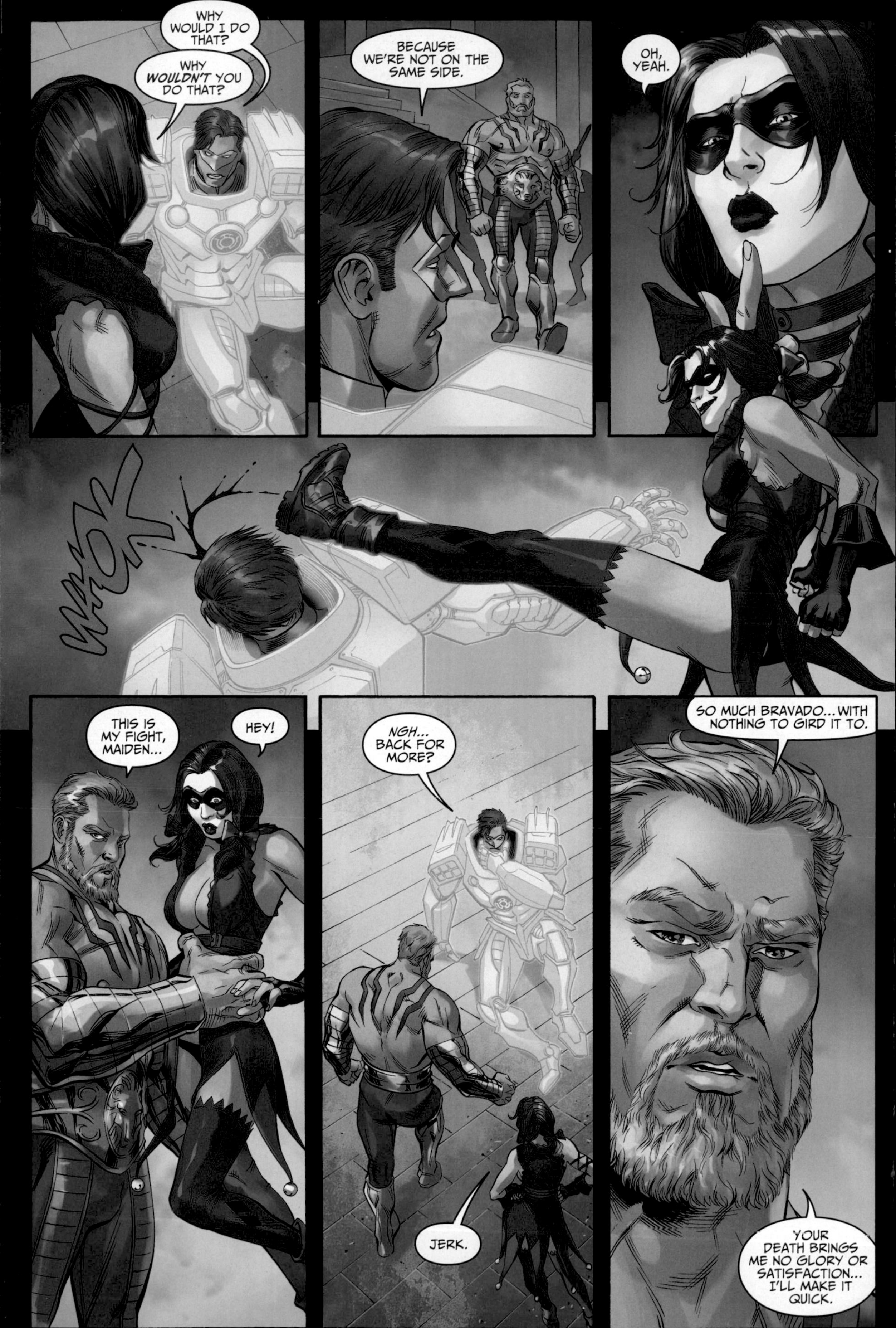
WHY WOULD I DO THAT?
WHY *WOULDN'T* YOU DO THAT?
BECAUSE WE'RE NOT ON THE SAME SIDE.
OH, YEAH.
WHOK
THIS IS MY FIGHT, MAIDEN...
HEY!
NGH... BACK FOR MORE?
JERK.
SO MUCH BRAVADO...WITH NOTHING TO GIRD IT TO.
YOUR DEATH BRINGS ME NO GLORY OR SATISFACTION... I'LL MAKE IT QUICK.

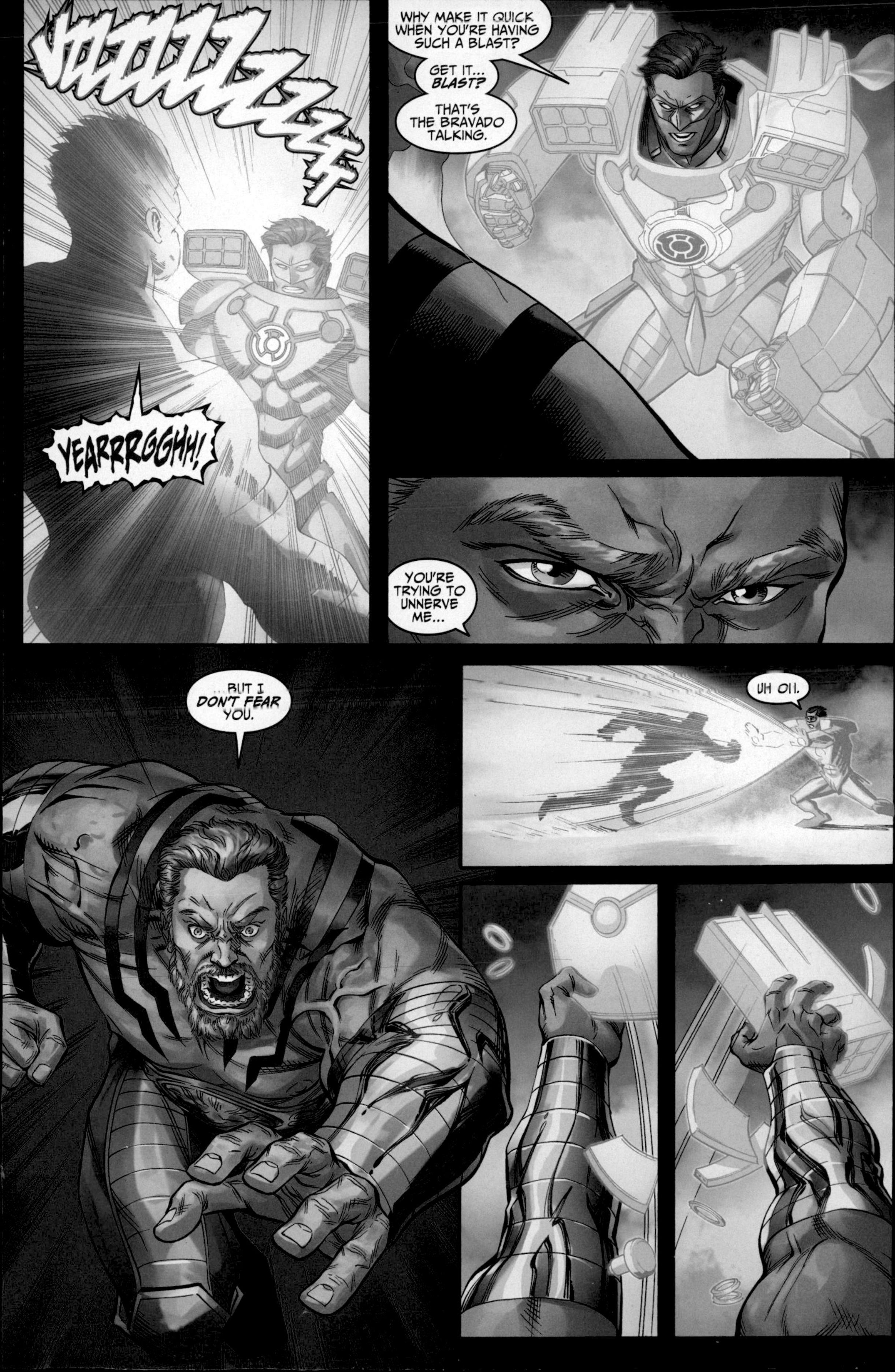

VVRRRZZZH
YEARRRGGHH!
WHY MAKE IT QUICK WHEN YOU'RE HAVING SUCH A BLAST?
GET IT... BLAST?
THAT'S THE BRAVADO TALKING.
YOU'RE TRYING TO UNNERVE ME...
...BUT I DON'T FEAR YOU.
UH OH.

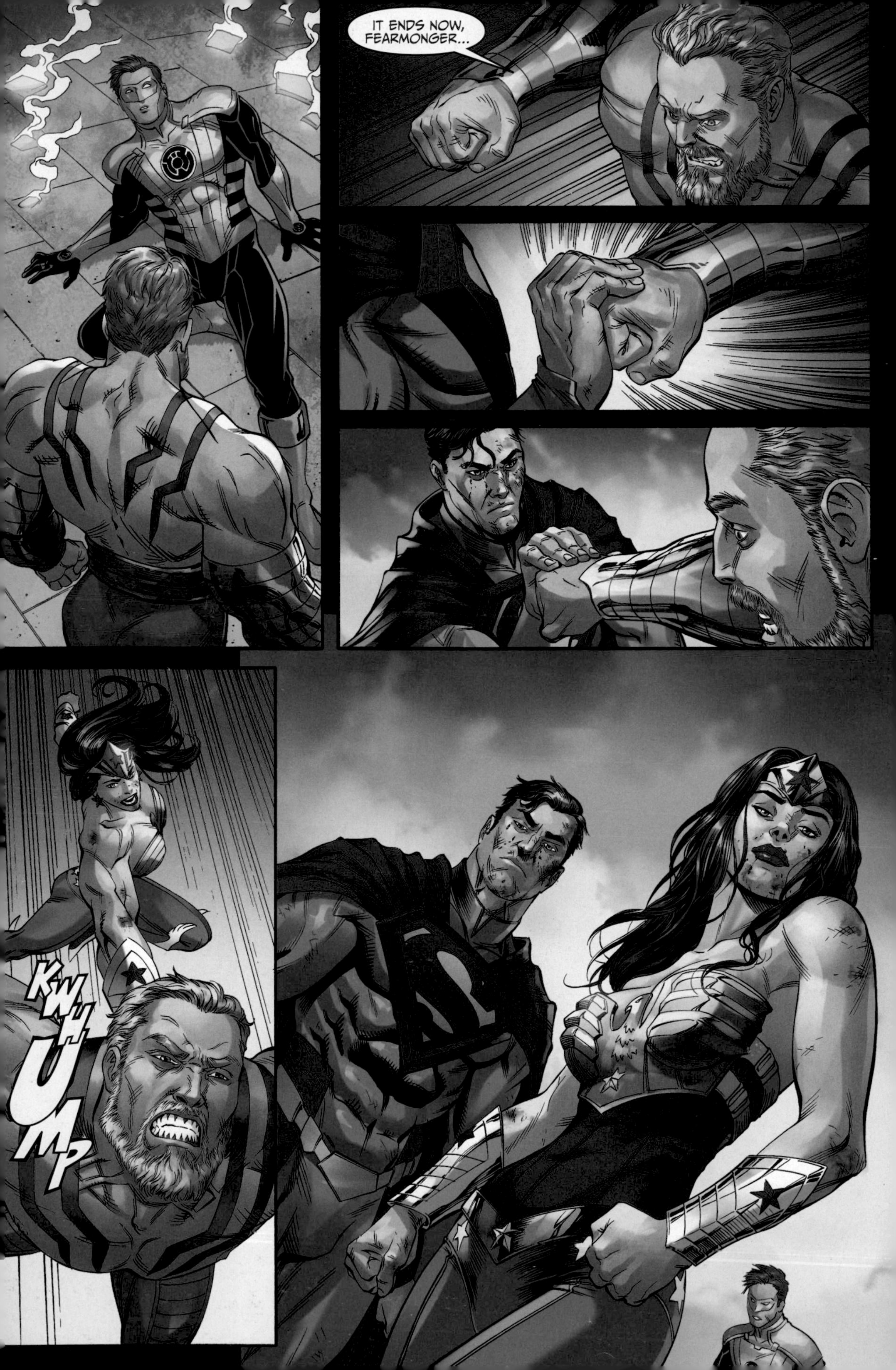
IT ENDS NOW, FEARMONGER...
KWHUMP

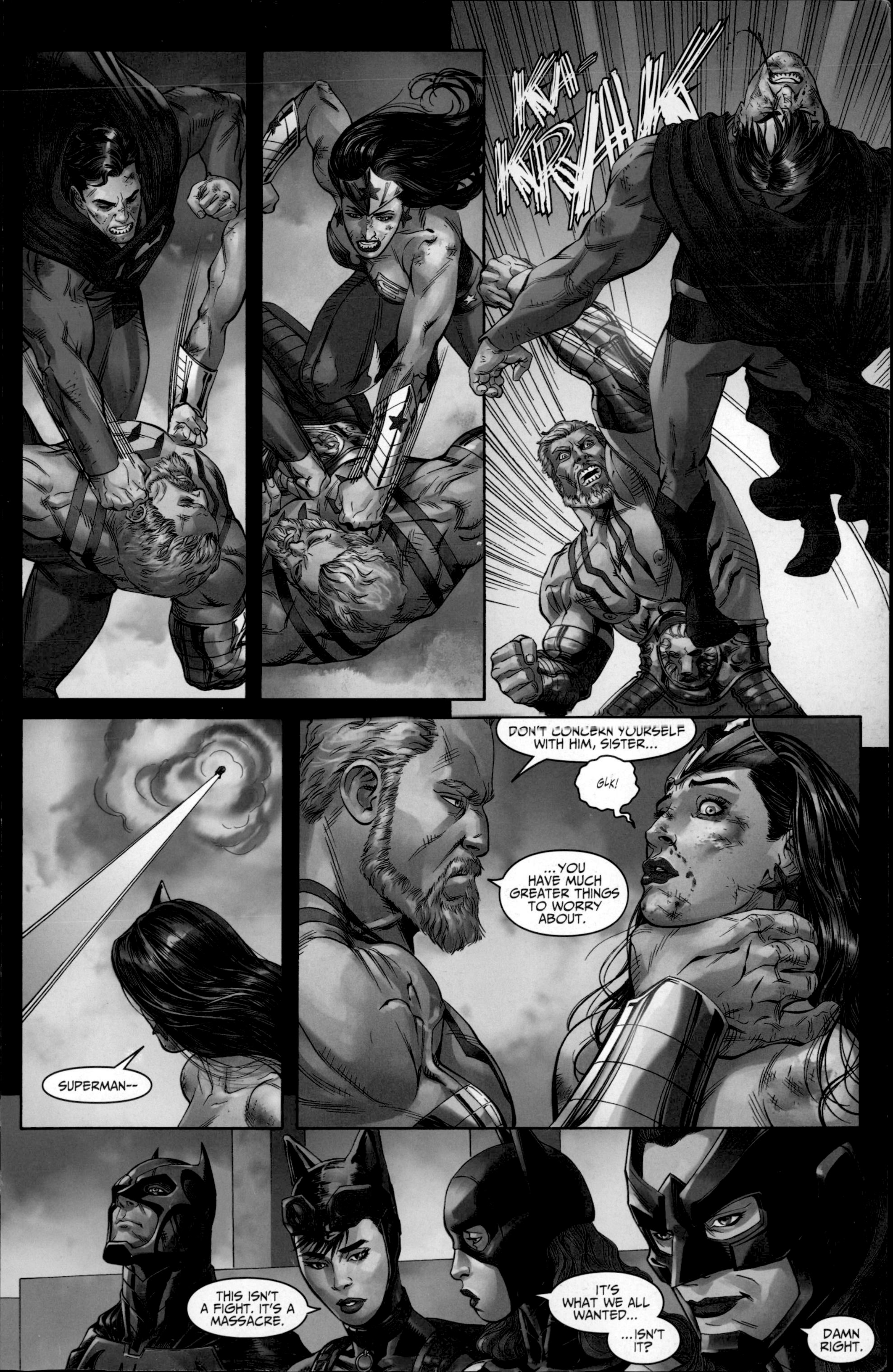
KA-KRAKK
SUPERMAN--
DON'T CONCERN YOURSELF WITH HIM, SISTER...
GLK!
...YOU HAVE MUCH GREATER THINGS TO WORRY ABOUT.
THIS ISN'T A FIGHT. IT'S A MASSACRE.
IT'S WHAT WE ALL WANTED...
...ISN'T IT?
DAMN RIGHT.

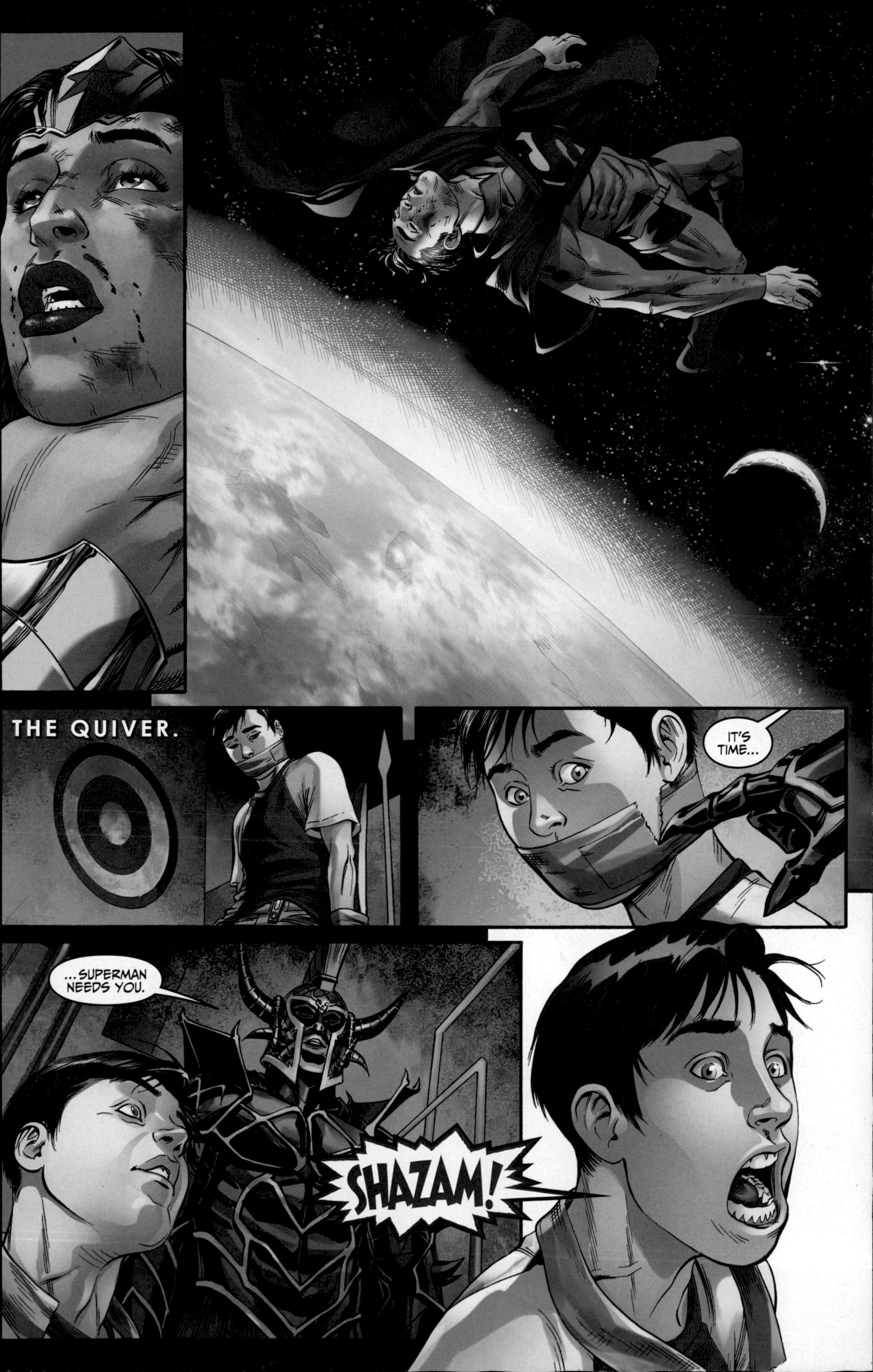
THE QUIVER.
IT'S TIME...
...SUPERMAN NEEDS YOU.
SHAZAM!

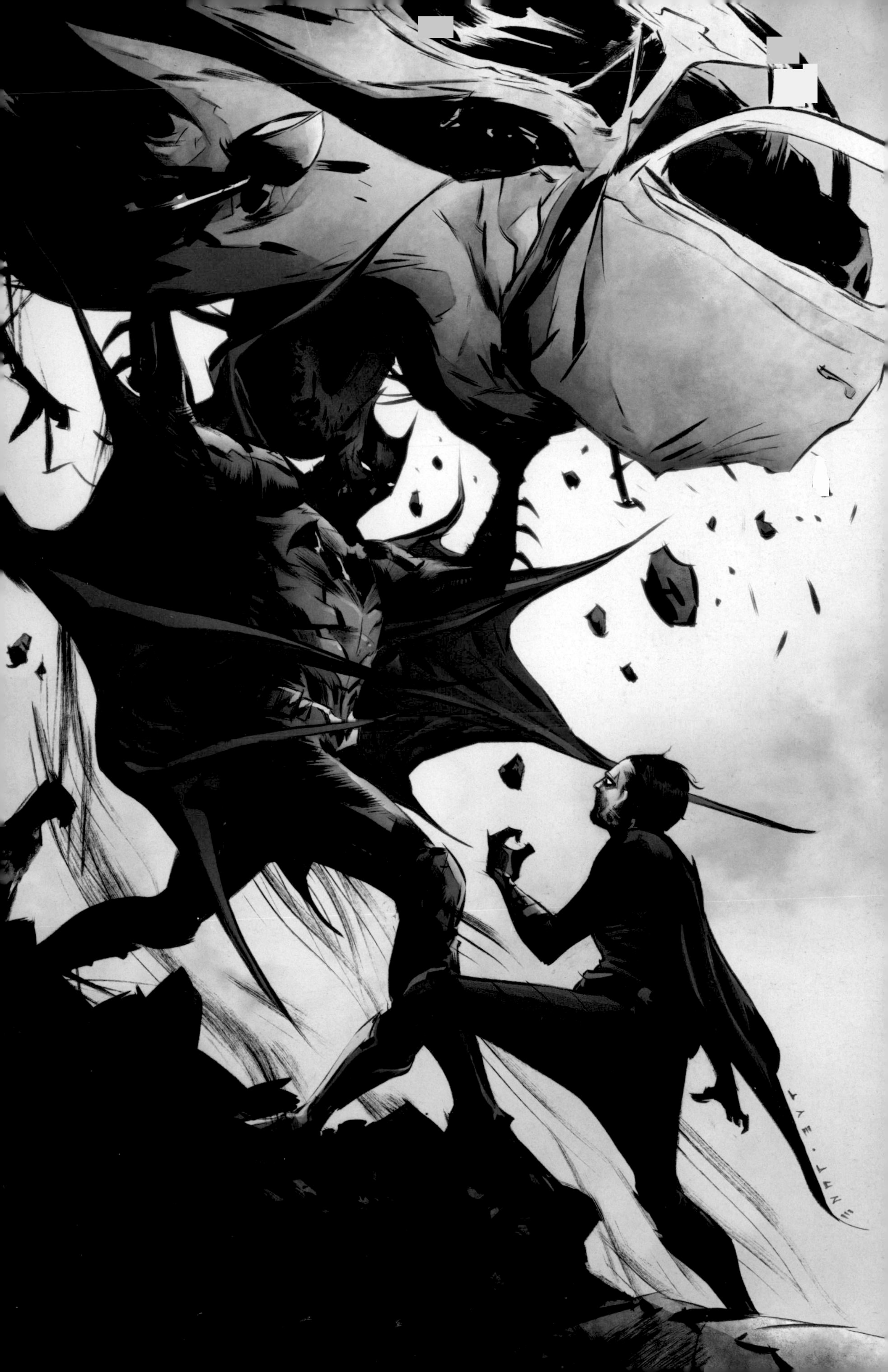

"Strength of Hercules" **Bruno Redondo** Penciller **Juan Albarran** Inker **Rex Lokus** Colorist
"The Old and the New" **Xermanico & Tom Derenick** Artists **Rex Lokus** Colorist
Cover Art by **Jae Lee & June Chun**

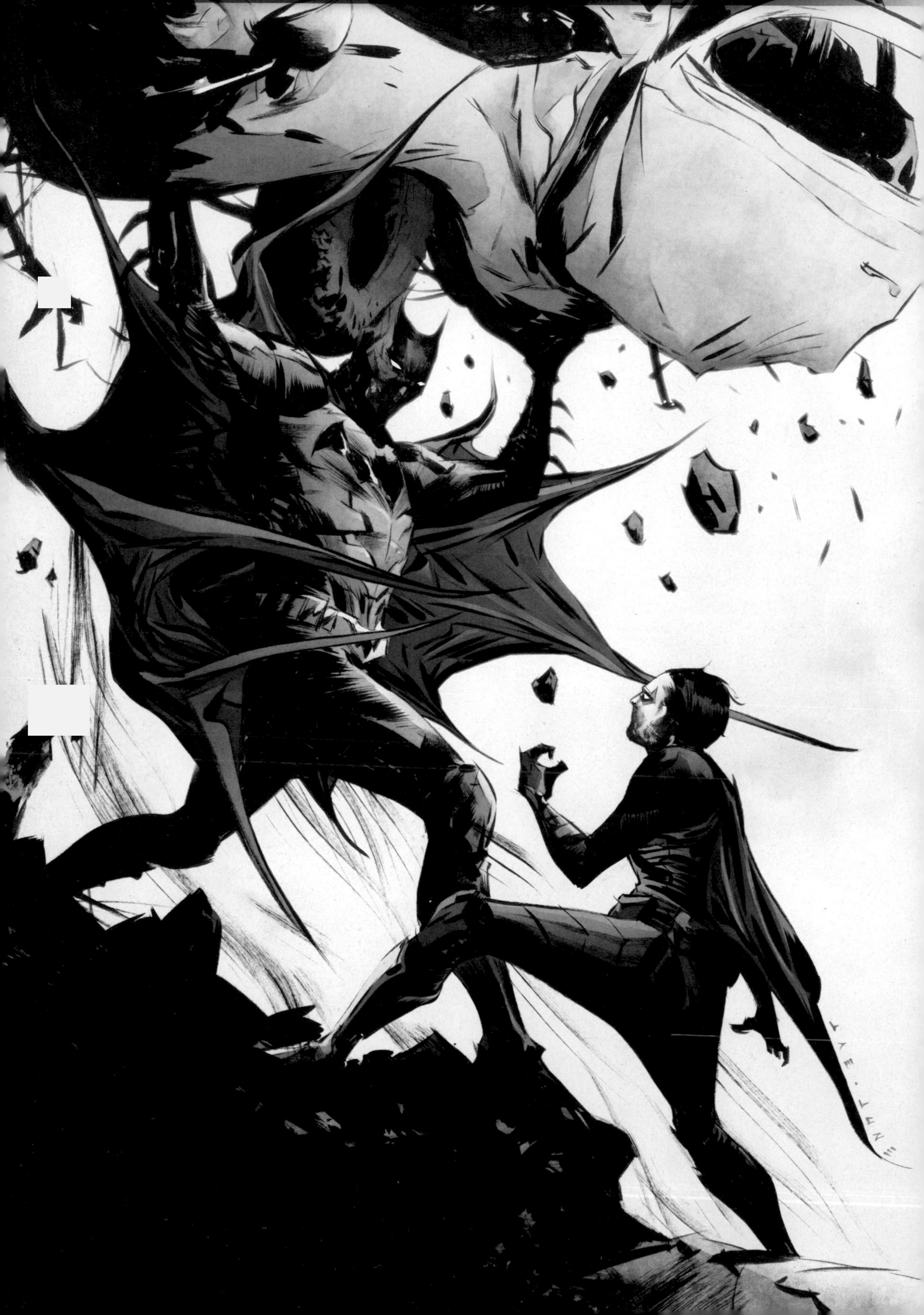

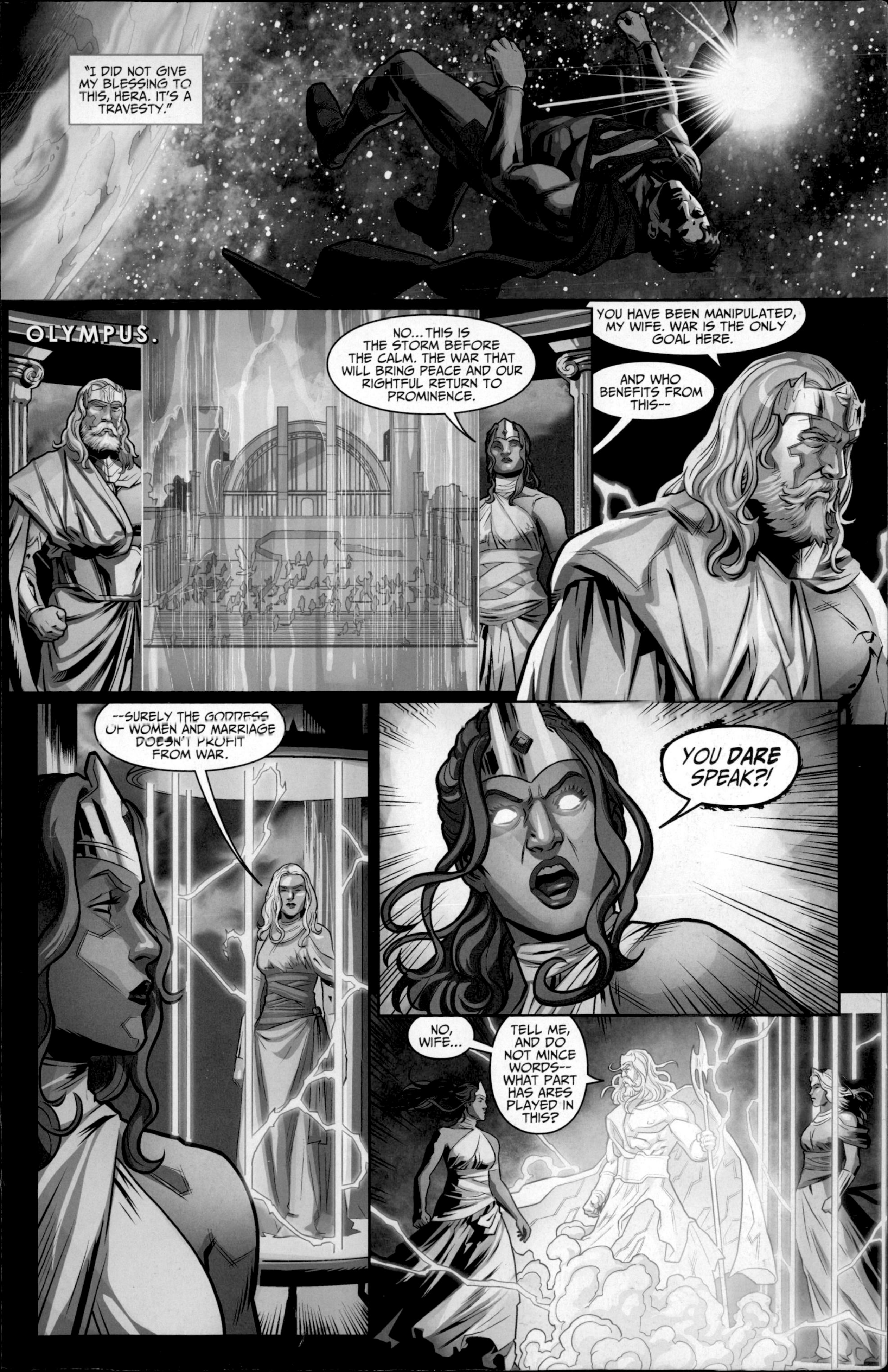
"I DID NOT GIVE MY BLESSING TO THIS, HERA. IT'S A TRAVESTY."
OLYMPUS.
NO...THIS IS THE STORM BEFORE THE CALM. THE WAR THAT WILL BRING PEACE AND OUR RIGHTFUL RETURN TO PROMINENCE.
YOU HAVE BEEN MANIPULATED, MY WIFE. WAR IS THE ONLY GOAL HERE.
AND WHO BENEFITS FROM THIS--
--SURELY THE GODDESS OF WOMEN AND MARRIAGE DOESN'T PROFIT FROM WAR.
YOU DARE SPEAK?!
NO, WIFE...
TELL ME, AND DO NOT MINCE WORDS-- WHAT PART HAS ARES PLAYED IN THIS?

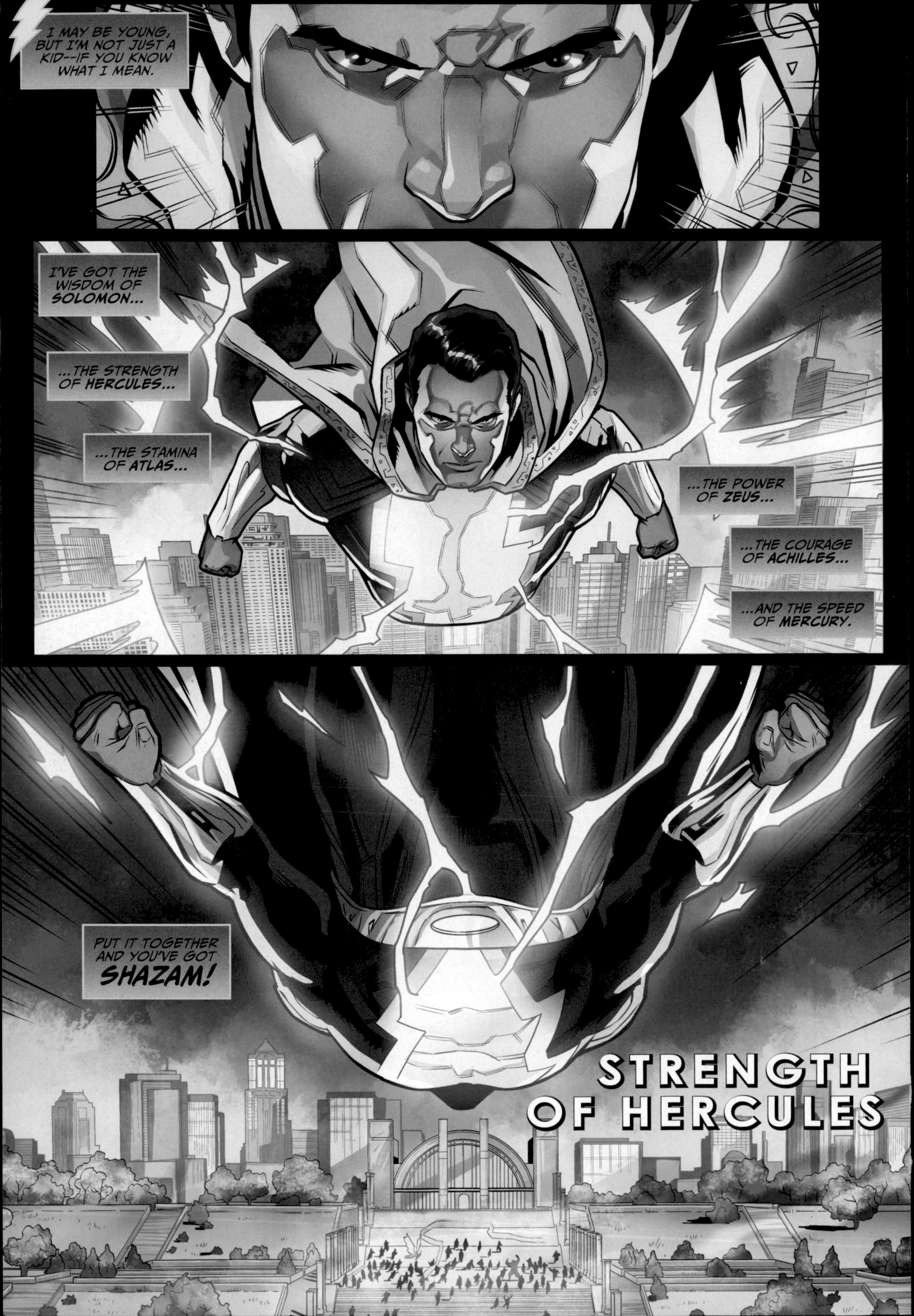

I MAY BE YOUNG, BUT I'M NOT JUST A KID--IF YOU KNOW WHAT I MEAN.
I'VE GOT THE WISDOM OF SOLOMON...
...THE STRENGTH OF HERCULES...
...THE STAMINA OF ATLAS...
...THE POWER OF ZEUS...
...THE COURAGE OF ACHILLES...
...AND THE SPEED OF MERCURY.
PUT IT TOGETHER AND YOU'VE GOT SHAZAM!
STRENGTH OF HERCULES

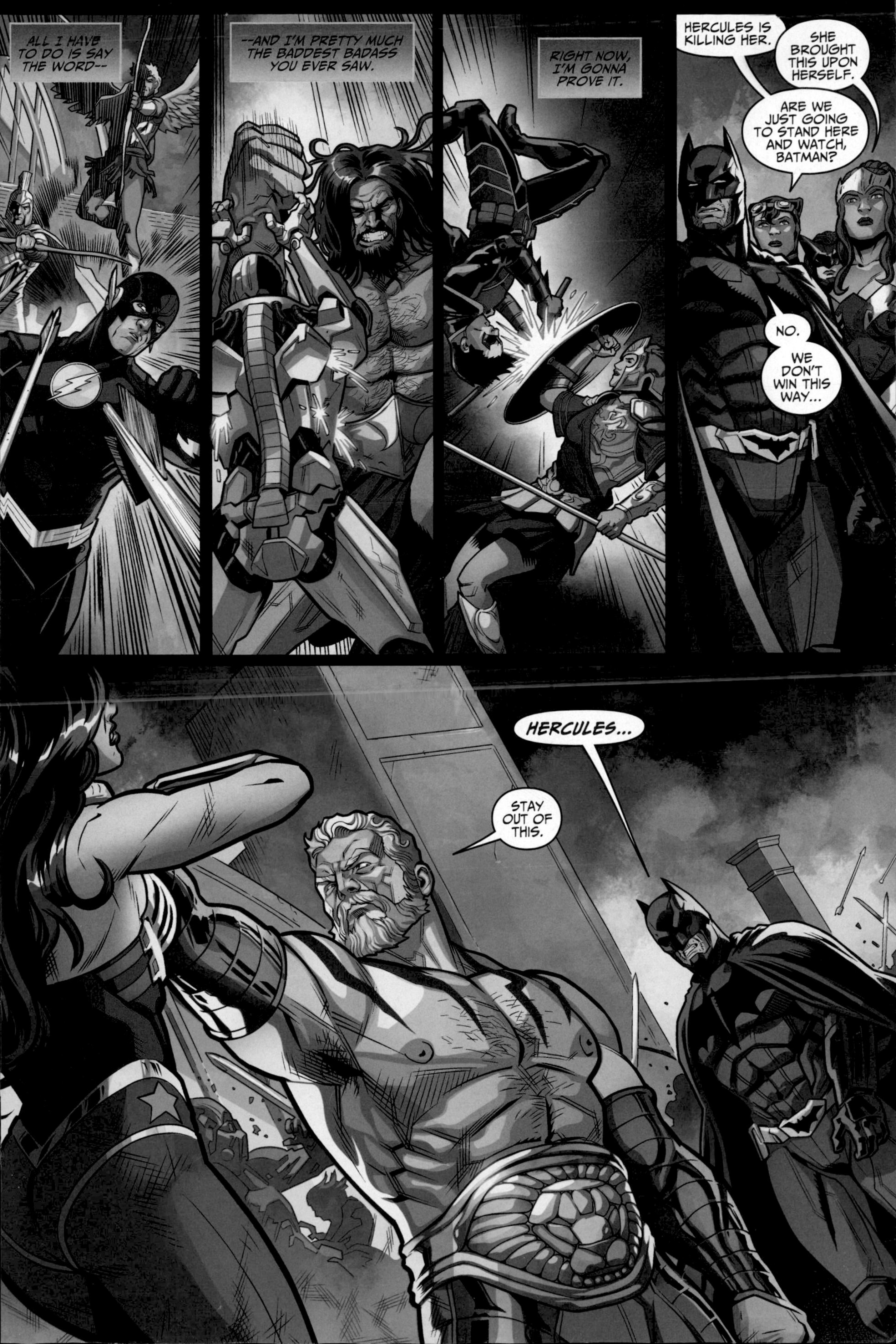
ALL I HAVE TO DO IS SAY THE WORD--
--AND I'M PRETTY MUCH THE BADDEST BADASS YOU EVER SAW.
RIGHT NOW, I'M GONNA PROVE IT.
HERCULES IS KILLING HER.
SHE BROUGHT THIS UPON HERSELF.
ARE WE JUST GOING TO STAND HERE AND WATCH, BATMAN?
NO.
WE DON'T WIN THIS WAY...
HERCULES...
STAY OUT OF THIS.

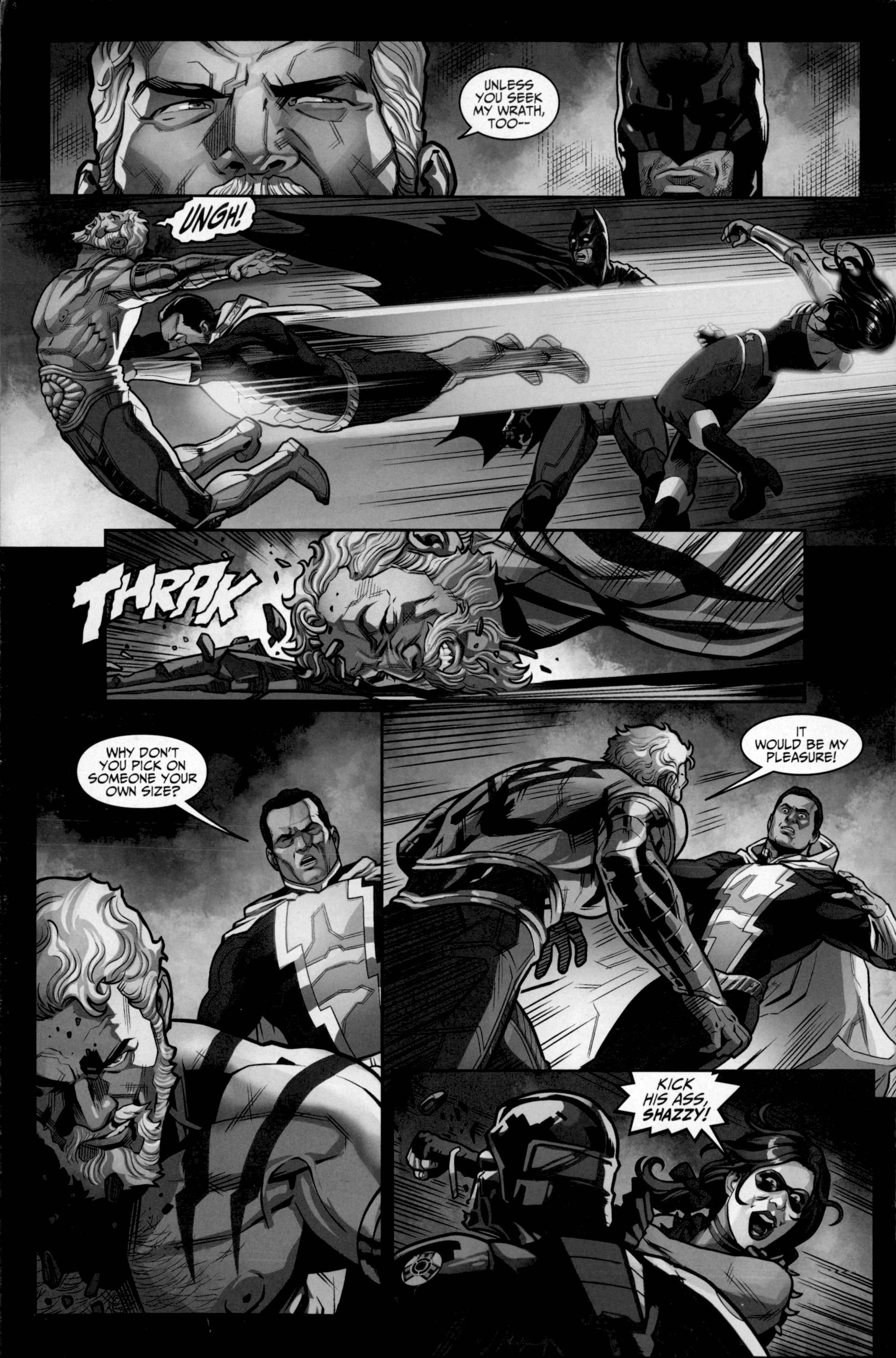
UNLESS YOU SEEK MY WRATH, TOO--
UNGH!
THRAK
WHY DON'T YOU PICK ON SOMEONE YOUR OWN SIZE?
IT WOULD BE MY PLEASURE!
KICK HIS ASS, SHAZZY!

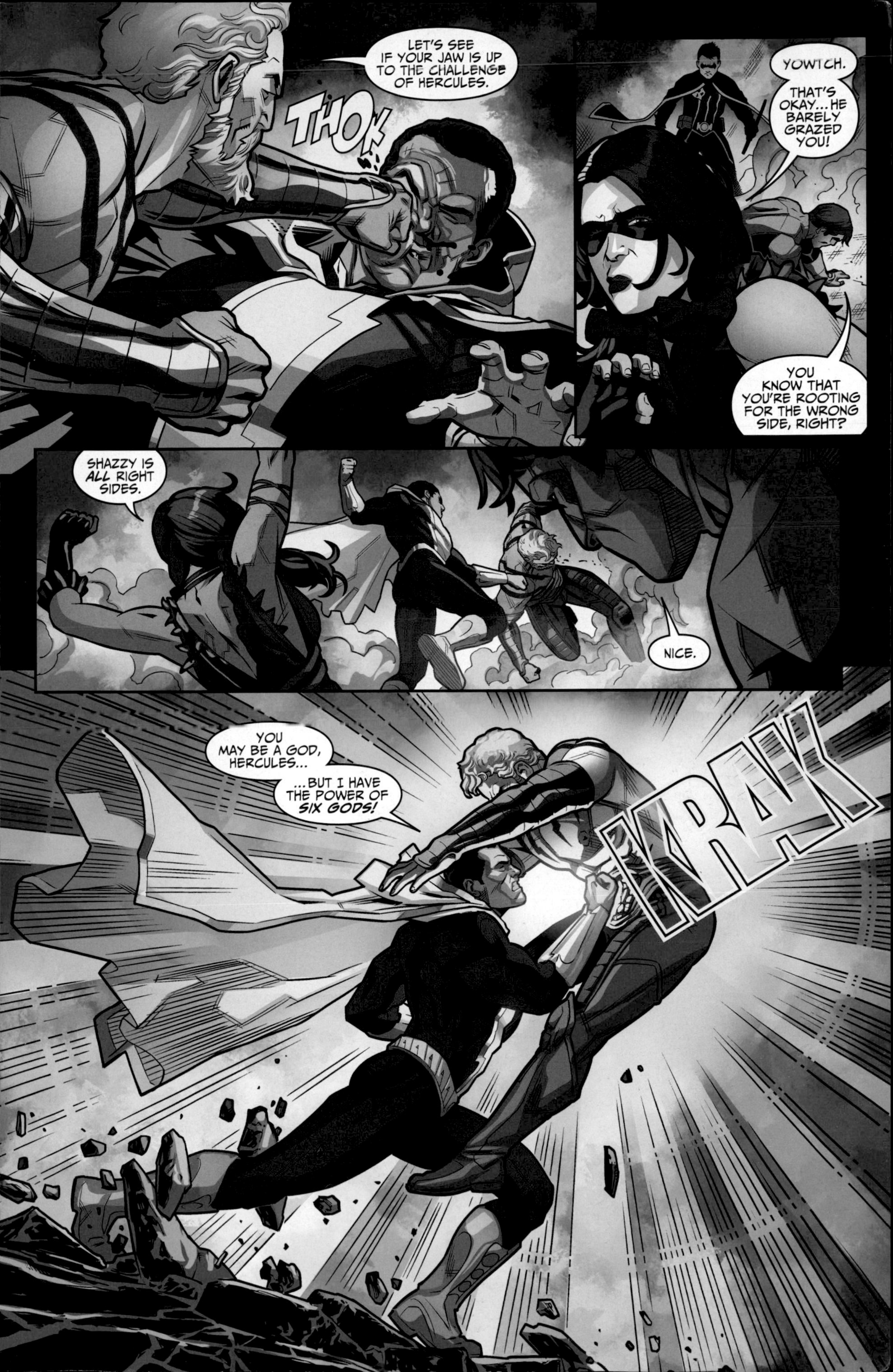
LET'S SEE IF YOUR JAW IS UP TO THE CHALLENGE OF HERCULES.
THOK
YOWTCH.
THAT'S OKAY... HE BARELY GRAZED YOU!
YOU KNOW THAT YOU'RE ROOTING FOR THE WRONG SIDE, RIGHT?
SHAZZY IS ALL RIGHT SIDES.
NICE.
YOU MAY BE A GOD, HERCULES...
...BUT I HAVE THE POWER OF SIX GODS!
KRAK

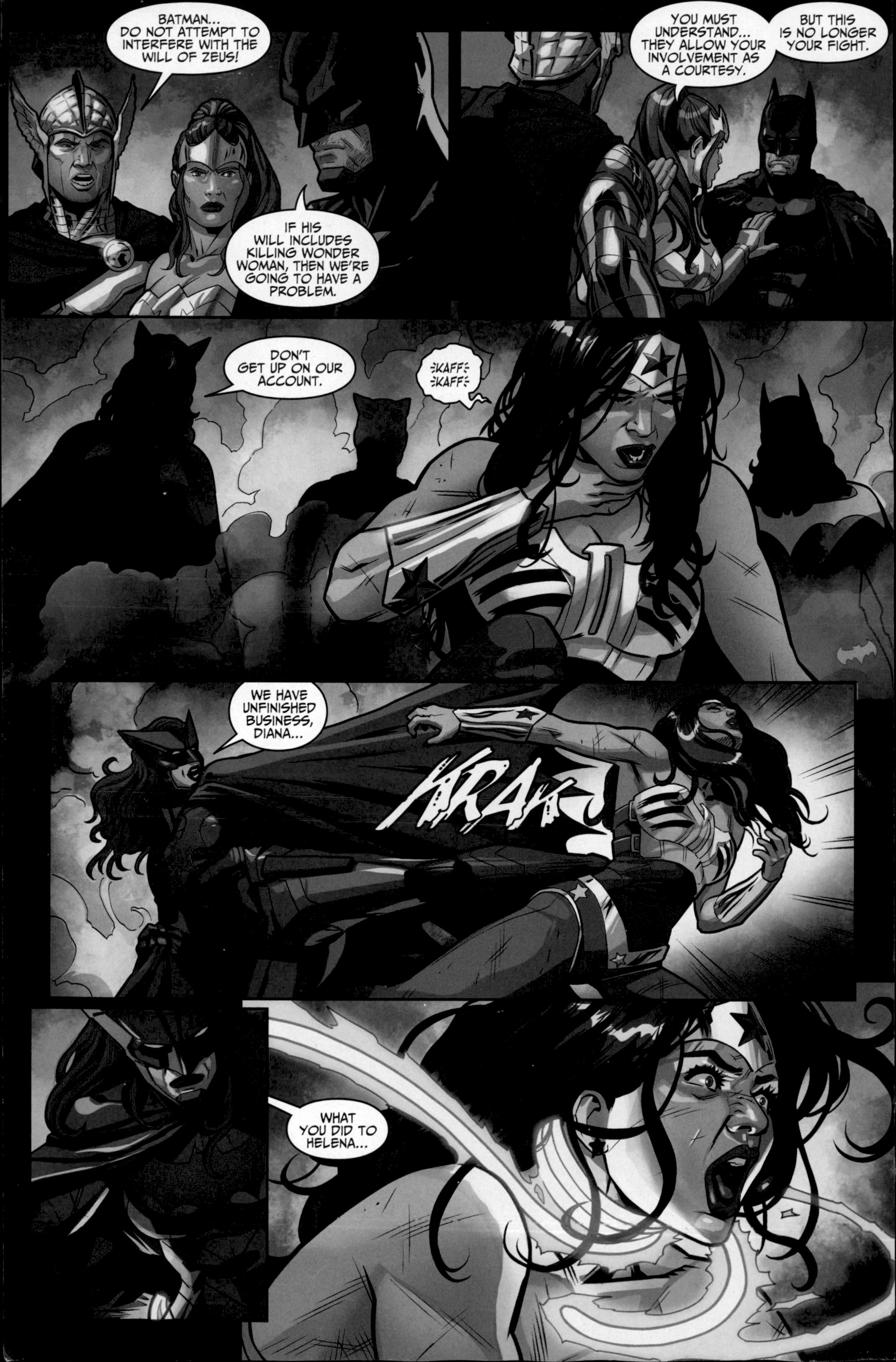
BATMAN... DO NOT ATTEMPT TO INTERFERE WITH THE WILL OF ZEUS!
IF HIS WILL INCLUDES KILLING WONDER WOMAN, THEN WE'RE GOING TO HAVE A PROBLEM.
YOU MUST UNDERSTAND... THEY ALLOW YOUR INVOLVEMENT AS A COURTESY.
BUT THIS IS NO LONGER YOUR FIGHT.
DON'T GET UP ON OUR ACCOUNT.
KAFF KAFF
WE HAVE UNFINISHED BUSINESS, DIANA...
KRAK
WHAT YOU DID TO HELENA...

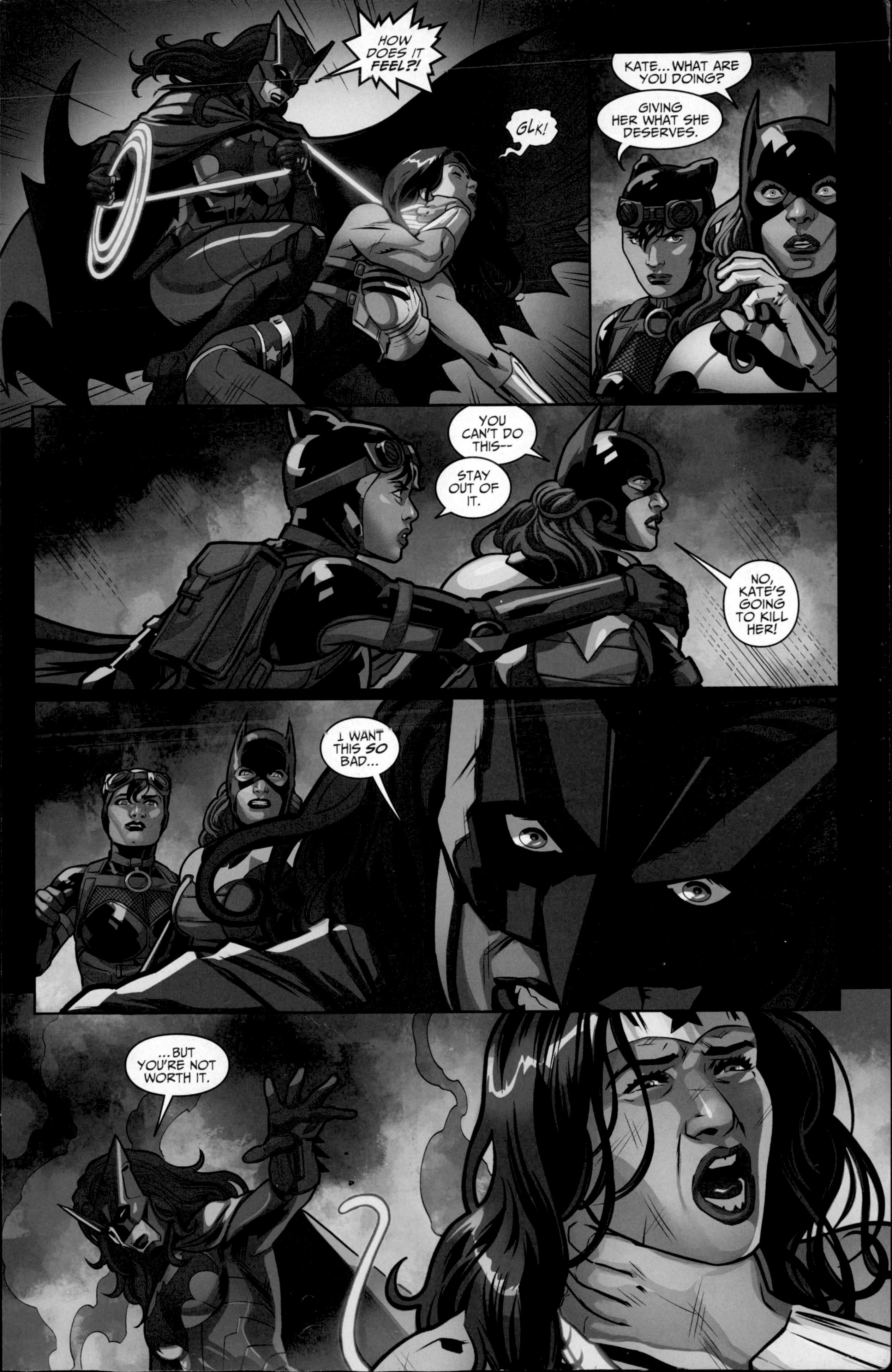
HOW DOES IT FEEL?!
GLK!
KATE... WHAT ARE YOU DOING?
GIVING HER WHAT SHE DESERVES.
YOU CAN'T DO THIS--
STAY OUT OF IT.
NO, KATE'S GOING TO KILL HER!
I WANT THIS SO BAD...
...BUT YOU'RE NOT WORTH IT.

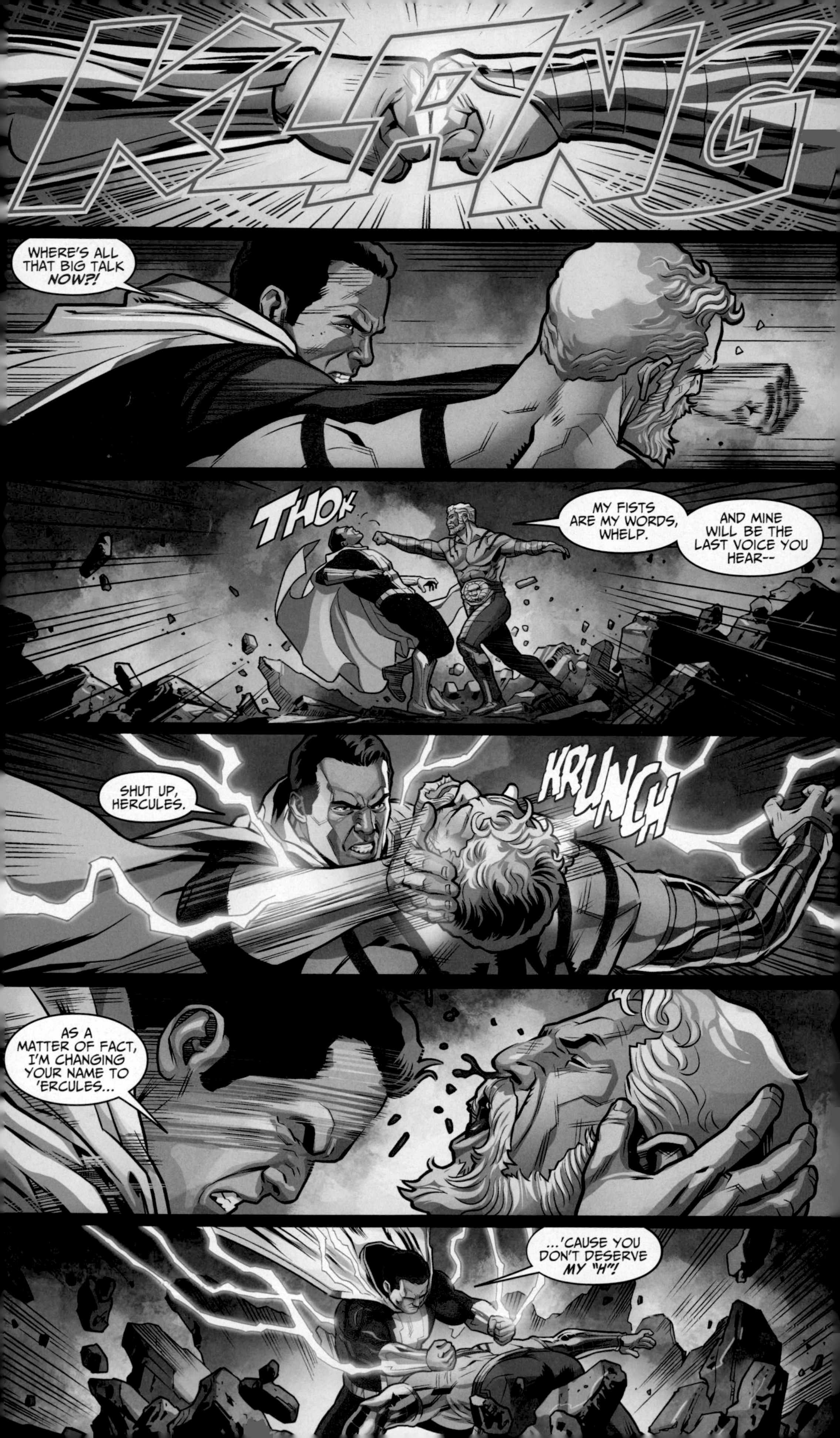

KLANG
WHERE'S ALL THAT BIG TALK NOW?!
THOK
MY FISTS ARE MY WORDS, WHELP.
AND MINE WILL BE THE LAST VOICE YOU HEAR--
SHUT UP, HERCULES.
KRUNCH
AS A MATTER OF FACT, I'M CHANGING YOUR NAME TO 'ERCULES...
...'CAUSE YOU DON'T DESERVE MY "H"!

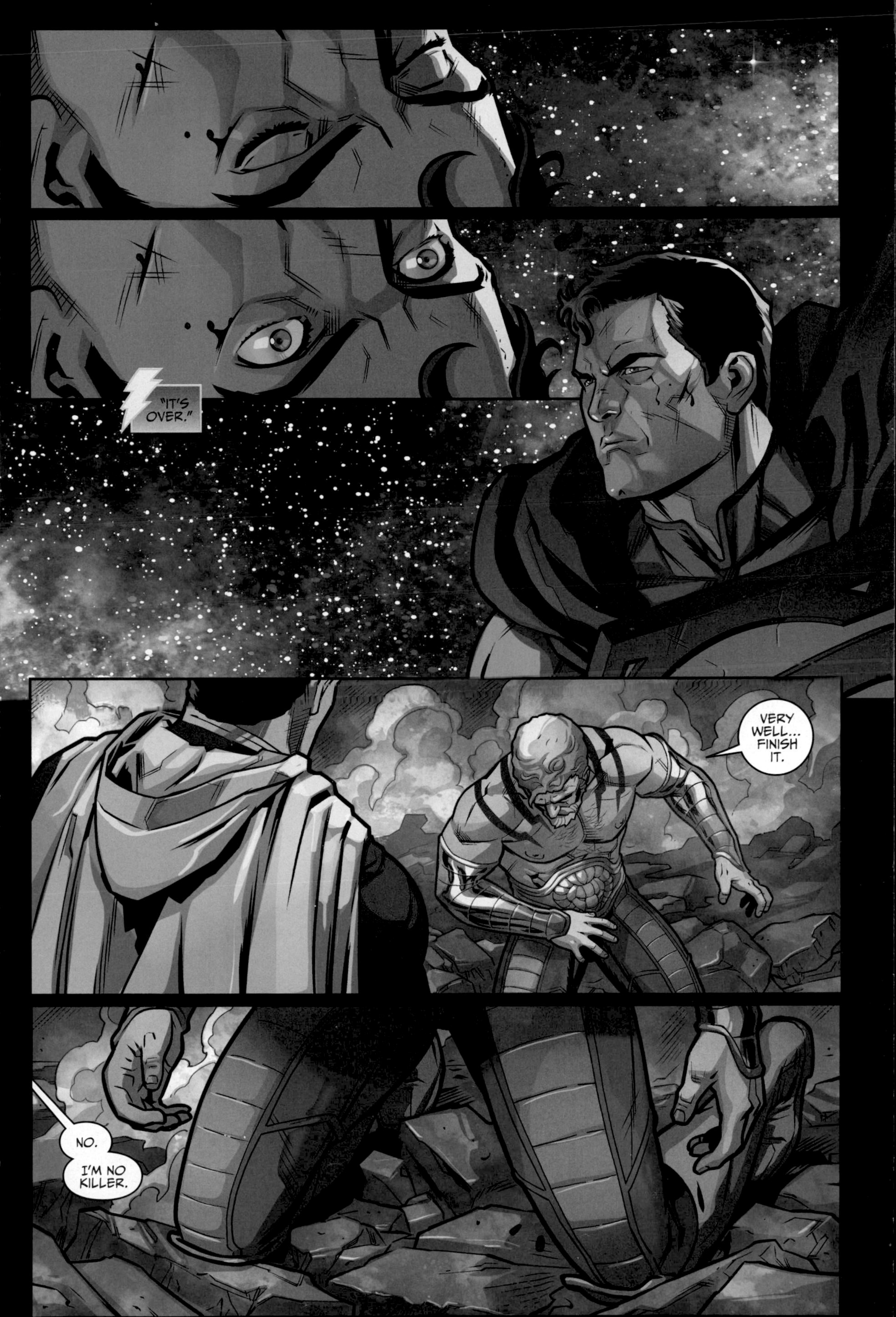
"IT'S OVER."
VERY WELL... FINISH IT.
NO.
I'M NO KILLER.

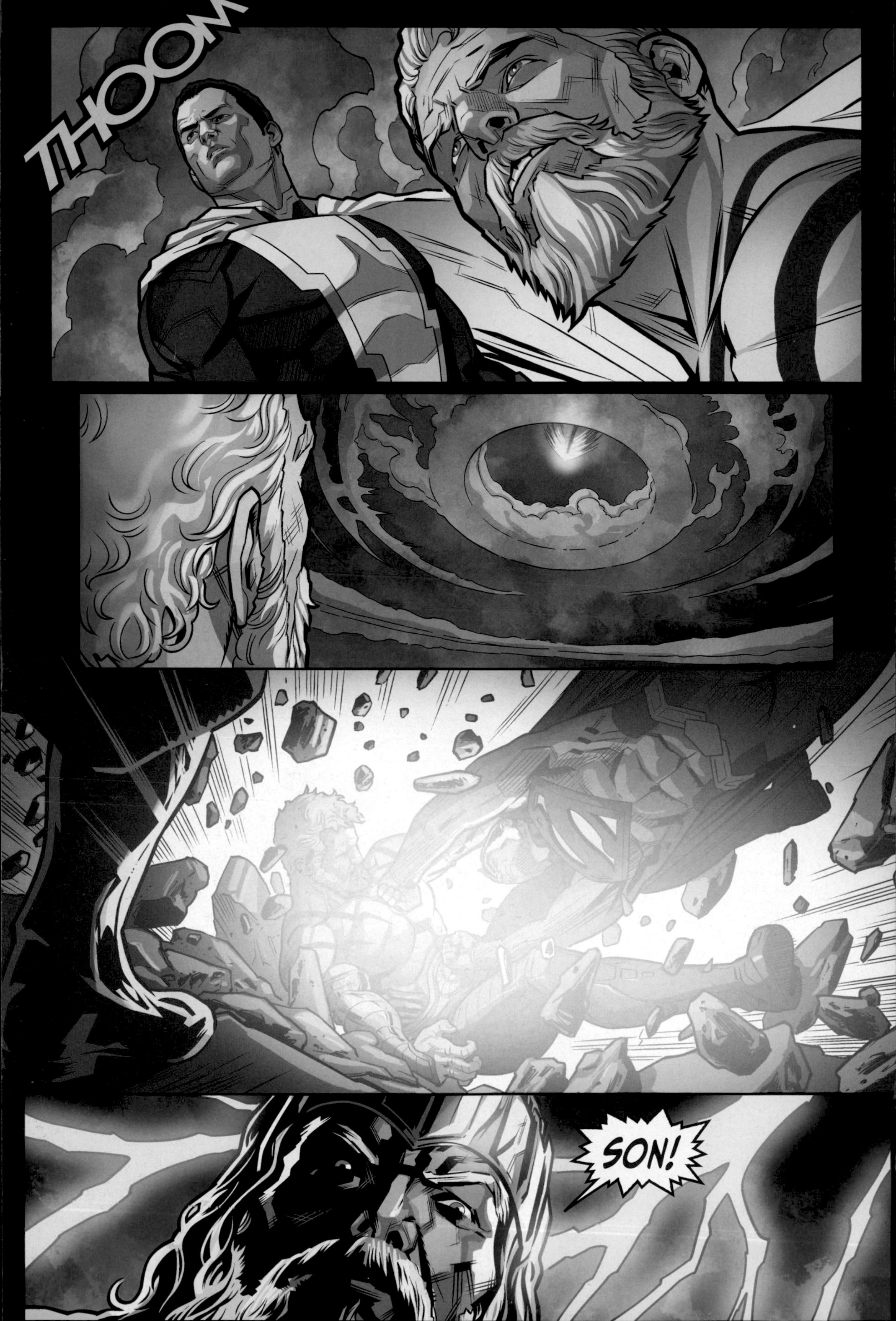
THOOM
SON!

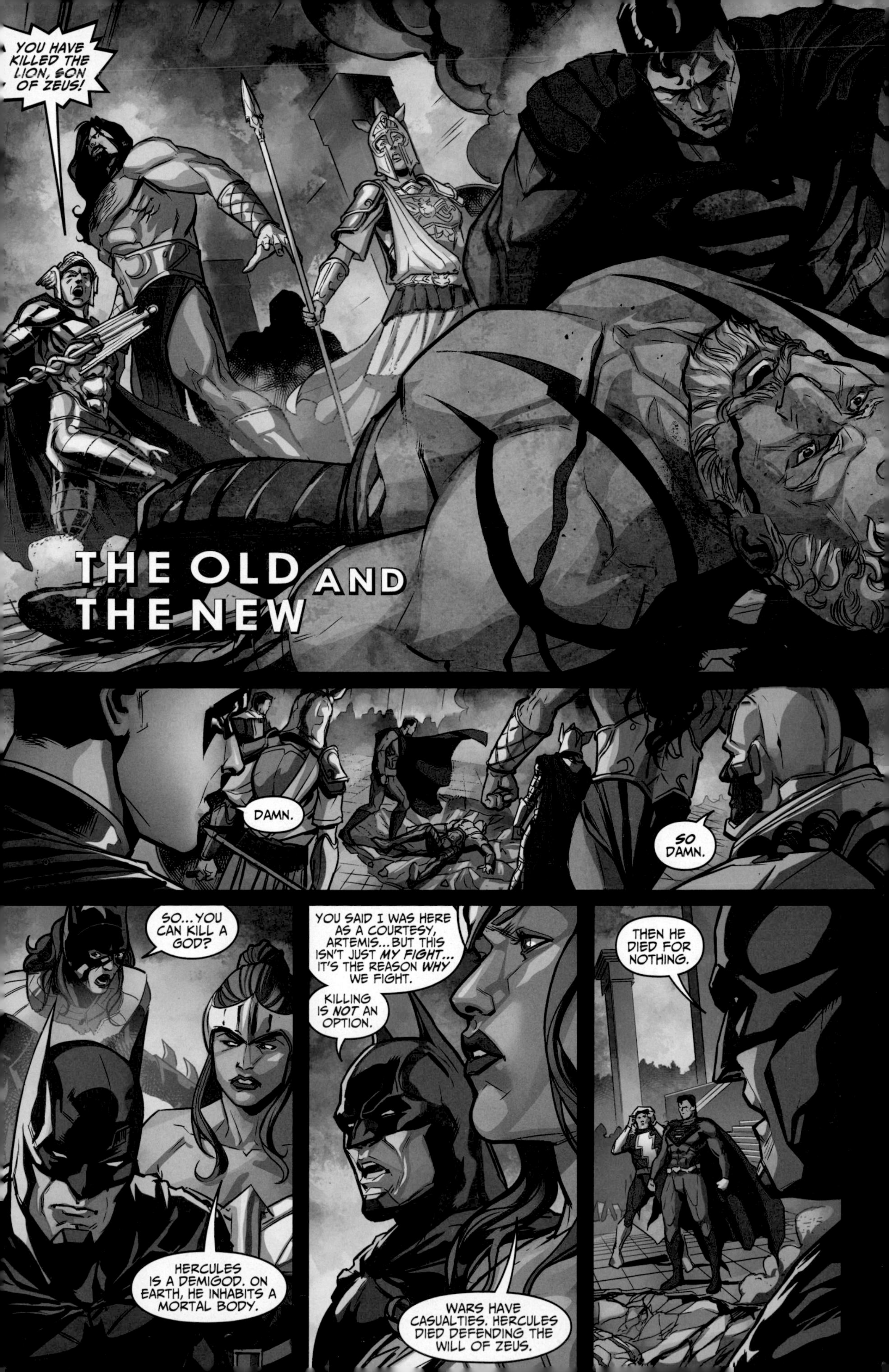

YOU HAVE KILLED THE LION, SON OF ZEUS!
THE OLD AND THE NEW
DAMN.
SO DAMN.
SO... YOU CAN KILL A GOD?
HERCULES IS A DEMIGOD. ON EARTH, HE INHABITS A MORTAL BODY.
YOU SAID I WAS HERE AS A COURTESY, ARTEMIS... BUT THIS ISN'T JUST MY FIGHT... IT'S THE REASON WHY WE FIGHT.
KILLING IS NOT AN OPTION.
WARS HAVE CASUALTIES. HERCULES DIED DEFENDING THE WILL OF ZEUS.
THEN HE DIED FOR NOTHING.

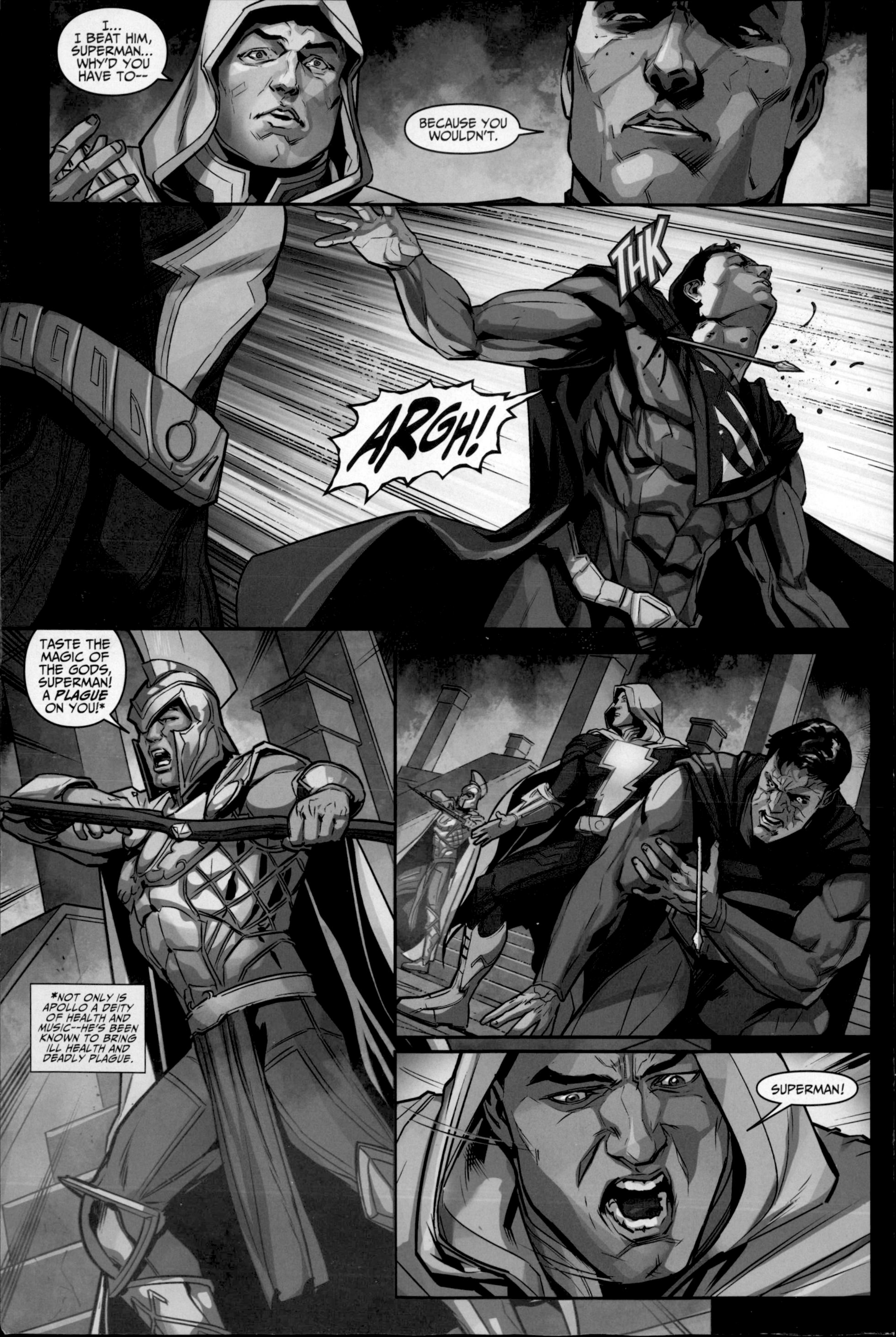
I... I BEAT HIM, SUPERMAN... WHY'D YOU HAVE TO--
BECAUSE YOU WOULDN'T.
THK
ARGH!
TASTE THE MAGIC OF THE GODS, SUPERMAN! A PLAGUE ON YOU!*
*NOT ONLY IS APOLLO A DEITY OF HEALTH AND MUSIC--HE'S BEEN KNOWN TO BRING ILL HEALTH AND DEADLY PLAGUE.
SUPERMAN!

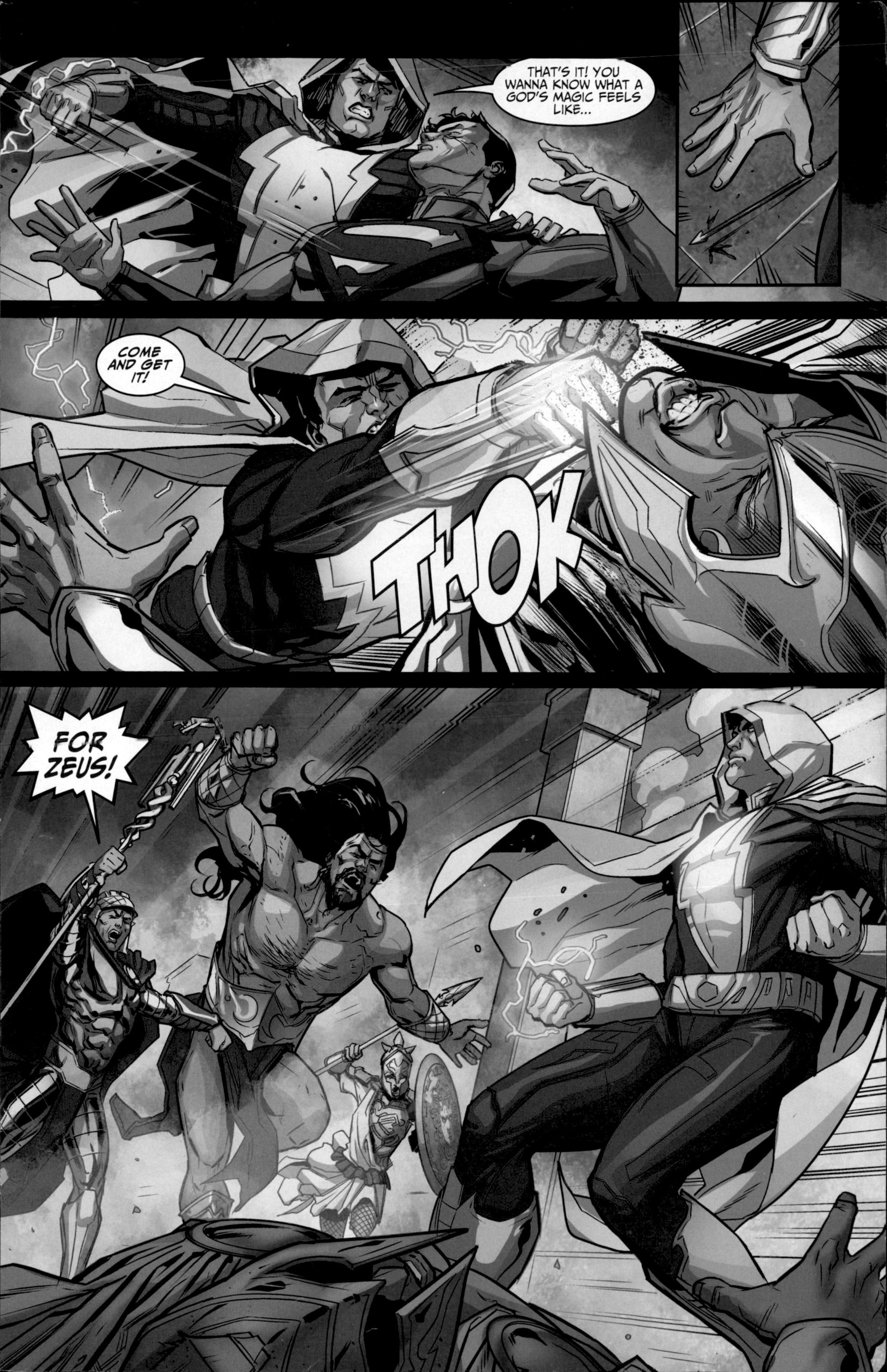
THAT'S IT! YOU WANNA KNOW WHAT A GOD'S MAGIC FEELS LIKE...
COME AND GET IT!
THOK
FOR ZEUS!

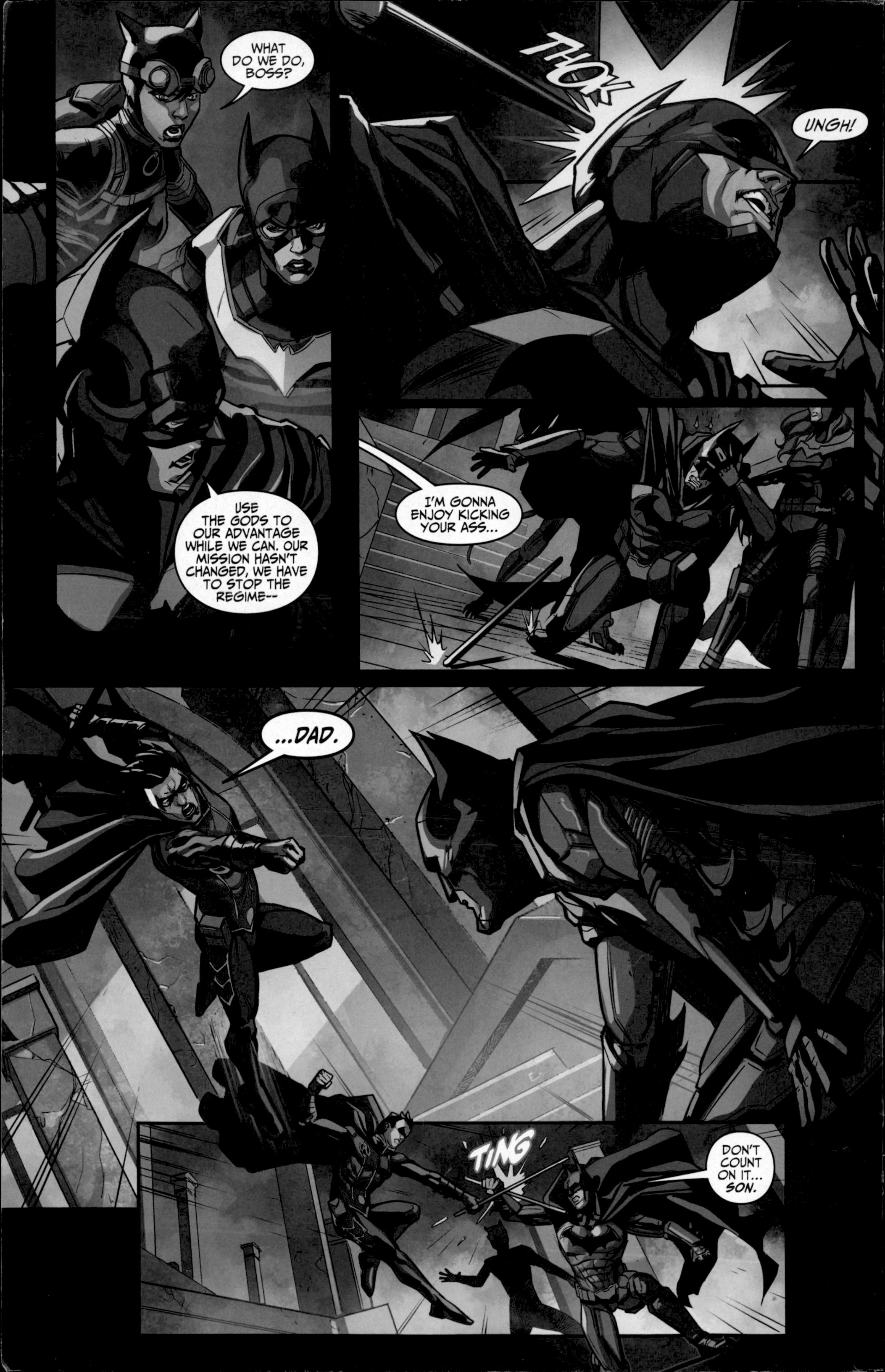
WHAT DO WE DO, BOSS?
USE THE GODS TO OUR ADVANTAGE WHILE WE CAN. OUR MISSION HASN'T CHANGED, WE HAVE TO STOP THE REGIME--
THOK
UNGH!
I'M GONNA ENJOY KICKING YOUR ASS...
...DAD.
TING
DON'T COUNT ON IT... SON.

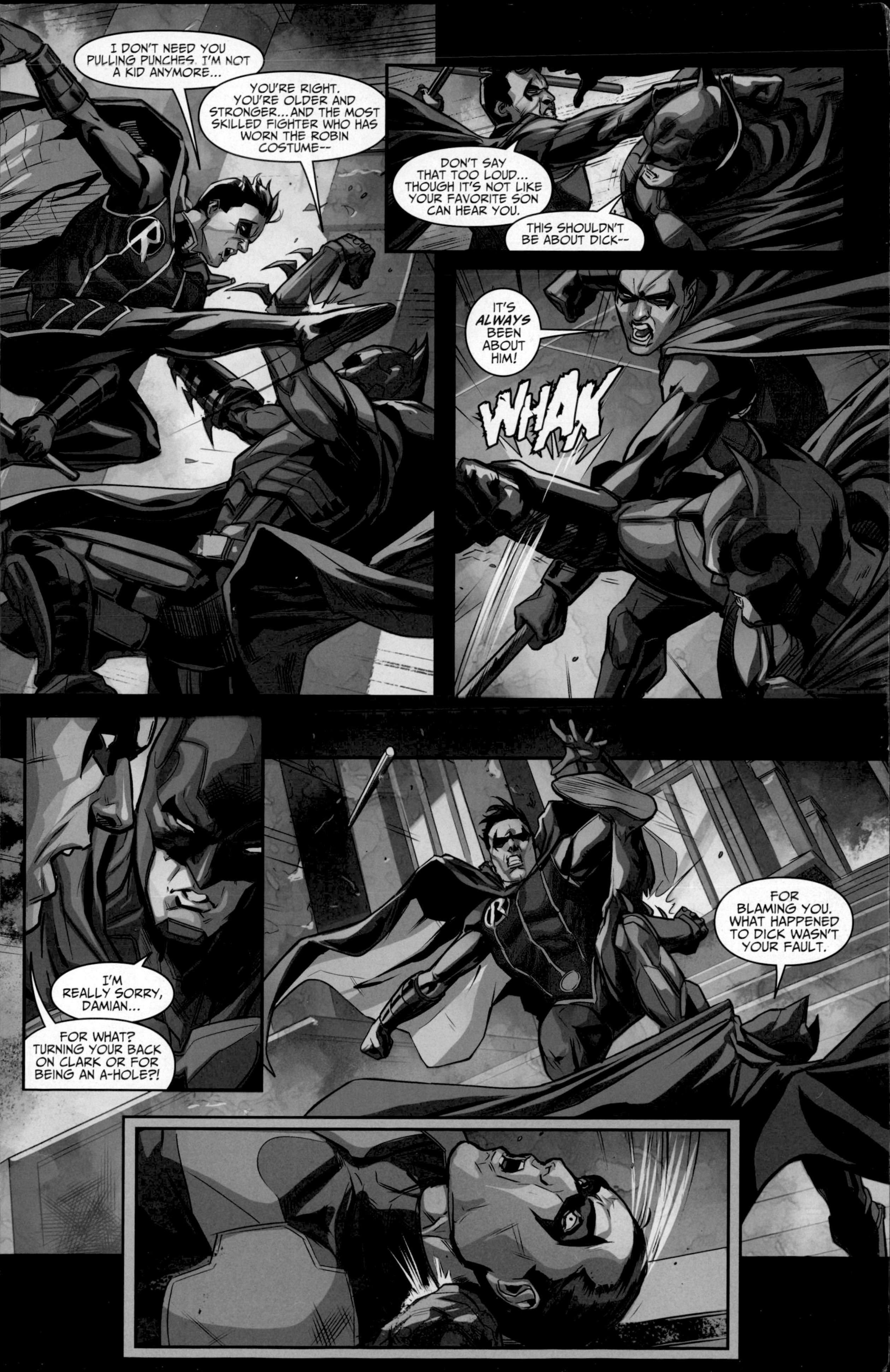
I DON'T NEED YOU PULLING PUNCHES. I'M NOT A KID ANYMORE...
YOU'RE RIGHT. YOU'RE OLDER AND STRONGER... AND THE MOST SKILLED FIGHTER WHO HAS WORN THE ROBIN COSTUME--
DON'T SAY THAT TOO LOUD... THOUGH IT'S NOT LIKE YOUR FAVORITE SON CAN HEAR YOU.
THIS SHOULDN'T BE ABOUT DICK--
IT'S *ALWAYS* BEEN ABOUT HIM!
WHAK
I'M REALLY SORRY, DAMIAN...
FOR WHAT? TURNING YOUR BACK ON CLARK OR FOR BEING AN A-HOLE?!
FOR BLAMING YOU. WHAT HAPPENED TO DICK WASN'T YOUR FAULT.

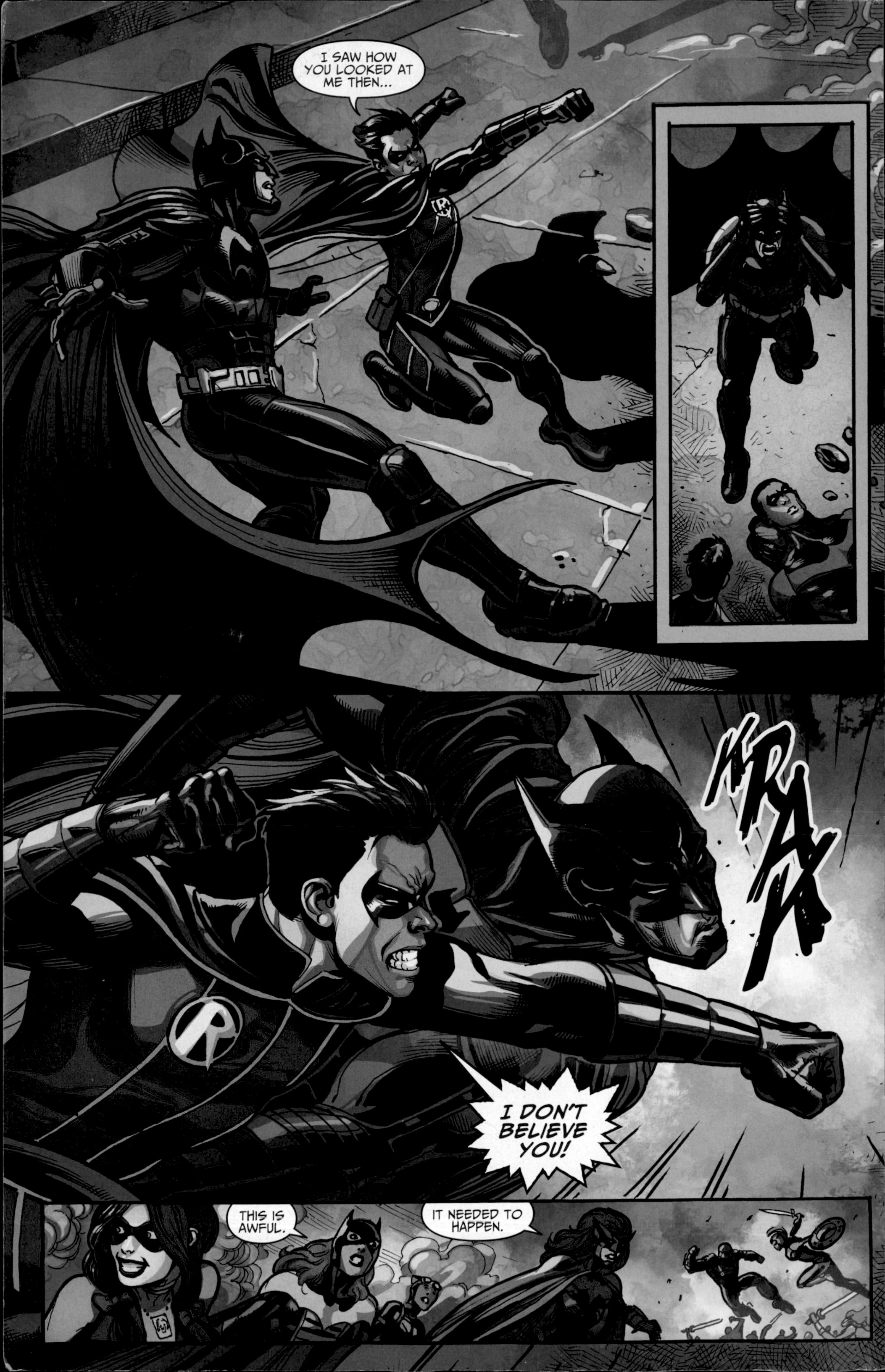
I SAW HOW YOU LOOKED AT ME THEN...
I DON'T BELIEVE YOU!
THIS IS AWFUL.
IT NEEDED TO HAPPEN.

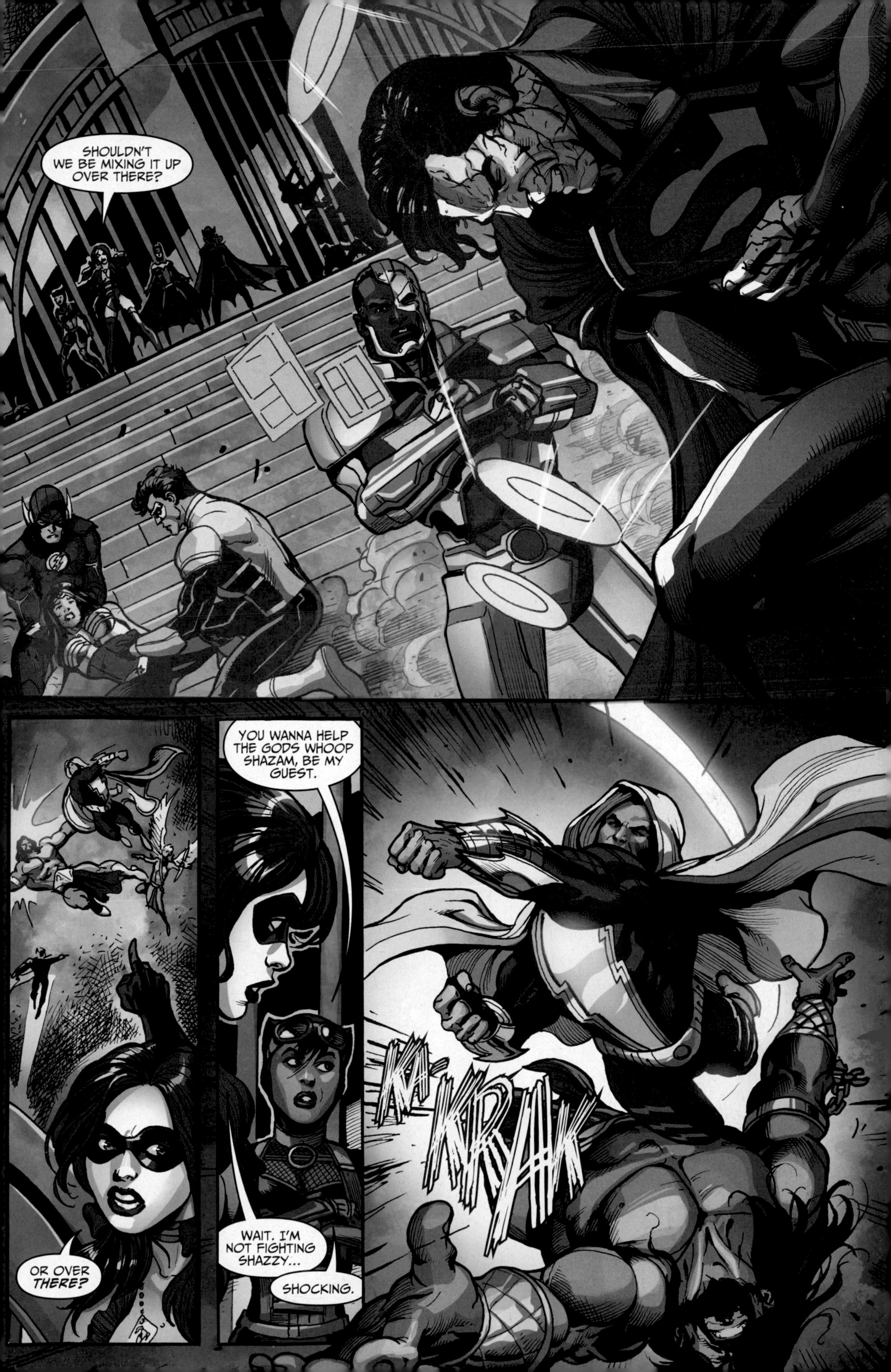
SHOULDN'T WE BE MIXING IT UP OVER THERE?
OR OVER *THERE?*
YOU WANNA HELP THE GODS WHOOP SHAZAM, BE MY GUEST.
WAIT. I'M NOT FIGHTING SHAZZY...
SHOCKING.
KA-KRAKK

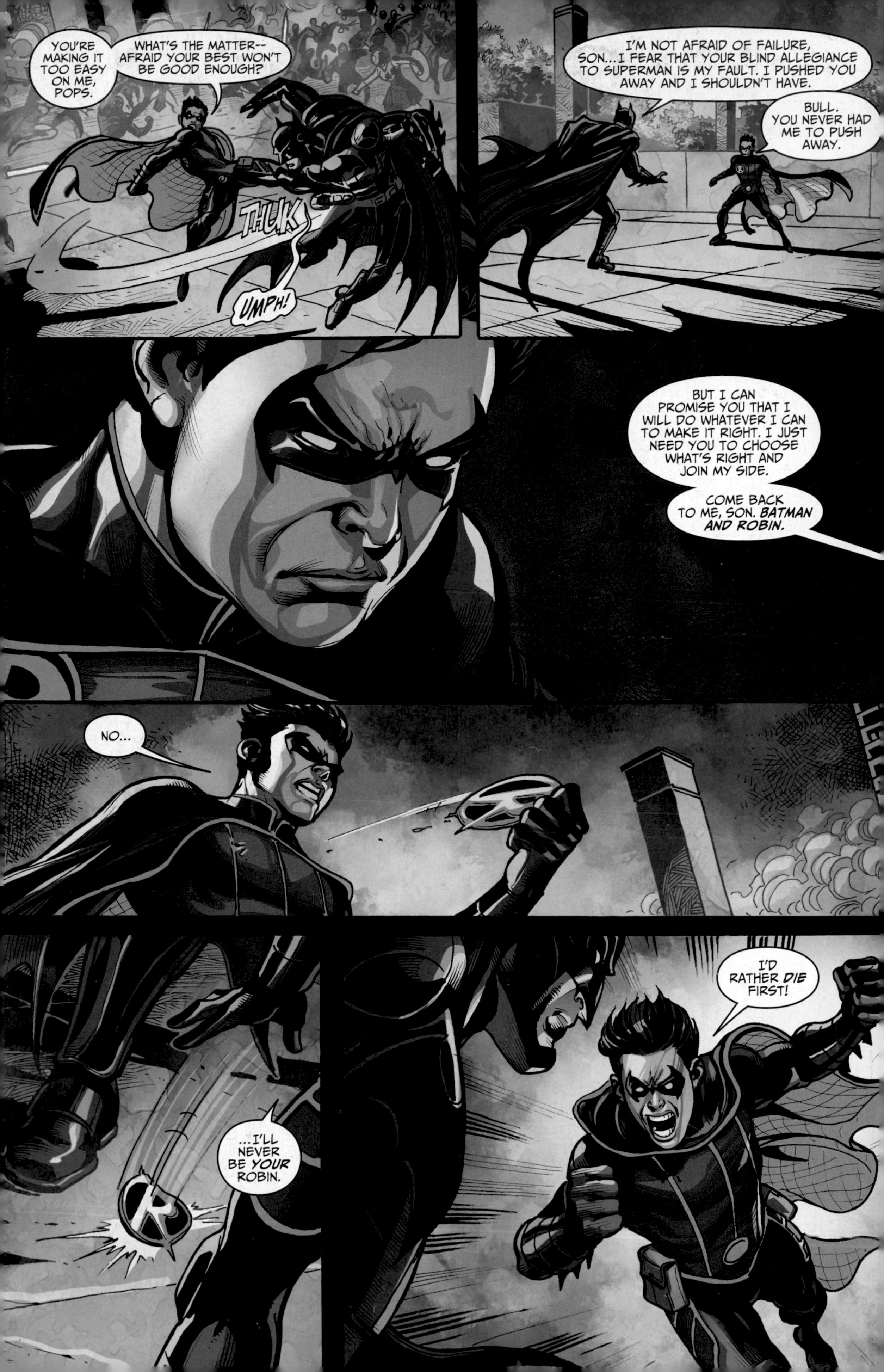
YOU'RE MAKING IT TOO EASY ON ME, POPS.
WHAT'S THE MATTER-- AFRAID YOUR BEST WON'T BE GOOD ENOUGH?
THUK
UMPH!
I'M NOT AFRAID OF FAILURE, SON... I FEAR THAT YOUR BLIND ALLEGIANCE TO SUPERMAN IS MY FAULT. I PUSHED YOU AWAY AND I SHOULDN'T HAVE.
BULL. YOU NEVER HAD ME TO PUSH AWAY.
BUT I CAN PROMISE YOU THAT I WILL DO WHATEVER I CAN TO MAKE IT RIGHT. I JUST NEED YOU TO CHOOSE WHAT'S RIGHT AND JOIN MY SIDE.
COME BACK TO ME, SON. BATMAN AND ROBIN.
NO...
...I'LL NEVER BE YOUR ROBIN.
I'D RATHER DIE FIRST!

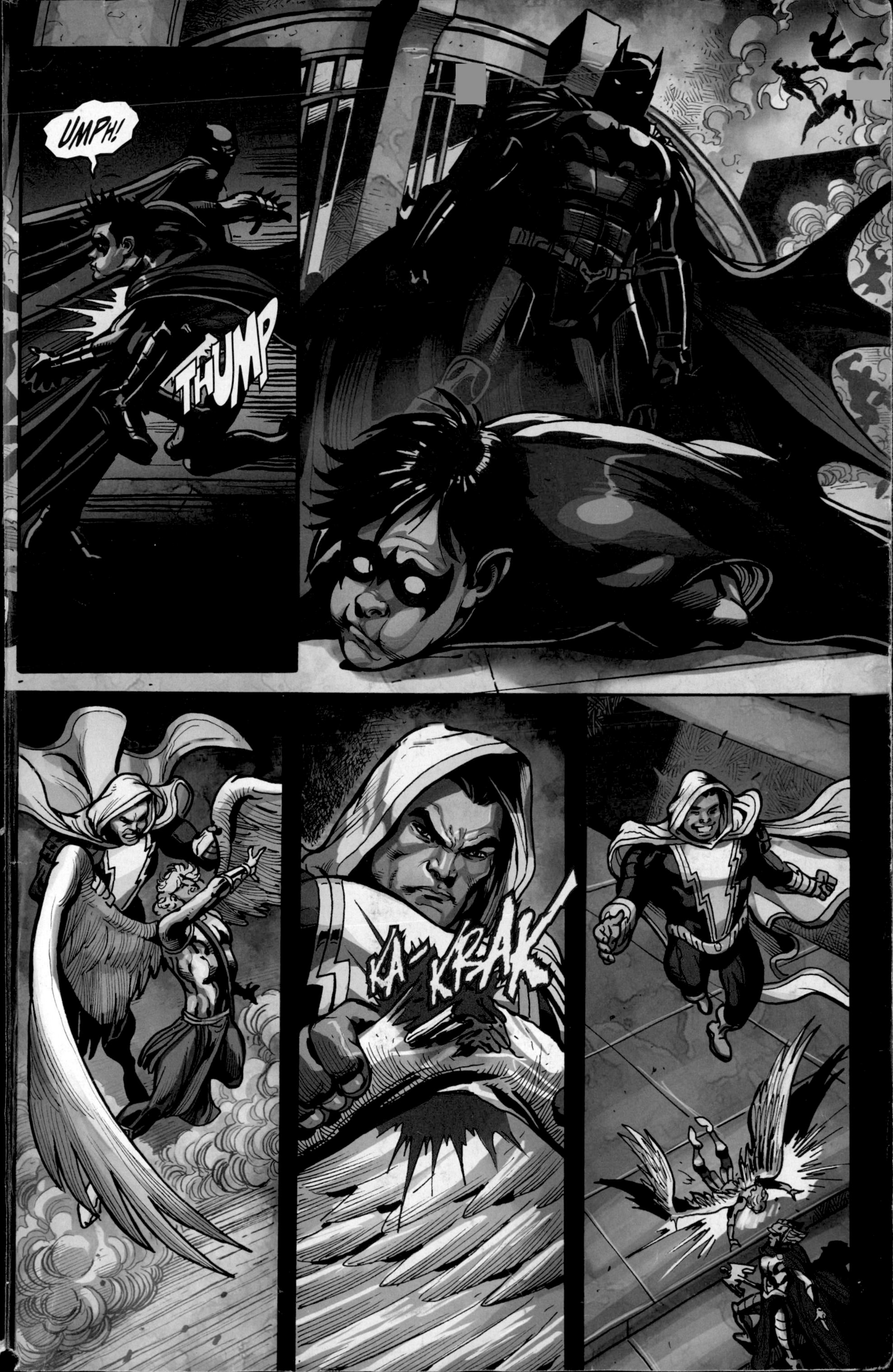
UMPH!
THUMP
KA-KRAK

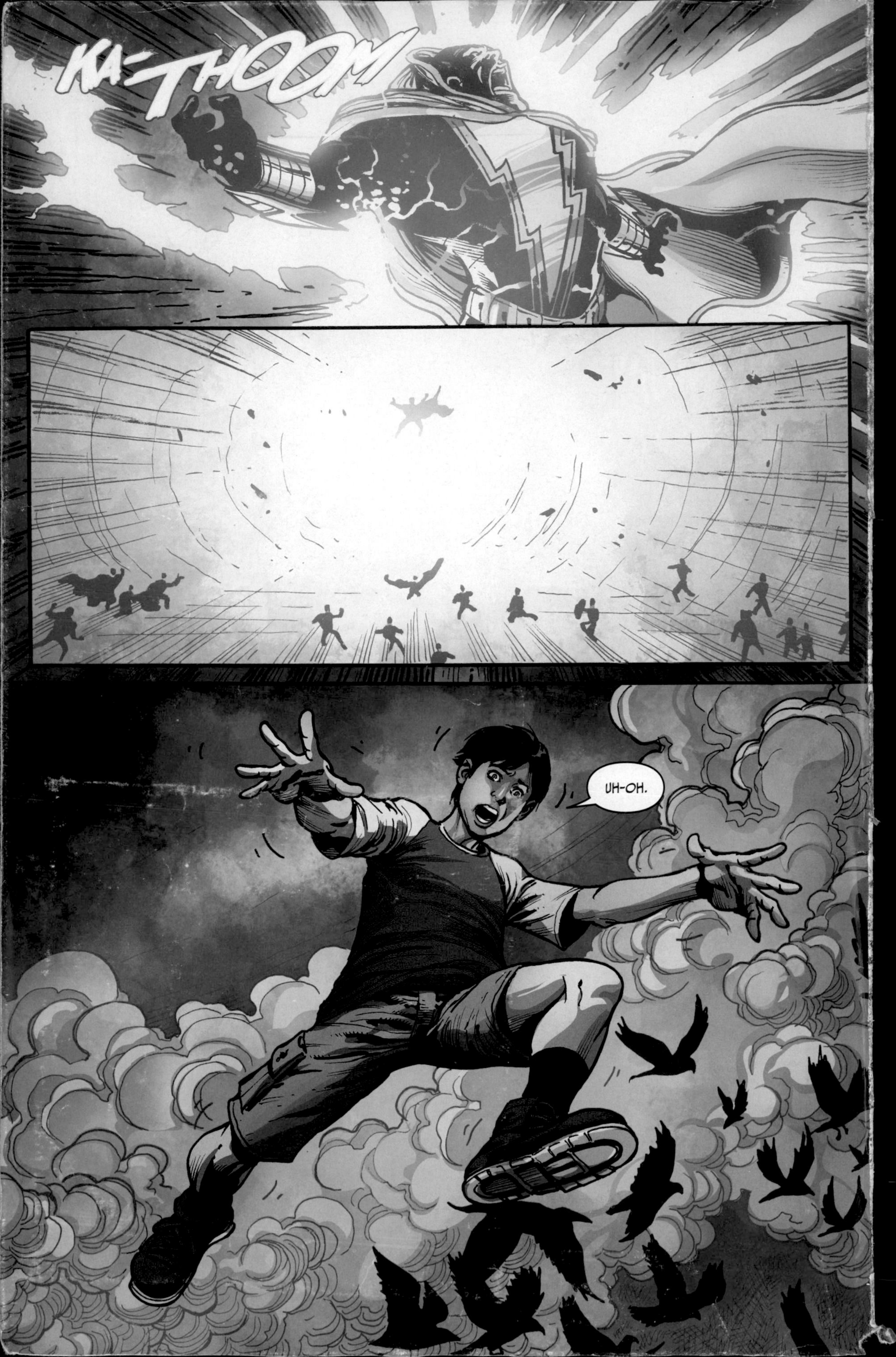
KA-THOOM
UH-OH.